**Perspectives on Regional
Transportation Planning**

Perspectives on Regional Transportation Planning

Edited by
Joseph S. DeSalvo

Lexington Books
D.C. Heath and Company
Lexington, Massachusetts
Toronto   London

Library of Congress Cataloging in Publication Data
Main entry under title:

Perspectives on regional transportation planning.

    Revised versions of nine papers originally delivered at the Conference
on Regional Transportation Planning, Santa Monica, Calif., 1971.
    1. Transportation—United States—Congresses.
2. Regional planning—United States—Congresses.
I. DeSalvo, Joseph S., ed.   II. Conference on Regional Transportation
Planning, Santa Monica, Calif., 1971.
HE203.P45   380.5'0973   72-7024
ISBN O-669-84343-1

213336

Second printing January 1974.

Published simultaneously in Canada.

Printed in the United States of America.

International Standard Book Number: 0-669-84343-1

Library of Congress Catalog Card Number: 72-7024

3-1303-0004-8835

Contents

v

List of Tables

List of Figures

Preface

The papers constituting this book developed from a Conference on Regional Transportation Planning held at the Rand Corporation in January 1971, under the sponsorship of the U.S. Department of Transportation. The PROCEEDINGS of the Conference were subsequently published as a Rand Corporation Report.

The Conference explored the question of whether or not some form of transportation planning entity should be created between two existing levels of planning—the national level and the individual states or smaller jurisdictions. The objective was to consider the advantages and disadvantages, in economic and administrative terms, of conducting transportation planning on a "regional" basis.

The present volume consists of revised versions of the nine papers originally delivered at the Rand Conference and a new Introduction. The lively exchange of ideas that took place during the Conference—among authors and invited guests from DOT, Rand, and the National Academy of Sciences—and the subsequent criticisms from colleagues and others who read the papers led the authors to revise their work, in some cases rather substantially, from the original versions as well as from the versions that appeared in the Rand Report. An Introduction, written by the editor, presents in detail the reasons for the study, how the various papers fit into the overall structure of the study, summaries of the individual papers, and an attempt to synthesize some of the main themes.

As might be imagined in an endeavor stretching over two years and involving two major institutions—Rand and DOT—and nine papers by authors spread out over the U.S. from Cambridge, Massachusetts, to Pullman, Washington, there are a number of people to whom the authors owe thanks: the secretaries who typed and retyped the innumerable revisions, the editors at Rand and D.C. Heath who tried to improve our prose, the administrative staffs of Rand, DOT, and D.C. Heath who smoothed the way from initial DOT contract to final D.C. Heath book, and all the many friends and colleagues who read and criticized the papers. Unfortunately, we cannot thank them all by name. We must mention, however, Robert E. Burns and Lee W. Huff of the U.S. Department of Transportation, who probably came closest to being the intellectual fathers of the enterprise, though they should not be held accountable for the way the child finally turned out. Thanks are also due Alan Carlin of the Environmental Protection Agency and James P. Stucker of Rand who were the Rand "referees" of the original papers and, therefore, are largely responsible for the later revisions. Of course, we did not always take their advice, so we cannot allow them to share the blame for what we finally produced. Finally, we must thank John P. White of Rand who provided administrative expertise—i.e., threats, cajolery, a shoulder to cry on—from the very beginning to the very end of this endeavor.

The work was done as a part of the Rand Corporation's domestic research program.

Joseph S. DeSalvo

Milwaukee, Wisconsin

**Perspectives on Regional
Transportation Planning**

Introduction

The idea of regional transportation planning has existed for some time and has manifested itself in various ways. Most regional planning has involved regional *transportation* planning as well, and several regional planning or regional transportation planning entities have existed or currently exist in the United States. As Ralph Gakenheimer points out in his contribution to this volume, regional planning has taken place within a number of administrative forms: metropolitan agencies, the Northeast Corridor Project, various state agencies, the Economic Development Regions, and various port authorities. Moreover, the idea of establishing regional transportation planning entities of a more permanent nature and exhaustive of the entire country has cropped up from time to time. For example, in the Ninety-first Congress, Senators Pell and Magnuson both introduced bills that, if passed, would have required the establishment of regional transportation planning authorities.

Probably the main idea motivating the desire for regional transportation planning is that the planning and decision-making process for the provision of transportation facilities has not been well structured for achieving balance and coordination in transportation, particularly at the federal level. This in turn impinges on the states' capabilities to plan effectively and to coordinate transportation developments. But since much of transportation crosses state lines, strengthening the decision-making role of the states is not sufficient and some kind of regional or national decision-making is required. It is sometimes further argued that since the burden of inadequate transportation is regional, the means and capability to cope with the problems should be regional. Moreover, there are decisions that can be taken without involving national coordination. For example, the proposed VTOL and STOL aircraft would involve essentially a regional operation, as would high speed ground transportation.

On the other hand, it can be argued that there are several difficulties with the idea of regional transportation planning. There is the problem of actually defining the boundaries of a region for transportation planning purposes. What should be the considerations relevant to defining workable transportation regions? Should they be drawn differently for freight problems and passenger problems, for air versus surface transport, land versus water, etc.? If regions are permitted to do their own transportation planning, might not they attempt to achieve balanced growth within their own region to the possible detriment of the nation because of the nonexploitation of regional comparative advantage? Is it not also the case that many important matters would be beyond the legitimate powers of regional authorities, e.g., transport regulation, tax policies, and trust fund decisions? Is not regional *transportation* planning too narrow a view? Would it not be better to treat transportation as merely an aspect of a larger regional plan? Would it not be preferable to avoid the creation of another bureaucratic level?

1

Clearly, then, there are serious questions as to the efficacy of regional transportation planning. It is the purpose of this book to address some of these. A fundamental issue is the economic rationale for transportation planning. Under what conditions should we have planning at all? Do these conditions prevail for transportation? It would seem that only when these questions are answered should the more narrow question of the efficacy of regional transportation planning be addressed. The first chapter, therefore, discusses the economic rationale for transportation planning. Another important issue is the relationship between transport regions and transport markets, an issue that is closely related to the thorny problem of defining transport regions for planning purposes. Chapters 2, 3, and 4 confront this topic, with individual chapters on delimiting regions for transportation planning, the territorial basis of national transportation planning, and markets and planning regions for transportation. Since there exists or has existed a number of actual cases of regional planning, it would seem useful to draw on this experience with an eye toward the likely success of regional transportation planning. In addition, a great deal of governmental effort, regulatory and promotional, has been directed toward transportation in this country. Again, it would seem useful to assess this experience and its relevance for regional transportation planning. Chapters 5, 6, and 7 present critiques of present and past policies regarding transportation and regional planning. In particular, there are separate chapters on the effect of regional planning policies on the relationship among regional development, resource allocation, and transportation; a critique of governmental intervention in transport; and a critical review of a number of cases of regional transportation planning. Chapter 8 addresses the important issue for regional transportation planning of future changes in transport demand, population, and technology. Finally, Chapter 9 considers the political and administrative aspects of regional planning. Given this overall view of the structure of the book, we now turn to more detailed summaries of the papers, emphasizing their conclusions and recommendations. In a subsequent section, we try to synthesize the major themes of the study.

Summaries of Papers

The Economic Rationale for Transportation
Planning: Chapter 1

The first chapter, by Joseph S. DeSalvo, examines the circumstances under which economic theory provides a rationale for planning and examines empirical analyses to determine whether and to what extent these circumstances prevail in transportation. The implications of these findings for regional transportation planning are explored. This paper serves, therefore, as a guide to the kinds of issues with which transportation planning might usefully be concerned and as an introduction to the other papers constituting the study.

Although the private competitive market is a wonderful device for attaining the efficient use of scarce resources under certain conditions, when these conditions are not present or are violated, a rationale for planning exists. Certain general principles concerning planning and markets emerge from the analysis in this chapter. Where competitive markets exist, or could exist, there should be no government interference with market determined prices, outputs, and investment decisions. Where competitive markets do not exist because of (1) incomplete information, (2) technologies of increasing returns to scale large relative to the market, (3) externalities, (4) public goods, and (5) market concentration, then, to the extent benefits exceed cost, the government should (1) provide information, (2) subsidize firms, (3) internalize externalities, (4) provide and finance public goods through user charges, and (5) dissolve firms in highly concentrated industries.

A competitive market structure (that is, one that would very likely be competitive in the absence of regulation) seems to exist for trucking, which is characterized by constant returns to scale, low market concentration, and easy entry conditions. Inland waterway transportation could probably also be competitive except in markets that are small relative to the scale of an efficient firm. It is more difficult to judge the probable competitiveness of rail, air, intercity bus, and intracity bus transportation, for market concentration is high and entry is difficult (perhaps because of regulation) although cost structures indicate that competition is possible (except for rail, where empirical research on returns to scale is mixed). Given intermodal competition, however, deregulation appears appropriate, but a watchful eye should be kept on merger activity with the use of current anti-trust legislation if necessary. Finally, pipeline transportation has all the characteristics of a natural monopoly, and continued regulation would appear to be in order.

The only externality of transportation for which there is enough empirical analysis to support a recommendation is congestion. The empirical work necessary to determine social congestion costs has been performed for auto, air, and inland water. Experimenting with toll schemes might be tried. More research on demand, on other methods to internalize congestion, and on the proper use of the proceeds of tolls is needed, as is research on pollution and noise.

On the issue of transport public goods, no operational recommendations can be made with respect to the decision about whether or not to provide the goods. At present, this is handled by elected representatives, with little guidance concerning social demand. The financing of such goods, once provided, should be done through user charges under a benefit theory of taxation, but real problems emerge in determining how much various users should contribute. More research must be performed on this issue.

All of the preceding recommendations relate to planning in general. No information is given on the appropriate planning level. In fact, DeSalvo was unable to draw such conclusions from the analysis, probably due to its a-spatial and a-institutional nature and to the absence of an explicit planning function in economic analysis. Thus, there is no rationale for regional transportation planning, although a rationale for transportation planning per se has been established. It seems that in order to judge whether regional transportation planning is better than planning at some other level, more must be known about the cost of planning at various levels.

Delimitation of Regions for Transportation
Planning: Chapter 2

In his paper on delimiting regions for transportation planning, Karl A. Fox designates an exhaustive and mutually exclusive set of 24 regions for regional passenger transportation purposes. (See Figure 2-17.) Fox defines four levels of transport areas. The basic subregions are called Functional Economic Areas (FEAs) and Metropolitan Subareas. An FEA is delineated on the basis of the actual transportation behavior of employed members of the labor force with respect to the journey to work. Fox aggregates FEAs and Metropolitan Subareas into regions, called National Metropolitan Regions. These regions have a radius of about 200 miles and are organized around major cities. Above this level, the United States might be delineated into five large regions, oriented towards New York City, Chicago, Los Angeles, and, perhaps, Dallas-Fort Worth and Atlanta. The final level would be the nation as a whole with New York City and Washington serving, respectively, as economic and political capitals.

Out of this analysis, Fox suggests the following view of the United States for purposes of passenger transportation planning. First, local transportation planning would take place within each of some 500 Functional Economic Areas and Metropolitan Subareas, involving motor vehicles for the most part. Second, national transportation planning would take place at the level of about 24 widely separated cities, involving air travel for the most part. Finally, regional transportation planning within each of some 24 National Metropolitan Regions would take place, involving motor vehicles, light planes, and perhaps some inter-urban transit by rail.

The Territorial Basis of National Transportation
Planning: Chapter 3

In the third chapter, John Friedmann and Barbara Stuckey examine the territorial basis of national transportation planning. They attempt to answer the question: How might the planning and related activities of the Department of

Transportation be organized in space to meet the needs for transport in different parts of the country more effectively? They approach this question by examining the existing pattern of spatial organization, including the division of powers among the several levels of government, the pattern of regions established for economic development and general administration, the distribution of population and activities, and the distribution of levels of economic and social well being.

As a result of their survey of the territorial basis of national transportation planning, Friedmann and Stuckey develop five major recommendations. First, they maintain that the definition of regions for transportation planning in the United States is best approached through an ordering of specific activities in space. Second, developmental functions of transport services are best planned in close coordination with other developmental considerations. The Economic Development Regions of the country are the logical foci for evolving comprehensive strategies of regional development. Third, the facilitating roles of transport services arise in connection with an already existing or projected demand that is generated independently of the provision of these services. In this case, an intersectoral planning approach is needed less than one emphasizing intermodal coordination. Fourth, intermodal coordination is called for especially where the provision of transport services within a given area does not require repeated and successive decision-making and where the complexity of the transport system requires continuing attention. In the first case, planning can generally be accomplished on an ad hoc basis, without designating special transport regions. In the second place, however, several distinct situations must be considered. At the level of metropolitan-centered regions, transport planning should be integrated with already existing Metropolitan Associations of Government in order to strengthen their coordinating powers. At state levels, improved intermodal coordination requires the creation of Departments of Transportation that would be capable of bringing the various state transport services together, achieve greater political accountability, and secure a substantial saving of resources. At the level of inter-state urban corridors—such as the Northeast or the corridor areas linking Milwaukee with Chicago, Detroit, Buffalo, and Pittsburgh—special transportation measures should be established. Their fifth recommendation is that all other transport planning activities should continue to be carried out essentially at the national level, except that certain routine functions, such as grant processing, should be decentralized to the already existing administrative regions for better coordination with other federal programs.

Markets and Planning Regions for Transportation:
Chapter 4

In his study of markets and planning regions for transportation, William Alonso concludes that it would not be wise to divide the nation into a permanent set of large transportation regions and to create an authority for each region charged with comprehensive transportation planning. He advances several reasons for this position. Alonso feels that no simple regionalization of information gathering, forecasting, and decision-making can serve a nation which is as complexly structured as the United States. Moreover, since transportation is only an instrumental function, i.e., not desired for itself but as an instrument, its planning structure must be adapted to the structure and needs of the larger system. He further argues that large-scale regions are not optimal for comprehensive transportation planning. Instead of an exhaustive and permanent set of regions, we need mechanisms that are adapted to the complex crosscurrents of sectors and areas of the society to be served, that provide forums for diverse viewpoints and information, and that allow cost and benefit negotiations. This set of mechanisms should be established in the context of existing governmental structure.

To achieve this goal, we should improve transportation planning at the national level. This should be based to a large degree on long-range forecasting and on the consistency of transportation policies with other relevant national policies (in particular, national goals and procedures to deal with the spatial distribution of the national population). The Department of Transportation should consider formation of regional desks to serve as clearing houses for the vertically organized divisions and for the independent regulatory boards and those divisions of other departments that have to do with transportation. Moreover, planning by the Executive Branch of the Federal Government should be done in consultation with members of key Congressional committees.

In addition to strengthening transportation planning at the national level, an attempt should be made to improve the performance of already existing regional agencies. Federal law and administrative practice could be used to assist the participation of these bodies in the planning of transportation for their regions and to integrate transportation into the other sectors of their consideration.

Finally, from time-to-time there may be a need to establish special transportation planning districts or special project agencies. This is particularly true where the territory that must be considered for transportation planning differs significantly from the region as defined for other purposes or where general purpose regional bodies do not exist. It is recommended, however, that when such special transportation districts or special project agencies are established, a terminal date be included in their charters. This is designed to maintain flexibility that is necessary to permit adaptation to changing circumstances.

Regional Development, Resource Allocation,
and Transportation: Chapter 5

Chapter 5 is a critical survey of regional development, resource allocation, and transportation by John H. Cumberland. Transportation generates important positive and negative economic externalities. Because of the geographic and spatial distribution of these transport-related externalities, regional economic development is significantly affected by transportation, and regional development in turn significantly affects transportation objectives. Recognition of the close interdependence between transportation systems and regional development is indicated by recent proposals to establish regional agencies for the coordination of transportation planning. The purpose of Cumberland's survey is to examine some aspects of the U.S. experience in regional development in order to assess possible opportunities for improving performance in the fields of both transportation and regional development.

Cumberland points out several shortcomings in United States regional development. (1) There is a general tendency to neglect and to override the rights of minority groups and the disadvantaged. (2) There is a general reluctance to undertake the necessary detailed identification of objectives, evaluation of benefits and costs of alternative programs, and specific comprehensive planning required to assure that both national and regional goals are reconciled and achieved through a total systems approach. (3) There is a basic tendency to emphasize the quantitative, aggregative aspects of development, rather than the qualitative aspects, and the tendency towards an unselective proliferation of programs. (4) There is a failure to protect the nation's environment.

Given these shortcomings of United States regional development, Cumberland has one general recommendation. The nation urgently needs to formulate a national transportation policy based upon a clear identification of objectives and an appraisal of the benefits and costs of alternative programs for achieving these objectives. Nevertheless, rational design of transportation policy must be related to national policies in the associated areas of regional and urban development, land use, natural resource management, technology assessment, and environmental protection.

With this general recommendation in mind, some more specific recommendations are proposed. First, the major need in regional development policy is to abandon the concept of ubiquitous acceleration of economic growth in all regions in favor of moving toward improvement in the quality of regional and urban life through concentrating resource allocation according to the priority of objectives. This requires the identification of growth and non-growth areas. Cumberland suggests the following candidates for non-growth areas: all seashores; rivers and stream banks; flood plains; highest peaks and deepest valleys; wilderness areas; areas of unique geological, ecological, environmental, recreational, and historic significance; regions with potentially hazardous soil, seismic, drought, storm, meteorological, and brush fire conditions. It is recommended, second, that the pressure on regions to pursue economic development be lessened by revenue sharing, by federal guidelines for development priorities, by more detailed federal and state physical planning, and by requirements that local authorities refer their plans to higher levels of government for coordination of regional and national interests. Third, no region should suffer economically from economic response to changes in national priorities. Policy should give top priority to human welfare problems and provide generous assistance to people and to regions that experienced economic distress as a result of changes in national goals, technology, or market forces.

The fourth specific recommendation is the use of life-cycle resource planning to reduce irreversible damage and misallocation of investments. This concept would require that prior to the beginning of operations, a comprehensive plan be submitted for all phases of the operations, including exploration, development, and eventual restoration of the area. Fifth, economic incentives to achieve environmental quality should be provided by national policies of taxation, subsidy, and regulation to encourage recycling, prevent discharges into common property resources, and to develop environmentally neutral technology. Sixth, it is recommended that the performance characteristics of transport systems be spelled out in advance. The Federal Government should exercise control over this through its research and development, regulatory, and other functions. Seventh, planning and transportation systems should involve the active participation not only of those groups that would produce and use them, but also of all those that would be affected by them.

An eighth specific recommendation concerns the use of public guidelines to prevent the overuse of environmental resources. More detailed planning, physical design, and specification of guidelines will be necessary by federal and state agencies, in contrast to the latitude that was previously left to local and private planning. Ninth, rather than establish a single set of regions for transportation planning, flexible systems of regions should be established from small-area building blocks that can be combined in various ways to represent all of the governmental levels and units, including international, which are affected by the system involved. Transportation is more likely to serve general social goals if, instead of setting up separate transportation planning regions, transportation planning is carried on in conjunction with established regional planning units. The final specific recommendation is that consideration be given to the phasing out of trust funds, so that every transport mode and every transportation program or project could be considered on its merits with its net social benefits compared with those of alternative programs. Coupled with this recommendation would be the requirement that transport systems pay their full social costs and internalize external diseconomies.

A Critique of Governmental Intervention in Transport: Chapter 6

In this paper, James C. Nelson divides his critique of governmental intervention in transportation into two parts. The first part deals with the regulatory policies and standards of the Federal Government with respect to transportation. The second part deals with the government's promotion of transportation by investments and subsidies. Analysis of both parts of the problem lead to several recommendations, first, with respect to regulatory policies and standards, and second, with respect to governmental promotion of transportation.

Nelson provides cogent arguments for the removal of regulatory policies and standards that have adverse rate and service effects and that have induced a misallocation of traffic and resources. He feels that the major uneconomical effects of regulation are due to the application of minimum rate and entry control regulation to the naturally competitive modes. There is a spectrum of alternatives for improving the efficiency of transportation. At one extreme would be the deregulation of transport modes. At the other extreme would be the change of statutory mandate and policy statements to direct the Interstate Commerce Commission to modify its entry, merger, and minimum rate policies so as not to be in conflict with an economic organization of the transport industries, efficient competitive pricing, and economic competition between modes. An alternative somewhat midway between these two extremes would be partial deregulation, involving either abandonment of regulations for the naturally competitive modes or elimination of the specific regulatory tools, entry and minimum rate regulation, that lessen competition and bring about inefficient market structures. Nelson appears to believe that the policy of deregulation is not likely to be a realistic alternative. Consequently, he proposes partial deregulation.

To be successful, partial deregulation would require four major characteristics. First, there would have to be a repeal of minimum rate regulations for motor and water carriers. Minimum rate regulations would be used sparingly for railroads. Second, there would have to be no control on entry into motor and water transportation. Third, there would need to be restrictions on the powers of the Interstate Commerce Commission to (1) control rate and service discrimination and maximum rates; (2) secure joint rate and service arrangements to promote coordination where voluntary action by carriers fails to meet reasonable standards of efficiency; (3) control integration and securities to prevent impairment of competition and investor injury; (4) prevent railroads from engaging in activities designed to destroy competition of other agencies. The final requirement for partial deregulation is the abandonment of the tacit acceptance of rate bureaus and other association activities to fix rates in favor of the active enforcement of the anti-trust laws.

Given the political difficulties of changing regulatory statutes (which the above recommendations would require) and the transitional income effects of converting regulated transport markets into competitive markets, the possibility that the Interstate Commerce Commission might be induced to change its own administrative standards in order to make more efficient use of the present regulatory structure and standards might be considered. The changes that would need to be made under this alternative are as follows. First, the Interstate

Commerce Commission should make minimal use of the minimum rate power. Second, much discretion was left to the Interstate Commerce Commission to utilize the logical tests of economics in determining the cost standards to apply in judging whether competition is economic or "destructive" in each situation. Nelson suggests that the Interstate Commerce Commission could remove much of the protective coloring and fair-sharing traffic allocations that its past full-cost standards have introduced. In this way, the Interstate Commerce Commission could release intermodal competition to do its real work in distributing traffic efficiently and lessening the misallocating effects of minimum rate regulations. Third, and finally, the Interstate Commerce Commission should move more rapidly to remove the waste-producing and competition-limiting effects of its operating authority restrictions. The Commission could order additional blanket liberalization of certificate restrictions limiting efficiency.

The second major class of recommendations has to do with the promotion of transportation by government investments and subsidies. The government has played a strong role as a public entrepreneur in ownership and operation of transport facilities and in giving financial aid and subsidies for transport investment. Nelson feels that this has been the controlling factor in shaping the development of the entire transportation system. The result of this role of the Federal Government has been overinvestment in airports, airways, highways, and inland waterways, with detrimental effects on railroads. Reforming regulatory policy will not solve this problem. It requires major change in promotional and investment policies of state and Federal government, and it requires substantial adjustment of the state and federal user-fee policies.

Nelson proposes several recommendations with respect to the issue of governmental promotion of transportation investment. All state and federal transportation projects should be subjected to uniform and competent application of fully economic investment criteria. This is needed to avoid double counting of benefits, subject indirect or social benefits to tests equivalent to the willingness of particular consumers to pay for the services of each project, avoid underestimation of the future costs of the carriers using public transport facilities, count all social costs, and insure the use of realistic interest and discount rates. If such applications of investment criteria were applied to prospective transport projects, a list of individual transportation projects could be established, ranked from high to low in terms of net benefits. Then, investments in specific transport projects could be undertaken in that order.

Another class of recommendations concerns the power of the U.S. Department of Transportation. Nelson feels that the Department of Transportation's jurisdiction over the investment planning activities of inland waterways and of the merchant marine should be extended. He also recommends an increase in the Department of Transportation's power to subject federal public investment planning for all modes to common and relevant economic investment criteria and to coordinate the investment recommendations of all action agencies.

In addition to strengthening the U.S. Department of Transportation, Nelson recommends the establishment of State Departments of Transportation, with powers to plan and integrate statewide transport development for all modes in which state investments are made or to which state aid is given. At present, thirteen such State Departments of Transportation exist. In addition to these organizations, if urban, state, and federal planning agencies that already exist or that could be established did not sufficiently account for regional considerations, some regional planning organizations could be organized to serve a useful study and planning function. It seems far from clear to Nelson that any wholesale establishment of such regional planning organizations would be justified at this time.

Another set of recommendations concerns user charges. Congress should enact suitable and sufficient user fees or tolls for the inland waterways in order to recover at least all annual maintenance and operating costs of present waterways and all costs of new waterways. Highway user fees should be adjusted to increase the payments of large and heavy vehicles to more closely approximate their long-run marginal construction, maintenance, and operating costs. Finally, congestion tolls or fees should be charged for use of streets and highways.

Nelson's final recommendation concerns the transportation trust funds. It is recommended that these trust funds and other revenues be pooled to be used for investments in whatever mode of transport can be economically justified.

Regional Transportation Planning Experience in
the United States: A Critical Review of Selected
Cases: Chapter 7

Ralph Gakenheimer and his associates attempt an evaluation of the actual experience of metropolitan regions, corridor regions, states, economic development regions, and focal regions. They look at actual cases of regional transportation planning in terms of the domains of transportation planning activities and in terms of the administrative form by which the regional agencies function. Regional transportation agencies are also evaluated in terms of their purposes and the strategies and techniques used. The authors conclude that the U.S. is in no condition at the present time "to develop a comprehensive national transportation system." The states are too strong and mediation among their interests is very difficult. The intermodal and intersectoral problems remain largely unsolved, both analytically and institutionally. The paper does, however, indicate a series of key options in the development of regional transportation planning. These are summarized below, followed by a summary of recommendations.

Regions which are highly coherent from the administrative point of view (e.g., the states) offer much better means of implementation, more responsiveness to client users, and better opportunities for intersectoral collaboration. The functional regions, those which better encompass problems (e.g., the corridors and metropolitan regions), provide greater leverage on analytic solution and may be the only means of solving the more important problems, but they suffer unfortunate implementation disadvantages. Evidence suggests that the states are the most promising regions for the problems they encompass. It is also apparent that regions that compromise between the criteria of functional and administrative coherence, those that have some of each but not a great deal of either (e.g., the economic development regions), have special problems.

The option of identifying a concrete, necessarily simplistic problem for the purpose of policymaking (e.g., the metropolitan areas and corridors), as opposed to creating a general purpose agency that conducts an open search for regional policies (e.g., the economic development regions) is another important alternative. Among the latter, the states again promise the most effective agencies. The situation suggests the advisability of special, short term agencies with rather specific problem missions as a means of accomplishing multi-state regional planning.

Another option is to create change-oriented agencies that strive for qualitatively different forms of the involved social or physical situations (such as the Appalachian attempt at social change or the Northeast Corridor emphasis on technological change), as opposed to agencies more concerned with the allocation of investment along existing lines to keep related transport and economic activities in equilibrium (e.g., metropolitan and most state planning agencies). To the extent that consensus on priority policy issues is great, change-oriented planning is the more possible.

With respect to the particular agency types reviewed, it is suggested that state planning should be advanced toward the accomplishments that the states' ample breadth of powers makes possible. This is the area where the deficit of good analytical tools and strategic procedure is most evident and would profit most quickly from contributions of this sort. It is clear that guidance for interstate collaboration is needed from the Federal Government, but except in special cases this appears not to imply multi-state agencies, which would add another level to the hierarchy.

Metropolitan transportation planning appears in a state of limbo. It needs to be retooled. But we must wait for evidence to be produced by such creative undertakings as the Boston Restudy to be sure of appropriate directions. Meanwhile, methodological studies on the matter are very worthy of attention. Care must be taken with the natural tendency for metropolitan planning techniques to be exported to the regional planning agencies, so that recipients are aware of limitations on these techniques which have been discovered in previous use. Whether the current concerns will produce metropolitan regions that are larger than present ones, and of a scale interesting to regionalization at the multi-state level, remains to be seen. Investigations of the usefulness of such larger metropolitan regions would repay the effort. In view of the coherence of the regions, and the size of the investment at stake, metropolitan planning clearly must be continued.

Corridor planning is clearly confined in applicability to the Northeast Corridor and the Lower Great Lakes region. Any further "corridors" would be planned by means basically different from these and would appear to have very doubtful prospects of success. But the Northeast Corridor—or the sections of it above and below New York City, if one prefers—is as viable a planning region as can be established on the multi-state level. Its important contributions to choice of technology may well constitute an important contribution to the field and improve the feasibility of various kinds of regional transportation planning in the future.

The experiment of economic development regions is not yet complete. There have been important evolutionary changes in their approaches which require further evaluation and the generating of further evidence before they can be properly qualified as transportation planning regions. The fact that they are organized to meet the highest priority problems of policy at this scale recommends the use of resources to give them the best possible opportunities for success. These remarks apply, however, only to the most viable of them. There seems little hope for a number of additional ones to attain a good level of effectiveness.

Little basis is found for encouragement toward the creation of much more widespread regionalization for transportation planning, such as an exhaustive regionalization of the United States.

The Future and Its Implications for Regional Transportation Planning: Chapter 8

In Chapter 8, John R. Meyer assesses the future and its implications for regional transportation planning. The design of a proper framework for transportation planning has never been well understood for several reasons, one of which is the simple fact that transport technologies have hardly been static, so that any specification of the underlying behavioral relationships could quickly become dated. The paper discusses the implications of future development—ranging from transportation technology to population distribution to changes in industrial location—that may have implications for the efficacy of regional transportation planning.

Meyer argues that different modes and functions require different levels of planning. Transport facilities serve many purposes, and the proper level of planning for some purposes may be quite different from that for others. He further argues that increasing environmental concern will heighten the demand for more local participation, even if technological or efficiency arguments suggest a shift toward higher level planning. This suggests that the planning process be devised so as to ensure consultation for involvement of the very many different constituencies that are likely to be affected. Meyer suggests identifying constituencies, in rising order of scale or of geographic coverage: for example, neighborhood, city (or commuter watershed), urban conurbation or megalopolis, ecological or environmental region, nation, and, finally, the international community. He points out that this is not an exhaustive list, and that there is no need to define constituencies on geographical grounds. They could be defined along functional lines or on some other basis.

Meyer sees the main problem of transport planning as externalities created by transportation. This means many groups get involved and claim they need to be consulted about transport development before these developments occur. The essential problem in transport planning, then, is to identify these relevant interests or constituencies and devise means to represent their views *without unduly restricting or immobilizing the entire planning process.* The essential challenge for transportation planning in the next few years will be the development of planning services at different levels of government to serve different modes and functions in such a way that these are properly articulated, coordinated, and nevertheless are aware of many diverse interests.

Political and Administrative Realities of
Regional Transportation Planning: Chapter 9

The ultimate decisions with respect to whether there will be regional planning, what its characteristics may be, what regional boundaries may be drawn, how the planning might be accomplished, what its objectives and methods might be, and related issues are all public sector or governmental decisions and can only be understood in the context of the political decision-making process. This process is the focus of Norman Wengert's paper, which examines the institutions, forces, and factors that influence and shape decisions with respect to regional transportation planning.

Wengert's recommendations concerning regional transportation planning seem to fall into two main categories: (1) those characteristics requisite for successful planning, and (2) the proper role for regionalization in transportation planning. Under the first heading, Wengert argues that planning is impossible without first determining goals. Decisions on goals and means of achieving them are political; that is, they require knowledge concerning the allocation of benefits and the distribution of costs. Thus they need legitimation through support and acceptance of proposed courses of action. Planning must take account of the views and interests of all the people affected by plans and proposals. This requires careful research and analysis, opinion surveys, simulation of social decision-making, organization and encouragement of groups not presently expressing their views, advocacy planning and use of ombudsmen, adversary proceedings, and hearings. Ultimately decisions must be made by administrators and planners weighing citizens' views. Wengert does not regard "participation" as the whole process.

The author regards benefit-cost analysis as an important tool in helping administrators reach decisions concerning planning. He argues that benefit-cost analysis should be used on investment decisions but emphasizes the distribution of benefits and costs for determining policies as among regions. It is not enough to know that a proposed project is justified on narrow benefit-cost grounds; the impact of a project's benefits and cost on different income groups and on different regions is necessary also for correct decision-making.

Concerning the issue of regionalization, Wengert points out that the creation of boundaries has far-reaching implications because political boundaries tend to become rigidly fixed and because boundaries drawn for today's purposes may not fit tomorrow's needs. Once boundaries are determined, they must be stable for purposes of analysis and appraisal, although fluid boundaries might seem preferable. Consequently, decisions to establish boundaries must be taken with great care and based on clear perception of goals and thorough analysis.

Another point relevant to the issue of regionalization concerns whether the regional organization will be a unit of government or simply a department or agency of government. Wengert points out that a unit of government typically has the following characteristics: territory; independent financial authority; and a popularly elected, independent governing body. Many problems may be regional in character and scope, and may be amenable to regional solutions, but simply creating regional administrative agencies or commissions does not guarantee that they will be dealt with more effectively. One might contemplate regional government with clear governing authority and responsibility to the people through designated officials. These might be elected specifically for this purpose. On the other hand, the Representatives and/or Senators from the region might be constituted as the regional governing legislature. Perhaps regional committees of Congress could be set up. (These would lack adequate governing authority, however.) Wengert contends that unless the issue of power can be resolved, one must be skeptical about what regionalization can accomplish.

In particular, Wengert questions the desirability of the approach to regional transportation planning contained in Senator Magnuson's Bill, S.2425, introduced in the 91st Congress, 1st Session. Instead, he suggests that regionalization under the Intergovernmental Cooperation Act and the Budget Bureau Circular A-95 may come nearer dealing effectively with pressing transportation problems. The Intergovernmental Cooperation Act of 1968 is designed to ". . . establish coordinated intergovernmental policy and administration of development assistance programs." Title IV sets out a national policy of considering local, regional, and state interests in administering federal aid programs for local development.

This Title of the bill was implemented by the Budget Bureau Circular A-95 on July 24, 1969. The Circular emphasizes the need for sound and orderly development of urban and rural areas of the nation. It directs that "to the maximum extent possible, consistent with national objectives, all federal aid for development purposes shall be consistent and further the objectives of state, regional, and local planning."

Major Themes of the Study

This section pulls together a few of the major themes growing out of the individual papers. The themes discussed are regionalization, planning and the market, efficiency versus equity, and the role of "participation." This section synthesizes the paper discussions, although no attempt is made to cover up disagreements among individual authors.

Regionalization

The major theme of the study was aptly stated by Friedman and Stuckey. The issue of regionalization can be posed in two ways: (1) as a search for some uniform set of criteria that may be used to divide the nation into a set of mutually exclusive and exhaustive regions, or (2) as a search for a complex pattern of regions corresponding to different purposes and needs, which regions may be overlapping and superimposed on one another.

If one chooses the first approach, he is led to the type of regions proposed by Fox. Fox sees his FEA as a fundamental building block for general purpose regions. The FEA, then, is the culmination of the search described in the first approach to regionalization. Fox says, "The fundamental community of 1970 in metropolitan areas is coextensive with the commuting field. It is delineated on the basis of actual transportation behavior of employed members of the labor force with respect to the journey to work. It is of great potential value as a general-purpose social, economic, and political community, with capabilities for transportation planning and general urban-regional planning within its boundaries."

If one chooses the second approach, then, as Friedmann and Stuckey point out, he is led to the question how might the planning and related activities be organized in space so as to meet the needs for transport in different parts of the country more effectively. That is, the issue becomes not designing regions for transportation planning but rather designing transportation planning for regions.

While most of the authors are opposed to establishing permanent and mutually exclusive multi-state regions exhaustive of the United States, as proposed, for example, in the Magnuson bill, they are, nevertheless, aware of the advantages of such a regionalization. Wengert, in particular, points out the importance of unit boundaries; namely, that most government activity takes place within rigidly defined spatial units and that substantial data collection occurs only within boundaries. For purposes of implementation, operation, and assessment, boundaries are almost a necessity.

Nonetheless, the arguments against such regions appear overwhelming and are discussed by several authors. For example, Alonso makes the following points. Transportation regions are blurred and difficult to bound. They are essentially nodal for which it is relatively easy to identify a core or spine, but from this center they diffuse through space so that bounding is arbitrary. They change over time with changes in technology and the structure of the economy; thus any initial regionalization of the country will become obsolete at a later time. Clear jurisdictional boundaries would conflict with the reality of transportation markets whose tendency is to overlap, interpenetrate, and interlock. A regionalization based on the large-scale regional structure of the transport system would cut across the grain of other bases of regional definition, e.g., North-South Appalachian region for economic development versus the East-West flow of transportation. Those people residing outside a region but who are affected by its policies may be unable to get redress of grievances. For these reasons, elaborated in the following chapters, an exhaustive and permanent regionalization of the U.S. for transportation planning purposes would not seem desirable.

Planning and the Market

Another theme of the study was the extent to which planning could be left to markets. It should be understood that no author advocates *laissez-faire*; all realize that some governmental intervention in otherwise free markets will often be required to achieve the most efficient use of economic resources. In his paper, DeSalvo explicitly considers situations in which planning is necessary and desirable, where "planning" is taken to mean any governmental intervention in private market operations. Economic theory and empirical work dictate certain prescriptions concerning planning in addition to providing a rationale for it. These prescriptions have not always been followed in practice, however; this is particularly so for transportation planning. Nelson shows this to be true for transportation and proposes policy changes to improve the use of resources in transportation.

While the economist is able to provide a pretty impressive framework for policy prescription in transportation, planners nevertheless feel that there is more scope for planning than the economist perceives. Alonso, for example, says transport markets are controlled and regulated *but unplanned*. In other words, he sees some functions different from regulation and control that may be legitimately called planning. These other planning functions comprise collection of information, forecasting, and the development and evaluation of alternatives for action.

This is not an uncommon view among planners and others; however, a reconciliation between the views of economists and planners was not made in any of the papers, and unless this is eventually done, the knowledge of economists and planners will be difficult to mesh. It seems that progress toward a resolution would be achieved by the explicit introduction into economic theory of a "planning function" analogous to the production function relating firm inputs to firm outputs. Without such a function in economic analysis, there will of course be no role for "planning" as Alonso uses the term. Since it is obvious that such a planning function exists (otherwise how is governmental intervention implemented?), its inclusion in economic analysis would go a long way toward reconciling economics with planning.

Efficiency versus Equity

A distinction is often made between "efficiency" and "equity" as objectives of economic policy. Efficiency is producing the most goods and services with the resources at our disposal. (A rigorous definition is provided in the DeSalvo paper.) Once a collection of goods and services is produced, it may be distributed in a variety of ways, e.g., all to one person, none to the rest; equally to all; etc. An equitable distribution is one that is socially acceptable.

The importance of this distinction for purposes of this volume is the predominance of the efficiency objective in policy prescriptions. Benefit-cost analysis, for example, is a method for deciding whether to undertake a public investment project. Choosing a project on the basis of benefit-cost ratios (or similar criteria) ensures an *efficient* use of resources. It says nothing about the distributional effects of the project. A project justified on benefit-cost grounds could in fact make the rich richer and the poor poorer.

The contributors to this book recognize this problem and attempt to propose solutions. Several authors propose that prospective benefits and costs of public investment projects be arrayed by income class of recipient (or bearer, in the case of costs) or by region, or by any other variable that reflects the distributional impact of the prospective project. In this way the analyst would not impose on policymakers his own ethical views concerning distribution, nor imply that there were no distributional effects. The proposal would not remove the difficulty of making a choice, but at least the choice would not solely be made on efficiency grounds. This was an issue the authors felt strongly about, as indicated by its inclusion in nearly all the papers.

Participation

Several of the papers call for participation in regional planning decisions by those likely to be affected by such decisions. It is particularly stressed in the papers by Cumberland and Meyer. The call for "participation" is undoubtedly predicated on democratic principles, but the operational meaning of the term is not always adequately considered. Wengert's paper explores this issue.

"Participation" should have operational significance: not like, "the right of people to participate in decisions which affect their lives is a central value of democracy," but rather like "no taxation without representation." To achieve an operational "participation," methods must be used to establish a two-way flow of communication. But, in addition, identifying those affected by plans and programs requires careful research and analysis. Wengert's proposals, elaborated in detail in his chapter, would seem to go a long way toward achieving real participation.

1

The Economic Rationale for Transportation Planning

Joseph S. DeSalvo,
University of Wisconsin–Milwaukee

This paper examines the circumstances under which economic theory provides a rationale for planning and surveys empirical analyses to determine whether and to what extent these circumstances prevail in transportation. The implications of these findings for regional transportation planning are explored. It serves, therefore, as a guide to the kinds of issues with which transportation planning might usefully concern itself and as an introduction to the other papers constituting this study.

The discussion is divided into six sections. The first treats the nature of planning: its definition and arguments pro and con. The next section specifies the conditions under which a competitively organized economy can produce maximum economic efficiency without planning. Since these conditions are stringent and may be violated in practice, a rationale for planning emerges in the third section. The fourth section surveys empirical research bearing on the violation of these efficiency conditions. Here the analysis narrows to the field of transportation. The conjunction of empirical transportation analyses with the theoretical rationale for planning produces a synthesis leading to a rationale for transportation planning, contained in the fifth section. Finally, in the last section, the implications of the preceding for *regional* transportation planning are explored, and some of the myriad special considerations for such planning are mentioned. Some of these considerations are taken up in subsequent papers.

The Nature of Planning

"Planning" has been variously defined. It has been called "action-oriented thought,"[1] "the application of intelligence to the future,"[2] "preparation for work,"[3] and so on. An adequate single definition that encompasses most of the others has been provided by Seeley.[4] He views planning as a formal or ordered process in which men seek by forethought to affect action so as to bring about more desired states than it is anticipated would otherwise occur. This definition captures the essence, implicit or explicit, of other definitions: thoughtful action to produce desired change. Moreover, its generality permits almost any kind of planning (economic, social, intra-firm, etc.) and any kind of planning organization (national government, state government, regional planning authorities, the PTA, etc.).

For the purposes of this paper, it is *economic* planning that is of interest. That is, the actions that are sought to be affected by planning are economic ones (saving, investment, production and consumption of commodities, and so on) and the more desired states to be brought about are economic (growth and development, price stability, full employment, and an equitable income distribution).

Also, for the purposes of this paper, the planning agency will be assumed to be a government or some agency created by a government or to which a government has granted certain rights and duties. The reason for this is that such an authority would possess the power to ensure accordance with its decisions. There are clearly types of planning that do not require the planning agency to be a unit or agent of government. Because of the pervasiveness of economic variables, however, it is unlikely that economic planning could succeed without the power of government behind it. Consequently, we view economic planning as governmental intervention into otherwise free markets.

Whether government should engage in economic planning has been the subject of debate for a number of years. The noneconomic arguments usually revolve around the question of freedom under planning. The economic arguments concern themselves with whether or not planning is the best way of attaining desired economic objectives.

The debate over freedom under planning still continues. Nevertheless, most of the issues were brought out a quarter of a century ago by F.A. Hayek[5] and Barbara Wootton.[6] Hayek holds that economic planning is inevitably totalitarian and inimical to freedom. Wootton's position is that, although there are dangers, economic planning is compatible with freedom. Both would agree that no plan can give people what they actually want as distinct from what somebody else thinks they want or ought to want.

The issue of freedom under planning continues to be debated, and it is not the purpose of this paper to enter that debate. However, it should be noted that much of the case against planning rests on a view of the private market mechanism as an efficient allocator of resources. The private market is seen as a great organizer of consumption and production decisions. The very multitude of such decisions is a powerful argument against planning, for it is said that no planner can hope to possess the information necessary to make the decisions that the market makes unaided. In this view, all that is needed to achieve the best use of scarce economic resources is a hands-off policy by government that should content itself with national defense, police functions, and other presumably noneconomic activities.

This faith in the free market has existed at least since the time of Adam Smith (1776) who used the term "invisible hand" to describe its workings. It is only recently, however, that the "invisible hand" theorem has been rigorously proved and the conditions under which the theorem holds spelled out carefully. To the extent those conditions are not fulfilled in practice, the case against planning is much weakened, for decentralized decisionmaking cannot achieve desired economic goals when the conditions are violated. Some other method is then required.

The following section presents a careful statement of the "invisible hand" theorem and its requisite conditions.

Economic Efficiency Without Planning

One of the greatest achievements of economic theory has been the elucidation of the conditions under which competitive markets produce the best resource use. Although, as mentioned earlier, the idea of the "invisible hand" dates back at least to the time of Adam Smith, it was not until fairly recently that the conditions under which the theorem holds were satisfactorily worked out.[7]

Some Definitions

Before stating the basic results of this section, it is necessary to define certain concepts that will be used throughout this paper. These concepts are *resource allocation, distribution of income, efficiency, equity*, and *competition*.

Resource Allocation and Income Distribution. The economic system, whether competitive or not, produces an allocation of resources among its members. That is, the final consumption goods and services, intermediate goods used by firms in their own production, capital goods used in production, labor services, raw materials, and so forth, are all at any given instant allocated in some fashion among the economic units, households and firms, comprising the economy. This is another way of saying that at any given time the income of the economy is distributed in some fashion among the members. Although at any given moment in time there is an allocation of resources or distribution of income, it is also true that resources are allocated over time. How an economy chooses to allocate resources over time determines to a great extent the rate at which that economy will grow and develop. Resource allocation, at a moment in time and over time, results from the operation of the economic system: through the expenditures of wages and salaries, dividends, profits, interest, and so on, which are in turn obtained from the sale or "rental" of labor, goods, services, materials, and savings.

Efficiency. An allocation of resources is "efficient" (or, alternatively, Pareto optimal, Pareto efficient) if there is no other allocation that would make at least one person better off without making anyone else worse off ("better off" in terms of each individual's own preferences not as these are perceived by someone else). Thus, if an alternative allocation of resources would be preferred by one individual and would leave all others as well off as the present allocation, then the present allocation is not efficient. This definition applies to an economy at any given moment in time as well as over time. It is conceivable for an economy to operate efficiently at successive moments in time but for the time path of allocation to be inefficient. Note that the "desired economic objectives" mentioned earlier, except equitable income distribution, are included in the single objective of efficiency.

Equity. The preceding is a definition of optimal resource use with which few people could quarrel. It should be pointed out, however, the many efficient allocations may exist at the same time. Choices between these would require strong ethical judgments because movement from one efficient allocation to another would of necessity make at least one person worse off and at least one better off. In other words, an allocation of resources could be efficient, but the distribution might be undesirable from society's viewpoint. Equity exists when the allocation of resources is efficient and the associated distribution of income is acceptable to society.

Competition. Competition exists when individual consumers and firms regard the prices of commodities and of productive inputs to be unalterable by their own consumption and production decisions. Under competition, the consumer can purchase all he wants of any commodity without affecting its price, and the firm can purchase all it wants of productive inputs without affecting their prices. Furthermore, competition requires the price of each commodity and each productive input to be the same for each consumer and producer. All consumers pay the same price for the same item, and all producers pay the same price for the same productive input. These conditions implicitly assume that everybody knows all prices and that charging prices does not itself use up resources.

Competitive Equilibrium and Efficiency

A competitive market will produce an equilibrium in which individual consumers obtain maximum satisfaction from expenditure of their incomes on commodities, individual firms achieve maximum profits from their expenditures on factor inputs and production and sale of outputs, and consumer purchases are consistent with firms' sales (i.e., markets clear).[8]

Two propositions about competitive markets are of special importance for our purposes: (1) *a competitive equilibrium is efficient* and (2) *any efficient allocation of resources can be achieved by competitive markets, given a suitable reallocation of initial resources.* The results apply to an economy at any given time as well as over time. Consequently, a competitive economy will produce an efficient pattern of capital accumulation as well as an efficient allocation of goods and services among its members.[9]

These characteristics of competitive markets provide a rationale for decentralized decision-making by individuals and firms without government intervention. This is basically Adam Smith's invisible hand. Private self-interest on the part of consumers and producers in a competitive environment results in the best use of scarce resources. Also, if we can decide on some socially desired distribution of incomes and a mechanism for attaining it, then the competitive market can be used to obtain an efficient allocation of resources consistent with the desired distribution of income. This means decisions regarding equity can be separated from the efficient operation of an economy; the latter can be left to private competitive markets.

These propositions provide the intellectual rationale for private enterprise operating through competitive markets. Nevertheless, these powerful propositions are based on certain assumptions that may not hold for particular economies. When they do not hold, the basic propositions justifying decentralized decision-making no longer hold, and there is then a need for some kind of collective decision-making designed to produce efficiency.

Impediments to Attaining Efficiency Without Planning

Competitive markets may fail to be economically efficient for a number of reasons, and, of course, there is no presumption that non-competitive markets will be efficient. Hence, there are two broad issues with which to deal. The first concerns those factors that prevent otherwise competitive markets from achieving efficiency. What are these factors, and what can be done about them? The second concerns non-competitive market structures and what can be done about attaining efficiency with them.

Existence of Competitive Markets and Increasing Returns to Scale. Since competitive markets are so important to the efficient operation of a decentralized economy, the first question one might raise is whether or not such markets can in fact work. In other words, can individual consumers and producers, when left alone to purchase and sell at market-determined prices, produce an equilibrium in the economy such that their actions are mutually consistent? It is not obvious that a competitive equilibrium can exist, and, if it cannot, the normative role of competitive markets collapses.

It turns out that a competitive equilibrium depends on the absence of increasing returns to scale large relative to the market.[10] When a firm expands its scale of operation by increasing all its productive inputs proportionately and its output consequently rises in a proportionately greater amount, the firm is said to enjoy increasing returns to scale. Also, if the prices the firm must pay for its productive inputs are unchanged as it expands its scale of operations, then its average production costs decline as output increases. Such a situation may not permit the operation of competitive markets, for the firm would be induced to expand its production until it were one of a few firms or the only firm occupying the market, unless the range of increasing returns to scale was small relative to the size of the market. However, if only one or a few firms operated in a single market, each would have some control over price. Such "high concentration" would violate the requirement for competition that specifies no control over price. Firms with increasing returns to scale large relative to the market are often called "natural monopolies."

Externalities. Thus, the absence of increasing returns large relative to the market means that a competitive equilibrium is possible. There are, however, other conditions that may not permit such a competitive equilibrium to be efficient. Perhaps the most important of these is the presence of externalities.[11] Externalities are interdependencies between economic units for which no market exists. The best examples are by-products of production that affect other producers or consumers, such as smoke, noise, and noxious odors. These interdependencies are a barrier to achieving economic efficiency because there is no market mechanism to value them. The smoke emitted by the steel manufacturer may increase the cleaning bills of neighboring households, but the producer does not perceive this cost. Hence, the social cost of steel production is greater than the private cost. If it were possible to make the producer bear the full social cost of his output, the production of steel (and consequently smoke) would be less. In fact, the amounts of these products would be optimal in the sense of efficient resource use. Where there exists no way of "internalizing" externalities, the private competitive market will result in inefficient resource use. In the example, there would be too many resources devoted to steelmaking.

There are many interdependencies between consumers and producers, consumers and other consumers, and producers and other producers. All of these are not externalities, however, because some arrangement is made to internalize them, either through legal, contractual, pricing, or other means. One reason externalities exist is that the cost of internalizing the interdependency would exceed the gains of doing so, and a voluntary arrangement cannot be made between the affected parties.

Public Goods. Aside from increasing returns, where competition may not exist, and externalities, where if competition exists it cannot be efficient, there is a special kind of commodity that the market may not produce in appropriate amounts. This kind of commodity is called a public or collective good. It is a good that can be consumed by more than one person at the same time at no extra expense, and it actually costs something to exclude potential consumers.[1 2]

When an ordinary commodity is consumed, the units consumed are thereby denied to others. For public goods, however, it may be impossible or very costly to exclude people from consumption. National defense is often given as an example of a good from which it is impossible to exclude consumption, but there are less extreme examples for which exclusion would be possible but costly. (People are in fact excluded from certain kinds of national defense, e.g., by location of ABM sites.) Television reception is a public good, but it is conceivable that television set owners could be excluded from obtaining a particular program by scrambling the signal and levying a charge for an unscrambler. Similarly, live concerts, plays, and so on, are public goods because the performance is available to all in about the same amount (although some people may have better seats than others). It is possible to exclude non-payers by erecting walls and supervising admission.

The key to the public good problem is the costliness of excluding consumption. In those instances where the cost of exclusion exceeds the gain, private enterprise will not produce the good, even though it may be desired by consumers, because consumers cannot be made to pay their fair share for its provision. Thus, in an economy with demand for public goods, these demands may not be satisfied by private enterprise even when competitive markets prevail. There is therefore a possible role for collective action in the provision of such goods.

Uncertainty and Information. Implicit in the definition of a competitive market were two assumptions: (1) certainty and (2) complete information.[1 3] These were implied when it was said that every economic agent faced constant and identical prices. Uncertainty, a lack of knowledge of which state of nature will prevail in the future, is not in and of itself inconsistent with competition. People can make contracts contingent on the occurrence of certain possible outcomes. Insurance is an example of these kinds of contracts; common stocks may also be an example. It is not, therefore, uncertainty itself that is inimical to competitive markets or to efficiency.[1 4] This is true, however, only when the events insured are not controllable by individual behavior. There are, of course, situations in which the fact of insurance affects the insured's behavior (called "moral hazard" in the insurance literature). Examples are hospitalization insurance, where the insured will tend to spend more on hospital services than he would if uninsured, and automobile collison insurance, where the insured may drive more recklessly than when uninsured and possibly spend more on auto repairs. In such cases competitive markets result in overconsumption, since the price paid by the consumer is artificially low. Inefficiencies may therefore occur in otherwise competitive markets because of uncertainty.[1 5]

This type of uncertainty is closely related to lack of information. Apart from uncertainty about states of the world, however, lack of information itself leads to inefficiency. Participants in the economic system are assumed to have full knowledge of prices and availability of commodities and factor inputs. Clearly this assumption does not hold in the real world. It is approximated in many situations (for example, commodities that are repeatedly purchased) but not in others (for example, the one-time purchase of a durable consumption item). Where there is incomplete information, there is no reason to believe the market outcome will be efficient.

Imperfect Competition. The previous discussion has dealt with the assumptions underlying competitive equilibrium and with the other conditions that, while not inconsistent with competition, result in inefficiency. Now, there is no presumption that non-competitive market structures will be efficient. Strictly speaking, since non-increasing returns is a sufficient condition for competitive equilibrium, then, if the economy does not attain a competitive equilibrium, that must be due to increasing returns. Thus, while it is logically possible to boil down cases of non-competitive markets to cases of increasing returns, it is nevertheless useful to look at specific conditions that have been associated with imperfect competition.

Seller concentration is the primary characteristic of imperfect markets, the extreme being monopoly (one firm selling a product for which there are no close substitutes) but with gradations from monopolistic competition (many firms selling slightly differentiated products) to oligopoly (few firms selling identical or slightly differentiated products). The inefficiency resulting from these market forms manifests itself in higher prices and smaller outputs than would result under competitive organization.[16]

Besides economies of scale, the major factors giving rise to seller concentration are product differentiation and barriers to entry. Product differentiation is present when consumers form different preferences for individual brands of a product. Since the products, though they may be physically identical, are different in the minds of consumers, the pressure to sell at the same price is lessened. (Product differentiation may be due to incomplete information on the part of consumers.) There are as a consequence fewer sellers of each slightly differentiated product. Barriers to entry constitute such things as patent controls over strategic techniques or products, monopolistic ownership of strategic resource supplies, pricing to discourage or prevent entry of new firms, and strong stable buyer preferences.[17]

Whatever the particular cause of concentration and whatever the degree of concentration (from monopolistic competition to monopoly), the allocation of resources through these markets will be inefficient. To the extent that market forces do not themselves tend to mitigate these non-competitive conditions, there is a role for government in this area.

Summary. There are a number of reasons why a market economy may not achieve efficient utilization of resources. In otherwise competitive markets, externalities, public goods, uncertainty, and incomplete information render the market solution inefficient. With these factors absent, increasing returns, and non-competitive markets in general, render the competitive market solution inoperative, the resulting market solution being inefficient. Hence, the powerful forces of the invisible hand are stymied when certain conditions prevail. The case for decentralized decision-making is weakened, and the case for governmental planning is strengthened. Given the goal of efficient use of scarce resources, what actions can be taken to restore efficiency in the face of these adverse conditions? This is the issue taken up next.

Economic Efficiency Under Planning

Extent of Centralization and Second Best Policy Prescriptions

Two issues arise in this connection before one gets down to specific methods for eliminating or mitigating the factors blocking the achievement of economic efficiency. The first of these concerns the alternative to decentralization when it is not possible for decentralized decisions to result in efficiency. What is the requisite extent of centralization? In principle this is easy to answer. It is that amount of centralization just necessary to restore efficient resource use. In practice, the answer is not so easy. Instead of answering the question it is assumed here that the minimum required centralized agency can be established to handle the problem or, alternatively, that the minimum required actions will be taken by the centralized agency already established. The most important type of centralized decision-maker is, of course, a government or governmental agency.

The second preliminary issue concerns the efficacy of correcting one disparity from efficient resource use in a world of many such disparities. This is an issue that has come to be called the problem of "second best."[18] It is simply not true in general that perceived policies for eliminating some sources of inefficiency result in an assured increase in efficiency.

An example from international economics illustrates the principle. Economists agree that free trade (no tariff or other barriers to imports or exports) results in world efficiency in resource use. Nevertheless, the reduction or elimination of a single tariff when there are many others may not increase efficiency. Suppose country A buys a commodity from country B since it is the cheapest source even after duty is paid. Now suppose country C, which also produces the item but at a higher cost than country B, lowers its tariff on the goods to such an extent that the total cost to country A is less than it would be if bought from country B. Country A then imports the item from country C, causing a reallocation of resources in country C from other goods to that imported commodity and a reallocation in country B away from the goods formerly exported to A. This result does not increase the efficiency of world trade, even though a tariff has been reduced. It would be more efficient in terms of resources expended for country B to produce the good, and, if there were no tariffs at all, this is what would result.

One wonders whether any policy prescriptions can be safely made in the face of such a situation. The problem of second best is certainly a blow to piece-meal policy changes, but it is important to understand that it is not the death knell. The second-best theorem does not mean that there are no piece-meal policy prescriptions that if adopted will lead to more efficient resource use. In particular, whenever there is a deviation from efficiency-producing behavior and the decisions of the deviant economic unit depend only on prices and variables under its control, then piece-meal policy is all that is required to correct the deviation.[19] It would seem a good deal of antitrust policy could proceed on a piece-meal basis without running afoul of second best problems. Whenever subsets of economic units are interrelated, however, through externalities or by other means that cause their decisions to be affected by non-price variables not directly under their controls, then the policymaker must consider the entire subset of units to avoid undesirable consequences. It is with respect to these latter cases that very little of a general nature can be said about policy prescriptions. Whether or not the "standard" treatments will in fact produce a more efficient allocation of resources must be settled on a case-by-case examination.

Redistribution of Income

We noted earlier that efficiency in the use of resources did not necessarily imply equity in the distribution of resources. It was also noted that, when competitive markets exist, any desired distribution of resources can be attained by such markets, given a suitable reallocation of initial resources. Consequently, even if all the requisite conditions for the operation of competition were fulfilled, there might still be a rationale for government planning to attain the socially desired distribution of income.

Despite the importance of income redistribution, we will say very little more about it in what follows. No prescriptions regarding the appropriate actions of government in redistributing incomes will be presented. The reason for this is that the justification for any particular distribution of incomes depends on value judgments about the relative worth or need of individuals. Although such judgments are implicit in many existing governmental programs—e.g., public housing, grants-in-aid to state and local governments, Medicare, unemployment payments—and in private charity, they are subject to serious disagreement. Prescriptions concerning efficiency, on the other hand, are likely to achieve wide agreement, for they are based merely on the proposition that, if an action makes at least one person better off and no one worse off, then it *should* be taken. In what follows, therefore, we restrict ourselves to efficiency-improving prescriptions only.

Uncertainty and Incomplete Information

From what has been said before about uncertainty and information, it would seem that government would have a role to play in reducing uncertainty and increasing the dissemination and availability of information. In fact, governments already do these things in varying amounts.

Our Federal Social Security System may be viewed as a method for sharing risk among individuals in order to reduce the uncertainty of future states of the world. It illustrates our point well because it is a system of insurance that would probably not be provided by individuals acting alone.

Government disseminates a wide variety of information, ranging from food quality grading to consumer price indices. The Federal Trade Commission tries to see that manufacturers and sellers do not mislead the consumer on the characteristics and prices of products.

That the government already performs these services is not to say it should do so nor that, if it should, it is doing so correctly. The theory tells us that there is a likely role for government in the presence of uncertainty and incomplete information, but the issue still to be addressed is when and how the government should intervene in private markets to mitigate the effects on efficiency of the presence of these conditions.

As already pointed out, the market handles some aspects of these problems. Information is produced through various kinds of advertising, and this no doubt goes some way toward informing consumers and producers about prices and the availability of commodities and inputs. Some uncertainties are handled by insurance. It would seem, then, inappropriate for government to interfere where markets exist for these items and where these markets are adequately doing the job. Nevertheless, as we have stressed above, there are likely cases where markets do not exist or are not doing an adequate job. It is here that government may make an efficiency-improving change. In this case, a whole gamut of possibilities opens up. At one extreme, the government could provide the service necessary for efficiency (e.g., provide information, collectively insure); at the other, it could attempt to establish markets to handle these problems or improve existing markets. Whatever approach is taken should depend in part on empirical questions concerning the characteristics of the problems (How adequate are private markets handling the problems? What are the cost conditions underlying the problem? Is the commodity or service a public good?) and in part on empirical questions concerning the relative costs of correcting the problem by various methods.

Increasing Returns and Non-Competitive Markets

Other conditions favoring a role for government in otherwise free markets are increasing returns and non-competitive market conditions. These will be discussed together because the remedies usually proposed for each are the same in some circumstances. Increasing returns, if large relative to the market, can result in the concentration of that market (i.e., a relatively large share of the market being held by the few largest firms); concentrated markets can arise for other reasons as well. The proposed remedies are regulation or dissolution and merger prevention. Regulation (that is, setting prices, rates of return, or outputs) is usually favored for so-called natural monopolies, firms whose product technology is such that the most efficient scale of operation is so large that it precludes other firms from operating in the same market. Either dissolution (that is, the breakup of one firm into several smaller ones) or prevention of mergers is favored where the monopoly does not rest on scale economies, so that several individual firms could produce as cheaply as one large one and through competition have lower prices and a greater total output than if the market were highly concentrated.

Although some economists have questioned these policy prescriptions, they are generally accepted in broad outline.[20] Difficulties arise primarily over empirical questions. Is the technology such that increasing returns prevail? What is the extent of concentration in markets? Is there a clear correlation between high rates of return and high concentration?

There is an argument, however, on both theoretical and empirical grounds, concerning the role of highly concentrated industries in economic growth and development. It is argued by some that large size is necessary for research directed toward discovering new products and techniques and the development of these new ideas.[21] Others hold that such is not the case. Unfortunately, empirical evidence on this issue is conflicting. Since there is no clearcut answer, a cloud hangs over the policy prescriptions discussed earlier.

Dissolution of a highly concentrated industry might make for more efficient resource use in the near term, but it might also reduce the amount of new products and techniques (and, hence, result in less efficient resource use) in the future. Thus, in recommending policy with respect to highly concentrated industries, one should bear in mind both issues. In individual cases, it might be possible to determine the relative importance of size for innovation and size for inefficient resource use.

Public Goods

The question here is not one of restoring efficiency in the presence of public goods but, rather, one of recognizing the collective desire for such goods and arranging the provision of them.

The provision of some public goods ends up in the private sector because it is profitable to exclude some potential users and charge prices to others. Examples are movies, plays, sporting events, and concerts. On the other hand, there are public goods that are not produced voluntarily by private enterprise because exclusion of potential users is too costly. Consequently, even should there be a demand for this type of good, it may go unproduced.

There would seem to be a role for government in the provision of public goods.[22] However, this raises two issues: (1) How is it to be recognized that there is a demand for such goods? and (2) What role should the government play? Neither question has been adequately answered.

To cover the first question would take us into some complex issues on the borderline between economics and political science. Rather than get into these issues, let us assume that somehow community desires become known. This is of course what happens in the real world: a community desire for national defense has been recognized and a public good has been provided.

This still leaves us with the issue of what is the government's role. How much of the public good should be produced and how should it be priced? Conceptually, answers have been found for these questions, but their practical application leaves much to be desired. In principle, an amount of the public good should be produced that will bring the social demand for the good into equality with its marginal cost.[23] In other words, if less than the optimal amount were produced, consumers would value an additional unit at more than its additional cost, and more of the good should be produced. Likewise, if a greater than optimal amount were produced, the additional cost of a unit of the public good would be greater than the additional value consumers attach to it, and less of the good should be produced. Only when consumers value the last unit of the good at its additional cost (that is, when social demand equals marginal cost) will there be no improvement in producing either more or less of the good. Furthermore, to pay for the good, in accordance with the benefit principle of taxation, taxes should be collected from consumers equal to their individual valuations of the good at the level it is provided. (This normative statement goes beyond efficiency in that it says how the cost should be distributed, whereas all that is required for efficiency is that social demand equal marginal cost of the public good.)

Although it might be possible to estimate the marginal cost of a public good, it would be practically impossible to estimate the individual valuations necessary for "pricing" the good and determining its optimal amount. This is particularly complicated by the individual consumer's self interest in not accurately revealing the value to him of the public good, for, if it is available to others, it is available to him as well.

Externalities

We are on somewhat firmer ground with respect to policy prescriptions in the face of externalities than we are for public goods. Most economists agree that certain externalities give rise to situations that, if uncorrected, lead to inefficient resource allocation. It is agreed that correction should take place. There is disagreement, however, on how the correction should take place.

The usual recommendation given in a case where there is a divergence between social cost and private cost (e.g., the steel mill example given earlier) is that action should be taken to bring the two into equality.[24] That is, the externality should be internalized in some way so that social cost becomes private cost. If an activity results in diseconomies not paid for by the producer, then he should be made to pay for them. Unless such action is taken, too much of the activity will be undertaken. On the other hand, if an activity results in benefits to others not recouped by the producer, then such an activity should be encouraged to expand by rewarding it in some manner. The traditional method proposed for achieving the equality of private and social costs and thus the increase or decrease in the activity is through use of taxes and subsidies. Put a tax on the activity producing external diseconomies and a subsidy on the activity producing external economies. This, however, is not the only, nor perhaps the best, way of internalizing an externality.[25] In fact, in practice, externalities are handled through governmentally imposed prohibitions, directives, and regulations. Which is the best technique would seem to depend on the specific problem.

Some economists maintain that government need take no action in the face of interdependencies, for markets in them will arise. These economists argue that the presence of an interdependency will give rise to mutually agreeable bargaining between the source and recipient of the external effect. Coase cites, as an example of how this might work, the case of neighbors living in adjoining houses.[26] One neighbor remodels his house by extending to a greater height the wall adjoining the other's house, thereby blocking the latter's chimney so that smoke backs down it into his house. Although the case was settled in court in favor of the neighbor who remodeled and against the one whose house became smokey, Coase contends that, *given the possibility of costless market transactions*, a mutually beneficial trade could have been arranged between the two neighbors. Specifically, he suggests the man with the smoking chimney would presumably be willing to pay a sum equal to the monetary worth to him of eliminating the smoke, and this would therefore become for the wall-builder a cost of continuing to have a high wall. If such bargaining took place and resulted in mutually beneficial trades, the result would be desirable. As a practical matter, however, it seems unlikely that this happens often. It may not be possible to reach bargains in situations like this or, if reached, they may be unstable, even when transactions are costless. Of course, transactions often take time and money in the real world. In recommending specific policy prescriptions, however, it would seem wise to keep in mind the possibility of such markets arising. If they could be expected to arise, then there would be no need for other ways of handling economic interdependencies.

In any case, whether or not to internalize the externality, or which method to use, depends on the costs and benefits of the alternative arrangements and must be answered in the context of a particular problem.

Empirical Studies in Transportation

To summarize to this point, we have examined those factors giving rise to a rationale for government intervention into otherwise free markets. We saw that imperfect competition, increasing returns, externalities, public goods, uncertainty, and incomplete information could each give rise to a need for centralized as opposed to decentralized decision-making for the sake of economic efficiency. Moreover, we discussed in general terms what actions a central authority might take to restore economic efficiency in the face of these factors and pointed out some of the difficulties of proposed policies. To this point, the discussion has been conceptual; no indication, except through examples, has been given concerning the existence of any of these factors in real-world markets. Clearly, if we are to say anything applicable to real markets, we must remedy this deficiency.

Our concern in this paper is with transportation. Hence we must seek to apply the preceding concepts to transport markets to deduce the appropriate role of government in such markets. To do this, we must know whether and to what extent the efficiency-impeding factors are present in transportation.

In this section, we draw on the large body of empirical research on transportation. While there is a wealth of literature, it does not, unfortunately, provide us with answers to all the questions we raise. This is especially so with respect to the issues of public goods, uncertainty, and incomplete information, and less so with respect to the issues of imperfect competition, increasing returns, and externalities. Consequently, what we say about the first three factors will be less reliable than what we say about the latter three.

Our procedure will be similar to that followed previously. We first examine the evidence bearing on the existence and magnitude of the six factors. Later, we discuss corrective policies for situations where such policies seem appropriate.

Returns to Scale in the Transportation Industries

We begin by examining the returns to scale of various transport modes. We start here for two reasons. First, there is more empirical work in this area than in any other, and, second, increasing returns, in addition to providing a rationale for government intervention alone, may also give rise to imperfect competition by facilitating concentration. Thus it seems that the issue of increasing returns is logically prior to the issue of market structure.

We shall draw inferences concerning returns to scale in transportation from various cost and production studies performed over the years. A number of such studies exist, but they are not always directed toward the issue of economies of scale. Their approaches have differed as well.

The empirical literature on this subject usually contains estimates of either production functions or cost functions or both. A production function is a relationship between productive inputs and the output of the transport mode. It states the maximum output that can be obtained from any specified quantity of inputs. For a railroad, we might have output measured in freight ton-miles per year related to inputs such as track mileage, number of locomotives and cars, hours of various types of labor, etc. And, for any combination of specific quantities of these inputs, the production function would give the maximum output of the firm or other productive unit.

When a production function has been estimated, we may examine it to determine the existence and extent of scale economies. If all inputs are increased in the same proportion (say, doubled) and output increased in a greater proportion (say, tripled), then the production function exhibits *increasing returns to scale*. When output rises by the same proportion in which inputs are increased, the production function exhibits *constant returns to scale*. Finally, when output increases by a smaller proportion than the increase in inputs, the production function exhibits *decreasing returns to scale*. The extent or magnitude of returns to scale, or course, may vary. Production functions may exhibit very greatly increasing returns or slightly increasing returns. Similarly, decreasing returns to scale may be great or small.

A (total) cost function, on the other hand, is a relationship between the total costs of production and the rate of output produced. It states the minimum cost of producing a specified rate of output. For a railroad, total annual costs might be stated as a function of freight ton-miles transported per year.

A distinction is made between long-run and short-run cost functions. The former shows the relationship of costs to output when each output level is produced with the optimum scale of plant for that output level. A short-run cost function displays the relationship between cost and output for a particular scale of plant. To determine the type and extent of returns to scale from cost functions, we must have estimates of long-run cost functions.

If total costs rise faster than the rate of increase in output (a 1-percent increase in output results in a greater than 1-percent increase in costs), then the cost function exhibits *decreasing returns to scale*. If total costs rise at the same rate as output, the cost function exhibits *constant returns to scale*. Finally, if total costs increase more slowly then output (a 1-percent increase in output results in less than a 1-percent increase in costs), then the cost function exhibits *increasing returns to scale*. Alternatively, average cost (total cost divided by output level) may be used to determine returns to scale. If average cost falls (rises) as output increases, returns to scale are increasing (decreasing). If average cost is constant as output increases, returns to scale are constant.

Some empirical studies of returns to scale have not estimated cost or production functions. Instead, they have categorized various firms into size groups. Then, using cost and output data for each firm, these studies calculate a unit cost figure for each firm. These unit costs are then averaged for all firms comprising a given size group. By comparing the level of size-group averages with size, one can determine the existence and extent of returns to scale.

We turn now to brief discussions of the empirical work on returns to scale for transport modes. The following modes are discussed: inland water, rail, air, highway, and pipeline. Readers uninterested in the details may turn directly to the summary table at the end of each subsection. These tables give the name of the researcher, the date the study was published, the type of study (statistical cost function, size-group average, engineering production function, and so forth), the country to which the findings refer, and the returns-to-scale findings.

Inland Waterway Transportation. Efforts to estimate inland waterway production and cost functions are fairly recent. Charles Howe has produced a number of papers, published and unpublished, that address the issue of inland waterway scale economies.[27] These have been recently pulled together into one volume, along with a good deal of other analyses pertaining to inland waterway transportation.[28] This volume represents the most extensive analysis of the economics of inland waterway transportation published to date. We also have available a recent study by L.S. Case and L.B. Lave on inland waterway scale economies.[29]

Howe's work treats both barge linehaul operations and the bargeline firm. His analysis of the linehaul process proceeds by developing production and cost functions for the linehaul operations of a barge tow. This function is obtained by solving for equilibrium tow speed two statistically estimated engineering relationships—effective push and resistance functions—that are functions of tow and waterway characteristics such as waterway width, depth, and stream velocity and tow-boat horsepower, tow length, breadth, and draft. Given the last three variables, the cargo weight of the tow is determined, and the speed function can be transformed into a production function—ton-miles per hour as a function of waterway and tow characteristics. Howe finds increasing returns to scale for the linehaul operations of barge tows.

Given cost data on tow operations, Howe is able to derive, with the help of his linehaul production function, a cost function for the barge tow. He finds that, as the scale of the tow (larger towboats) is increased, increasing returns to scale exist only up to a point after which decreasing returns prevail.

Howe attributes the observed decreasing returns to scale to the fact that the size of the waterway itself is being held constant as the scale of the tow increases. He finds, however, that the advantages of increasing the size of the waterway are exhausted when its depth is four times the draft of the tow and its width is twice that of the tow.

Howe's analysis is for a tow operating at equilibrium speed and encountering no delays. This is clearly not even a complete description of the linehaul operations of tows, which typically encounter numerous delays for locking, dropping and adding barges, adverse waterway conditions, and so on.[30] Analysis based on actual operating data can better reflect these conditions than the analysis just described, which was based on engineering relationships.

Leininger's statistical production function for tow linehaul operations—relating ton-miles per hour to tow draft, length, breadth; direction of travel (upstream or downstream); presence of Kort nozzles on towboat; and season—finds increasing returns to scale for the spring season, when rivers are open and locking is not required, and decreasing returns to scale for the fall season, when rivers are at pool stage and locking is required. These findings do not conflict with those of Howe, who finds cost advantages to deeper and wider waterways. We might tentatively conclude from these studies that, for a given waterway, increasing returns are followed by decreasing returns, the point or range where the one begins and the other ends is a function of waterway size, the larger the waterway the greater the range of increasing or constant returns to scale.

The analyses discussed above concern themselves only with production and cost relations for the linehaul operations of barge tows. This is, of course, only one aspect of the operations of a bargeline firm. Omitted are considerations of other activities such as terminaling and scheduling as well as various management operations. Now, it is conceivable that these other aspects of the firm's behavior could be built into the above analyses of linehaul operations, but in fact this has not been done. Rather, studies addressing the issue of the economies of scale of the bargeline firm have estimated statistical production and cost relationships that are self contained. We discuss these now.

Howe estimates both a production function and what he calls a planning function for the linehaul operations of bargeline firms. The former is concerned only with the firm's utilization of its stocks of boats and barges since at any given time only a portion of the firm's entire stock of capital equipment is utilized. The planning function, on the other hand, is designed to account for the idle stocks. The distinction allows Howe to determine whether increasing or decreasing returns to scale are due to scheduling or other dynamic factors.

A multi-equation model is estimated, using data on three firms operating in three different types of waterway environments. The model consists of a production function and two input demand equations. The production function relates cargo ton-miles to barge and towboat utilization variables. The barge and towboat input demand equations relate the quantity demanded of each input to the firm's output and the input's operating cost and utilization rate in a previous period. The findings, though statistically weak, indicate increasing returns to scale that decrease with the increasing restrictiveness of the waterway.

The planning function is estimated as part of a five-equation model similar to that of the production function model but differing primarily in its use of stock variables rather than utilization variables. Data are cross-section and time-series observations for six large firms. Results indicate decreasing returns with respect to the stocks of boats and barges, although the statistical reliability is slight. This means that as firm size increases firms encounter difficulties in scheduling their barges and boats and, consequently, suffer increasing unit costs.

In addition to the production and planning function analysis, which only refer to the firm's linehaul operations, Howe and his associates estimate a cost function for the bargeline firm, encompassing all costs. Costs are statistically related to output. Both costs (total waterline operating expenses) and output (total tonnage carried) are obtained from the Interstate Commerce Commission's published statistics. The results indicate increasing returns to scale. They are clouded, however, by the inability to distinguish real technological economies of

Table 1-1
Returns to Scale in Inland Waterway Transportation: Summary

Researcher	Date	Type	Country	Finding
Leininger	1963	SPF	U.S.A.	IRTS, linehaul operations in spring DRTS, linehaul operations in fall
Howe	Jan. 1964	EPF & ECF	U.S.A.	IRTS, linehaul production function IRTS followed by DRTS, linehaul cost function
Howe	July 1964	SPF	U.S.A.	IRTS, flow variables DRTS, stock variables
Howe, et al.	1969	SCF	U.S.A.	IRTS
Case & Lave	1970	SCF	U.S.A.	IRTS

Key:
EPF, engineering production function
ECF, engineering cost function
SPF, statistical production function
SCF, statistical cost function
IRTS, increasing returns to scale
DRTS, decreasing returns to scale

Note: Date of Howe's research is its earliest appearance.

firm expansion from reductions in input prices obtained by larger firms. Lower input prices cause lower unit costs that may magnify or diminish whatever returns to scale exist.

Case and Lave have also estimated the bargeline firm's cost function by statistically relating unit cost to a measure of current output and firm size variables. They also adjust for time trend, seasonality, and inter-firm differences. Using quarterly data on five firms for the period 1962-66, Case and Lave find substantial economies of scale for bargeline firms: a 10-percent increase in firm size will lead to only about a 3-percent increase in total cost.

In summary, the linehaul process shows increasing returns to scale, at least up to a point and under favorable waterway conditions. The bargeline firm enjoys increasing returns to scale also. The study by Howe finding decreasing returns is fairly weak statistically and emphasizes the stocks of boats and barges as variables. The Case-Lave study, however, also uses stock variables and is statistically better than Howe's. Consequently, the tentative conclusion is that bargeline firms operate with a technology that produces increasing returns to scale.

Railway Transportation. Railroad costs have long been a subject for study, but surprisingly few of the studies are relevant to our purpose. Initially the major concern was whether or not increasing returns characterized the industry, but, as explained later, these early studies are suspect. Research attention has been directed in recent years to development of estimates of long-run marginal costs for particular movements and of costing procedures; unfortunately, these do not fit our needs.

A discussion of the findings of early railway cost studies may be found in an article by Borts.[31] The emphasis, as already mentioned, was on the extent of increasing returns in the railway industry. The degree of increasing returns was felt to be indicated by the ratio of variable costs to constant cost for the rail firm. The smaller this ratio, the greater was the extent of increasing returns.

As Borts points out, much of the work on rail costs was done before the long-run cost function of economic theory had been developed. There is, therefore, little distinction in these studies between long-run and short-run costs. Borts feels that the dichotomy between "variable" costs and "constant" costs is identical to the current economics usage only when the short-run cost function is linear. Otherwise, the early railway economists were including some variable costs in their constant cost category. The extent of increasing returns, as this term was used by the early railway economists, referred to the relationship between fixed and variable costs and is not returns to scale resulting from firm size. Consequently, these early studies are of no use for our purposes.

Meyer, Peck, Stanason, and Zwick sought to present an approach to rail cost analysis that would answer some of the criticisms leveled at earlier studies and particularly the Interstate Commerce Commission method of rail costing, which was an outgrowth of some of the earlier methods.[32] The approach is to estimate cost, by component cost categories, as a function of output and plant size. The output variable is usually gross ton-miles, and the size variable is usually track mileage or number of cars. Cross-sectional cost functions are estimated for several different cost accounts for twenty-five Class I U.S. railraods. Both freight and passenger costs are analyzed.

No single cost function emerges from this work. Rather, the result is a large number of cost equations for various cost categories, namely, maintenance of way and structure, maintenance of equipment, administration and legal expenses, selling and marketing, station, yard, and linehaul. However, the authors obtain an estimate of long-run marginal cost by summing the estimated coefficient on the output variable from all equations.

Although the constancy of marginal costs implies constant returns to scale, this conclusion is not a result of the analysis but is, rather, implicit in it. Given the way the authors chose to synthesize an estimate of marginal cost, only a constant could result. Consequently, we cannot use this analysis to draw inferences concerning economies of scale in railway operations.

The Canadian railroads have gone farther with the above approach than did Meyer and his associates.[33] Through the use of statistical methods and engineering analysis, the variability of cost components is investigated in detail. Again, however, the result is not a conclusion concerning economies of scale. This was not the purpose; rather, it was to develop an accurate costing technique for pricing decisions.

Borts has attempted to estimate the long-run cost function for railways.[34] Using cross-section data for 1948 from Interstate Commerce Commission records and stratifying by region, Borts estimates a relationship between freight operating expenditures, total loaded and empty freight car miles, and total freight carloads. He finds that decreasing returns to scale prevail only in the Eastern region, although increasing and constant returns occur in both the South and the West.

One of the two statistical estimations of rail production functions to be found in the economics literature is also the work of Borts.[35] His study is designed to determine whether increasing returns exist in the railway industry. A model of production is specified for two processes in railway technology, and a production function is estimated from cross-section data for each process.

In both models, four variable inputs are specified. For the linehaul process they are: (1) labor services, (2) fuel consumption, (3) flow of equipment services, and (4) flow of track and structure services. The outputs are represented by (1) loaded freight car miles, (2) carloads of freight, and (3) empty freight car miles. The fixed inputs are represented by (1) total tractive capacity of freight locomotives and (2) miles of mainline track.

In the switching process the variable inputs used are the same as for linehaul except, of course, they are specified to yard operations. The outputs are represented by (1) yard switching locomotive miles, (2) yard switching locomotive hours, and (3) carloads of freight. The fixed inputs are: (1) miles of yard switching track, (2) total tractive capacity of yard locomotives, and (3) average number of freight cars standing in line.

Using Interstate Commerce Commission data for 1948 on observations of seventy-six Class I railways, Borts estimates both models and derives their implications for returns to scale. He finds that the switching process exhibits constant returns to scale. For the linehaul process, he gets conflicting results depending on which of two model specifications he uses. One indicates constant returns, whereas the other indicates increasing returns to scale for the linehaul process.

Klein estimated a production function for railroads in 1936.[36] The production function relates net ton-miles of freight carried to net passenger miles, man-hours of employment, tons of fuel consumed (in coal equivalents), and train-hours utilized. The inclusion of net passenger miles is due to Klein's treatment of freight and passenger carriage as joint outputs for a railroad firm. Because of the jointness of product, Klein cannot simply regress net ton-miles of freight on the other variables. He avoids this problem, however, by using a two-step estimation procedure: he first uses input prices to estimate the minimum cost levels for each railroad; then these are used to estimate parameters associated with the outputs. The result is a railroad production function indicating increasing returns to scale.

Another study sometimes cited in connection with rail scale economies is by Mansfield and Wein.[37] These authors estimate a rail freightyard cost function. Cost per day is assumed to be a linear function of the number of cuts switched per day (a "cut" is a group of cars that rolls as a unit onto the same classification track in a switching yard) and the number of cars delivered per day. Data consist of sixty-one days' experience during the summer of 1956 for a freightyard located in Toledo, Ohio. Since the equation is linear in the size variable, marginal cost is a constant. But, since the intercept's standard error is not reported, one cannot tell whether constant returns to scale describe the freightyard process.

Healy examines the scale effects of railroads by first accounting for density and regional differences among railroad systems and then relating cost adjusted for density and region to scale.[38] He does this for several expense categories—investment, wages, maintenance, transportation (train, yard, and station operations), and selling and administration—but believes that the rate of return on capital is most suggestive for measuring scale effects.

For investment, Healy finds there is a lower capital investment per unit of output for the smaller rail systems—5,000 to 19,000 employees—than for the larger systems. The difference is as much as 14 percent in favor of the smaller systems. For scales below 5,000 employees, the unit investment is higher. For wages, he finds as scale increases wages per unit of output increase, with about 13-percent increase in wages per unit with an increase in scale from 10,000 to

80,000 employees. For maintenance, Healy finds no significant relationship with scale. But, for transportation expenses, he finds an increase of 12 percent in unit expense as scale increases from 10,000 to 80,000 employees. The only expense category for which unit expenses decrease with increases in scale is administration and sales expense. Finally, Healy finds a decreasing return on capital with increasing scale above 10,000 employees and a decrease also below 5,000. On balance, then, Healy's study indicates decreasing returns to scale for the railroad industry.

The author has estimated a linehaul production function for a railway by using engineering relationships very much in the way Howe did for barge tows.[39] His production function relates the ton-miles per hour output of a freight train to (1) characteristics of the locomotives: number of locomotives, horsepower of each, number of axles of each; (2) characteristics of freight cars: number of cars; number of axles of each car, each car's load limit, cargo capacity, and proportion loaded; (3) characteristics of commodities transported: weight of each commodity per unit volume; and (4) characteristics of the route: gradient of terrain and track curvature.

Investigation of the production function for economies of scale reveals that when the locomotive and freight car inputs are increased in the same proportion, output increases in a greater proportion. Increasing returns to scale prevail throughout the whole range of output levels examined, although apparently only slight economies persist beyond a certain output level.

As with Howe's production function for tows, these findings refer to a specific vehicle and route; the levels of cost and the point at which most economies of scale are exhausted would vary with different vehicles (e.g., different types of freight cars and locomotives) and routes. Nevertheless, this analysis of the linehaul production function seems clearly to reveal economies of scale.

To investigate what happens to firm costs due to linehaul operations, DeSalvo and Lave apply the Meyer, Peck, Stanason, and Zwick non-linehaul costs to the linehaul costs generated by the DeSalvo function.[40] Again, it is found that increasing returns are associated with the linehaul movement throughout the entire range of output levels investigated.

In a recent critique of rail cost studies which were conducted by the Cost Finding Section of the Interstate Commerce Commission, Griliches finds much smaller economies of scale than reported by the I.C.C.[41] His purpose is to criticize the I.C.C.'s use of deflated and irrelevant data in its cost analyses, rather than provide an elaborate cost analysis himself. Consequently, he uses only simple (weighted and unweighted) linear and log-linear regressions between total cost per railroad and gross ton-miles, deflating these variables by miles of road operated in some cases and not deflating in others. Altogether, Griliches uses 1957-1961 averaged data on ninety-seven Class I U.S. railroads, divided into two groups: those roads with less than 500 miles of track operated in 1957 and those

Table 1-2
Returns to Scale in Railway Transportation: Summary

Researcher	Date	Type	Country	Finding
Borts	1952	SPF	U.S.A.	CRTS, switching process CRTS or IRTS, linehaul process
Klein	1953	SPF	U.S.A.	IRTS
Borts	1960	SCF	U.S.A.	DRTS, Eastern Region CRTS or IRTS, Southern and Western Regions
Healy	1961	SCF	U.S.A.	DRTS
DeSalvo & Lave	1968	S-ECF	U.S.A.	IRTS
DeSalvo	1969	EPF & ECF	U.S.A.	IRTS, linehaul process
Griliches	1972	SCF	U.S.A.	IRTS, much less pronounced for larger roads

Key:
SPF, statistical production function
SCF, statistical cost function
S-ECF, statistical-engineering cost function
EPF, engineering production function
ECF, engineering cost function
CRTS, constant returns to scale
IRTS, increasing returns to scale
DRTS, decreasing returns to scale

with more than 500. By splitting the data into two groups based on size of railroads, Griliches is able to show that economies of scale were much less pronounced for the larger roads.

In summary, it would seem that, despite the large body of analysis of railways, only a small fraction of it is relevant to the issue of scale economies. Of these, results are mixed. Borts' finding for the Eastern region and Healy's study indicate decreasing returns to scale. Borts' other work is consistent with constant or increasing returns to scale for the railway firm. Griliches and Klein find increasing returns to scale. DeSalvo and Lave also find increasing returns to scale for particular linehaul movements. Given this diversity as well as the sampling errors in the statistical analyses, it is impossible to draw a firm conclusion on scale economies in railroading, but the evidence favors increasing returns to scale.

Airlines. Early studies of airline costs compared the average costs of domestic carriers in various size classes. If the average cost of the "small" carriers was higher than the average cost of the "large" carriers, one could say that increasing returns to scale were present in the airline industry. John B. Crane, using 1940 and 1941 data, and Harold D. Koontz, using 1949 data, produce essentially the same results: there are large economies of scale evident for medium and large sized firms relative to very small firms, but there are little, if any, economies of scale in the medium to large range.[42] These economies appear to come from ground operations and general and administrative operations.

Caves, using 1958 data, comes to essentially the same conclusion as do the earlier investigators.[43] He relates average costs to available ton-miles, finding no significant relation between size and average costs among trunklines (the largest firms) but very substantial diseconomies of small scale for the local service carriers (the smallest firms). Moreover, the minimum size at which firms can enjoy the lowest average costs is itself found to be rather small.

Some airline cost studies use multiple regression analysis, recognizing that many factors other than size affect an airline's costs. One of the first of these, by Proctor and Duncan, encounters numerous difficulties in trying to relate total operating expenses per revenue ton-mile to seven independent variables.[44] Their primary problem is the high correlation between independent variables that frustrates their attempt to distinguish the individual contribution to cost of each variable.

Using simple correlations, Cherington finds average costs to be significantly influenced by the airline's proportion of coach traffic and its average length of passenger journey, but not by its scale of operations.[45] Wheatcroft, using scatter diagrams between average cost and a composite variable reflecting the size and speed of aircraft operated, finds that average cost decreases as the size and speed of aircraft increases.[46]

Table 1-3
Returns to Scale in Airline Transportation: Summary

Researcher	Date	Type	Country	Finding
Crane	1944	SGA	U.S.A.	IRTS, from small to medium and large-sized firms DRTS or CRTS, from medium to large-sized firms
Koontz	1951; 1952	SGA	U.S.A.	IRTS, from small to medium and large-sized firms
Wheatcroft	1956	SD	U.S.A.	CRTS
Cherington	1958	SC	U.S.A.	CRTS
Caves	1962	SGA	U.S.A.	IRTS, local service CRTS, trunklines
Eads, Nerlove, & Raduchel	1969	SCF	U.S.A.	IRTS, slight, local service
Murphy	1969	SCF	U.S.A.	CRTS

Key:
SGA, size-group average
SC, simple correlation
SD, scatter diagram
SCF, statistical cost function
IRTS, increasing returns to scale
DRTS, decreasing returns to scale
CRTS, constant returns to scale

The existence of substantial increasing returns to scale as firm size increases from very small to medium has been called into question in a recent study by Eads, Nerlove, and Raduchel.[47] These researchers estimate a long-run cost function for local service carriers, using statistically sophisticated techniques and data consisting of quarterly observations on twelve local service carriers over a nine-year period from 1958 to 1966. Their finding with respect to scale economies is that no evidence indicates that the local service airline industry is subject to substantial increasing returns. Their conclusion is that the industry is subject only to slightly increasing returns to scale.

In another recent study, using multiple regression analysis but not confined to local service carriers, Murphy finds constant returns to scale for the airline industry.[48] His data are for 1965 and 1966 and apply to eleven domestic trunk lines and thirteen local service carriers.

In summary, there appears to be agreement among researchers that there are no economies or diseconomies of scale beyond the smallest size firm in the U.S. airline industry. There is disagreement, however, about whether or not there are substantial economies of scale obtainable in size increases from the smallest. The most sophisticated study performed to date finds only minor scale economies for local service carriers. It would seem, on balance, that a fairly safe conclusion would be that the U.S. airline industry exhibits constant returns to scale.

Highway Transportation. The issue of economies of scale in trucking has over its roughly thirty-year history engendered a good deal of controversy. A number of articles and books contain discussions of the role of economies of scale in trucking, but only nine of these contain empirical estimates of the existence and extent of such economies. Only those works in which empirical work on the issue has been performed are discussed here.[49]

The earliest empirical study of returns to scale in trucking is apparently that of Cadbury.[50] He compares unit costs of three different categories of road transport in England. The data consist of observations on 150 trucks, but no date is given for the observations. Computing size-group averages, Cadbury concludes that "the larger concerns have no special advantage, and indeed that for limited mileages, the small man seems to be able to operate more cheaply than his rivals."[51]

Most of the studies of returns to scale in trucking employ the method of grouping firms into size classes and computing an average unit cost for each class. Clearly, unless other variables are controlled, this method is prone to serious error. One of the earliest studies, however, did produce a cost curve estimated by simple linear regression.[52] Edwards' analysis is based on data for fifteen Class I carriers of general freight with similar average hauls. The linearity of the cost function is interpreted to imply constant returns to scale, although there is some departure from linearity at lower outputs. (Linearity does not ensure constant returns to scale unless the intercept is not significantly different from zero. No information is given on this point by Edwards.)

It was not until nearly a decade later that the next studies of trucking returns to scale were published.[53] Roberts uses data for 114 Class I carriers of general commodities operating primarily over regular routes and entirely within Illinois, Indiana, Ohio, and lower Michigan in an attempt to obtain a high degree of service and geographic homogeneity. Average cost per vehicle-mile is calculated for each carrier. Also size-group averages are computed for small, medium, and large firms. Although the size-group average costs show a general decline with size, upon examination of the individual firm unit costs, Roberts concludes that small firms are as efficient as large ones. Nelson groups 102 Class I carriers by intercity revenue class and compares them on the basis of cost per vehicle-mile and cost per ton-mile. He attempts to standardize operating characteristics by studying carriers with similar average hauls and loads. No evidence of economies of scale is found.

The first use of multiple regression analysis in the study of trucking returns to scale was by Chisholm.[54] His data are from 384 contractors hauling milk from farms in England and Wales during 1955-56. Chisholm divides his data into three size categories on the basis of gallons of milk carried. For each category he performs a regression of cost per gallon on gallons collected per vehicle-mile, gallons collected per farm, and the number of vehicles as a percentage of that expected on the basis of annual mileage run. This and further analysis of the data lead Chisholm to conclude that no economies and perhaps slight diseconomies of scale are present.

Schenker compares the efficiency of trucking in England under private enterprise, when most of the firms were small, and under nationalization, which produced a tremendous increase in scale.[55] Using various measures of efficiency, including cost per ton-mile, Schenker concludes that nationalization did not reduce efficiency but neither did it raise it; i.e., constant returns to scale.

Most of the studies discussed to this point found constant returns to scale for trucking, but none of them used very advanced statistical procedures. Warner performed an analysis of scale economies in trucking, paying careful attention to the statistical methodology.[56] A long-run cost function is estimated using annual data on seventy-two firms for the years 1955 to 1960. Warner finds that increasing returns to scale are overstated due to measurement errors. After correcting for measurement errors in the variables, it is found that increasing returns to scale are still present but small.

The only study to find substantial increasing returns to scale for trucking is reported by Emery.[57] His data consist of 233 Middle Atlantic Class I and II motor carriers of general commodities for 1960. Seven size groups are established based on revenue, equipment, employees, and assets. Average operating expenses per ton-mile are calculated for each category, and average costs fall substantially with size.

The most recent study of truck scale economies is by Koshal.[58] He estimates linear cost functions for the trucking industry by relating total costs to truck kilometers or ton-kilometers, using data for nine publicly-owned Indian truck

Table 1-4
Returns to Scale in Highway Transportation—Truck: Summary

Researcher	Date	Type	Country	Finding
Cadbury	1935	SGA	U.K.	IRTS, smaller firms CRTS, beyond smallest
Edwards	1947	SCF	U.S.A.	CRTS
Roberts	1956	SGA	U.S.A.	CRTS
Nelson	1956; 1959	SGA	U.S.A.	CRTS
Chisholm	1959	SGA	U.K.	CRTS or slight DRTS
Schenker	1965	SGA	U.K.	CRTS
Warner	1965	SCF	U.S.A.	IRTS, slight
Emery	1965	SGA	U.S.A.	IRTS, substantial
Koshal	1972	SCF	India	IRTS, distances below 1000 kilometers CRTS, distances beyond 1000 kilometers

Key:
SGA, size-group average
SCF, statistical cost function
IRTS, increasing returns to scale
CRTS, constant returns to scale
DRTS, decreasing returns to scale

companies for the fiscal year 1965-66 and for three privately-owned truck companies for the fiscal year 1958-59. He finds increasing returns to scale for the publicly-owned firms and also for one group of privately-owned firms, the latter operating primarily over distances of 500 kilometers. Constant returns are found for another group of firms operating primarily over longer distances. Koshal's conclusion is that the Indian trucking industry enjoys economies of scale provided the operation is restricted to distances below 1,000 kilometers.

In summary, only one study reports substantial increasing returns to scale. Most report either slight increasing returns over a large range of firm sizes or increasing returns for only the smallest firms or shortest routes, or constant returns. Only one study reports slight decreasing returns, but constant returns are reported also in the same study. Since the studies, for the most part, employ naive statistical methods, additional weight should probably be given to the studies of Edwards, Warner, and Koshal. Schenker's study, since it deals with such a massive increase in scale, should probably also receive more weight. Consequently, it seems fair to say that the best evidence suggests the existence of constant returns to scale for trucking. If any economies of scale exist, they are surely very slight.

Probably the first study of bus economies of scale was performed by Johnston.[59] He uses cross-section data for a group of twenty-four different sized firms in England for 1951. Instead of using regression analysis to relate expenses to output, Johnston explores various partial correlations among the variables: total expenses per car-mile, car miles, and the percentage of the fleet using fuel oil as opposed to gasoline. His conclusion is that, although there is some indication that long-run average costs decline with output, the hypothesis that long-run average costs do not vary with output cannot be rejected; i.e., constant returns to scale.

Meyer, Kain, and Wohl estimate bus operating costs.[60] The purpose, however, is not to obtain information on scale economies but to compare costs of different modes. Assuming fixed factor proportions and estimating operating costs per vehicle-mile additively by taking representative unit costs for each input, Meyer and his associates necessarily produce a constant marginal cost, which thereby implies constant returns to scale by definition.

More recently, Lee and Steedman use forty-four observations on municipal bus operations in Britain for 1967 to estimate a cost function.[61] Dependent variables are component cost categories (power costs, repair and maintenance costs, management and general expenses, and traffic operations costs) as well as total expenses per bus mile. Various regressors are used to represent the following dependent variables: size, factor prices (although data are cross-sectional, different geographical areas have different factor prices), homogeneity of output, physical and traffic environment, and accounting (to allow for different accounting procedures between firms). The analysis supports the hypothesis of constant returns to scale in municipal bus operations. Although there is evidence of increasing returns in traffic operations and in maintenance and repair activities, these are not sufficient to be reflected in total expenses.

Koshal presents some findings on bus scale economies using Indian data.[62] The data are for the fiscal year 1963-64 and refer to twenty-six state companies of the nationalized portion of the Indian bus transport industry, which constitutes about 35 percent of the whole industry. Koshal analyzes the behavior of total cost and its components: personnel, materials, overhead, depreciation, and interest. His output measure is seat-kilometers, a measure which takes into account size of bus. Simple linear regressions of cost on output are performed for each category. The consistent finding, for all cost components and for all types of service, is constant returns to scale.

Miller estimates a long-run cost function for urban bus transport relating bus operating cost to output, factor prices, and city setting.[63] The unique aspect of this study is its use of city-setting variables: in particular, schedule speed, which reflects the degree of congestion present in a city; total annual vehicle miles per route-mile served, a variable that is intended to distinguish cities on the basis of their "spreadoutness" or compactness; and a dummy variable for city age, which

Table 1-5
Returns to Scale in Highway Transportation—Bus: Summary

Researcher	Date	Type	Country	Finding
Johnston	1960	PC	U.K.	CRTS
Lee & Steedman	1970	SCF	U.K.	CRTS
Koshal	1970	SCF	India	CRTS
Miller	1970	SCF	U.S.A.	DRTS, slight
Koshal	1972	SCF	U.S.A.	CRTS

Key:
PC, partial correlation
SCF, statistical cost function
CRTS, constant returns to scale
DRTS, decreasing returns to scale

is intended to capture city differences in adaptation to rubber-tired transport technology. The data consist of observations on bus operations in thirty-three U.S. cities in 1963. The estimated function exhibits the presence of slight diseconomies of scale.

The most recent study of bus scale economies is by Koshal.[64] He estimates a linear cost function relating total cost to total bus miles using data on ten U.S. bus companies operating in metropolitan areas in 1969. No evidence of any economies or diseconomies of scale is found.

In conclusion, it seems safe to say that intra- and intercity busing display constant returns to scale; if there are any decreasing returns, they are very slight.

Pipeline Transportation. Two engineering type production functions have been obtained for pipeline transportation, one for gas and one for petroleum products. Although neither study is particularly recent, apparently no others have been performed. Both find substantial increasing returns to scale.

Chenery derives a production function for the process of gas transmission.[65] It is based on engineering relationships between the two basic capital inputs, pipe and compressors. After deriving the production function, input prices are

Table 1-6
Returns to Scale in Pipeline Transportation: Summary

Researcher	Date	Type	Country	Finding
Chenery	1949; 1953	EPF	U.S.A.	IRTS
Cookenboo	1954; 1955	EPF	U.S.A.	IRTS

Key:
EPF, engineering production function
IRTS, increasing returns to scale

used along with the production function to obtain a long-run average cost function of gas pipeline transportation. The average cost curve is downward sloping throughout, indicating increasing returns to scale for pipelines of larger capacity. Very great economies appear at low to medium capacities and smaller economies at larger capacities.

A similar technology exists for the transportation of crude oil, refined petroleum products, and, more recently, coal and ore in semiliquid form. Cookenboo derives a production function for crude oil pipelines, and, as one would expect, substantial scale economies are found.[66] In this case, horsepower of pumping equipment and pipeline diameter are the major inputs in the production of pipeline throughput. The long-run cost curve obtained from the production function is downward sloping throughout, indicating substantial economies.

Summary and Conclusions on Scale Economies in Transportation. In a cursory fashion we have examined the presence and extent of scale economies for the major transport modes currently in operation. In short, the following modes appear to possess increasing returns to scale: inland waterway transportation, pipeline, and probably rail. Constant returns to scale are exhibited by the following modes: airline (certainly trunk lines and probably local service lines), intercity trucking, and intercity and intracity busing.

Our purpose for reviewing these findings was to draw an inference with respect to the role of planning in transportation. *Other things equal*, government transportation planning of transport modes should occur only for modes that exhibit increasing returns to scale large relative to their markets. The evidence cited above indicates that pipeline and, to a less extent, inland waterway transportation and rail transportation are industries with technologies producing increasing returns to scale. Consequently, in those markets where demand for pipeline, inland waterway, and rail transportation is small relative to the minimum size of an efficient firm, competition will not result in efficient resource use and some sort of government intervention is necessary for the sake of economic efficiency.[a] As indicated by the emphasis on "other things equal" above, this is not the whole story. Below we discuss some of the other things that affect this policy prescription, namely, market structure and intermodal competition.[67]

---

[a]We do not take up the issue of cost levels and the rational allocation of transportation. A competitive economy without increasing returns for any transport mode would produce a rational allocation of transport resources. Such an allocation might mean the elimination of certain modes presently operating. (See Meyer, Peck, Stenason, & Zwick, pp. 145-167 for their view of the rational allocation to prevail under competition.) However, the presence of increasing returns to scale, even under perfect competition, requires government regulation of some sort, and this is the issue with which we are concerned.

Market Structure of Transportation Industries

Assessing the structure of markets is necessary as discussed earlier to determine whether industries can be expected to operate competitively in the absence of government regulation. Since transport industries are currently regulated, it is impossible to divorce their present structure from the regulatory behavior of government; the structure is determined largely by regulation. Consequently, we must look at the structure as it exists, bringing in additional information such as cost structure and entry conditions, and attempt to deduce whether or not the industries could be competitive in the absence of regulation.

Market Structure of Railroads. Although there is still a large number of railroads, the industry is highly concentrated. At the end of 1970 there were seventy-three Class I railroads and 282 Class II railroads in the United States. (Class I railroads, as defined by the I.C.C., are those having annual revenues that average $5 million or more over a three-year period; Class II railroads are those with operating revenues under $5 million.) The Class I companies own some 86 percent of the total miles of road and operate on some 9 percent more.[68] These firms also pay out about 93 percent of total railroad employee compensation.[69] Moreover, the ten largest Class I railroads produce over 62 percent of the total operating revenues of Class I roads.[70]

In addition, the market for rail service is not nationwide but consists of a large number of individual origin-destination points. Consequently, competition between railroads occurs only when two or more roads operate between the same points. Clearly, if rail transportation markets are defined this way, there are very few routes that have more than one railroad operating on them. This situation is mitigated to some extent because a given movement may use several different roads and at various points along the way may traverse routes on which several railroads operate.

Capital costs for prospective new entrants into the industry are very high. In 1970 Class I railroads owned road and equipment valued at about $34 billion, or about $192,000 per mile of road.[71] Of course, under regulation, entry is controlled by the I.C.C.

Railroads, though competitive to some extent, and subject to competition from other modes, clearly constitute an oligopolistic industry: a few firms selling identical or similar products. Such a market, as previously discussed, could not be expected, if unregulated, to produce an efficient allocation of resources as would an industry more closely approximating pure competition.

Market Structure of Trucking. In 1970 there were 1,571 Class I motor carriers of property required to report to the I.C.C., 2,061 Class II carriers, and 11,468 Class III carriers.[72] (Class I carriers are those with annual gross revenues of $1 million or more; Class II, those with between $300,000 and $1 million; and Class

III, those with revenues less than $300,000.) Although this is a substantial number of companies, there are even more that are not required to report to the I.C.C. Locklin reports, for example, that in 1964 there were 15,895 motor carriers of property subject to the authority of the Public Utilities Commission of California.[73]

There are, of course, some very large firms in the trucking industry. In 1969 there were thirty-four Class I carriers whose total operating revenues were over $50 million annually. Of 408 firms reporting to the I.C.C. and earning over $5 million annually, these thirty-four firms earned together almost 40 percent of total operating revenues.[74]

Entry conditions into the industry are very easy. Locklin reports, for example, that in California in 1964 there were over 4,300 motor carriers for hire that operated only one truck each and over 3,000 with only two trucks each. Moreover, these two classes of carriers comprised over half of the for-hire truckers in the state.[75]

Therefore, despite the existence of some very large firms, the trucking industry itself is very unconcentrated. Although there is no scientific method of determining the minimum number and size distribution of firms sufficient for pure competition, it seems safe to say that trucking approximates these conditions. As with railroads, however, the relevant market is the origin-destination route. It may well be that on some routes trucking falls into the oligopoly market structure.

Market Structure of Intercity and Intracity Passenger Buses. In 1969 seventy Class I carriers of passengers (those earning over $1 million annually) reported to the I.C.C., but over 60 percent of the total operating revenues of these companies was earned by Greyhound Lines, Inc.[76] In addition to the high degree of industry-wide concentration, there appears to be high concentration in individual markets, where between most of the important city-pairs there are only one or two firms operating. It would not appear this concentration is due to economies of large scale. Rather, the observed concentration is probably due to early franchises obtained by Greyhound, resulting in an entry barrier for newcomers. (The author is indebted to James C. Nelson for this point.)

Intracity busing is characterized by municipally sanctioned monopoly in most cases and, consequently, by high concentration and difficult entry.

Market Structure of Pipeline Transportation. In 1970 there were 101 oil pipelines reporting to the I.C.C. These companies owned 175,735 miles of pipeline, with only three firms owning 10,000 or more miles each.[77] Seven firms earned total operating revenues of $50 million or more, together contributing about 40 percent of total operating revenues of the 101 firms.[78] The pipeline industry is, therefore, highly concentrated, and there is also virtual monopoly in individual markets. This situation is undoubtedly due to the characteristics of the technology, producing very large increasing returns to scale. Consequently, pipelines are the closest thing to a natural monopoly in the transportation industries. This means that a competitive market structure could not be sustained in the long run and in the short run would result in a less efficient allocation of resources than would a regulated monopoly.

Market Structure of Air Transportation. Trunk airlines transporting passengers between major U.S. cities constitute a highly concentrated sector of the airline industry. There are at present eleven trunk lines. Even within this small group there is extreme concentration among the four largest, which handle about two-thirds of all trunk carrier revenue ton-miles.[79] In addition, there do appear to be large entry costs for the airline industry, especially for firms desiring to compete with trunklines. Of course, entry into the airline industry is regulated by the C.A.B., but one student of the industry has recently concluded that the industry would probably be oligopolistic even in the absence of regulation.[80] This is the same conclusion reached in an earlier study.[81] High entry costs and the economies of passenger density (the volume of traffic related to a given route) are given as the main reasons for the expected concentration of an unregulated airline industry.[82] This is not to say that a substantial increase in carriers could not be sustained by the market. Jordan estimates that between four and twelve times the actual number of certificated carriers could have existed over the period 1949 to 1965 than in fact did exist had there been no regulation.[83]

The local service airlines also constitute a highly concentrated sector of the airline industry. There are now nine of these airlines.[84] And because market size is small, each line is a virtual monopolist in its area, receiving large government subsidies. (In 1969 the Federal subsidy to local service carriers was over $44.5 million or about 9 percent of overall operating revenues of these carriers.)[85]

Market Stucture of Inland Waterway Transportation. Inland waterway transportation is at present a rather unconcentrated industry. There are about 1,700 firms operating on the inland waterways of the United States. Of this total 113 are certificated by the Interstate Commerce Commission as common carriers, 32 are permitted to operate as contract carriers, 1,150 are permitted to operate unregulated because of the nature of the commodities hauled, and about 400 are private carriers.[86]

It has been estimated that 90 percent of inland waterway transportation is carried by the unregulated firms. The remaining traffic is spread among the common, contract, and private carriers. It seems unlikely, therefore, that the regulated, non-private firms could be very concentrated, or that entry conditions could be very stringent. Of the 188 annual reports filed by carriers subject to the jurisdiction of the Interstate Commerce Commission in 1969, 59 had annual operating revenues exceeding $500,000, 31 exceeding $100,000 but not more than $500,000, and 98 with $100,000 or less.[87]

Summary. Observed concentration in the transportation industries appears to be either very high or very low. High concentration is found in rail, intercity and intracity bus, pipeline, and air transportation. Low concentration is found in truck and inland waterway transportation. The observed high concentration seems to be the result of one or more of several factors. Part is due to increasing returns to scale (pipeline), part to high entry costs (rail and air transportation), and part to regulation itself (rail, intracity bus, and air). High concentration in intercity busing appears to be the result of a head start by Greyhound due to franchises.

Intermodal and Intramodal Competition

The preceding two sections have presented summaries of research into the issues of returns to scale and concentration for individual transport modes. The existence of non-increasing returns to scale and low concentration means that the mode is, or could likely be, competitive. Similarly, the existence of increasing returns to scale and high seller concentration means that the mode is unlikely to be competitive.

There is, however, another issue to be considered here. We have treated each mode individually in assessing the extent of scale economies and concentration. Consequently, our conclusions concerning the likely competitiveness of the mode only apply to intramodal competition, not intermodal competition. Nonetheless, when one is dealing with industries that produce essentially the same product—transportation—there is surely competition between industries as well as within industries. To the extent that such competition exists between transportation industries, it mitigates the conclusion of probable non-competitive behavior based on an examination of modal returns to scale and concentration.

The emphasis on intramodal competition in this paper is for two reasons. First, it is much easier to measure intraindustry concentration in general and for transportation in particular and to estimate returns to scale for one transport mode than for several whose technologies differ markedly. Second, intraindustry competition is very important. The reason for its importance was summed up by Meyer and his associates as follows:

It is only in competition between firms in the same industry that each competitor has similar cost structures and products, so that each can come near to duplicating a rival's prices and service. In contrast, interindustry competition must always be limited, for the differences in cost structures from one industry to another provide sheltered markets in which one industry has an inherent advantage over all rivals. For this reason, competition within an industry is considered necessary in both the literature of economics and the interpretations of the antitrust laws in order to provide the competitive pressures necessary to fully promote efficiency, progress, and lower prices.[88]

Externalities of Transportation

As previously discussed, externalities are interdependencies between economic units for which there exist no markets. Clearly transport modes produce externalities in conjunction with transportation. The most important of these are the external diseconomies of air pollution and congestion. Very little empirical work of the type we are interested in has been performed for air pollution. Much has been written about air pollution, of course, and there have even been attempts to measure its effects, but there do not appear to be any empirical analyses measuring the divergence between private and social costs. This measurement is necessary in order to draw policy inferences about the phenomenon. On the other hand, such analyses have been performed with respect to congestion. Congestion from highway, air, and inland water transportation has been studied, and it is these studies we report here.

Highway Congestion. Of the three transportation modes that have been studied in connection with congestion externalities, most research has been performed for highway congestion. Most of the analysis of this issue has been performed in the last ten years, and, although the research is fairly large and of high quality, relatively little is empirical. What empirical work there is has pretty much followed the same general approach. Since this is so, and since we are interested in general findings rather than the results of specific studies, we will not describe the individual findings.[8][9]

The empirical work on road congestion has been primarily concerned with estimating the costs of highway travel as these are related to traffic density. The demand side of the picture has been neglected primarily because of the difficulties involved in estimating such a relationship.

The studies of congestion costs typically begin with a relationship between traffic volume (measured, say, in vehicles per hour) and vehicle speed. This relationship can be transformed into a travel-time function related to traffic volume (say, minutes per mile as a function of vehicles per hour). The latter relationship is usually meant to represent the travel time of a typical or average vehicle, and its parameters are either based on engineering studies or statistical (usually linear regression) relationships for vehicle and roadway characteristics.

To get travel costs as a function of traffic volume, the traveltime relationship is used in conjunction with estimates of vehicle operating costs and estimates of the value of time of the vehicle occupants. Usually both of these estimates are assumed to be constants per unit of time or distance or, alternatively, are quite simple relationships to time or distance. Studies differ markedly regarding how many types of operating costs are included and how they are obtained as well as regarding the determination of value of time to vehicle occupants. In any case, once such costs are determined, the relationship between vehicle travel costs and traffic volume can be obtained.

The function thus obtained is meant to represent the travel costs of an average vehicle. From such a relationship can be determined the *total* travel costs of all vehicles operating on the road in any particular traffic volume. And, from the total cost function, the marginal travel cost function can be derived. This function gives the travel cost added by one more vehicle. That is, it is the aggregate of cost increases added to all vehicles due to the entrance of an additional vehicle. If there were no congestion on the road, the new entrant would only raise total cost by its own travel cost, so, where there is congestion, the marginal cost is the new entrant's cost *plus* what he imposes on all others. Thus the difference between average travel costs and marginal travel costs is the cost of congestion.

All the empirical studies dealing with highway congestion have attempted to estimate these two important relationships—average and marginal travel costs—as a function of traffic volume. All have found that average and marginal travel costs are equal up to a certain traffic volume after which congestion causes marginal travel costs to rise much more rapidly than average travel costs.

Some idea of the relation between marginal and average travel costs may be gained from Wohl's figures, shown in Table 1-7.

Table 1-7
Travel Costs for One-Mile Vehicle Trips on Central London Roadways (in U.S. cents)

Vehicles per Hour	Average Travel Costs	Marginal Travel Costs
200	19.46	20.26
600	21.29	24.41
1000	23.70	30.70
1400	27.73	41.69
1800	32.64	59.89
2000	36.37	75.26
2200	40.65	97.60
2400	46.77	133.55
2600	54.91	195.34
2800	68.70	318.70
3000	93.70	618.70

Source: M. Wohl, "The Short-Run Congestion Cost and Pricing Dilemma," *Traffic Quarterly*, Vol. 20, No. 1, January 1966, Table 2, p. 58.

Air and Inland Waterway Congestion. Although most of the empirical work on congestion has been performed for highways, there has been one study we know of for air congestion[90] and there have been two for inland waterway congestion.[91] These studies are similar to those for highways in that they estimate congestion cost functions. However, they differ in that there is an important queueing aspect for air and inland waterway transportation. Aircraft must often wait to take off and land because other aircraft are ahead in the queue. Similarly, barge tows operating on the inland waterway systems must often wait in line at locks while other tows are being serviced. Thus, most of the congestion occurs at fixed points; whereas, for cars, although there are some queueing aspects, congestion usually means a slower speed.

Carlin and Park, in their study of airport congestion, find that delay costs are a function of the absolute service time (how many minutes it takes for the aircraft to take off or land in the absence of congestion), the number of operations (takeoffs or landings) over a given busy period, and the cost per minute of delay (operating costs of the aircraft and value of passenger time lost). Since it is difficult to estimate the first two of these, Carlin and Park use relative service times (e.g., the proportion of a large jet's service time required by a small aircraft) and the proportions of various types of operations (e.g., the percentage of all landings by large jets). They are able to get data on all these variables for LaGuardia and John F. Kennedy Airports.

Table 1-8 presents marginal delay costs found by Carlin and Park for LaGuardia Airport. These are given as a function of the time of day and are different for arrivals and departures and for commercial air carriers and general aviation. The figures are average values of the delay costs imposed on other users by incremental operations at any time of day. Carlin and Park find some very high congestion costs. For example, an additional carrier arrival between 3 and 4 p.m. will impose delay costs of over $1,000 on other users. Marginal delay costs for general aviation operations during the same hour are over $500.

The two studies of inland waterway congestion use two different methods for estimating delay time and costs. Lave and DeSalvo use an analytical queueing model to estimate waiting times at locks on the Illinois Waterway.[9][2] Howe and his associates construct a simulation model for portions of the Ohio River. There are advantages and disadvantages of both methods. The queuing model is simple and seems to predict well while requiring less data, whereas the simulation model is capable of handling a considerable number of waterway and tow variables and is more "realistic" in its assumptions.

Lave and DeSalvo assume the arrival rate of tows at a lock to be a random variable approximated by the Poisson distribution and service time to be a random variable approximated by an exponential distribution. These assumptions permit the use of very simple waiting time and service time formulas obtained from queueing theory. With these formulas, one can investigate the effect of increasing the number of tows operating on the waterway. Table 1-9 presents average and marginal locking times as a function of the number of tows operating on the waterway. These results are not waterway-dependent; they are simply the results of working out the implications of the queuing formulas. (The results hold only for a single lock. If the methodology is extended to portions of

Table 1-8

Marginal Delay Costs for Arrivals and Departures at La Guardia Airport, New York City, 1967-1968 (Dollars per incremental operation)

Hour of Day	Air Carrier		General Aviation	
	Arrivals	Departures	Arrivals	Departures
0000-0700	0	0	0	0
0700-0800	60	52	32	28
0800-0900	270	232	146	124
0900-1000	271	233	146	125
1000-1100	162	140	88	75
1100-1200	93	80	50	43
1200-1300	245	211	132	113
1300-1400	594	511	321	173
1400-1500	694	597	375	319
1500-1600	1090	937	588	501
1600-1700	963	829	520	443
1700-1800	786	676	424	361
1800-1900	607	522	328	279
1900-2000	364	313	196	167
2000-2100	159	137	86	73
2100-2200	59	50	32	27
2200-2300	14	12	8	7
2300-2400	3	3	2	2

Source: A. Carlin and R.E. Park, *The Efficient Use of Airport Runway Capacity in a Time of Scarcity*, The Rand Corporation, RM-5817-PA, p. 96.

Note: Data are for the period April 1967 through March 1968.

waterways with more than one lock, then the locks must be far enough apart so that dependence effects are absent. In fact, the formulas were applied to five locks on the Illinois Waterway and predicted locking times pretty well.) It is clear that, even at relatively low traffic densities, the additional locking time (waiting and service) that each tow must suffer as a new tow enters the waterway is fairly large and grows larger as traffic density becomes greater.

Although Lave and DeSalvo do not transform these delay times into costs,[b] Howe does present such costs obtained from his simulation model of a waterway similar to a stretch of the Ohio River. These are shown in Table 1-10. Howe's simulation model generates tow arrivals into the system by a pseudo-random process based on the Poisson distribution. Tows pass through the waterway according to a predetermined itinerary. Assumptions about tow characteristics and waterway characteristics are also necessary to the model.

[b]This is done to get the optimal tolls, but only the tolls themselves are presented in the article. These will be discussed in a later section.

Table 1-9
Marginal and Average Locking Time at a Single Lock

Number of Tows (Annual)	Locking Time (Hours/tow)	
	Average	Marginal
1	1.00	1.00
100	1.01	1.02
1000	1.13	1.28
2000	1.30	1.69
3000	1.52	2.31
4000	1.84	3.39
5000	2.33	5.43
6000	3.18	10.11
7000	4.98	24.80
8000	11.52	132.71

Source: L.B. Lave and J.S. DeSalvo, "Congestion, Tolls, and the Economic Capacity of a Waterway," *Journal of Political Economy*, Vol. 76, No. 3, May-June 1968, adapted from Table 1, p. 382.

Travel times, other than delays, are generated by the tow production function discussed earlier. Thus, a portion of a river and its traffic are simulated. Applying operating costs to the delay times generated produces the figures shown in Table 1-10. Again we see the rather high costs due to congestion.

Table 1-10
Marginal and Average Delay Costs on a Three-Dam River System

Daily Arrival Rate of Tows	Delay Costs (Dollars/tow)	
	Average	Marginal
10	38	—
12	50	101
14	80	265
16	120	382
18	199	938
20	484	3035

Source: C.W. Howe, et al., *Inland Waterway Transportation: Studies in Public and Private Management and Investment Decisions*, Resources for the Future, Inc., Washington, D.C., 1969, adapted from Table 17, p. 90.

Summary. All the empirical work reviewed above has in common the quantification of the theoretical relationship between average and marginal delay costs. These findings, for highway, air, and inland water transport modes all show a rise in average travel cost, and a faster rise in marginal travel cost, attributable to congestion.

Economic Rationale for Transportation Planning

On the basis of the preceding discussion, we should be able now to bring together the economic principles relating to efficient resource use and, with the help of the empirical work on transportation, to apply these principles to transportation.

Economic Principles

Although much of what has been said to this point has dealt with the situations impeding the competitive market solution to economic efficiency, we should not lose sight of the usefulness of the forces of competition. The first economic principle drawn from our analysis is that where competitive markets exist, or could exist, there should be no government interference with market determined prices, outputs, and investment decisions.

The test of viability of competitive markets would seem to involve four aspects. First, there must be a large enough number of buyers and sellers so that neither group has control over price. Generally speaking, for most products, this reduces to low seller concentration since there are typically enough buyers to avoid buyer control over prices. Second, buyers and sellers must be well informed about the characteristics of the product and productive inputs as well as about their prices. Third, the technology must be such that there are no increasing returns to scale large relative to the market. Finally, no important externalities must be present from the production and consumption of the product.

As we have seen, where any of these four aspects of markets are present, the competitive solution either will not exist, in which case imperfect competition results, or will exist in conjunction with one of the market aspects mentioned above. In either case, the resulting allocation of resources will be inefficient. It is here that there is a rationale for economic planning, and the economic principles discussed below are designed to produce efficient resource use where that would not be forthcoming without some kind of non-market interference. (Public goods, the demand for which may give rise to government provision, do not fit neatly into the framework set out here. There are, however, economic principles relating to public goods, and these are given later.)

That incomplete information, market concentration, increasing returns, and externalities cause inefficient resource use and provide a case for planning does not mean that government should correct these problems at any cost. Government planning is not costless and neither are the proposed solutions to inefficient resource use. Consequently, there is one overriding principle, and that is that specific policies should only be undertaken when there is assurance that benefits will exceed the costs. In other words, all of the principles discussed below must, in practice, be subjected to a benefit-cost analysis to be justified. We now discuss each impediment to efficiency and the possible actions government can take toward each.

Incomplete information impedes the operation of competitive markets. Therefore, government planning agencies should provide information in those areas where the benefits of so doing are very likely to exceed the costs. Probably the best example of governmental information is the U.S. Government's aid to farmers. The information provided farmers includes such things as new crop varieties, bookkeeping methods, and even how to buy clothes. Perhaps some would argue that this supply of information over a number of years has had more to do with the efficiency of farming in the U.S. than any other single thing. It is unclear, however, whether all of it would have been found justified on benefit-cost grounds.

Concentrated markets are unlikely to be competitive, and where the benefits of fragmenting them would exceed the costs, this should be done (if non-increasing returns prevail) either by dissolving existing firms or by lowering or removing entry barriers. These are *ex post* measures. *Ex ante* measures would include prevention of mergers.

Technologies characterized by increasing returns to scale large relative to the market are also a problem for planning. Ideally, output should be produced as cheaply as possible. With products produced under increasing returns to scale, this means that a single firm is the most efficient size for the market. For efficiency's sake, the firm should produce one more unit of output as long as the addition to total cost of that unit is less than the price consumers would be willing to pay for it. In the terminology of economic theory, the firm should produce that output level that equates marginal cost and price. Although this would be the most efficient output and use of resources, it could not be sustained by the firm since the price would be less than its average production costs. (When each successive unit of output adds less to total cost than the former units, the average cost declines but remains above marginal cost.) Consequently, if we stick with the price-equals-marginal-cost pricing rule, the firm must be subsidized on each unit of output for the difference between average cost (including a "competitive" return on capital) and marginal cost.

The next principle relates to externalities: externalities should be "internalized" by making the private cost of providing the commodity or service that gives rise to the externality equal to the social cost from the provision of the good and its externality. When the external effect is an external diseconomy, the principle says that private cost should be raised to reflect the cost imposed on others by the externality. When the external effect is an external economy, the principle says that private cost should be lowered to reflect the benefit conferred on others by the externality. There are various ways to bring about the equality of private and social costs. The one most frequently mentioned by economists is taxation, in the case of an external diseconomy, or subsidization, in the case of an external economy, of the agent producing the externality.

A word on public goods is necessary here. The economic principles for public goods refer to their amount and their financing. The correct amount of a public good is the quantity that brings the marginal cost of providing it into equality with total consumer demand for it; a pricing rule is to charge each consumer his dollar valuation of the good at the quantity provided (i.e., how much he would be willing to pay for the provided amount if that could somehow be elicited from him). The difficulty with these principles with respect to public goods lies in the practical achievement of them. There is at present no way of measuring the total demand for a public good so that, in conjunction with its marginal cost, the optimum level can be determined. Rather, the determination of the quantities of public goods that are provided at present is made through our political system. In addition, there is no way of measuring the individual consumer demands making up total demand or, alternatively, there is no way of eliciting from consumers the amount each would be willing to pay toward the provision of the public good. Consequently, financing of public goods takes place through a variety of methods from general taxation to user charges. These issues are important in transportation. We turn now to applying the principles of efficient resource use to transportation.

Transportation Planning

In trying to specify the role for transportation planning, we shall proceed in three steps. First, each transport mode will be examined with respect to returns to scale, concentration, and entry conditions. From this can be drawn a conclusion as to whether or not the mode could be expected to operate competitively in the absence of current regulation and what should be done if it cannot be expected to operate competitively. Second, the issue of externalities will be taken up. Congestion externalities and a method for internalizing them will be discussed. Finally, the issue of public goods will be addressed. The major public goods provided for each mode, if any, will be discussed along with present and proposed financing arrangements.

Competition and Regulation. Competitive intramodal market structures (that is, those that would very likely be competitive in the absence of regulation) seem to exist for trucking, inland water transportation, and intercity busing. The competitive nature of the following modes is uncertain: intracity busing, trunk and local service air transportation, and rail. Because of large increasing returns to scale and high concentration, it would seem pipeline transportation could not be competitive intramodally. These conclusions are based on the empirical evidence surveyed earlier relating to economies of scale, concentration, and entry conditions. Those modes exhibiting constant or decreasing returns to scale, low concentration, and easy entry conditions are said to possess competitive structures. Those exhibiting increasing returns to scale, high concentration, and difficult entry conditions are said to possess non-competitive structures. Of course, observed concentration and entry conditions are often due to current and past regulatory policy. What we really would like to know is the likely concentration and entry condition for a mode in the absence of regulation. In some cases, judgments can be made; in others, not. Moreover, intermodal competition, as discussed earlier, mitigates the non-competitiveness indicated by our findings of increasing returns to scale, market concentration, and entry conditions.

Our survey showed that trucking probably possesses constant returns to scale (or very slight increasing returns), that even under present regulatory policies it exhibits low concentration, and that entry into the industry is easy. Trucking, as will be seen, presents the clearest evidence for a competitive structure of any of the transport modes. Inland waterway transportation appears to produce its transport under conditions of constant or increasing returns to scale (there is conflicting evidence on this point), possesses low concentration, and entry is moderately easy. Intercity bus transportation exhibits a technology of constant returns to scale and easy entry, but because of the dominance of Greyhound concentration is high, although there are many firms. Intracity busing possesses very much the same characteristics as intercity busing, the concentration being high in this case because of municipally-granted monopoly. Airlines, both local service and trunk, display constant returns to scale (although there is some evidence of increasing returns for local service carriers), rather high concentration, and large threshold costs. Studies of rail transportation are conflicting with respect to returns to scale, but tend to favor increasing returns. Rail also exhibits high concentration and difficult entry conditions. Pipelines possess substantial scale economies, high concentration, but probably easier entry than, say, rail.

It seems clear that trucking could operate competitively, and it seems pipelines could not. In between, the conclusions are less straightforward, although the evidence favors competition. This is so because of the evidence on returns to scale and entry, as well as the existence of intermodal competition. The present level of concentration is not entirely market determined but is in large measure due to current regulatory policy. Consequently, where constant or slightly increasing returns are coupled with ease of entry, as in inland water and bus transport, a case can be made for competition even in the presence of high concentration as is exhibited by bus transportation. The case is harder to make for airlines because of higher entry costs and the likely persistence of concentration even under competition. In general, however, the evidence favors competition. This does not mean that high concentration in these industries should be tolerated if it interferes with efficient resource use. Instead, the antitrust laws currently on the books could be used against transport firms as they are against non-transport firms. Thus, most of transportation could be unregulated but watched.

Given the extreme increasing returns to scale in the pipeline industry, it would seem that consolidation and regulation thereafter as natural monopolies would be in order. However, even for pipelines things are not so clearcut, except where pipelines are not integrated as part of the shipper firm. Where they are, there would seem to be room for regulation on the grounds that the pipeline economies could lead to excessive profits and consolidation by shippers.[93]

The preceding discussion is based on empirical and theoretical results that are rather general. It leads, nevertheless, to a rationale for government transportation planning for the transport industries with respect to regulation of the operation of those industries. The types of regulatory policies rationalized have been sketched broadly but not in detail.[94]

Externalities. Although several externalities are created by transportation, congestion has been the most studied of possible transport externalities and is produced at one time or another by almost all transport modes. We have seen evidence of some of its impacts on highway, waterway, and air transportation. There is a role for government in the internalization of such externalities.

To get some idea of the magnitudes involved, look back to Tables 1-7 to 1-10. It is the difference between marginal delay cost and average delay cost that must somehow be brought to bear on the producer of the congestion. The most frequently proposed method is for the government to charge a toll for the use of the facility. The toll would be set equal to the difference between marginal and average delay cost that would exist at the optimal level of traffic (i.e., that level of traffic for which demand equals marginal cost).

One difficulty with this proposal is knowing the demand for traffic on the facility as a function of travel costs. No one has as yet estimated such a demand function, although as we have seen several estimates of congestion costs as a function of traffic flow have been estimated. Without the demand function, the proper toll cannot be determined *ex ante*. Instead, there would have to be a period of trial and error, starting from the toll associated with the pre-toll level of traffic. It is conceivable that demand functions could be estimated, and it is also conceivable that trial and error would lead to the proper toll.

Another issue concerns what to do with the revenue obtained from the toll. It must be returned to the consumer in order for the resulting allocation to be efficient, but there is little agreement over the form in which it should return. Some have proposed the revenue be used to expand facilities or otherwise benefit the users; others have proposed it be spent elsewhere. A final point concerns the partial nature of the analyses, attention being confined to the effects of the toll on traffic on one facility only without analyzing the effects elsewhere.

All of these criticisms, and some others not included here, represent points that should be considered by analysts and by policymakers considering the imposition of tolls. They are not, in the opinion of this writer, sufficient to vitiate the desirability of internalizing congestion through the use of tolls.

Congestion, then (as well as other externalities of transportation such as pollution and noise), provides a rationale for transportation planning: to estimate demands and costs so as to determine and then impose the correct tolls necessary to internalize congestion costs and achieve more efficient use of resources.

Public Goods and Their Financing. Many of the most vexing problems relating to transportation arise from the difficulties associated with the provision and financing of public goods. Of particular importance seem to be the government's provision of "roadbed" (highways, waterways, airways, and airports) and the underwriting of research and development for new transport vehicles. Both of these are public goods because they are available to all once provided and involve very high exclusion costs. Certainly the knowledge gained through research and development is available to all once provided. And this is true to a lesser extent for "roadbed" as well. Only when the "roadbed" becomes congested is the publicness of the good hampered, but we have already dealt with this issue. Here the concern is not the efficient use of the public good once provided but the decision to provide it in the first place and its financing thereafter.

One need only read the newspapers to recognize the difficulties in the provision of public goods for transportation: How much is to be spent on highways? Where should they be put? Should New York City have another airport? Should the federal government spend more on the development of a supersonic transport aircraft? Unfortunately, at this stage of the development of economics, there is little the economist can say regarding the optimal amount of such expenditures. He can perform benefit-cost analyses, but these must be incomplete since the user benefits cannot be measured if the total demand function cannot be estimated. (In benefit-cost analysis the demand function is used to obtain an estimate of user benefits.) And the benefits of the public good prestige (as, for example, with the space program and the SST) are difficult if not impossible to measure even if real. Consequently, decisions regarding the provision of public goods get made in the arena of politics, where elected representatives implicitly try to estimate the level of total demand for the public good, the provision of which it is their duty to decide. The recent Congressional decision on the SST is a good example of the process described here.

Once the decision to provide the public good has been made, there remains the issue of financing. In the case of air, water, and highway transportation, governments provide the "roadbed" and finance it out of tax revenues. Only the railroads must raise their own capital for investment in "roadbed." There is no charge for tows using the inland waterways of the U.S. Airline, trucking, and busing firms do contribute to the financing of their respective "roadbeds" through user charges, but it is unclear whether they pay what they "should."

As already seen, the theory of public goods, coupled with the principle of benefit taxation, provides an answer in principle to the question of financing such goods. According to the theory, everyone's valuation of the good must be known for any given amount of it. The theory makes no distinction, often found in transportation, between users and non-users; anybody who attaches some value to the good is a "user." In other words, people who do not even ride on the highways, if they attach some value to the existence of highways, should be asked to contribute toward their financing. In fact, this is done for highway finance. User charges from gasoline and other taxes do not adequately cover the costs of highways; tax revenues from non-users make up the difference. This is true, even more forcefully, for other modes.

In practice, then, the issue of financing transportation public goods breaks into two parts: (1) estimating the costs; (2) allocating the costs (a) between users and non-users and (b) among users. The cost issue would not appear to be too difficult, given the experience with financing and operating highways, waterways, and airports in this country. As has already been indicated, it is the second part that is very difficult. Even if, as some have argued, there is no need nor desirability to have non-users bear the costs,[95] there still remains the thorny problem of cost allocation among users. This would probably be easiest for waterway transportation because of the minimal variety of users and the existence of means to exclude non-payers from the waterways, which is more difficult for air transportation because of the large number of non-commercial vehicles using airspace and airports, and probably most difficult for highway transportation because of the variety of users and the non-existence of "natural" points of excludability, especially for city streets.

Summary

At this point, it seems safe to conclude that a rationale for transportation planning has been provided. It is consistent with economic theory and empirical studies and should serve to indicate those aspects of transportation with which planning might usefully serve to improve welfare by achieving efficient resource use. Briefly, we have taken the position that planning should be confined to that set of problems and activites that cannot be handled by private competitive markets. It should concern itself with the appropriate regulation of transportation in those markets where competition is not likely to prevail and with the policing of competitive markets to ensure their continued competitiveness. It should concern itself with devising congestion tolls (and the investigation of other externalities, particularly pollution and noise) that would serve efficiently to allocate users to transport facilities. It should concern itself with determining the need for and amount of public expenditures for public goods in transportation and the financing of such expenditures through user charges.

Regional Transportation Planning

No distinction has yet been made in this paper between levels of transportation planning, except for a brief earlier discussion of the extent of centralization. In particular, we now want to explore the role of *regional* transportation planning.

Most intercity trips are for 500 miles or less, and the Northeast Corridor project predicts that average intercity trips in the Northeast Corridor for the year 1975 will be about 75 miles for auto, 125 miles for rail, and 175 miles for conventional air travel.[96] There is reason to believe similar conditions prevail elsewhere. This, coupled with the deficiences in short- and intermediate-range transportation in the last few years, would seem to be evidence that regional transportation needs are great and, perhaps, dominate national needs. To the extent that transportation issues such as regulation, externalities, and public goods are regional, then we have established a rationale for transportation planning for regions. However, this is not the same thing as saying that regional transportation problems should be administered by regional authorities.

Given that there are regional transportation problems, is there anything in the preceding analysis that would lead to the conclusion that transportation planning should be done at the regional level as opposed to some other level or levels? If there is, it would not appear to be found in the economic principles themselves. Reference is here made to the normative or prescriptive principles stated in the previous section. The principles themselves would appear to be a-spatial as well as a-institutional. As an example, take congestion externalities caused by airplanes at airports. The economic principle that such externalities should be turned into private costs assessed on the aircraft causing the congestion (assuming the principle is correct) does not appear to depend on whether the aircrafts are traveling solely within the region in which the airport is located; the principle applies even if the aircrafts' origins are outside the region in which the airport is located. Moreover, the economic principle is silent on the institutional aspects of the problem except insofar as they would affect the congestion costs or demand. As long as the appropriate toll were charged and an appropriate disbursement of toll revenue made, economic efficiency is served whether jurisdiction over toll collection and disbursement is local, regional, or national. Similar remarks could be made about the other economic principles also. (This assumes that alternative institutional set-ups are equally costly in terms of economic resources used for their administration.)

Nor does there appear to be found in the empirical analyses reported above any basis for regional planning as opposed to any other kind of planning. It is true, as already alluded to earlier, that transport markets appear to be largely regional. It is also true that the impacts of transport externalities are local or regional, though perhaps not usually as large as multi-state regions. Congestion, for example, is fairly localized, whereas air pollution is more widespread. Also, the impacts of public goods—highways, airports, waterways—are local or regional rather than national. While granting all this, it does not appear one must grant that planning should be regional in its administration, although it must clearly consider issues of markets, externalities, and public goods that may be largely local or regional.

Thus, it would seem that, in the context of this paper, there is no rationale for regional transportation planning, although a rationale for transportation planning *per se* has been established. To avoid misunderstanding, neither has there been established in this paper a rationale for local, county, or state transportation planning as opposed to any other form.

Since there appears to be a basis for transportation planning established in this paper but no basis one way or the other regarding *regional* transportation planning, one might wonder under what circumstances a rationale for regional transportation planning would emerge. It seems to this writer that a case for regional transportation planning can be made if it can be shown that the costs of transportation planning are lower for regional administration than for its alternatives.

R.A. Nelson has argued that the planning and decisionmaking process for the provision of transportation facilities has not been well structured for achieving balance and coordination in transportation, particulary at the Federal level. This in turn impinges on the states' capabilities to plan effectively and to coordinate transportation developments. But since much of transportation crosses state lines, strengthening the decisionmaking role of the states is not sufficient and some kind of regional or national decisionmaking is required. Nelson has further argued that, since the burden of inadequate transportation is regional, the means and capability to cope with the problems should be regional. Moreover, there are decisions that can be taken without involving national coordination. For example, the proposed VTOL and STOL aircraft would involve essentially a regional operation, as would high speed ground transportation.[97]

On the other hand, it has been argued that there are several difficulties with the idea of regional transportation planning. There is the problem of actually defining the boundaries of a region for transportation planning purposes. What should be the considerations relevant to defining workable transportation regions? Should they be drawn differently for freight problems and passenger problems, for air versus surface transport, land versus water, etc.? If regions are permitted to do their own transportation planning, might not they attempt to achieve balanced growth within their own region to the possible detriment of the nation because of the non-exploitation of regional comparative advantages? Is not it also the case that many important matters would be beyond the legitimate powers of regional authorities, e.g., transport regulation, tax policies, and trust fund decisions? Is not regional *transportation* planning too narrow a view? Would not it be better to treat transportation as merely an aspect of a larger regional plan? Finally, is not the creation of another bureaucratic level preferably avoided.[98]

As these conflicting viewpoints indicate, there are several issues that need to be settled before it can be determined whether regional transportation planning is preferable to any alternative, given that there exists a rationale for transportation planning. These would seem to involve the following issues: What is the relation between transport markets and regions, and how are regions to be delineated for transportation planning purposes? What has been the record of governmental intervention in transport markets, and what are its implications for the success of regional transportation planning? What has been the record of regional (non-transportation and transportation) planning, and what are its implications for the success of regional transportation planning? What are the issues likely to be faced by the transportation planner in the future, and how are these likely to be handled by regional transportation planning? What are the political and administrative problems that regional transportation must confront, and is it likely they can be resolved at the regional level?

It is these issues that the other papers in this study explore.

Notes

1. Y. Dror, "Dimensions of Planning," in C.J. Friedrick and S.E. Harris (eds.), PUBLIC POLICY, Vol. VII, Harvard Graduate School of Public Administration, Cambridge, 1956, p. 112.

2. J. Friedmann, "Planning as a Vocation (Part I)," PLAN, Vol. 6, No. 3, April 1966, pp. 99-100.

3. J.D. Millett, MANAGEMENT IN THE PUBLIC SERVICE, McGraw-Hill Book Company, Inc., New York, 1954, p. 55.

4. J.R. Seeley, "Central Planning: Prologue to a Critique," in R. Morris (ed.), CENTRALLY PLANNED CHANGE: PROSPECTS AND CONCEPTS, National Association of Social Workers, New York, 1964, p. 43.

5. F.A. Hayek, THE ROAD TO SERFDOM, University of Chicago Press, Chicago, 1944.

6. B. Wootton, FREEDOM UNDER PLANNING, University of North Carolina Press, Chapel Hill, 1945.

7. The most complete presentation is found in G. Debreu, THEORY OF VALUE: AN AXIOMATIC ANALYSIS OF ECONOMIC EQUILIBRIUM, John Wiley and Sons, Inc., New York, 1959. Also see T.C. Koopmans, "Allocation of Resources and the Price System," in THREE ESSAYS ON THE STATE OF ECONOMIC SCIENCE, McGraw-Hill Book Company, Inc., New York, 1957, and K.J. Arrow, "An Extension of the Basic Theorems of Classical Welfare Economics," in J. Neyman (ed.), PROCEEDINGS OF THE SECOND BERKELEY SYMPOSIUM ON MATHEMATICAL STATISTICS AND PROBABILITY, University of California Press, Berkeley, 1951.

8. That such a competitive equilibrium is possible has been proved. See K.J. Arrow and G. Debreu, "Existence of an Equilibrium for a Competitive Economy," ECONOMETRICA, Vol. 22, No. 3, July 1954, pp. 265-290; D. Gale, "The Law of Supply and Demand," MATHEMATICA SCANDINAVICA, Vol. 3, 1955, pp. 155-169; L.W. McKenzie, "On the Existence of General Equilibrium for a Competitive Market," ECONOMETRICA, Vol. 27, No. 1, January 1959, pp. 54-71.

9. See Debreu for proofs of these assertions; also, see R. Dorfman, P.A. Samuelson, and R.M. Solow, LINEAR PROGRAMMING AND ECONOMIC ANALYSIS, McGraw-Hill Book Co., Inc., New York, 1958, Ch. 12; and E. Malinvaud, "Capital Accumulation and Efficient Allocation of Resources," ECONOMETRICA, Vol. 21, No. 2, April 1953, pp. 233-268, reprinted with corrections in K.J. Arrow and T. Scitovsky, READINGS IN WELFARE ECONOMICS, Richard D. Irwin, Inc., Homewood, Illinois, 1969.

10. See M.J. Farrell, "The Convexity Assumption in the Theory of Competitive Markets," JOURNAL OF POLITICAL ECONOMY, Vol. 67, No. 4, August 1959, pp. 377-391; J. Rothenberg, "Non-Convexity, Aggregation, and Pareto Optimality," JOURNAL OF POLITICAL ECONOMY, Vol. 68, No. 5, October 1960, pp. 435-468; and R.M. Starr, "Quasi-Equilibria in Markets with Non-Convex Preferences," ECONOMETRICA, Vol. 37, No. 1, January 1969, pp. 25-38.

11. The classical discussion of externalities may be found in A.C. Pigou, THE ECONOMICS OF WELFARE, 4th ed., Macmillan and Co., Ltd., London, 1932, Part 2, Ch. 9.

12. The implications of the existence of such goods for attainment of efficiency by private markets were presented by P.A. Samuelson in three articles in the REVIEW OF ECONOMICS AND STATISTICS: "The Pure Theory of Public Expenditure," Vol. 36, No. 4, November 1954, pp. 387-389; "Diagrammatic Exposition of a Theory of Public Expenditures," Vol. 37, No. 4, November 1955, pp. 350-356; and "Aspects of Public Expenditure Theories," Vol. 40, November 1958, pp. 332-338. All are reprinted in J.E. Stiglitz (ed.), THE COLLECTED SCIENTIFIC PAPERS OF PAUL A. SAMUELSON, 2 vols., The M.I.T. Press, Cambridge, Massachusetts, 1966. The definition used in the text is adopted from R.N. McKean, PUBLIC SPENDING, McGraw-Hill Book Co., New York, 1968.

13. Also implicit is the assumption that transactions themselves are costless. Nevertheless, transactions cost will not be treated separately in this paper, for it is intimately bound up with all of the other problems hindering the competitive solution. It can be argued, for example, that, if transactions costs were zero, there would be no externality problem, for a market in the externality could always be formed. Similar arguments may be presented for economies of scale, imperfect competition, public goods, and information. See R.H. Coase, "The Problem of Social Cost," JOURNAL OF LAW AND ECONOMICS, Vol. 3, October 1960, pp. 1-44. The basic idea due to Coase has been expanded and elaborated by H. Demsetz. See his "The Exchange and Enforcement of Property Rights," JOURNAL OF LAW AND ECONOMICS, Vol. 7, October 1964, pp. 11-26; "Why Regulate Utilities?" JOURNAL OF LAW AND ECONOMICS, Vol. 11, April 1968, pp. 55-66; and "Contracting Cost and Public Policy," in THE ANALYSIS AND EVALUATION OF PUBLIC EXPENDITURES: THE PPB SYSTEM, Vol. 1, U.S. Government Printing Office, Washington, D.C., 1969.

14. For proofs that this type of uncertainty is consistent with Pareto efficiency and decentralized competitive markets, see K.J. Arrow, "The Role of Securities in the Optimal Allocation of Risk Bearing," REVIEW OF ECONOMIC STUDIES, Vol. 31 (2), No. 86, April 1964, pp. 91-96; R. Radner, "Competitive Equilibrium Under Uncertainty," ECONOMETRICA, Vol. 36, No. 1, January 1968, pp. 31-58. But see J.E. Stiglitz, "On the Optimality of the Stock Market Allocation of Investment," QUARTERLY JOURNAL OF ECONOMICS, Vol. 86, No. 1, February 1972, pp. 25-60.

15. See K.J. Arrow, "The Economics of Moral Hazard: Further Comment," AMERICAN ECONOMIC REVIEW, Vol. 58, No. 3, Part 1, June 1968, pp. 537-539.

16. See any intermediate microtheory text, e.g., E. Mansfield, MICROECO-NOMICS: THEORY AND APPLICATIONS, W.W. Norton and Co., Inc., New York, 1970, pp. 268-270, 299-300, 329-330.

17. For a discussion of barriers to entry, see J.S. Bain, INDUSTRIAL ORGANIZATION, John Wiley and Sons, Inc., New York, 1959, pp. 210-265. Scale economies can also serve as barriers to entry, for the market might not be large enough to support a new firm at a scale large enough to permit it to enjoy costs as low as its competitors.

18. See R.G. Lipsey and K. Lancaster, "The General Theory of Second Best," REVIEW OF ECONOMIC STUDIES, Vol. 24 (1), No. 63, December 1956, pp. 11-32.

19. See O.A. Davis and A.B. Whinston, "Welfare Economics and the Theory of Second Best," REVIEW OF ECONOMIC STUDIES, Vol. 32 (1), No. 89, January 1965, pp. 1-14.

20. For a standard discussion of these points in the context of U.S. practice, see R. Caves, AMERICAN INDUSTRY: STRUCTURE, CONDUCT, PERFORM-ANCE, Prentice-Hall, Inc., Englewood Cliffs, New Jersey, 1964, pp. 54-75. A

challenge to the view that natural monopolies should be regulated is H. Demsetz, "Why Regulate Utilities?," JOURNAL OF LAW AND ECONOMICS, Vol. 11, April 1968, pp. 55-56. A challenge to deconcentration prescriptions is Y. Brozen, "The Antitrust Task Force Deconcentration Recommendation," JOURNAL OF LAW AND ECONOMICS, Vol. 13, No. 2, October 1970, pp. 279-292.

21. J.A. Schumpeter, CAPITALISM, SOCIALISM, AND DEMOCRACY, 3rd ed., Harper and Brothers Publishers, New York, 1950, pp. 81-86.

22. It is unclear whether there is efficient provision of public goods by private markets when exclusion is possible. One writer has argued that there is overevaluation and overproduction of collective goods produced and sold in purely competitive markets, but he recognizes some possible qualifications to his arguments. See E.A. Thompson, "The Perfectly Competitive Production of Collective Goods," REVIEW OF ECONOMICS AND STATISTICS, Vol. 50, No. 1, February 1968, pp. 1-12. Critics have attacked this analysis on a number of grounds. See comments by B.M. Owen, J.D. Rogers and S.K. Ganguly, all in the REVIEW OF ECONOMICS AND STATISTICS, Vol. 51, No. 4, November 1969, pp. 475-479.

23. Technically, "social demand" is the vertical sum of consumers' marginal rate of substitution functions between the public good and a numeraire good. Samuelson has recently called these "pseudo demand curves." See P.A. Samuelson, "Pure Theory of Public Expenditure and Taxation," in J. Margolis and H. Guitton (eds.), PUBLIC ECONOMICS, Macmillan and Co., Ltd., London, 1969.

24. See Pigou, Part 2, Ch. 9.

25. For a discussion of difficulties with the classical tax-subsidy prescription, see J.M. Buchanan, "Politics, Policy, and the Pigovian Margins," ECONOMICA, Vol. 29, No. 113, February 1962, pp. 17-28; J.M. Buchanan and W.C. Stubblebine, "Externality," ECONOMICA, Vol. 29, No. 116, November 1962, pp. 371-384, reprinted in Arrow and Scitovsky; R. H. Coase, "The Problem of Social Cost," JOURNAL OF LAW AND ECONOMICS, Vol. 3, October 1960, pp. 1-44; O.A. Davis and A. Whinston, "Externalities, Welfare, and the Theory of Games," JOURNAL OF POLITICAL ECONOMY, Vol. 70, No. 3, June 1962, pp. 241-262. Counterarguments may be found in S. Wellisz, "On External Diseconomies and the Government-Assisted Invisible Hand," ECONOMICA, Vol. 31, No. 124, November 1964, pp. 345-362. The issue of what to tax in order to internalize an externality has been discussed in C.R. Plott, "Externalities and Corrective Taxes," ECONOMICA, Vol. 33, No. 129, February 1966, pp. 84-87.

26. Coase, pp. 11-13.

27. See C.W. Howe, "Process and Production Functions for Inland Waterway Transportation," Institute for Quantitative Research in Economics and Management, Krannert Graduate School, Purdue University, Institute Paper No. 65, January 1964; "Models of a Bargeline: An Analysis of Returns to Scale in Inland Waterway Transportation," Institute for Quantitative Research in Economics and Management, Krannert Graduate School, Purdue University, Institute Paper

No. 77, July 1964; "Methods for Equipment Selection and Benefit Evaluation in Inland Waterway Transportation," WATER RESOURCES RESEARCH, Vol. 1, No. 1, First Quarter 1965, pp. 25-39; "Mathematical Model of Barge Tow Performance," JOURNAL OF THE WATERWAYS AND HARBORS DIVISION, AMERICAN SOCIETY OF CIVIL ENGINEERS, Vol. 93, No. WW4, Proc. Paper 5588, November 1967, pp. 153-166.

28. C.W. Howe, et al., INLAND WATERWAY TRANSPORTATION: STUDIES IN PUBLIC AND PRIVATE MANAGEMENT AND INVESTMENT DECISIONS, Resources for the Future, Inc., Washington, D.C., 1969. An earlier effort by W.J. Leininger, "An Empirical Production Function for Barge Towing Operations on the Ohio River," unpublished Ph.D. dissertation, Purdue University, August 1963, has also been incorporated in the Howe, et al., volume. Also, some of A.P. Hurter's work, previously unpublished, has been incorporated into the Howe study. See A.P. Hurter, Jr., "Production Relationships For Inland Waterway Operations on the Mississippi River: 1950, 1957, 1962," The Transportation Center, Northwestern University, 1965; "Cost Relationships for Inland Waterway Operations on the Mississippi River: 1950, 1957, 1962," The Transportation Center, Northwestern University, 1965.

29. L.S. Case and L.B. Lave, "Cost Functions for Inland Waterways," JOURNAL OF TRANSPORT ECONOMICS AND POLICY, Vol. 4, No. 2, May 1970, pp. 181-191.

30. See J.S. DeSalvo and L.B. Lave, "An Analysis of Towboat Delays," JOURNAL OF TRANSPORT ECONOMICS AND POLICY, Vol. 2, No. 2, May 1968, pp. 232-241. It would be possible to incorporate delays into Howe's production function, but this has not as yet been done so as to yield information on returns to scale, although Howe has incorporated locking time into a waterway simulation model. See Howe, et al., pp. 73-109.

31. G.H. Borts, "Increasing Returns in the Railway Industry," JOURNAL OF POLITICAL ECONOMY, Vol. 62, No. 4, August 1954, pp. 316-333.

32. J.R. Meyer, M.J. Peck, J. Stenason, and C. Zwick, THE ECONOMICS OF COMPETITION IN THE TRANSPORTATION INDUSTRIES, Harvard University Press, Cambridge, Massachusetts, 1960.

33. W.J. Stenason and R.A. Bandeen, "Transportation Costs and Their Implications: An Empirical Study of Railway Costs in Canada," TRANSPORTATION ECONOMICS, National Bureau of Economic Research, New York, 1965.

34. G.H. Borts, "The Estimation of Rail Cost Functions," ECONOMETRICA, Vol. 28, No. 1, January 1960, pp. 108-131.

35. G.H. Borts, "Production Relations in the Railway Industry," ECONOMETRICA, Vol. 20, No. 1, January 1952, pp. 71-79.

36. L.R. Klein, A TEXTBOOK OF ECONOMETRICS, Row, Peterson and Co., Evanston, Illinois, 1953, pp. 226-236.

37. E. Mansfield and H.H. Wein, "A Regression Control Chart for Costs," APPLIED STATISTICS, Vol. 7, No. 1, March 1958, pp. 48-57. See citation in

A.A. Walters, "Production and Cost Functions: An Econometric Survey," ECONOMETRICA, Vol. 31, No. 1-2, January-April 1963, pp. 1-66.

38. K.T. Healy, THE EFFECTS OF SCALE IN THE RAILROAD INDUS-TRY, Committee on Transportation, Yale University, 1961.

39. J.S. DeSalvo, "A Process Function for Rail Linehaul Operations," JOURNAL OF TRANSPORT ECONOMICS AND POLICY, Vol. 3, No. 1, January 1969, pp. 3-27.

40. J.S. DeSalvo and L.B. Lave, A STATISTICAL-ENGINEERING AP-PROACH TO ESTIMATING RAILWAY COST FUNCTIONS, The Rand Corporation, P-3781, March 1968.

41. Z. Griliches, "Cost Allocation in Railroad Regulation," BELL JOURNAL OF ECONOMICS AND MANAGEMENT SCIENCE, Vol. 3, No. 1, Spring 1972, pp. 26-41.

42. J.B. Crane, "The Economics of Air Transportation," HARVARD BUSI-NESS REVIEW, Vol. 22, No. 4, Summer 1944, pp. 495-509; H.D. Koontz, "Economic and Managerial Factors Underlying Subsidy Needs of Domestic Trunk Line Air Carriers," JOURNAL OF AIR LAW AND COMMERCE, Vol. 18, No. 2, Spring 1951, pp. 127-156; H.D. Koontz, "Domestic Airlines Self-Suffi-ciency: A Problem of Route Structure," AMERICAN ECONOMIC REVIEW, Vol. 42, No. 1, March 1952, pp. 103-125.

43. R.E. Caves, AIR TRANSPORT AND ITS REGULATORS: AN INDUS-TRY STUDY, Harvard University Press, Cambridge, 1962, pp. 55-65.

44. J.W. Proctor and J.S. Duncan, "A Regression Analysis of Airline Costs," JOURNAL OF AIR LAW AND COMMERCE, Vol. 21, No. 3, Summer 1954, pp. 282-292.

45. P.W. Cherington, AIRLINES PRICE POLICY: A STUDY OF DOMES-TIC AIRLINE PASSENGER FARES, Graduate School of Business Administra-tion, Harvard University, Boston, 1958.

46. S. Wheatcroft, THE ECONOMICS OF EUROPEAN AIR TRANSPORT, Manchester University Press, Manchester, England, 1956.

47. G. Eads, M. Nerlove, and W. Raduchel, "A Long-Run Cost Function for the Local Service Airline Industry: An Experiment in Non-Linear Estimation," REVIEW OF ECONOMICS AND STATISTICS, Vol. 51, No. 3, August 1969, pp. 258-270.

48. N.B. Murphy, "Sources of Productivity Increases in the U.S. Passenger Airline Industry," TRANSPORTATION SCIENCE, Vol. 3, No. 3, August 1969, pp. 233-238.

49. The following works are often cited in connection with economies of scale in trucking, but they contain no original empirical work on that subject: H. Kolsen, "Structure and Price Determination in the New South Wales Road Haulage Industry," ECONOMIC RECORD, Vol. 32, November 1956, pp. 291-304; E.W. Smykay, "An Appraisal of the Economics of Scale in the Motor Carrier Industry," LAND ECONOMICS, Vol. 34, No. 2, May 1958, pp. 143-148;

R.N. Farmer, "Motor Vehicle Pricing in Lebanon," JOURNAL OF INDUS-TRIAL ECONOMICS, Vol. 7, No. 3, July 1959, pp. 199-204; W. Adams and J. Hendry, "Trucking Mergers, Concentration and Small Business: An Analysis of Interstate Commerce Commission Policy, 1950-1956" in U.S. Senate Select Subcommittee on Small Business, TRUCKING MERGERS AND CONCENTRA-TION, U.S. Government Printing Office, Washington, D.C., 1956; G.W. Wilson, "The Nature of Competition in the Motor Transport Industry," LAND ECO-NOMICS, Vol. 36, No. 4, November 1960, pp. 387-391; A.A. Walters, "Econ-omies of Scale in Road Haulage: A Comment," OXFORD ECONOMIC PAPERS, Vol. 13, No. 1, February 1961, pp. 116-118; A.J. Harrison,"Economies of Scale and the Structure of the Road Haulage Industry," OXFORD ECONOMIC PAPERS, Vol. 15, No. 3, November 1963, pp. 287-307; G.N. Dicer, "Economies of Scale and Motors Carrier Optimum Size," QUARTERLY REVIEW OF ECONOMICS AND BUSINESS, Vol. 11, No. 1, Spring 1971, pp. 31-37; G. Walker, ROAD AND RAIL: AN ENQUIRY INTO THE ECONOMICS OF COMPETITION AND STATE CONTROL, rev. ed., George Allen and Unwin, Ltd., London, 1947; L.A. Schumer, "Road Transport," in Australian Institute of Political Science (John Wilkes, ed.), AUSTRALIA'S TRANSPORT CRISIS, Angus and Roberts, Sydney, 1956, pp. 134-158; J.R. Meyer, M.J. Peck, J. Stenanson, and C. Zwick, THE ECONOMICS OF COMPETITION IN THE TRANSPORTATION INDUSTRIES, Harvard Univ. Press, Cambridge, 1964, pp. 86-101; J.R. Sargent, British Transport Policy, Clarendon Press, Oxford, 1958. P.S. Henman, "The Economics of Goods Transport by Road," INSTITUTE OF TRANSPORT JOURNAL, Vol. 29, March 1962, pp. 259-270.

50. L.J. Cadbury, "Large and Small Firms: A Note on Costs in the Road Transport Industry," ECONOMIC JOURNAL, Vol. 45, No. 180, December 1935, pp. 789-793.

51. Cadbury, p. 790.

52. F.K. Edwards, "Cost Analysis in Transportation," AMERICAN ECO-NOMIC REVIEW, Vol. 37, May 1947, pp. 441-461.

53. M.J. Roberts, "Some Aspects of Motor Carrier Costs: Firm Size, Efficiency, and Financial Health," LAND ECONOMICS, Vol. 32, No. 3, August 1956, pp. 228-238; R.A. Nelson, "The Economies of Scale in the Motor Carrier Industry: A Reply," LAND ECONOMICS, Vol. 35, No. 2, May 1959, pp. 180-185. Nelson's work was originally reported in "The Economic Structure of the Highway Carrier Industry in New England," MOTOR FREIGHT TRANSPORT FOR NEW ENGLAND, New England Governors' Committee on Public Trans-portation, Boston, 1956.

54. M. Chisholm, "Economies of Scale in Road Goods Transport? Off-Farm Milk Collection in England and Wales," OXFORD ECONOMIC PAPERS, Vol. 11, No. 3, October 1959, pp. 282-290.

55. E. Schenker, "Technical Efficiency of British Motor Transport Under Nationalization," TRANSPORTATION JOURNAL, Vol. 4, No. 3, Spring 1965, pp. 5-11.

56. S.L. Warner, "Cost Models, Measurement Errors, and Economies of Scale in Trucking," in M.L. Burstein, et al., THE COST OF TRUCKING: ECONOMETRIC ANALYSIS, Wm. C. Brown Co. Publishers, Dubuque, Iowa, 1965, pp. 1-46.

57. P.W. Emery, II, "An Empirical Approach to the Motor Carrier Scale Economies Controversy," LAND ECONOMICS, Vol. 41, No. 3, August 1965, pp. 285-289.

58. R.K. Koshal, "Economies of Scale. I. The Cost of Trucking: Econometric Analysis. II. Bus Transport: Some United States Experience," JOURNAL OF TRANSPORT ECONOMICS AND POLICY, Vol. 6, No. 2, May 1972, pp. 147-153.

59. J. Johnston, STATISTICAL COST ANALYSIS, McGraw-Hill Book Co., Inc., New York, 1960, pp. 84-86.

60. J.R. Meyer, J.F. Kain, and M. Wohl, THE URBAN TRANSPORTATION PROBLEM, Harvard University Press, Cambridge, 1966, pp. 216-218.

61. N. Lee and I. Steedman, "Economies of Scale in Bus Transport: I—Some British Municipal Results," JOURNAL OF TRANSPORT ECONOMICS AND POLICY, Vol. 4, No. 1, January 1970, pp. 15-28.

62. R.K. Koshal, "Economies of Scale in Bus Transport: II—Some Indian Experience," JOURNAL OF TRANSPORT ECONOMICS AND POLICY, Vol. 4, No. 1, January 1970, pp. 29-36.

63. D.R. Miller, "Differences Among Cities, Differences Among Firms, and Costs of Urban Bus Transport," JOURNAL OF INDUSTRIAL ECONOMICS, Vol. 19, No. 1, November 1970, pp. 22-32.

64. R.K. Koshal, "Economies of Scale. I. The Cost of Trucking: Econometric Analysis. II. Bus Transport: Some United States Experience," JOURNAL OF TRANSPORT ECONOMICS AND POLICY, Vol. 6, No. 2, May 1972, pp. 147-153.

65. H.B. Chenery, "Engineering Production Functions," QUARTERLY JOURNAL OF ECONOMICS, Vol. 63, No. 4, November 1949, pp. 507-531. Also see his "Process and Production Functions from Engineering Data," in W. Leontief, et al., STUDIES IN THE STRUCTURE OF THE AMERICAN ECONOMY, Oxford University Press, New York, 1953.

66. L. Cookenboo, Jr., "Costs of Operating Crude Oil Pipelines," RICE INSTITUTE PAMPHLETS, Vol. 41, No. 1, April 1954, pp. 35-113. Also, by the same author, CRUDE OIL PIPELINES AND COMPETITION IN THE INDUSTRY, Harvard University Press, Cambridge, Massachusetts, 1955.

67. James C. Nelson's paper in this volume takes up some additional regulatory issues.

68. Interstate Commerce Commission, EIGHTY-FOURTH ANNUAL REPORT ON TRANSPORT STATISTICS IN THE UNITED STATES, 1970, U.S. Government Printing Office, Washington, D.C., 1972, Part I, p. 3.

69. Ibid., p. 19.

70. Calculated from data in ibid., pp. 118-286.

71. Ibid., p. 53. Although large capital costs are not in themselves entry barriers, when coupled with high concentration they can be entry barriers because of higher interest rates due to the risk of possible retaliation from existing firms.

72. Ibid., Part 7, p. 127.

73. D.P. Locklin, ECONOMICS OF TRANSPORTATION, 7th ed., Richard D. Irwin, Inc., Homewood, Illinois, 1972, p. 647.

74. Interstate Commerce Commission, EIGHTY-THIRD ANNUAL REPORT ON TRANSPORT STATISTICS IN THE UNITED STATES, 1969, U.S. Government Printing Office, Washington, D.C. 1970. Calculated from data contained in Part 7, pp. 56-64.

75. Locklin, p. 650.

76. I.C.C., EIGHTY-THIRD ANNUAL REPORT . . . , 1969. Calculated from data in Part 7, p. 98.

77. I.C.C., EIGHTY-FOURTH ANNUAL REPORT . . . , 1970. Based on data in Part 6, p. 6.

78. Based on data in ibid., Part 6, pp. 16-18.

79. Civil Aeronautics Board, HANDBOOK OF AIRLINE STATISTICS, 1969 Edition, U.S. Government Printing Office, Washington, D.C. 1970, p. 4.

80. W.A. Jordan, AIRLINE REGULATION IN AMERICA: EFFECTS AND IMPERFECTIONS, John Hopkins Press, Baltimore, 1970, p. 13.

81. Meyer, Peck, Stenason, and Zwick, p. 228.

82. Ibid.

83. Jordan, p. 27.

84. C.A.B., HANDBOOK . . . , p. 4.

85. Ibid., p. 205.

86. These figures are for 1964 and were obtained from BIG LOAD AFLOAT, The American Waterways Operators, Inc., Washington, D.C., 1965, p. 3.

87. I.C.C., EIGHTY-THIRD ANNUAL REPORT . . . , 1969, Part 5, p. 1. These figures include carriers operating in the following areas: Atlantic and Gulf Coast, Great Lakes, Mississippi River and Tributaries, Pacific Coast, and Intracoastal.

88. Meyer, Peck, Stenason, and Zwick, pp. 240-241.

89. See A.A. Walters, "The Theory and Measurement of Private and Social Costs of Highway Congestion," ECONOMETRICA, Vol. 29, No. 4, October 1961, pp. 676-699; A.A. Walters, "Empirical Evidence on Optimum Motor Taxes for the U.K.," APPLIED STATISTICS, Vol. 10, No. 3, November 1961, pp. 157-169; M.B. Johnson, "On the Economics of Road Congestion," ECONOMETRICA, Vol. 32, No. 1-2, January-April 1964, pp. 137-150; J. Hewitt, "The Calculation of Congestion Taxes on Roads," ECONOMICA, Vol. 31, No. 121, February 1964, pp. 72-81; H. Mohring, "Relation Between Optimum Congestion Tolls and Present Highway User Charges," in Highway Research Board, "Traffic

Congestion as a Factor in Road-User Taxation: 6 Reports," HIGHWAY RESEARCH RECORD, No. 47, 1964; M. Wohl, "The Short-Run Congestion Cost and Pricing Dilemma," TRAFFIC QUARTERLY, Vol. 20, No. 1, January 1966, pp. 48-70; A.A. Walters, THE ECONOMICS OF ROAD USER CHARGES, World Bank Staff Occasional Papers, No. 5, International Bank for Reconstruction and Development, 1968.

90. A. Carlin and R.E. Park, THE EFFICIENT USE OF AIRPORT RUNWAY CAPACITY IN A TIME OF SCARCITY, The Rand Corporation, RM-5917-PA, August 1969. Some of the analysis contained in this Rand Memorandum has been published in A. Carlin and R.E. Park, "Marginal Cost Pricing of Airport Runway Capacity," AMERICAN ECONOMIC REVIEW, Vol. 60, No. 3, June 1970, pp. 310-319; and A. Carlin and R.E. Park, "A Model of Delays at Busy Airports," JOURNAL OF TRANSPORT ECONOMICS AND POLICY, Vol. 4, No. 1, January 1970, pp. 37-54.

91. Howe, et al.; L.B. Lave and J.S. DeSalvo, "Congestion, Tolls, and the Economic Capacity of a Waterway," JOURNAL OF POLITICAL ECONOMY, Vol. 76, No. 3, May-June 1968, pp. 375-391.

92. The model and its application to the Illinois Waterway are contained in J.S. DeSalvo and L.B. Lave, "An Analysis of Towboat Delays," JOURNAL OF TRANSPORT ECONOMICS AND POLICY, Vol. 2, No. 2, May 1968, pp. 232-241. The economic efficiency implications of the analysis are worked out in Lave and DeSalvo.

93. See Meyer, Peck, Stenason, and Zwick, p. 249.

94. Detailed recommendations are given in Meyer, Peck, Stenason, and Zwick, pp. 242-273. See also James C. Nelson's paper in this volume.

95. FINAL REPORT OF THE HIGHWAY COST ALLOCATION STUDY, prepared by the Federal Highway Administrator for the U.S. Department of Commerce, House Document No. 54, 87th Cong., 1st Sess., U.S. Government Printing Office, Washington, D.C., 1961.

96. Testimony by R.A. Nelson in HEARINGS BEFORE THE COMMITTEE ON COMMERCE, ON S. 924 and S. 2425, 91st Cong., 2nd Sess., U.S. Government Printing Office, Washington, D.C., 1970, p. 114.

97. All of these points were made in the testimony by R.A. Nelson, already cited, p. 114.

98. All of these points were made by Secretary of Transportation J.A. Volpe in his testimony before the Senate, cited above, pp. 237-238.

Bibliography

Adams, W., and J. Hendry, "Trucking Mergers, Concentration and Small Business: An Analysis of Interstate Commerce Commission Policy, 1950-1956," in U.S. Senate Select Subcommittee on Small Business, TRUCKING MERGERS AND CONCENTRATION, U.S. Government Printing Office, Washington, D.C., 1956.

THE ANALYSIS AND EVALUATION OF PUBLIC EXPENDITURES: THE PPB SYSTEM, Vol. 1, U.S. Government Printing Office, Washington, D.C., 1969.

Arrow, K.J., "The Economics of Moral Hazard: Further Comment," AMERICAN ECONOMIC REVIEW, Vol. 58, No. 3, Part 1, June 1968, pp. 537-539.

_____, "An Extension of the Basic Theorems of Classical Welfare Economics," in J. Neyman (ed.), PROCEEDINGS OF THE SECOND BERKELEY SYMPOSIUM ON MATHEMATICAL STATISTICS AND PROBABILITY, University of California Press, Berkeley, 1951.

_____, "The Role of Securities in the Optimal Allocation of Risk Bearing," REVIEW OF ECONOMIC STUDIES, Vol. 31 (2), No. 86, April 1964, pp. 91-96.

_____, and G. Debreu, "Existence of an Equilibrium for a Competitive Economy," ECONOMETRICA, Vol. 22, No. 3, July 1954, pp. 265-290.

_____, and T. Scitovsky, (eds.), READINGS IN WELFARE ECONOMICS, Richard D. Irwin, Inc., Homewood, Ill., 1969.

Aumann, R.J., "Existence of Competitive Equilibria in Markets with a Continuum of Traders," ECONOMETRICA, Vol. 34, No. 1, January 1966, pp. 1-17.

Bain, J.S., INDUSTRIAL ORGANIZATION, John Wiley and Sons, Inc., New York, 1959.

Beckmann, M., C.B. McGuire, and C.B. Winston, STUDIES IN THE ECONOMICS OF TRANSPORTATION, Yale University Press, New Haven, Conn., 1956.

BIG LOAD AFLOAT, The American Waterways Operators, Inc., Washington, D.C., 1965.

Borts, G.H., "The Estimation of Rail Cost Functions," ECONOMETRICA, Vol. 28, No. 1, January 1960, pp. 108-131.

_____, "Increasing Returns in the Railway Industry," JOURNAL OF POLITICAL ECONOMY, Vol. 62, No. 4, August 1954, pp. 316-333.

_____, "Production Relations in the Railway Industry," ECONOMETRICA, Vol. 20, No. 1, January 1952, pp. 71-79.

Brozen, Y., "The Antitrust Task Force Deconcentration Recommendation," JOURNAL OF LAW AND ECONOMICS, Vol. 13, No. 2, October 1970, pp. 279-292.

Buchanan, J.M., "Politics, Policy, and the Pigovian Margins," ECONOMICA, Vol. 29, No. 113, February 1962, pp. 17-28.

Buchanan, J.M., and M.Z. Kafoglis, "A Note on Public Goods Supply," AMER-
ICAN ECONOMIC REVIEW, Vol. 53, June 1963, pp. 403-414.

_____, and W.C. Stubblebine, "Externality," ECONOMICA, Vol. 29, No. 116,
November 1962, pp. 371-384.

Burstein, M.L., A.V. Cabot, J.W. Egan, A.P. Hurter, Jr., and S.L. Warner, THE
COST OF TRUCKING: ECONOMETRIC ANALYSIS, Wm. C. Brown Co.
Publishers, Dubuque, Iowa, 1965.

Cadbury, L.J., "Large and Small Firms: A Note on Costs in the Road Transport
Industry," ECONOMIC JOURNAL, Vol. 45, No. 180, December 1935, pp.
789-793.

Carlin, A., and R.E. Park, THE EFFICIENT USE OF AIRPORT RUNWAY
CAPACITY IN A TIME OF SCARCITY, The Rand Corporation,
RM-5817-PA, August 1969.

_____, and _____, "Marginal Cost Pricing of Airport Runway Capacity,"
AMERICAN ECONOMIC REVIEW, Vol. 60, No. 3, June 1970, pp. 310-319.

_____, and _____, "A Model of Delays at Busy Airports," JOURNAL OF
TRANSPORT ECONOMICS AND POLICY, Vol. 4, No. 1, January 1970, pp.
37-54.

Case, L.S., and L.B. Lave, "Cost Functions for Inland Waterways," JOURNAL
OF TRANSPORT ECONOMICS AND POLICY, Vol. 4, No. 2, May 1970, pp.
181-191.

Caves, R.E., AIR TRANSPORT AND ITS REGULATORS: AN INDUSTRY
STUDY, Harvard University Press, Cambridge, 1962.

_____, AMERICAN INDUSTRY: STRUCTURE, CONDUCT, PERFORM-
ANCE, Prentice Hall, Inc., Englewood Cliffs, N.J., 1964.

Chenery, H.B., "Engineering Production Functions," QUARTERLY JOURNAL
OF ECONOMICS, Vol. 63, No. 4, November 1949, pp. 507-531.

_____, "Process and Production Functions from Engineering Data," in W.
Leontief, et al., STUDIES IN THE STRUCTURE OF THE AMERICAN
ECONOMY, Oxford University Press, New York, 1953.

Cherington, P.W., AIRLINE PRICE POLICY: A STUDY OF DOMESTIC
AIRLINE PASSENGER FARES, Graduate School of Business Administration, Harvard University, Boston, 1958.

Chisholm, M., "Economies of Scale in Road Goods Transport? Off-Farm Milk
Collection in England and Wales," OXFORD ECONOMIC PAPERS, Vol. 11,
No. 3, October 1959, pp. 282-290.

Civil Aeronautics Board, HANDBOOK OF AIRLINE STATISTICS, 1969 Edition, U.S. Government Printing Office, Washington, D.C., 1970.

Coase, R.H., "The Problem of Social Cost," JOURNAL OF LAW AND
ECONOMICS, Vol. 3, October 1960, pp. 1-44.

Cookenboo, L., Jr., "Costs of Operating Crude Oil Pipelines," RICE INSTITUTE
PAMPHLETS, Vol. 41, No. 1, April 1954, pp. 35-113.

_____, CRUDE OIL PIPELINES AND COMPETITION IN THE OIL INDUS-
TRY, Harvard University Press, Cambridge, 1955.

Crane, J.B., "The Economics of Air Transportation," HARVARD BUSINESS REVIEW, Vol. 22, No. 4, Summer 1944, pp. 495-509.

Davis, O.A., and A.B. Whinston, "On Externalities, Information, and the Government-Assisted Invisible Hand," ECONOMICA, Vol. 33, No. 131, August 1966, pp. 303-318.

_____, and _____, "Externalities, Welfare and the Theory of Games," JOURNAL OF POLITICAL ECONOMY, Vol. 70, No. 3, June 1962, pp. 241-262.

_____, and _____, "Welfare Economics and the Theory of Second Best," REVIEW OF ECONOMIC STUDIES, Vol. 32 (1), No. 89, January 1965, pp. 1-14.

Debreu, G., THEORY OF VALUE: AN AXIOMATIC ANALYSIS OF ECONOMIC EQUILIBRIUM, John Wiley and Sons, Inc., New York, 1959.

Demsetz, H., "Contracting Cost and Public Policy," in THE ANALYSIS AND EVALUATION OF PUBLIC EXPENDITURES: THE PPB SYSTEM, Vol. 1, U.S. Government Printing Office, Washington, D.C., 1969.

_____, "The Exchange and Enforcement of Property Rights," JOURNAL OF LAW AND ECONOMICS Vol. 7, October 1964, pp. 11-26.

_____, "Why Regulate Utilities?" JOURNAL OF LAW AND ECONOMICS, Vol. 11, April 1968, pp. 55-66.

DeSalvo, J.S., "A Process Function for Rail Linehaul Operations," JOURNAL OF TRANSPORT ECONOMICS AND POLICY, Vol. 3, No. 1, January 1969, pp. 3-27.

_____, and L.B. Lave, "An Analysis of Towboat Delays," JOURNAL OF TRANSPORT ECONOMICS AND POLICY, Vol. 2, No. 2, May 1968, pp. 232-241.

_____, and _____, A STATISTICAL-ENGINEERING APPROACH TO ESTIMATING RAILWAY COST FUNCTIONS, The Rand Corporation, P-3781, March 1968.

Dicer, G.N., "Economies of Scale and Motor Carrier Optimum Size," QUARTERLY REVIEW OF ECONOMICS AND BUSINESS, Vol. 11, No. 1, Spring 1971, pp. 31-37.

Dorfman, R., P.A. Samuelson, and R.M. Solow, LINEAR PROGRAMMING AND ECONOMIC ANALYSIS, McGraw-Hill Book Co., Inc., New York, 1958.

Dror, Y., "Dimensions of Planning" in C.J. Friedrich and S.E. Harris (eds.), PUBLIC POLICY, Vol. VII, Harvard Graduate School of Public Administration, Cambridge, 1956.

Eads, G., M. Nerlove, and W. Raduchel, "A Long-Run Cost Function for the Local Service Airline Industry: An Experiment in Non-Linear Estimation," REVIEW OF ECONOMICS AND STATISTICS, Vol. 51, No. 3, August 1969, pp. 258-270.

Edwards, F.K., "Cost Analysis in Transportation," AMERICAN ECONOMIC REVIEW, Vol. 37, May 1947, pp. 441-461.

Edwards, F.K., RAIL FREIGHT SERVICE COSTS IN THE VARIOUS RATE TERRITORIES OF THE UNITED STATES, 78th Congress, 1st Session, Senate Document No. 63, Washington, D.C., 1943.

Emery, P.W., II, "An Empirical Approach to the Motor Carrier Scale Economies Controversy," LAND ECONOMICS, Vol. 41, No. 3, August 1965, pp. 285-289.

Farmer, R.N., "Motor Vehicle Pricing in Lebanon," JOURNAL OF INDUSTRIAL ECONOMICS, Vol. 7, No. 3, July 1959, pp. 199-205.

Farrell, M.J., "The Convexity Assumption in the Theory of Competitive Markets," JOURNAL OF POLITICAL ECONOMY, Vol. 67, No. 4, August 1959, pp. 377-391.

FINAL REPORT OF THE HIGHWAY COST ALLOCATION STUDY, prepared by the Federal Highway Administrator for the U.S. Department of Commerce, House Document No. 54, 87th Congress, 1st Session, U.S. Government Printing Office, Washington, D.C., 1961.

Friedmann, J., "Planning as a Vocation (Part I)," PLAN, Vol. 6, No. 3, April 1966, pp. 99-124.

Gale, D., "The Law of Supply and Demand," MATHEMATICA SCANDINAVICA, Vol. 3, 1955, pp. 155-169.

Ganguly, S.K., "The Perfectly Competitive Production of Collective Goods: Comment," REVIEW OF ECONOMICS AND STATISTICS, Vol. 51, No. 4, November 1969, pp. 478-479.

Griliches, Z., "Cost Allocation in Railroad Regulation," BELL JOURNAL OF ECONOMICS AND MANAGEMENT SCIENCE, Vol. 3, No. 1, Spring 1972, pp. 26-41.

Harrison, A.J., "Economies of Scale and the Structure of the Road Haulage Industry," OXFORD ECONOMIC PAPERS, Vol. 15, No. 3, November 1963, pp. 287-307.

Hayek, F.A., THE ROAD TO SERFDOM, University of Chicago Press, Chicago, 1944.

Healy, K.T., THE EFFECTS OF SCALE IN THE RAILROAD INDUSTRY, Committee on Transportation, Yale University, 1961.

HEARINGS BEFORE THE COMMITTEE ON COMMERCE, ON S.924 AND S.2425, 91st Congress, 2nd Session, U.S. Government Printing Office, Washington, D.C., 1970.

Henman, P.S., "The Economics of Goods Transport by Road," INSTITUTE OF TRANSPORT JOURNAL, Vol. 29, March 1962, pp. 259-270.

Hewitt, J., "The Calculation of Congestion Taxes on Roads," ECONOMICA, Vol. 31, No. 121, February 1964, pp. 72-81.

Highway Research Board, TRAFFIC CONGESTION AS A FACTOR IN ROAD USE: 6 REPORTS, HIGHWAY RESEARCH RECORD, No. 47, 1964.

Howe, C.W., "Mathematical Model of Barge Tow Performance," JOURNAL OF THE WATERWAYS AND HARBORS DIVISION, AMERICAN SOCIETY OF

CIVIL ENGINEERS, Vol. 93, No. WW4, Proc. Paper 5588, November 1967, pp. 153-166.

————, "Methods for Equipment Selection and Benefit Evaluation in Inland Waterway Transportation," WATER RESOURCES RESEARCH, Vol. 1, No. 1, First Quarter 1965, pp. 25-39.

————, "Models of a Bargeline: An Analysis of Returns to Scale in Inland Waterway Transportation," Institute for Quantitative Research in Economics and Management, Krannert Graduate School, Purdue University, Institute Paper No. 77, July 1964.

————, "Process and Production Functions for Inland Waterway Transportation," Institute for Quantitative Research in Economics and Management, Krannert Graduate School, Purdue University, Institute Paper No. 65, January 1964.

————, J.L. Carroll, A.P. Hurter, Jr., W.J. Leininger, S.G. Ramsey, N.L. Schwatrz, E. Silberberg, and R.M. Steinberg, INLAND WATERWAY TRANSPORTATION: STUDIES IN PUBLIC AND PRIVATE MANAGEMENT AND INVESTMENT DECISIONS, Resources for the Future, Inc., Washington, D.C., 1969.

Hurter, A.P., Jr., "Cost Relationships for Inland Waterway Operations on the Mississippi River: 1950, 1957, 1962," The Transportation Center, Northwestern University, 1965.

————, "Production Relationships for Inland Waterway Operations on the Mississippi River: 1950, 1957, 1962," The Transportation Center, Northwestern University, 1965.

Interstate Commerce Commission, EIGHTY-FOURTH ANNUAL REPORT ON TRANSPORT STATISTICS IN THE UNITED STATES, 1970, U.S. Government Printing Office, Washington, D.C., 1972.

————, EIGHTY-THIRD ANNUAL REPORT ON TRANSPORT STATISTICS IN THE UNITED STATES, 1969, U.S. Government Printing Office, Washington, D.C., 1970.

Johnson, M.B., "On the Economics of Road Congestion," ECONOMETRICA, Vol. 32, No. 1-2, January-April 1964, pp. 137-150.

Johnston, J., STATISTICAL COST ANALYSIS, McGraw-Hill Book Co., Inc., New York, 1960.

Jordan, W.A., AIRLINE REGULATION IN AMERICA: EFFECTS AND IMPERFECTIONS, Johns Hopkins Press, Baltimore, 1970.

Klein, L.R., A TEXTBOOK OF ECONOMETRICS, Row, Peterson and Co., Evanston, Illinois, 1953.

Kolsen, H., "Structure and Price Determination in the New South Wales Road Haulage Industry," ECONOMIC RECORD, Vol. 32, November 1956, pp. 291-304.

Koontz, H.D., "Domestic Air Line Self-Sufficiency: A Problem of Route Structure," AMERICAN ECONOMIC REVIEW, Vol. 42, No. 1, March 1952, pp. 103-125.

Koontz, H.D., "Economic and Managerial Factors Underlying Subsidy Needs of Domestic Trunk Line Air Carriers," JOURNAL OF AIR LAW AND COMMERCE, Vol. 18, No. 2, Spring 1951, pp. 127-156.

Koopmans, T.C., THREE ESSAYS ON THE STATE OF ECONOMIC SCIENCE, McGraw-Hill Book Company, Inc., New York, 1957.

Koshal, R.K., "Economies of Scale in Bus Transport: II—Some Indian Experience," JOURNAL OF TRANSPORT ECONOMICS AND POLICY, Vol. 4, No. 1, January 1970, pp. 29-36.

_____, "Economies of Scale. I. The Cost of Trucking: Econometric Analysis. II. Bus transport: Some United States Experience," JOURNAL OF TRANSPORT ECONOMICS AND POLICY, Vol. 6, No. 2, May 1972, pp. 147-153.

Lave, L.B., and J.S. DeSalvo, "Congestion, Tolls, and the Economic Capacity of a Waterway," JOURNAL OF POLITICAL ECONOMY, Vol. 76, No. 3, May-June 1968, pp. 375-391.

Lee, N., and I. Steedman, "Economies of Scale in Bus Transport: I—Some British Municipal Results," JOURNAL OF TRANSPORT ECONOMICS AND POLICY, Vol. 4, No. 1, January 1970, pp. 15-28.

Leininger, W.J., "An Empirical Production Function for Barge Towing Operations on the Ohio River," unpublished Ph.D. dissertation, Purdue University, August 1963.

Leontief, W., et al., STUDIES IN THE STRUCTURE OF THE AMERICAN ECONOMY, Oxford University Press, New York, 1953.

Lipsey, R.G., and K. Lancaster, "The General Theory of Second Best," REVIEW OF ECONOMIC STUDIES, Vol. 24 (1), No. 63, December 1956, pp. 11-32.

Locklin, D.P., ECONOMICS OF TRANSPORTATION, 7th ed., Richard D. Irwin, Inc., Homewood, Illinois, 1972.

McKean, R.N., PUBLIC SPENDING, McGraw-Hill Book Co., New York, 1968.

McKenzie, L.W., "On the Existence of General Equilibrium for a Competitive Market," ECONOMETRICA, Vol. 27, No. 1, January 1959, pp. 54-71.

Malinvaud, E., "Capital Accumulation and Efficient Allocation of Resources," ECONOMETRICA, Vol. 21, No. 2, April 1953, pp. 233-268.

Mansfield, E., MICROECONOMICS: THEORY AND APPLICATIONS, W.W. Norton and Co., Inc., New York, 1970.

_____, and H.H. Wein, "A Regression Control Chart for Costs," APPLIED STATISTICS, Vol. 7, No. 1, March 1958, pp. 48-57.

Margolis, J., and H. Guitton, eds. PUBLIC ECONOMICS, Macmillan and Co., Ltd., London, 1969.

Meyer, J.R., J.F. Kain, and M. Wohl, THE URBAN TRANSPORTATION PROBLEM, Harvard University Press, Cambridge, 1966.

_____, M.J. Peck, J. Stenason, and C. Zwick, THE ECONOMICS OF COMPETITION IN THE TRANSPORTATION INDUSTRIES, Harvard University Press, Cambridge, 1960.

Miller, D.R. "Differences Among Cities, Differences Among Firms, and Costs of

Urban Bus Transport," JOURNAL OF INDUSTRIAL ECONOMICS, Vol. 19, No. 1, November 1970, pp. 27-32.

Millett, J.D., MANAGEMENT IN THE PUBLIC SERVICE, McGraw-Hill Book Company, Inc., New York, 1954.

Mohring, H., "Relation between Optimum Congestion Tolls and Present Highway User Charges," in Highway Research Board, TRAFFIC CONGESTION AS A FACTOR IN ROAD USE: 6 REPORTS, HIGHWAY RESEARCH RECORD, No. 47, 1964, pp. 1-14.

Murphy, N.B., "Sources of Productivity Increases in the U.S. Passenger Airline Industry," TRANSPORTATION SCIENCE, Vol. 3, No. 3, August 1969, pp. 233-238.

Nelson, R.A., "The Economic Structure of the Highway Carrier Industry in New England," MOTOR FREIGHT TRANSPORT FOR NEW ENGLAND, New England Governors' Conference on Public Transportation, Boston, 1956.

————, "The Economies of Scale in the Motor Carrier Industry: A Reply," LAND ECONOMICS, Vol. 35, No. 2, May 1959, pp. 180-185.

Neyman, J. (ed.), PROCEEDINGS OF THE SECOND BERKELEY SYMPOSIUM ON MATHEMATICAL STATISTICS AND PROBABILITY, University of California Press, Berkeley, 1951.

Owen, B.M., "The Perfectly Competitive Production of Collective Goods: Comment," REVIEW OF ECONOMICS AND STATISTICS, Vol. 51, No. 4, November 1969, pp. 475-476.

Pigou, A.C., THE ECONOMICS OF WELFARE, 4th ed., Macmillan and Co., Ltd., London, 1932.

Plott, C.R., "Externalities and Corrective Taxes," ECONOMICA, Vol. 33, No. 129, February 1966, pp. 84-87.

Proctor, J.W., and J.S. Duncan, "A Regression Analysis of Airline Costs," JOURNAL OF AIR LAW AND COMMERCE, Vol. 21, No. 3, Summer 1954, pp. 282-292.

Radner, R., "Competitive Equilibrium under Uncertainty," ECONOMETRICA, Vol. 36, No. 1, January 1968, pp. 31-58.

Rodgers, J.D., "The Perfectly Competitive Production of Collective Goods: Comment," REVIEW OF ECONOMICS AND STATISTICS, Vol. 51, No. 4, November 1969, pp. 476-478.

Roberts, M.J., "Some Aspects of Motor Carrier Costs: Firm Size, Efficiency, and Financial Health," LAND ECONOMICS, Vol. 32, No. 3, August 1956, pp. 228-238.

Rothenberg, J., "Non-Convexity, Aggregation, and Pareto Optimality," JOURNAL OF POLITICAL ECONOMY, Vol. 68, No. 5, October 1960, pp. 435-468.

Samuelson, P.A., "Aspects of Public Expenditure Theories," REVIEW OF ECONOMICS AND STATISTICS, Vol. 40, No. 4, November 1958, pp. 332-338.

Samuelson, P.A., "Diagrammatic Exposition of a Theory of Public Expenditure," REVIEW OF ECONOMICS AND STATISTICS, Vol. 37, No. 4, November 1955, pp. 350-356.

_____, "The Pure Theory of Public Expenditure," REVIEW OF ECONOMICS AND STATISTICS, Vol. 36, No. 4, November 1954, pp. 387-389.

_____, "Pure Theory of Public Expenditure and Taxation," in J. Margolis and H. Guitton (eds.), PUBLIC ECONOMICS, Macmillan and Co., Ltd., London, 1969.

Sargent, J.R., BRITISH TRANSPORT POLICY, Clarendon Press, Oxford, 1958.

Schenker, E., "Technical Efficiency of British Motor Transport under Nationalization," TRANSPORTATION JOURNAL, Vol. 4, No. 3, Spring 1965, pp. 5-11.

Schumer, L.A., "Road Transport," in Australian Institute of Political Science (John Wilkes, ed.), AUSTRALIA'S TRANSPORT CRISIS, Angus and Roberts, Sydney, 1956, pp. 134-158.

Schumpeter, J.A., CAPITALISM, SOCIALISM AND DEMOCRACY, 3rd ed., Harper and Brothers Publishers, New York, 1950.

Seeley, J.R., "Central Planning: Prologue to a Critique," in R. Morris (ed.), CENTRALLY PLANNED CHANGE: PROSPECTS AND CONCEPTS, National Association of Social Workers, New York, 1964.

Smykay, E.W., "An Appraisal of the Economics of Scale in the Motor Carrier Industry," LAND ECONOMICS, Vol. 34, No. 2, May 1958, pp. 143-148.

Starr, R.M., "Quasi-Equilibria in Markets with Non-Convex Preferences," ECONOMETRICA, Vol. 37, No. 1, January 1969, pp. 25-38.

Stenason, W.J., and R.A. Bandeen, "Transportation Costs and Their Implications: An Empirical Study of Railway Costs in Canada," TRANSPORTATION ECONOMICS, National Bureau of Economic Research, New York, 1965.

Stiglitz, J.E., "On the Optimality of the Stock Market Allocation of Investment," QUARTERLY JOURNAL OF ECONOMICS, Vol. 86, No. 1, February 1972, pp. 25-60.

_____, (ed.), THE COLLECTED SCIENTIFIC PAPERS OF PAUL A. SAMUELSON, 2 vols., The M.I.T. Press, Cambridge, Mass., 1966.

Thompson, E.A., "The Perfectly Competitive Production of Collective Goods," REVIEW OF ECONOMICS AND STATISTICS, Vol. 50, No. 1, February 1968, pp. 1-12.

_____, "The Perfectly Competitive Production of Collective Goods: Reply," REVIEW OF ECONOMICS AND STATISTICS, Vol. 51, No. 4, November 1969, pp. 479-482.

TRANSPORTATION ECONOMICS, National Bureau of Economic Research, New York, 1965.

Walker, G., ROAD AND RAIL: AN ENQUIRY INTO THE ECONOMICS OF COMPETITION AND STATE CONTROL, rev. ed., George Allen and Unwin, Ltd., London, 1947.

Walters, A.A., THE ECONOMICS OF ROAD USER CHARGES, World Bank Staff Occasional Paper No. 5, International Bank for Reconstruction and Development, 1968.

————,"Economies of Scale in Road Haulage: A Comment," OXFORD ECONOMIC PAPERS, Vol. 13, No. 1, February 1961, pp. 116-118.

————, "Empirical Evidence on Optimum Motor Taxes for the U.K.," APPLIED STATISTICS, Vol. 10, No. 3, November 1961, pp. 157-169.

————, "Production and Cost Functions: An Econometric Survey," ECONOMETRICA, Vol. 31, No. 1-2, January-April 1963, pp. 1-66.

————, "The Theory and Measurement of Private and Social Costs of Highway Congestion," ECONOMETRICA, Vol. 29, No. 4, October 1961, pp. 676-699.

Warner, S.L., "Cost Models, Measurement Errors, and Economies of Scale in Trucking," in M.L. Burstein, A.V. Cabot, J.W. Egan, A.P. Hurter, Jr., and S.L. Warner, THE COST OF TRUCKING: ECONOMETRIC ANALYSIS, Wm. C. Brown Co., Dubuque, Iowa, 1965, pp. 1-46.

Wellisz, S., "On External Diseconomies and the Government-Assisted Invisible Hand," ECONOMICA, Vol. 31, No. 124, November 1964, pp. 345-362.

Wheatcroft, S., THE ECONOMICS OF EURPOEAN AIR TRANSPORT, Manchester University Press, Manchester, England, 1956.

Wilson, G.W., "The Nature of Competition in the Motor Transport Industry," LAND ECONOMICS, Vol. 36, No. 4, November 1960, pp. 387-391.

Wohl, M., "The Short-Run Congestion Cost and Pricing Dilemma," TRAFFIC QUARTERLY, Vol. 20, No. 1, January 1966, pp. 48-70.

Wootton, B., FREEDOM UNDER PLANNING, University of North Carolina Press, Chapel Hill, 1945.

2

Delimitation of Regions for Transportation Planning

Karl A. Fox,
Iowa State University

Summary

The outline of our approach to delimiting transportation planning regions is as follows:

1. A transportation system exists to serve a community and is embedded in a community.
2. The communities relevant to transportation planning in the United States consist of a hierarchy of central places (successively larger cities) and their trade and service areas covering successively larger geographic territories.
3. Home-to-work commuting fields around cities of (typically) 25,000 or more people are the appropriate units for local transportation planning, and in nonmetropolitan areas such commuting fields often extend over several counties.
4. Larger regions for transportation planning should be made up of sets of contiguous commuting fields, and the set of larger regions itself should cover the entire continental United States.
5. The most promising large regions for transportation planning appear to be centered on about 24 major metropolitan areas.

A set of contiguous whole counties approximating a commuting field is called a functional economic area (FEA). Our largest metropolitan areas are equivalent in some respects to the close-packing of several or many FEAs, each centered on a regional shopping plaza or on the business district of a satellite city.

The larger regions, containing fifteen to 25 FEAs and metropolitan subareas in most cases, are referred to as National Metropolitan Regions (NMRs).

We arrive, then, at the following view of the United States for purposes of passenger transportation planning:

(a) *Local* transportation planning within each of some 500 multicounty FEAs and metropolitan subareas, involving motor vehicles for the most part.

(b) *National* transportation planning at the level of about 24 widely separated cities, mainly involving air travel.

(c) *Regional* transportation planning within each of some 24 NMRs, involving motor vehicles, (light) planes, and perhaps some interurban transit by rail.

State governments would be the most strategic units for implementing transportation plans (1) involving individual multicounty FEAs and (2) involving the improved linkage of two or more FEAs within an NMR. Some problems could be handled by a single state and others by two states; a limited number of NMR problems might involve three or more states.

If state governments had strong departments of transportation covering all modes, they should be in a good position to cooperate with each other on problems of intermodal transportation planning involving two or more states wholly or partly within an NMR.

A Transportation System Is Embedded In a Community: The Logic of Central Place Theory

Human communities have a strong tendency to organize themselves spatially according to "central place" principles. If all movement is on foot, the places used by community members in the rhythms of daily living must be conveniently accessible on foot. "Conveniently accessible" means that the amount of time per day used up in getting between places within the community requires only a tolerable fraction of the 24 hours. If a person's dwelling is so located with respect to the other relevant places in a community that his transportation time becomes intolerable, he will try to relocate further inside of the given community, or he will affiliate himself with a neighboring community if its services are accessible to him with a smaller expenditure of time. In this case, the person's dwelling is evidently located near the *de facto* boundary between two communities. If the stores, schools, churches, and other facilities in the two communities are equally attractive, the *de facto* boundary will be approximately equidistant from the centers of the two communities.

The area and population size of such a community will be determined within a socioeconomic equilibrium system that is approximately self-contained or closed with respect to a set of places (dwellings, work-places, stores, schools, etc.), the set of people who occupy those places, the set of economic and social activities conducted in those places, and the set of transportation facilities (roads, paths, sidewalks) that connect those places. The optimal capacity and design of each link in the transportation network would depend on the properties of the community as a whole.

Modifications of the pedestrian transportation network within the community would have few "spillover effects" on other communities; the costs and benefits would both accrue to residents of the same community. In general, the absence of spillover effects from a certain class of public decisions should favor clear thinking by members of the community about priorities for its public expenditures.

If (say) bicycles replaced walking as the universal means of getting around in a formerly pedestrian community, the earlier equilibrium would be upset. Perhaps 9 times as many children as before could be assembled at a single site without requiring any child to spend more time in transit. If schools with 270 pupils were distinctly superior to schools with 30 pupils, nine small schools might eventually be superseded by one large one. This factor of 9 (assuming 15 miles an hour on bicycles versus 5 miles an hour on foot) would be *permissive* with respect to the internal size and organization of every kind of establishment in the community, including bars and barber shops as well as food stores and factories. Bars and barber shops, depending upon their particular homeostatic pressures, might become larger by factors of 2 or 3, food stores and factories might expand by a factor of 9, and so on.

If our assumed "bicycle revolution" occurred simultaneously in all formerly pedestrian communities over a large region, the old community boundaries would become obsolete. People who lived and paid taxes in one jurisdiction could work, shop, and use public facilities in any or all of several other jurisdictions. Spillover effects would attend nearly all public (or private) decisions in each of the old jurisdictions; in fact, supermarket operators would be working hard to integrate a retail trade area 9 times as large as before, and factory managers would be working hard to integrate a labor market area and home-to-factory commuting field 9 times as large as before.

The logical implications are obvious. After a sufficiently long period, the typical community of daily life would cover 9 times as large an area as before. The journey-to-work would take about the same number of minutes as before but would average three times as many miles, as would other types of journeys to establishments which (for internal reasons) took advantage of the full permissive expansion factor of 9. The "local" transportation network would be coextensive with the new commuting field, and a certain class of public decisions would have to be made by an authority whose jurisdiction covered the entire commuting field *if* spillover effects were to be minimized.

It might turn out that some public decisions could still be made at the level of the old jurisdictions without major spillover effects. Considerable social activity would be organized around individual schools or churches. The problem in both public and private systems would be one of achieving an optimal pattern of decentralization of decision-making power.

A transportation planning authority covering a territory several times as large as the commuting fields of bicyclists might have perceived, well in advance, the probable impacts of the bicycle upon the sizes and internal structures of existing establishments and communities. If the hypothetical "bicycle revolution" were regarded as inevitable or desirable, or both, the problem of institutional adjustment could at least be brought into public discussion; the transition costs could be moderated as to amount and modified as to incidence.

Suppose, however, that the effects of the bicycle revolution were neither foreseen nor channeled. During a long transition period the actual locations of establishments would be a confused and confusing mixture of old and new. The old jurisdictions would continue to levy taxes and make expenditures for the same purposes despite increasing spillover effects into and from other jurisdictions. Evidences of community disorganization would increase, and the locations of establishments would appear to violate all principles of central place theory. Commuting patterns would seem equally *ad hoc*.

The foregoing is sufficient to introduce the line of argument of this chapter, which may be summarized as follows:

1. A passenger transportation system exists to serve a community, and is embedded in a community.
2. If the community is organized around a hierarchy of central places (for example, shopping centers of different levels), traffic flows will reflect this structure and different modes of transportation may be more efficient for connecting (say) Levels 3 and 4 than for connecting Levels 2 and 3 or 4 and 5.

If the same mode (and speed) of transportation is used to connect three or more levels, central places of Level n+1 will tend to be from 1/6 to 1/4 as numerous as central places of Level n; conversely, a trade and service area surrounding a center of Level n+1 will tend to be from 4 to 6 times as large (in area) as one surrounding a center of Level n. The *radius* of the trade area of a Level n + 1 center will tend to be from 2 to (say) 2-1/2 times as large as that of the trade area of a Level n center.

Any increase in average travel speeds will impose some stresses upon the central place hierarchy. If speeds are multiplied by two, the number of levels in the national hierarchy of central places may be reduced by one. Most establishments, however, can then be reached within a given number of minutes by about four times as many people; an innovator may threaten the survival of four existing establishments by opening a new one with four times their average capacity.

If average travel speeds are changing at different percentage rates over different sets of levels in the national central place hierarchy, pressures toward change in the numbers and sizes of establishments will be more intense at some hierarchical levels than at others.

Effects of the Automobile and Air Transport Revolutions
on the Central Place System of the United States

Since 1910, the automotive revolution has multiplied the speed of local travel in nonmetropolitan areas by 10 (as compared with travel by horse-and-buggy or on foot); it has multipled the area of the commuting field by 100! The average sizes of establishments of various sorts have increased by factors ranging as high as 100. The central city of a commuting field in 1972 is three levels higher in the urban hierarchy than the village that served the analogous functions in 1910.

The fundamental community of 1972 in nonmetropolitan areas is coextensive with the commuting field. It is delineated on the basis of the actual transportation behavior of employed members of the labor force with respect to the journey to work. It is of great potential value as a general purpose social, economic, and political community, with capabilities for transportation planning and general urban-regional planning within its boundaries. I have called this basic community (since 1961) a functional economic area or FEA.[1, 2]

The FEA concept also provides us with an important insight into the central place structure of a large metropolitan area. A large "regional" shopping plaza serving from 200,000 to 500,000 people stands on the same level in the central place hierarchy as does the *regional capital* of a nonmetropolitan FEA. The metropolitan area as a whole is equivalent to the close-packing of several or many FEAs.[2f, i, j, k, l] The retail trade and service activities of the metropolitan subarea surrounding a regional shopping plaza are equivalent to those of an FEA; however, many metropolitan residents are enabled, by rapid transit systems and freeways, to work outside of their subareas. Much of the present commuting in metropolitan areas is neither desirable nor necessary; the high cost of congestion in the metropolitan central business district (CBD) and the rapid deterioration of the industrial and residential areas adjacent to it favor the relocation of many employers to suburban sites.

The purposes to be served by passenger transportation *within* a metropolitan subarea are similar to those *within* an FEA, apart from the journey to work; as trade areas, the two types are equivalent. The commuting field of an FEA is essentially closed. The commuting field of a metropolitan subarea is open; the commuting field is approximately closed only for the metropolitan area as a whole.

FEAs and metropolitan subareas are the basic building blocks for larger regions; there are about 500 FEAs and metropolitan subareas in the United States.

The central place-oriented region next larger than the FEA has a radius of about 100 miles; it appears that travel between the central city of such a region and the central cities of its constituent FEAs would be mainly by automobile, although some interurban transit by rail might not be out of the question.

The type of region two stages above the FEA seems particularly important for intermodal transportation planning. Its radius (east of the Rocky Mountains) would be about 200 miles. Our tentative delineation suggests that the United States contains about 24 regions of this type organized around cities such as Minneapolis-St. Paul, Kansas City, St. Louis, and Denver. I have called this type of region (since October 3, 1970) a National Metropolitan Region (NMR), which would normally contain something like twenty FEAs and metropolitan subareas. Highway, rail, and air transportation may all have their places in moving passengers within an NMR.

Above the NMR level, the United States might be delineated into about five large regions, oriented toward New York City, Chicago, Los Angeles, and perhaps Dallas-Fort Worth and Atlanta. The final level would be the nation as a whole, with New York and Washington serving respectively as its economic and political capitals.

The top three levels of central places (NMR central cities and up) are connected primarily by air travel. There are approximately 24 cities in this set; with few exceptions, the cities are spaced at least 300 air miles apart.

We arrive, then, at the following view of the United States for purposes of passenger transportation planning:

(a) *Local* transportation planning within each of some 500 FEAs and metropolitan subareas, mainly involving motor vehicles;

(b) *National* transportation planning at the level of about 24 widely separated cities, mainly involving air travel; and

(c) *Regional* transportation planning within each of some 24 NMRs, involving motor vehicles, (light) planes, and perhaps some interurban transit by rail.

Integrating Transportation Systems for Goods with Transportation Systems for People

We turn now to the question of transportation planning for the movement of goods.

The NMR central cities, the regional metropolises next below them in the urban hierarchy, and the regional capitals (i.e., FEA central cities) are all involved in the wholesale distribution of finished manufactures to retailers. These goods usually move by truck over the same highways used for commuting and other passenger travel within an NMR; i.e., finished goods and people can be accommodated by the same central place-oriented transportation network.

The transportation of raw products from the extractive industries (farm and forest products, coal, crude oil, iron ore, and the like) to points of first processing and the transportation of semi-finished goods to points of final manufacture can usually be planned independently of transportation systems for passengers and finished goods. The NMR central cities are not primarily manufacturing centers, although much manufacturing takes place in them. At some point, finished *consumers' goods* must be transferred from the extractive and processing system to the wholesale and retail distribution system; the latter system is central place-oriented. *Producers' durable goods* (heavy construction materials, machine tools, heavy equipment, etc.) in a sense never emerge from the extractive and processing system.

Hence, comprehensive transportation planning might logically involve (1) a suboptimization for the central place-oriented subsystem, (2) a suboptimization for the extractive and manufacturing subsystem, and (3) a final joint optimization that should require only moderate revisions in the initial suboptima.

We might be justified in calling the first system a *consumption system* and the second a *production system.* The first system could be viewed as aggregating the demands of final consumers and transmitting them to the manufacturers of finished consumers' goods; the second could be viewed as a multistage transformation system that culminates in a production possibilities frontier for finished consumer goods. Equilibrium between the two systems would involve a point of tangency between the aggregate (consumer-derived) preference function of wholesalers and the aggregate production possibilities frontier of final-stage manufacturers.

The Home-to-Work Commuting Field or FEA as the Basic Unit for "Local" Transportation Planning in Nonmetropolitan Areas

This section describes the author's formulation of the FEA concept.

The New Multi-County Synthesis of Rural and Urban Society

The United States includes over 3000 counties and more than 18,000 incorporated places. About three-fourths of the incorporated places are towns with fewer than 2500 residents; more than half of the incorporated places have fewer than 1000 residents. The small size and close spacing of these places reflects their original function as retail trade and service centers for a dispersed farming population in a horse-and-buggy, five-miles-an-hour society. That society is gone, and in its place a new society has arisen with enormous untapped potentials.

What has happened is very simple. As of 1972 the passenger automobile is the almost universal means of transportation in rural areas. Our rural road systems are adapted to this. An automobile can travel ten times as fast as a horse-and-buggy, and the *area* from which workers and shoppers can reach a central place within one hour is roughly 5000 square miles—several times as large as a typical Midwestern county.

Each of these new trade areas is also a commuting field or labor market area. It includes a new kind of relatively self-sufficient community (a multi-county functional economic area) that represents a new synthesis of rural and urban society, increasingly urban in tone.

A solution to the problem of fragmented rural areas can be provided by urban-regional planning in terms of multi-county functional economic areas centered on cities with populations of 25,000 or more.

The central city of such a multi-county area is sometimes referred to as a "growth center" and includes the largest and most diversified array of jobs, retail shopping facilities, personal services, and professional services in the area. Research by Fox and by Berry has demonstrated that these growth centers are the centers of home-to-work commuting fields extending outward as far as 50 highway miles in all directions.

In sparsely populated regions, there may be gaps of mountain, desert, forest, or grazing land between commuting fields. In the more densely populated parts of the United States, cities are closer together and their commuting fields tend to overlap, sometimes in complicated ways. In such cases, it is useful to regard a set of two or more overlapping commuting fields as a consolidated urban region.

The individual towns and counties in a functional economic area are too small to provide their residents with a full range of public services of adequate quality at reasonable cost. Towns compete to attract industry, and main street businesses in different towns compete for the same customers. Small-town businessmen also compete with businessmen in the central city. Employers in all the various towns and the central city are alternative sources of employment for workers residing throughout the functional area.

No individual town or county in such an area has a significant degree of control over its own economic destiny. Even when the central city of a commuting field has fewer than 50,000 residents, the commuting field as a whole may have a population of 200,000 or more. Some functional economic areas in Iowa with central city populations of 30,000 to 35,000 have total area populations of about 150,000.

Economically and socially, these functional economic areas may be regarded as "low-density cities" or "urban community-of-interest areas." They are relatively self-contained labor markets in the short run. They contain a relatively complete array of consumer goods and services, including public services.

In brief, a functional economic area has all the economic and social potential of an independent city of similar population. All it lacks is official recognition, political encouragement, and a significant degree of area self-government, or at least, local initiative.

Such areas should be delineated and officially recognized by the states in which they are located. Federal funds should then be made available to encourage the creative planning of each such area to improve the quality of the environment and conditions of life for all residents of the area. Physical planning, including transportation planning, should reinforce the cohesiveness of the area as a functioning community.

We have also suggested in other places that the large metropolises should be restructured to emphasize viable communities (subareas of the metropolis) of not more than 500,000 population, each community having considerable autonomy and responsibility for improving its own physical, economic, and social qualities. [2i, j]

The multi-county functional areas in the rest of the country, despite the great difference in their visual characteristics, have essentially the same economic and social potential as the metropolitan subareas. The array of jobs in retail establishments, public school systems, local government agencies, and in personal and professional service occupations is much the same from one area to another. This commonality of consumer-oriented job structures produces a strong element of homogeneity in wage and salary income distributions in different functional economic areas.

There is great variation in the array of jobs that constitutes the export base from area to area. Most manufacturing plants are export-base activities. So are the government buildings in the state capital. So are major campuses of state universities. So are the home offices of businesses that operate in several or many functional economic areas. So, too, are federal military installations. The list is not exhaustive.

Obviously, differences among areas in the occupational distribution of workers in their export-base establishments result in differences among areas in wage, salary, and education-level distributions. Each area should have a good deal of local autonomy in determining what new or expanded export-base activities it wishes to encourage. Perhaps the best solution is healthy competition among areas to attract or develop activities that have high wage and salary structures and require high educational and skill levels. At the same time, firms will compete to locate in areas that are particularly attractive for their purposes.

A Visual Exposition of the Spatial Structure
of the United States Economy

The following illustrations will help us to visualize the U.S. economic structure as described above.[2i, j] Figure 2-1 shows the geographic distribution of the United States population in 1960. The locations of urbanized areas of 50,000 population or larger are specifically shown on the map; the location of a city of (say) 30,000 people would be represented by three small dots. Figure 2-2 shows the commuting fields of cities of different sizes. There are approximately 150

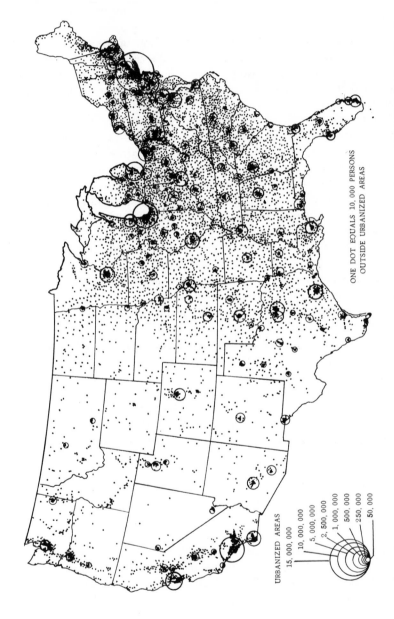

ONE DOT EQUALS 10,000 PERSONS
OUTSIDE URBANIZED AREAS

URBANIZED AREAS

15,000,000
10,000,000
5,000,000
2,500,000
1,000,000
500,000
250,000
50,000

Figure 2-1. Population distribution: 1960. Source: This map approximates the 1960 Population Map in CHARACTERISTICS OF THE POPULATION, Volume 1, United States Department of Commerce, Bureau of the Census, U.S. Government Printing Office, Washington, D.C., 1964, p. S 17.

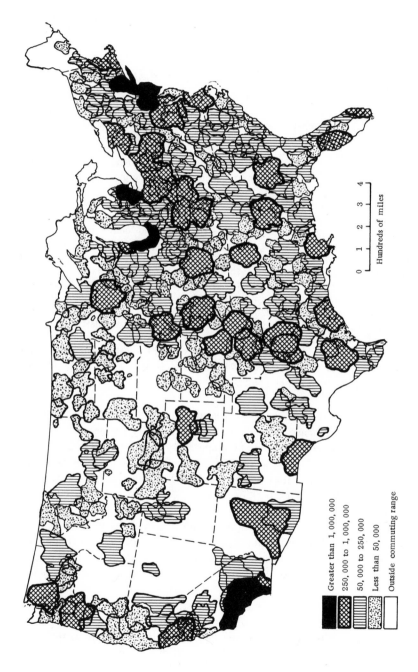

Figure 2-2. Areas within commuting range of cities of various size categories, 1960.

Greater than 1,000,000

250,000 to 1,000,000

50,000 to 250,000

Less than 50,000

Outside commuting range

0   1   2   3   4

Hundreds of miles

commuting fields with central cities (as of 1960) having less than 50,000 people and about 200 with central cities of 50,000 people or more.

Brian J.L. Berry[3] has characterized the spatial organization of the United States in terms of a national system of cities, as follows:

1. We live in a specialized society in which there is progressively greater division of labor and scale of enterprise, accompanied by increasing degrees of specialization.

2. There is an increasing diversity of people as producers. But as consumers they are becoming more and more alike from one part of the country to another, consuming much the same "basket of goods" wherever they may live, as well as increasingly large baskets because of rising real incomes.

3. The physical problem in the economic system is therefore one of articulation—insuring that the specialized products of each segment of the country are shipped to final consumers, seeing that consumers in every part of the country receive the basket of goods and services they demand and are able to purchase, and bringing demands and supplies into equality over a period of time.

4. Articulation requires flows of messages, of goods and services, and of funds. The flows appear to be highly structured and channeled and major metropolitan centers serve as critical articulation points. These flows are as follows: products move from their specialized production areas to shipping points in the locally dominant metropolitan centers; over the nation, products are transferred between metropolitan centers, with each metropolitan center shipping out the specialized products of its hinterland and collecting the entire range of specialized products from other metropolitan centers to satisfy the demands of the consumers residing in the area it dominates; distribution then takes place from the metropolis to its hinterland through wholesale and retail contacts. In the reverse direction move both requests for goods and services and funds to pay for goods and services received, so that the flows are not unidirectional.

The great majority of central cities of functional economic areas are wholesale centers and hence "articulation points" in Berry's sense.

Our Figure 2-2 is adapted from one prepared by Berry in 1967 and published (by the Bureau of the Census) in 1968.[4] Most cities of 50,000 population and over (and a good many cities of less than 50,000) are not only articulation points or wholesale centers for the flow of goods but are also centers of home-to-work commuting fields.

If we approximate the boundaries of commuting fields by means of clusters of whole counties, we obtain a politically-workable set of functional economic areas. Where central cities are close together and their commuting fields overlap, we may also look at groups of two or more overlapping areas as *consolidated urban regions.*

Figure 2-3 shows the central business district of a city of approximately 50,000 people and the location of all food supermarkets in the city as a whole. Residents of particular subareas of the city no doubt do much of their food shopping at the nearer supermarkets. Nearly all city residents depend on the

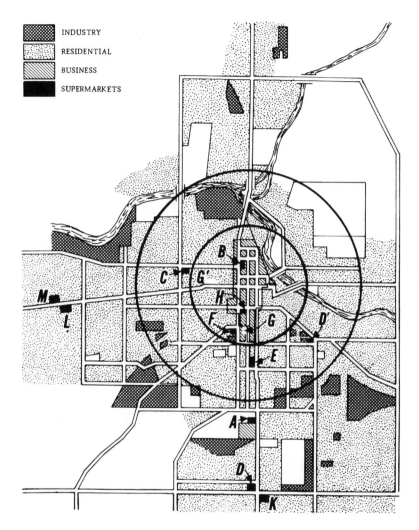

Figure 2-3. Map of Center City. Source: Bob R. Holdren, *The Structure of the Retail Market and the Market Behavior of Retail Units*, Prentice, Hall, Inc., 1960, adapted by permission.

central business district for a department store or stores and some highly specialized goods and services. The location of several of the supermarkets near the edge of the city suggests that their managers are very much aware of residents of the open country and smaller towns at some distance from the central city.

Figure 2-4 illustrates the distribution of town population sizes in a functional economic area having a central city population of 30,000 and a total area

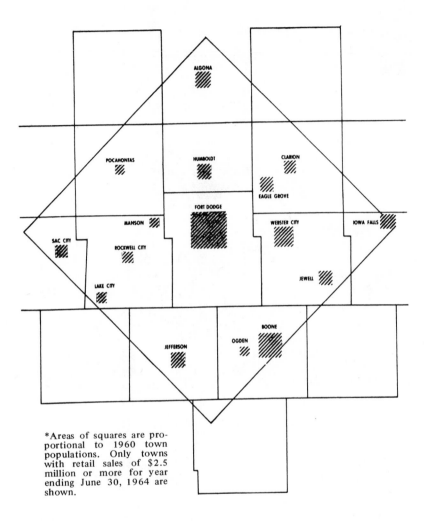

*Areas of squares are proportional to 1960 town populations. Only towns with retail sales of $2.5 million or more for year ending June 30, 1964 are shown.

Figure 2-4. Distribution of town population sizes in the Fort Dodge area, 1960.

population of 150,000. The central business district for the entire area is in Fort Dodge; facilities comparable to those in the Center City supermarket locations are found in a number of small cities scattered through the commuting field; and a few convenience-type establishments are found in each of the 60 or so small towns not shown on this map.

Figure 2-5 is adapted from a study by Borchert and Adams[5] of all towns and cities in an area that includes Minnesota and several states to the west. They

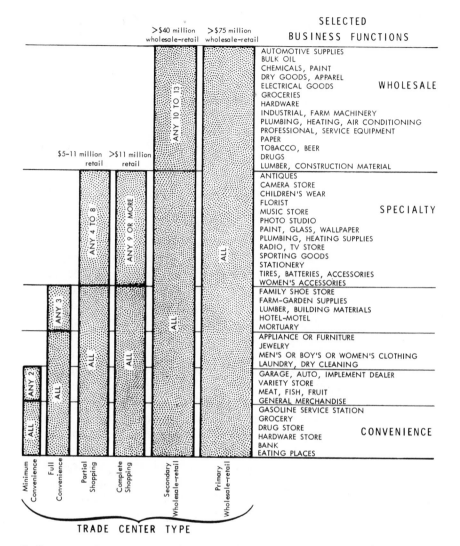

Figure 2-5. Trade center types defined by business functions.

Graphic summary of characteristics of six levels in the trade center hierarchy. Type of center is indicated at base of each bar. Types of business are listed in right-hand column. Businesses which were required and optional in defining each type of trade center are indicated by markings on each bar. Width of bar is proportional to dollar volume as indicated for partial shopping centers and above.

found a definite hierarchical pattern among towns of different sizes and locations, and Figure 2-5 classifies different-sized towns in terms of the arrays of goods and services available in them.

In general, Midwestern cities of 30,000 people or more as of 1960 would qualify as at least "secondary wholesale-retail centers" in Borchert's terminology. Most Midwestern cities of 50,000 or more would have met Borchert's criterion for a "primary wholesale-retail center."

Referring back to Figure 2-4, Fort Dodge is the only city within 100 road miles that qualifies as at least a "secondary wholesale-retail center." The other towns within 50 road miles of Fort Dodge occupy lower levels in the Borchert-Adams hierarchy. Figure 2-6 indicates that Fort Dodge is the center of a commuting field that is approximately coextensive with its wholesale and retail trading area. Figure 2-7 indicates schematically that, in a sense, small towns are small because they are made up of small establishments and large towns are large in order to accommodate larger, more complex establishments.

It is also true in general that the larger establishments require more customers and therefore larger trade areas. Establishments with many employees provide scope for specialization. Typically, they also require several hierarchical levels for their supervision and administration. The larger establishments, and therefore the larger towns, provide more remunerative top jobs that can attract and hold highly-trained and highly capable personnel.

Figure 2-7 also suggests why very small towns cannot hope to compete with larger towns or cities in attracting industry and providing stimulating environments for the managerial and professional personnel associated with large manufacturing plants. Cooperation among all towns on a multi-county basis can take advantage of the leadership capabilities in the central city as well as in other parts of the area; also, a new employer located anywhere in the commuting field increases job opportunities throughout the field as a whole.

Figure 2-8 suggests how functional economic areas in agricultural regions have emerged historically and why many residents of the farms and small towns in these areas do not fully understand the metamorphosis that has taken place.

As of 1915, the Midwest was dotted with relatively self-contained communities centered on towns of a few hundred to two or three thousand people, and with trade and labor market areas extending only five miles or so from the town itself—about the distance a pedestrian or a horse-and-wagon could travel in an hour's time.

During the past half century, the development of good roads and almost universal ownership of passenger automobiles has multiplied the rate of worker and customer travel by a factor of 10 and extended the feasible area of a self-contained labor market and trade area (in short, "community") by a factor of 100. In 1915, a typical Midwestern county contained ten or twelve retail trade areas; as of 1972, one functional economic area (which is both a commuting field and a retail trade area) extends over several counties.

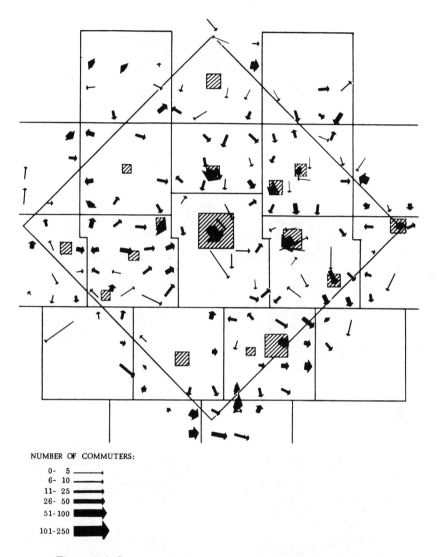

NUMBER OF COMMUTERS:

0- 5	
6- 10	
11- 25	
26- 50	
51-100	
101-250	

Figure 2-6. Commuting pattern in the Fort Dodge area, 1960.

Figure 2-9 shows 50-mile commuting area boundaries around each of Iowa's seven Standard Metropolitan Statistical Areas as of 1960. These are counties that contain central cities of 50,000 population or more. The shape and compass orientation of the commuting fields is based on the fact that Iowa has an almost complete grid of roads running east-west and north-south. Thus, from the center of any area in Figure 2-9 one can reach any of the four corners by traveling 50

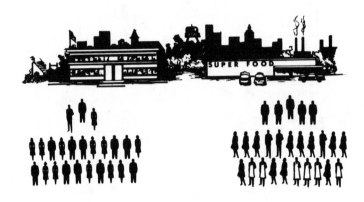

Figure 2-7. Job hierarchies in towns of different sizes.

109

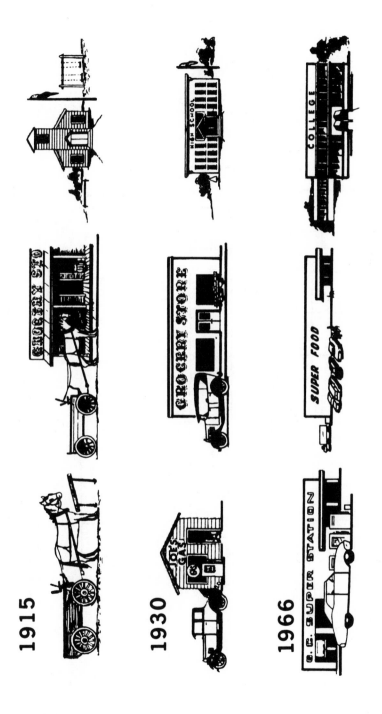

Figure 2-8. The automobile and rural social change, 1915-1966.

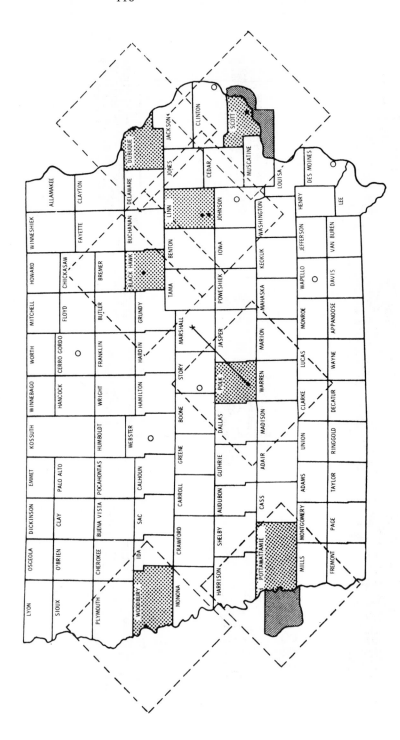

*Central cities of 50,000 people or more in 1960. Each shaded county or pair of shaded contiguous counties are SMSA's.

Figure 2-9. 50-mile commuting distances from the central business districts of Iowa SMSA central cities, 1960.

miles along an actual road. If one wishes to reach a point on (say) the northwestern boundary of such a square, however, one must travel 30 miles west and 20 miles north or 20 miles west and 30 miles north, etc.—a total of 50 miles.

Thus, each square in Figure 2-9 represents the projection of a 60-minute commuting circle upon a rectangular road grid over which we assume travel is possible in every direction at an average speed of 50 miles an hour.

Figure 2-10 shows 50-mile commuting perimeters around the seven SMSA central cities in Iowa. It also shows similar 50-mile perimeters around five other central cities that have populations of 35,000 or less. The squares include 80 percent of Iowa's area and 90 percent of Iowa's population.

These squares are only first approximations to the actual commuting fields. The outlines of actual commuting fields are somewhat irregular as suggested by Figure 2-2. Berry's research indicated that 96 percent of the United States population as of 1960 lived within urban-centered commuting fields.

Other Comments on the Nature of the FEA
in Nonmetropolitan Areas

Figure 2-11 shows percentage changes in the total populations of Iowa counties from 1950 to 1960. Within each of the 50-mile squares we see represented a process that might be called "creeping urbanization." In every case, population in the county containing the central city of the area increased more rapidly, or decreased less rapidly, than in the peripheral counties. Most of the peripheral counties lost population during the 1950s. With the exception of Wapello County, the population of each county containing an FEA central city increased quite significantly.

There is evidence that this centripetal process has been going on since about 1920. Farm population has been declining, but many of the young people who could not find adequate opportunities on farms have moved into the central city of the same functional economic area. Towns that had populations of 3,000 or more in 1920 have in most cases shown substantial growth, while towns and villages that had populations of less than 3,000 as of 1920 have in most cases remained stable or declined.

The durability of houses and the desire of many retired farm couples for low-rent housing have lent a somewhat specious stability to the populations of Iowa villages and small towns. The percentage of people over 65 years of age in such villages has increased rapidly and is higher than in any other size group of populated places. Main street enterprises in most villages of less than 1,000 have suffered severe declines because of competition from supermarkets and other enterprises in larger towns. The total number of job opportunities in villages of less than 1,000 has been supported in part by the increasing volume of purchased farm inputs handled in them, including commercial mixed feeds, oil

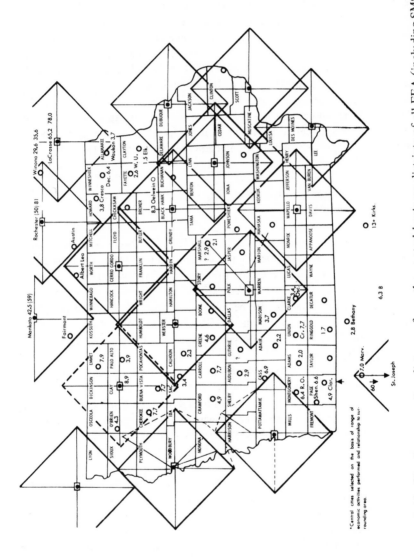

Figure 2-10. 50-mile commuting distances from the central business districts of all FEA (including SMSA) central cities in or near Iowa, 1960.

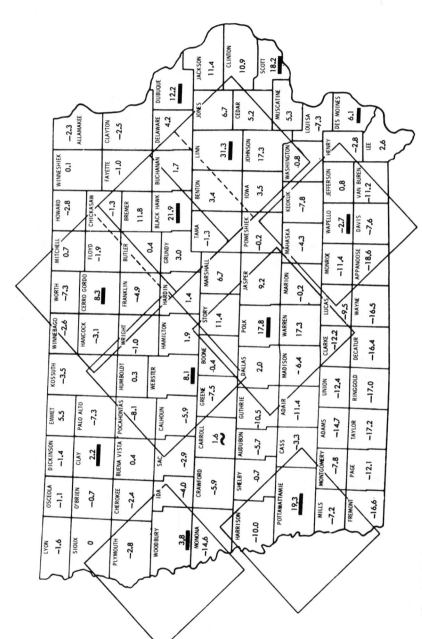

Figure 2-11. Percentage changes in total populations of Iowa counties, 1950-1960.

*Some of the 50-mile commuting perimeters are included to stress the redistribution of population occurring within functional economic areas.

and gasoline, seeds and fertilizers, farm machinery, replacement parts, repair services, and the like.

Figure 2-4 showed the distribution of town population sizes in the Fort Dodge area in 1960. The population of Fort Dodge itself (about 30,000) suggests that it is a city of a different hierarchical order and function than the other towns within 50 highway miles of it. Visits to Fort Dodge and the other towns strongly confirm this impression. Many specialized goods and services found in Fort Dodge are not available at any other town in the 50-mile commuting area.

In contrast, Figure 2-12 shows the distribution of town population sizes in an arbitrarily chosen area of six contiguous counties that includes the east-central portion of the Fort Dodge functional area. The six-county area has no central city of the Fort Dodge class. The configuration of town sizes immediately creates misgivings about the usefulness or viability of this area for purposes of administration or planning.

Figure 2-6 showed the home-to-work commuting pattern in the Fort Dodge area as of 1960. Each arrow represents workers who reside in a particular

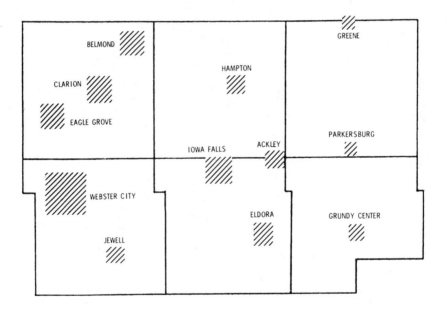

*Areas of squares are proportional to 1960 town populations. Only towns with retail sales of $2.5 million or more for year ending June 30, 1964 are shown.

Figure 2-12. Distribution of town population sizes in six contiguous counties, 1960.

township and who work in some county other than that in which their township is located. Where workers resident in a township work in two or more other counties, the arrow is a vector sum of the two or more real home-to-work commuting movements. The arrows indicate that the vast majority of workers living inside of the 50-mile square also work within its boundaries. At the same time, most workers living just outside the 50-mile boundary also work outside that boundary.

Figure 2-13 shows that the commuting pattern in the six contiguous counties of Figure 2-12 contrasts sharply with that in the functional economic area.

NUMBER OF COMMUTERS:

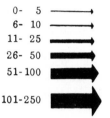

0- 5

6- 10

11- 25

26- 50

51- 100

101- 250

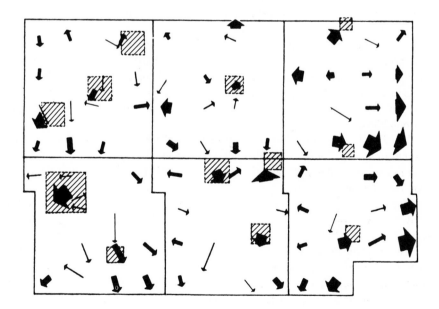

Figure 2-13. Commuting pattern in six contiguous counties, 1960.

Workers in the two eastern counties shown in Figures 2-12 and 2-13 are strongly oriented toward the city of Waterloo, and many workers along the southern borders commute toward other towns (Marshalltown, Nevada, and Ames) that are part of the Des Moines functional economic area. Workers in other portions of the six-county area commute toward Fort Dodge or Mason City. The six-county area, then, appears to be pulled in several different directions. It would be difficult to create a sense of common interest among the residents of such an area.

The Counterpart of the FEA in Metropolitan Areas

The same principles of human ecology and central place hierarchies determine the sizes and internal structures of multi-county functional areas and also of metropolitan subareas. "Central places" are usually taken to be towns and cities, but the same concepts can be applied to the locational patterns of shopping centers within the larger cities.

Berry and Harris[7] stated, as of 1968, "Most students suggest that the urban hierarchy has eight levels in advanced Western economies, roughly: the national [economic] capital; national metropolitan centers; regional metropolitan centers; regional capitals; small cities (e.g., county seats); towns; villages; and hamlets."

In the United States, a particular level in this hierarchy is strategic now for purposes of economic and social policy, namely the regional capital. The hamlets and villages are relics of the previously existing horse-and-buggy society; they have lost the bulk of their earlier consumer-oriented activities. The almost universal ownership of passenger automobiles has shaped the towns, small cities, and regional capitals into a three-level central place hierarchy. The area integrated around the regional capital is the home-to-work commuting field, the size of which is dictated (for the most part) by travel times in passenger automobiles.

In 1915, C.J. Galpin[6] found that the relatively self-contained "fundamental agricultural community" of his day was centered on a village; its modern counterpart is centered on a regional capital, three steps farther up in the Berry and Harris urban hierarchy.

The regional capitals about which functional economic areas are centered play strategic roles in the national system of cities. They are the basic points of articulation that link all such areas into a truly national economic system.

The distribution of shopping centers in metropolitan areas forms a three-stage hierarchy consisting of *regional, district,* and *neighborhood* centers. Let us call these R, D, and N-level centers, respectively. The shopping facilities of the regional centers are in most respects as complete as those of the central business district.

In non-metropolitan functional areas, the same three-stage hierarchy is found in the shopping facilities of the regional capital, the small cities, and the towns, respectively. In terms of *minutes*, including delays at traffic lights, parking lots, and the like, the effective "distances" between shopping centers of any given level in the metropolis are not much less than those between shopping centers of the same hierarchical level in non-metropolitan areas.

In non-metropolitan functional areas, the R-level trade area tends to coincide with the commuting field, forming what I have called a mononuclear FEA. A large metropolis is equivalent to the close-packing of several or many mononuclear FEAs; the residentiary activities of these FEAs are largely contained within the trade areas of R-level shopping centers, but the locations of export base employment for the residents of any given R-level trade area are scrambled and distorted by freeways and rapid transit systems.[2f, i, j]

The United States as a Comprehensive Set of Functional Economic Areas[a]

According to the 1960 Census, there were slightly over 60 million persons living in Standard Metropolitan Statistical Areas (SMSAs) with populations of one million or more. As of 1970, it seems probable that as many as 150 subareas, potential viable communities, could be delineated wholly or partly within the 24 largest metropolitan complexes.

Some multi-county commuting fields with central cities of 250,000 to 1,000,000 population might also prove to consist of two or more potentially viable communities rather than one. In addition, there are something like 250 functional economic areas with central cities of less than 250,000 population; in most cases, each such area constitutes a single economic community.

Including metropolitan and nonmetropolitan areas alike, there may be as many as 500 functional economic areas and/or viable communities in the United States. Nearly all the jobs in the United States are located within these 500 areas.

[a]The maps in this section are adapted from B.J.L. Berry, P.G. Goheen, and H. Goldstein, METROPOLITAN AREA DEFINITION: A REEVALUATION OF CONCEPT AND STATISTICAL PRACTICE, U.S. Bureau of the Census Working Paper 28, June 1968. This study was sponsored by the Social Science Research Council Committee on Areas for Social and Economic Statistics (1964-1967) under the Chairmanship of Karl A. Fox. The final report of this committee was summarized in Karl A. Fox, "Functional Economic Areas and Consolidated Urban Regions of the United States," SSRC ITEMS, Vol. 21, No. 4, December 1967, pp. 45-49 (2g). The background papers, maps, and final report which constitute Working Paper 28 were prepared by B.J.L. Berry and his associates at the University of Chicago during 1965-1967 under a contract between the Social Science Research Council and the U.S. Bureau of the Census. Berry and his associates made a comprehensive analysis of the commuting data from the 1960 Census of Population and Housing. Their basic units consisted of 43,000 places of residence (mostly townships) and 4,300 places of work (mostly counties). Their analysis strongly supported the validity and usefulness of the Functional Economic Area concept.

Figure 2-14 portrays the commuting fields of central cities; the boundaries are interpolated on the basis of data for 43,000 SLAs (Standard Location Areas of the township class). Figure 2-15 approximates these commuting fields in terms of clusters of contiguous whole counties.

Berry describes the definitions underlying these two figures:[b]

Considerable experimentation with the journey-to-work data led to the following set of definitions:

1. Commuting Field
   An area encompassing all standard location areas sending commuters to a designated workplace area. The field varies in intensity according to the proportion of resident employees in each SLA commuting to the workplace, and may be depicted cartographically by contours that enclose all areas exceeding a stated degree of commuting. Note: There will be as many commuting fields as there are designated workplace areas.
2. Labor Market
   All counties sending commuters to a given central county.
   a. Central County
      The designated workplace area for definition of a labor market.
   b. Central City
      The principal city located in a central county. Note: SMSA criteria 1 and 2 might be carried through to further specify 2a and 2b.
3. Functional Economic Area (FEA)
   All those counties within a labor market for which the proportion of resident workers commuting to a given central county exceeds the proportion commuting to alternative central counties.
   Note: There will be as many FEAs as there are central counties. The central city may also be located in more than one county so that criteria 2a may refer to two or more counties as the "Central County Unit."

Figure 2-16 shows the set of SMSAs used in the 1960 Census. Figures 2-14 and 2-15 (and Figure 2-2) clearly give a much fuller description of the spatial organization of the United States. Berry commented as follows:

An immediate contrast may be drawn between the map of the country's Standard Metropolitan Statistical Areas, as defined by the Bureau of the Budget, and the map showing areas within the commuting fields of cities in 1960 . . . Whereas two-thirds of the nation's population resided in the 1960 SMSAs, in fact 87 percent lived within the commuting area of one of the 1960 SMSAs' central cities (many within more than one such area). Another 9 percent lived in the commuting fields of somewhat smaller centers that filled the populated gaps between metropolitan labor markets. Only 4 percent of the population lived outside the labor markets noted [in Figures 2-2 and 2-14].

In fact, then, in 1960, the populated parts of the Nation were completely 'metropolitanized'—covered by a network of urban fields, and patterned socially and economically by them.

[b]Ibid., pp. 24-25.

119

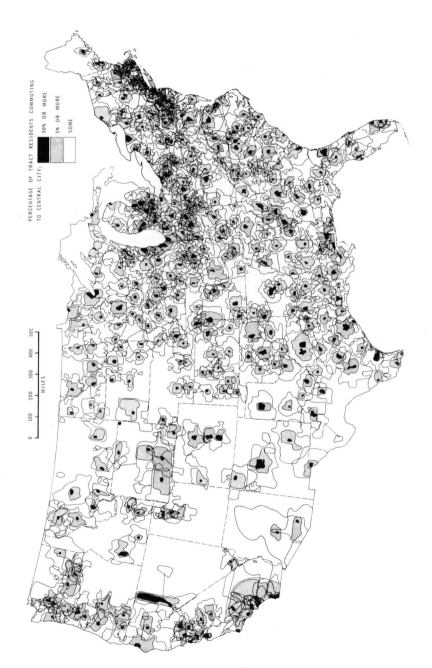

Figure 2-14. Commuting fields of central cities, 1960.

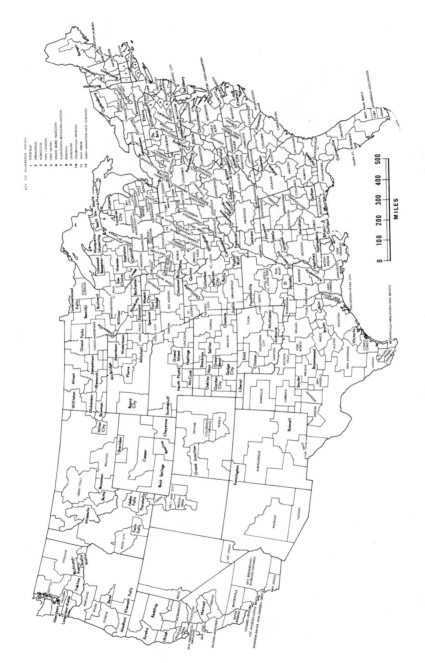

Figure 2-15. Functional Economic Areas of the United States, 1960.

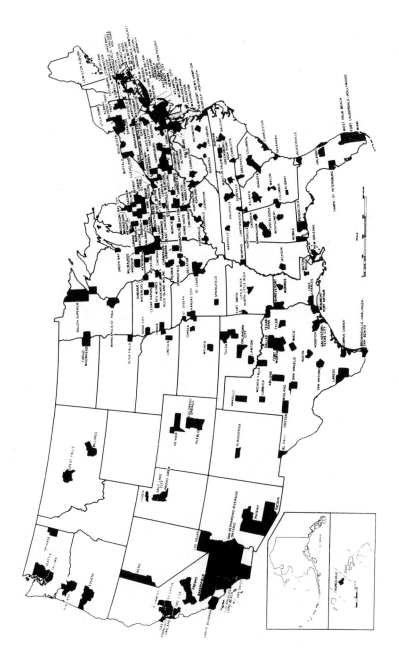

Figure 2-16. Standard Metropolitan Statistical Areas, 1960.

Berry's final recommendations to the Bureau of the Census were as follows:[c]

The proposed definitions will lead to a list of economically and socially integrated units, since they use the daily journey-to-work and identify relatively self-contained labor markets in the short run. One or another size criterion will shorten or lengthen the list of areas. Slight modifications in the process of defining FEAs, for example by 'cascading,' might sharpen allocation of marginal counties. Hierarchical allocation might be a preferable way of creating consolidated regions rather than cross-commuting between central counties. But each of these is a minor consideration compared with the prime issue that should now be apparent.

The regionalization used to create the 1960 SMSAs and the functional regionalization evidenced by commuting behavior are significantly different. A major choice must be made by the U.S. Bureaus of the Budget and Census, for the 1960 classification does *not* produce fully integrated areas with a large population nucleus even though this was the underlying concept. Is the intention to classify areas on the basis of *how they look*? In this case, continuation of present practice will suffice, and attention should be focused on the criteria of metropolitan character (although continuation of the practice of defining urbanized areas may be a more appropriate substitute). Alternatively, should the areas embrace people with *common patterns of behavior*? Then, commuting data dealing with daily links between place of residence and place of work are relevant, and indeed, they serve as proxies for a far wider set of geographic variations and connections.

Comparability is *not* the issue if county building blocks are used. Besides, there has been little consistency in definitional practice since inception of attempts to define metropolitan areas. Nor should consistency be expected in a dynamic socioeconomy in which patterns of organization and behavior are subject to continuing change.

There is a hard problem of choice, since there is a general agreement that some form of area classification will be required for publication of summary statistics for some time to come. As a result of the analysis and evaluation we have undertaken, we recommend the following steps be taken to revise metropolitan area definitional practice beginning in 1970:

1. County building-blocks or equivalent units be retained as the basis of any area classification, in all parts of the country.
2. County-to-county commuting data be the basis of the classification of counties into functional economic areas.
3. Functional Economic Areas be delineated around all central counties satisfying the existing SMSA criteria 1 and 2, and in addition be created for smaller regional centers of populations 25,000 to 50,000 in less densely populated parts of the country.
4. Where significant cross-commuting takes place, functional economic areas be merged by the creation of a consistent set of Consolidated Urban Regions
5. Consideration be given, for neatness of social accounting, to allocating all unallocated counties to one of the FEAs or CURs on the basis of additional criteria of regional interdependence.

---

[c]Ibid., p. 32.

The Hierarchy of Cities and Regions Between Functional
Economic Area and National Levels

We have identified the central city of the FEA as a *regional capital* in the Berry-Harris classification scheme. If we include equivalent metropolitan sub-areas together with mononuclear FEAs, we have approximately 500 areas of the FEA type in the United States.

Central place theory as such favors hierarchies of modulus six on a homogeneous plain *if* residents can travel in any direction without being restricted by roads and fences; it favors hierarchies of modulus four if movement is limited to a rectangular road grid. A number of geological, climatic, and historical factors have, it seems to me, favored east-west and north-south directions for major railroads and highways. These include the north-south orientation of the Mississippi River and the Rocky Mountains; the progressive increase in rainfall from the arid west to the humid east; and the progressive reduction in length of growing season from south to north. The path of settlement also moved from east to west.

In principle, air travel at a uniform speed would encourage a hexagonal pattern of central places at any given hierarchical level, and favor the emergence of one center at level n+1 for every six centers at level n. *De facto*, uniform air speed seems to apply at the upper two levels of the urban hierarchy, and to places that are at least 200 miles apart. Given the fixed cost (in time) of getting from home to airport and airport to business district, surface transportation seems to be preferred for most trips of 150 miles or less and for some longer ones. Nearly all goods move by surface transportation, and the location of some high level coordinating functions may still be influenced by this fact, even though the coordinating personnel may generally travel by air. Other factors, such as population density and the locations of the Great Lakes, also operate to prevent the emergence of any one pattern in all parts of the country.

All things considered, we have reason to expect that factors ranging from four to six connect the numbers of central places at successive hierarchical levels. Thus, if we come down from the national level by one step, we should find from four to six major cities and four to six regions served by them. At the next lower step, we should find from sixteen to 36 cities and the same number of regions served by them. There are reasons (mentioned above) for expecting that the actual number will be closer to sixteen than to 36. At the third stage, we might expect anywhere from 64 to 216 cities and regions. Given the existence of about 500 FEAs and equivalent metropolitan subareas, a number between 100 and 125 seems plausible.

The Pacific and Mountain States have a total area of about 1,200,000 square miles and less than 20 percent of the nation's population. The remaining states have an area of about 1,800,000 square miles and more than 80 percent of the nation's people. Supposing the latter area to contain 100 regions at the hierarchical level just above the FEA, their average area would be about 18,000 square miles. A πr^2 formula would yield an r (radius) of 75.7 miles. The hierarchical level two stages above the FEA should have something like 20 regions in the 1,800,000 square mile area, or an average of 90,000 square miles per region. Here, a πr^2 formula would yield a radius (r) of 169.3 miles. Roughly speaking, this would mean a pattern of central cities on the order of 300 air miles apart—less than one hour by air but at least five hours by car.

The next level above this would involve only a handful of cities (probably New York, Chicago, and Los Angeles plus, perhaps, Dallas-Fort Worth and Atlanta), each serving a large geographic division. At this level, airline distances between cities would be on the order of 700 air miles east of the Rockies and at least 1,500 air miles from Los Angeles to Chicago or Dallas-Fort Worth.

Travel among these five cities for business purposes is normally by air. At the next lower level, business travel among (say) 25 cities averaging 300 or more miles apart would also be by air in most cases. On the other hand, travel among cities averaging only 150 miles apart is normally by surface transportation (typically car).

It appears, then, that the important problems of intermodal planning for passenger transportation will be found *within* regions at the approximately 24 city-and-region level. A first approximation to such a set of regions is shown in Figure 2-17.[d] The underlying map of FEAs is identical to Figure 2-15.

In most of the 24 regions shown in Figure 2-17 there is one city that stands out from the rest. These regions and their central cities seem to be:

Region	Central City
1	Seattle
2	San Francisco
3	Los Angeles
4	Salt Lake City
5	Denver
6	Minneapolis-St. Paul
8	Kansas City
10	Dallas-Fort Worth
11	Houston
12	Chicago
13	St. Louis
14	Memphis
15	New Orleans

---

[d]I drew these boundaries after considerable study of a U.S. map entitled "Population Distribution, Urban and Rural, in the United States, 1960" (Bureau of the Census, United States Maps, GE50, No. 1, issued 1963). I took account of population data for the more populous FEAs together with location, and also of general information and personal observation about most of the cities from which selections might reasonably be made.

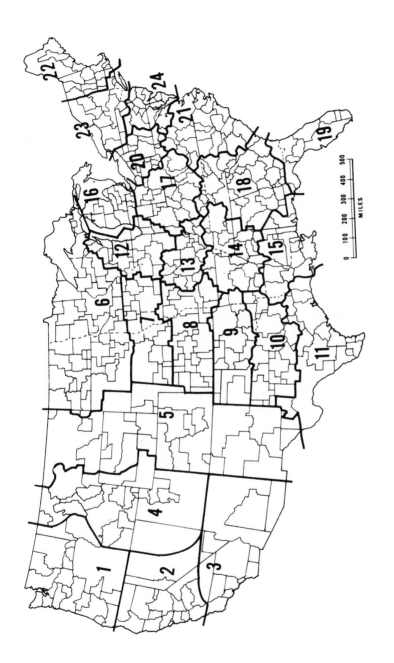

Figure 2-17. National Metropolitan Regions of the United States.

16	Detroit
17	Cincinnati
18	Atlanta
19	Miami
20	Pittsburgh
22	Boston
23	New York

The remaining regions in Figure 2-17 and their two or more principal cities are as follows:

Region	Principal Cities
7	Omaha, Des Moines
9	Oklahoma City, Tulsa
21	Richmond, Norfolk
24	Philadelphia, Baltimore, Washington

The delineations are, at this stage, highly tentative and intuitive. It is possible that regions 7 and 9 are not of "full rank"; if not, their component FEAs should be allocated to other regions. Also, regions 1, 17, 18, 19 and 20 contain other cities that are nearly as large as the ones listed.

We will defer naming these regions and suggesting objective methods for checking and improving their delineation until the next section. It seems unlikely, however, that the number of regions of this hierarchical level will be less than 20 or more than 30.

Figure 2-18 provides an interesting comparison with our tentative list of central cities. Each black area is a Consolidated Urban Region, defined by Berry[4] as follows:

Consolidated Urban Region (CUR): Two or more FEAs for which at least 5 percent of the resident workers of the central county of one commute to the central county of another.

Note: No prior determination of the number of CURs is possible, but application of the criterion to the 1960 data produced 31.

In sixteen of our 24 regions, Berry finds that the central metropolis is a CUR. These regions and their central cities follow:

Region	Central City
1	Seattle
2	San Fransisco
3	Los Angeles
4	Salt Lake City

127

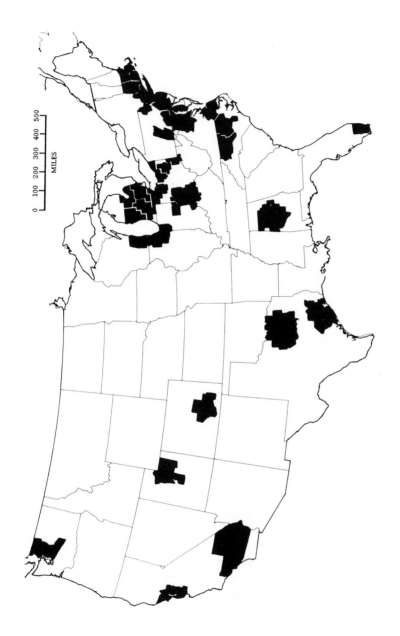

Figure 2-18. Consolidated Urban Regions, 1960.

Region	Central City
5	Denver
10	Dallas-Fort Worth
11	Houston
12	Chicago
16	Detroit
17	Cincinnati
19	Miami
20	Pittsburgh
21	Richmond, Norfolk
22	Boston
23	New York
24	Philadelphia, Baltimore, Washington

The eight exceptions are:

Region	Central City
6	Minneapolis-St. Paul
7	Omaha, Des Moines
8	Kansas City
9	Oklahoma City, Tulsa
13	St. Louis
14	Memphis
15	New Orleans
18	Atlanta

Consolidated Urban Regions are most likely to occur under Berry's definition in areas having both high population density and counties of small geographical area. These conditions are found most frequently from Chicago east to the Atlantic Seaboard. The "eight exceptions" listed above are all located in regions of lower population density and larger counties.

Geographical and historical factors no doubt also play a part. All the exceptions other than New Orleans are inland cities. Several of them are on the Mississippi-Missouri River system at points where these rivers are crossed by major transcontinental railroads. In general, these cities have been free to develop in a roughly circular pattern from the rail and river junction point. No other locations within a hundred miles or so of such cities had similar potentials as rail and river junctions, and the generally low population density of the surrounding agricultural areas also discouraged the emergence of nearby cities that might have become close competitors in terms of population size and central city functions performed.

Comparisons of Our Central City Choices With a
Classification Scheme by Duncan (1960)

After making the tentative regional delineation shown in Figure 2-17, I examined the book by Otis Dudley Duncan and his associates.[8] Duncan reviewed most of the pre-1960 literature on criteria of metropolitanism and classification schemes for cities toward the upper end of the population scale. He also presented, on page 271, his own classification of 56 Standard Metropolitan Areas with 1950 populations of 300,000 or more according to their metropolitan functions and regional relationships. Duncan's classification is reproduced as Table 2-1.

The central cities of seventeen of our regions fall in three of Duncan's categories, namely *national metropolis; regional metropolis;* and *regional capital, submetropolitan.* Four more of our central cities (Boston, Pittsburgh, St. Louis, and Cincinnati) are included in Duncan's category of *diversified manufacturing with metropolitan functions.* The three remaining cases in our 24 regions include Salt Lake City, which Duncan did not classify, as its SMA had a 1950 population of less than 300,000; Miami, which Duncan classifies under *special cases*; and our Region 21, within which Duncan classifies Richmond as a *regional capital, submetropolitan*, and Norfolk-Portsmouth as a *special case.*

On the other hand, none of our central cities is included in Duncan's categories of *specialized manufacturing* or of *diversified manufacturing with few metropolitan functions;* only one, Miami, is included in his category of *special cases.*

It is clear, then, that our array of central cities as of 1972 is drawn almost exclusively from a set in which Duncan had found "metropolitan functions" dominant or prominent as of 1950.

Duncan did not subject the five largest SMAs (Standard Metropolitan Areas) to detailed analysis, but he described the categories of *regional metropolis* and *regional capital, submetropolitan* as follows:

In the two categories now to be described are placed cities which are rather highly specialized for the most part, in industries representing 'metropolitan' functions. Trade functions are moderately to highly developed. Typically, though not without exception, there are profile manufacturing industries depending for important inputs on resource-extracting activities in the hinterland or a broader or still contiguous 'region.' Trade areas of moderate to large size can be more or less realistically identified, and there is clear evidence of the role of the center in integrating activities of such areas.

The distinction between the 'regional metropolis' and the 'regional capital' (with 'submetropolitan' characteristics)—as the two categories are named—turns in good measure on size. Denver, the smallest of the eight 'regional metropolises,' has a population of 564,000 while only three of the thirteen 'regional

Table 2-1

Classification of Standard Metropolitan Areas of 300,000 or More Inhabitants According to Metropolitan Functions and Regional Relationships

National Metropolis (N)

New York
Chicago
Los Angeles (Nd)
Philadelphia (Nd)
Detroit (Nm)

Diversified Manufacturing
with Metropolitan Functions (D)

Boston (Dn)
Pittsburgh (Dn)
St. Louis
Cleveland
Buffalo
Cincinnati

Diversified Manufacturing with
few Metropolitan Functions (D-)

Baltimore
Milwaukee
Albany-Schenectady-Troy
Toledo
Hartford
Syracuse

Specialized Manufacturing (M)

Providence
Youngstown
Rochester
Dayton
Allentown-Bethlehem-Easton
Akron
Springfield-Holyoke
Wheeling-Steubenville
Charleston, W. Va.

Regional Metropolis (R)

San Fransisco (Rn)
Minneapolis-St. Paul
Kansas City
Seattle
Portland
Atlanta
Dallas
Denver

Regional Capital,
Submetropolitan (C)

Houston
New Orleans
Louisville (Cd)
Birmingham (Cm)
Indianapolis (Cd)
Columbus (Cd)
Memphis
Omaha
Fort Worth
Richmond (Cd)
Oklahoma City
Nashville
Jacksonville

Special Cases (S)

Washington
San Diego
San Antonio
Miami
Norfolk-Portsmouth
Wilkes-Barre-Hazelton
Tampa-St. Petersburg
Knoxville
Phoenix

Source: Duncan, et al.[8], p. 271.

capitals' are this large. All the 'regional metropolises' have per capita wholesale sales in excess of $2,100 while six of the 'regional capitals' fall below this figure [see Figure 2-15]. However, the two groups are not perfectly distinguished on this criterion, for Omaha and Memphis have the highest per capita wholesale volume among the 56 SMAs. Their extreme development in this direction is partially discounted as a criterion of metropolitanism, since they are somewhat smaller than the 'regional capitals' with most nearly comparable per capita wholesale activity.

In brief, "metropolitan functions" in Duncan's terminology seem to be central place functions. As my own regions are based strictly on central place (plus population size) considerations, the close correspondence of my list of central cities with Duncan's list of SMAs having metropolitan functions is encouraging.

Duncan also summarized some findings of other investigators that are significant for our purposes.

The role of air transportation. On page 259 Duncan states:

Our data indicate a specialization in air transportation for some seventeen SMAs. By far the highest degree of specialization is manifested by Miami; this may be related in part to its functions as a tourist center with a sub-national if not national service area, as well as its advantageous location with respect to the Latin American traffic. Review of the remaining instances of industry profiles including air transportation points to no particular linkages worthy of note. It may simply be observed that such specialization is not characteristic of highly developed manufacturing centers. The inference drawn by Taaffe (1952, pp. 157-58)[9] is hardly contradicted by our data:

In general, air transportation seems to have followed rather than to have reshaped regional ties. This is indicated in the airlines' business traffic by the prominence of the wholesale cities and larger diversified cities in air traffic generation . . . It is possible that the concentration of air traffic on large centers may tend to increase the primacy of those cities. It is also possible, however, that air transportation has, to date, largely represented those activities which were already concentrated on large centers.

It hardly needs to be pointed out that air transportation assumes its greatest importance not in relating a center to its proximate, contiguous hinterland, but in facilitating relationships among widely separated centers. Appearance of specialization in air transportation, therefore, may be accepted as *prima facie* evidence of significant 'national' or at least 'inter-regional' functions.

Florence (1955)[10] on "metropolitan functions."

On pages 86-87, Duncan summarizes Florence's views concerning the "characteristic and distinctive functions" of the metropolis as follows:

. . . Analyzing employment data by means of location quotients, Florence (1955, p. 110ff.)[10] concludes that the following are among the more significant metropolitan functions: 'acting as headquarters of finance and of certain business services like accounting and technical advice'; communication, 'represented by the publishing of newspapers and of periodicals and books and by various publishing and printing services'; and 'leading scientific progress'—all of which functions 'suggest that the metropolis is a clearing house as well as a reserve or pool of distributable resources and a brain and nerve center for economic action.' But the metropolis also excels in economic activities catering to cultured and luxury tastes; it is a center of entertainment and specialized recreational services; and it provides a wide range of specialized professional services: 'The variety of activities of a metropolis . . . includes highly specialized activities which only it performs on any substantial scale.' In summary of his conclusions, Florence (1955, p. 116) presents the following scheme of 'the hierarchy of city functions':

Metropolitan Area (over 1,000,000 population)

Finance and business services
Book and periodical publishing and printing services
Science
Arts
Applied arts
Entertainment

Large City (200,000 to 1,000,000 population)

Wholesaling
Public services
Newspaper publishing

Middling City (25,000 to 200,000 population)

Public utilities
Commercial printing
Baking and bottling of beverages
Professional services (school teachers, general practitioners, and so on)
Eating and drinking locals
Retailing

In this scheme it is considered that the metropolitan area performs not only its own functions, but also those attributed to the large city and the middling city; whereas the large city performs functions of the middling city as well as those distinguishing it from the latter. No firm basis is given for the classifications in this scheme; but it does illustrate the possibility of treating metropolitan status as a particular level of functional specialization in an urban hierarchy.

*Forces Tending to Strengthen the Central Place
System Since 1945*

In reviewing classifications based on 1950 population data or on other data from the 1940s and early 1950s, it is important to recognize that a city's rank in the urban hierarchy need not remain fixed for all time. For example, the population of California in 1970 is three times as large as it was in 1940 and twice as large as in 1950. Several metropolitan centers have shown remarkable growth since 1940 or 1950. The total population of the United States has increased as follows:

1940	132,122,000
1945	139,928,000
1950	151,684,000
1970	204,800,000

Wartime restrictions on civilian transportation and construction were lifted in 1945-46. Total population has since increased by about 65,000,000, and includes about 95,000,000 children and young adults who were born after 1945. Since 1945 the automobile, the truck, and the airplane have had a full generation to exert forces that tend to strengthen the central place system. The automobile has strengthened the FEA pattern, the regional shopping plaza, and the metropolitan subarea; the truck has strengthened central place patterns in wholesale distribution at the two hierarchical levels next above the FEA; and the airplane has strengthened central place patterns at the level of approximately 24 large regions, the central cities of which constitute the top three levels of the urban hierarchy.

Meanwhile, rapid transit systems and passenger travel on railroads have lost ground; railroads have lost much of their middle-distance freight business to trucking firms. The railroads are still important for long distance hauling within the extractive and processing industries complex.

**The National Metropolitan Region as the Basic Unit
for "Regional" Transportation Planning**

After studying the spatial distribution and socioeconomic attributes of cities above the regional capital level, we have concluded that the United States can be delimited into approximately 24 National Metropolitan Regions. Our first, tentative delineation is shown in Figure 2-17. Each NMR is organized around a central city (or cities) that performs a certain array of central place functions for the NMR as a whole. Each NMR should, for transportation planning purposes, consist of a set of contiguous whole FEAs.

The central city of an NMR is two stages above the regional capital of an FEA (or the regional shopping plaza of a metropolitan subarea) in the urban hierarchy. Examples of NMR central cities are Minneapolis-St. Paul, Chicago, Kansas City, St. Louis, Dallas-Ft. Worth, and Atlanta (among others). In most cases, the central FEA of an NMR as of 1972 will contain from one to three million or more people.

Large population alone is not sufficient to qualify a metropolis as an NMR central city. To some extent, the NMR central cities must be regarded as a mutually related set; they cannot perform their central place functions efficiently if they are too close together. East of the Rocky Mountains, the NMR central cities tend to be 300 or more air miles apart; the distances are, of course, considerably greater than this in the arid West. A typical NMR in the humid area extends over about 100,000 square miles and includes a population of five to fifteen million or more people.

Perhaps five of the NMR central cities also perform functions a stage higher in the urban hierarchy; likely candidates include New York, Chicago, Los Angeles, Dallas-Ft. Worth, and Atlanta. New York City stands above the rest as the national (economic) capital and a "world city."

Passenger travel (i.e., business travel) among these 24 cities is mainly by air. At this level, passenger transportation planning seems to be primarily a matter of system design and balance within the air transportation mode.

There is a level of central places intermediate between the regional capitals of FEAs and the central cities of NMRs. In general, the FEAs containing such cities will have populations of 500,000 to 1,000,000 or somewhat larger. The regions corresponding to this level in the urban hierarchy are probably about five times as numerous as the NMRs, and east of the Rockies they would have average areas of about 20,000 square miles. The radius of such an area would be on the order of 100 highway miles, and the prevailing modes of transportation within the region would be passenger automobile and truck.

In contrast, a typical NMR would have a radius of 200 or more road miles. It appears that important problems of intermodal passenger transportation planning arise, and can be dealt with, within each NMR. There should be opportunities for combining automobiles, buses, light planes, and rails in more effective ways.

Socioeconomic Characteristics of the NMR Central Cities

All or nearly all of the 24 NMR central cities are "metropolitan areas" in Florence's sense, and perform the metropolitan functions that he lists—though with some differences in extent, emphasis, and quality. Most of the 24 cities do not exceed the NMR level in any major activity; half a dozen presumably have an additional level of functions; and New York City has traditionally been pre-eminent in finance, business coordination, publishing, advertising, and the arts.

Before actually delimiting NMRs for planning purposes, it would be wise to establish in greater depth and detail the distinctive economic, social, and cultural activities that distinguish this level in the urban hierarchy. In this process, we might decide that certain of the NMRs in our tentative list of 24 are not, as of 1972, of "full rank." If so, they should presumably be divided up (for transportation planning purposes) among the adjacent NMRs of full rank.

It might also turn out that certain of our regions that include two or more cities of more than 1,000,000 population should be subdivided for at least some transportation planning purposes. For example, population density might affect optimal transportation system design in addition to the level a region occupied in the national hierarchy.

A particularly interesting approach to identifying the characteristic activities of NMR central cities might be based on an analysis of the distribution of the approximately 64,000 names in *Who's Who in America*[11] by (1) FEA or SMSA of residence and (2) major career line. This list of names would include about 3 persons per 10,000 population. To the extent that they were selected because of career achievement and formal roles in large organizations, they must have been drawn from the highest levels of those organizations. Those named because of achievements in science, the arts, literature, entertainment and the professions have presumably achieved a level of visibility and social influence roughly equivalent to those of persons selected from business and other formal organizations.

In brief, a *Who's Who* tabulation might yield (1) "cultural profiles" or "cultural location quotients" for each FEA or SMSA considered to be of the NMR central city rank or higher and (2) absolute numbers of selectees in each occupation or category included in the profiles or quotients. Hypotheses concerning the existence (1) of distinct (cultural) hierarchical levels within the 24 NMR central cities and (2) of differences in cultural profiles between NMR central cities and other cities of the same population could be explored with such data.

Roughly equivalent profiles could no doubt be built up from other sources. Information would be required regarding the presence, quality, and amount of various cultural resources (museums, art galleries, theaters, symphony orchestras, zoos, and so on), not to mention professional athletic teams. This information would supplement the more conventional census data on occupations and industries that might or might not be sensitive enough to reflect significant differences in levels of cultural activities.

The point of the preceding paragraphs is that regional capitals and NMR central cities are centers of general social systems and not simply of economic systems. Travel patterns reflect social and cultural as well as economic objectives. In other papers, published and unpublished, I have suggested an approach to combining all outputs of a social system into a measure called the *gross social product* (GSP), which contains the gross economic product (GNP) and is expressed, for convenience, in dollar terms.[12, 13, 14] The object of passenger transportation planning within an FEA, an NMR, or the nation should be to maximize gross social product and not simply GNP.

Practical Methods for Delineating NMRs

Brian Berry[4] has recommended that a county be assigned to that FEA to the central county of which it directs the largest number of commuters. This is a simple, quantitative, reproducible criterion.

To the extent that nationwide data were available, it would seem desirable to allocate each FEA to that NMR to the central FEA of which it directs its largest number of passenger trips per year. Other measures might prove to be closely correlated with this one, for example, the volume of telephone calls during business hours between the regional capital of the FEA and the central cities of alternative NMRs. In some cases, the regional capital of an FEA might be linked by a preponderance of passenger trips and telephone calls to an FEA of 500,000 to 1,000,000 population, which in turn was strongly linked by travel and phone calls to the NMR central city. In such a case, the FEA would be allocated to the appropriate NMR on the basis of this two-stage linkage.

The criteria just mentioned, possibly including some supplementary rules for allocating areas of low population density (national forests, deserts, mountainous areas, and the like) should lead to reproducible delimitations of (1) an exhaustive set of FEAs, and (2) an exhaustive set of NMRs. Each FEA would consist of a set of contiguous whole counties, and each NMR would consist of a set of contiguous FEAs.

If such areas were used for planning and implementing public policies, some room for judgment should be provided at each of these two levels of delimitation. For example, the governor of Minnesota assigned some counties (for substate administrative purposes) to the specific central cities that were closest to them; other counties, located midway between two central cities, were given some time to decide with which administrative area to affiliate.

Probably the governor of each state should have some discretion in allocating the marginal counties among FEAs. Similarly, a national or multi-state authority should have some discretion in allocating marginal FEAs among NMRs.

These delineations, at both FEA and NMR levels, should be open to review from time to time. In general, the marginal counties and NMRs will have less population density and smaller central cities than the regional capital of the FEA or the central FEA of the NMR. Thus, the shifting of a marginal county or a marginal FEA should not change the basic nature of the transportation planning problem for the larger area of which it was a part.

Transportation Planning at Successive Levels:
Summary

Within each FEA, "local" transportation planning should lead to improved linkages among homes, workplaces, and the shopping and service facilities of towns, small cities, and the FEA central city (regional capital).

Within an NMR, "regional" transportation planning should emphasize improved linkages among the FEA central cities (regional capitals), the regional metropolises, and the central metropolis of the NMR.

Within the United States as a whole, "national" transportation planning should emphasize improved linkages among the central metropolises of the NMRs. There is also the problem of world transportation planning, which involves some NMR cities more than others.

The various levels of transportation planning are not wholly independent, and efficient interfacing of modes used at FEA, NMR, and national levels is important.

State governments are the key units for implementing transportation plans at both FEA and NMR levels. Plans for an FEA will rarely involve more than two states, and plans for an NMR will rarely involve more than three or four states. Strong departments of transportation in each state would facilitate planning and implementation at both FEA and NMR levels.

Notes

1. Papers based partly on March 1961 formulation of the functional economic area concept:
   a. Fox, K.A., THE CONCEPT OF COMMUNITY DEVELOPMENT, Iowa State University, March 1961, 42 pp. (mimeo.). Also in CAED Report 19, FUNDAMENTALS FOR AREA PROGRESS, Center for Agricultural and Economic Development, Iowa State University, 1963, pp. 13-39 (multilithed).
   b. _____, "The Study of Interactions Between Agriculture and the Non-Farm Economy—Local, Regional, and National," JOURNAL OF FARM ECONOMICS, Vol. 44, No. 1, February 1962, pp. 1-34.
   c. _____, "Delineating the Area," Proceedings of the CONFERENCE ON AREA DEVELOPMENT (multilithed), Institute of Community and Area Development, University of Georgia, January 1962, pp. 129-153. (Jointly sponsored by the Agricultural Policy Institute of North Carolina State University.)
   d. _____, "The Major Problem of Rural Society," CAEA Report 16, OUR RURAL PROBLEMS IN THEIR NATIONAL SETTING (multilithed), Proceedings of the Third Annual Farm Policy Review Conference, Center for Agricultural and Economic Development, Iowa State University, December 1962, pp. 9-26.
   e. _____, "On the Current Lack of Policy Orientation in Regional Accounting," comments stimulated by the Second Conference on Regional Accounts, Miami Beach, November 1962 (12 pp., mimeo.). Abridged version printed in W.Z. Hirsch (ed.), ELEMENTS OF REGIONAL ACCOUNTS, Johns Hopkins Press, Baltimore, 1964, pp. 80-85.
   f. _____, "Economic Models for Area Development Research," published in REGIONAL DEVELOPMENT ANALYSIS, Proceedings of the Workshop on Area Development sponsored by the Agricultural Policy Insti-

tute, North Carolina State University and the Great Plains Resource Economics Committee, May 1963, pp. 147-194. Reprinted, slightly abridged, in L.T. Wallace, D. Hobbs, and R.D. Vlasin (eds.), SELECTED PERSPECTIVES FOR COMMUNITY RESOURCE DEVELOPMENT, Agricultural Policy Institute, North Carolina State University, 1969, pp. 67-96.

g. Fox, K.A., INTEGRATING NATIONAL AND REGIONAL MODELS FOR ECONOMIC STABILIZATION AND GROWTH, paper presented at Conference on National Economic Planning, University of Pittsburgh, March 25-26, 1964, 27 pp. (mimeo.). Portions published in Section 12.1, K.A. Fox, J.K. Sengupta, and E. Thorbecke, THE THEORY OF QUANTITATIVE ECONOMIC POLICY, North-Holland Publishing Company: Amsterdam, and Rand McNally: Chicago, 1966.

2. Papers based partly on October 1964 formulation of the functional economic area concept:

a. Fox, K.A., and T. Krishna Kumar, "Delineating Functional Economic Areas," Chap. 1 in W.R. Maki and B.J.L. Berry (eds.), RESEARCH AND EDUCATION FOR REGIONAL AND AREA DEVELOPMENT, Iowa State University Press, Ames, 1966, pp. 13-55.

b. _____ , "The Functional Economic Area: Delineation and Implications for Economic Analysis and Policy," REGIONAL SCIENCE ASSOCIATION PAPERS, Vol. 15, 1965, pp. 57-85.

c. Fox, K.A., "Spatial Equilibrium and Central Place Hierarchies in Agricultural Regions Undergoing Rapid Changes in the Mode of Transport," 17 pp. (mimeo), 1965. Abstract in ECONOMETRICA, Vol. 34, No. 5, pp. 28-30, Supplementary Issue, 1966. (Abstract of paper presented at First World Congress of the Econometric Society, Rome, September 1965).

d. _____ , "The New Synthesis of Rural and Urban Society in the United States," in U. Papi and C. Nunn (eds.), ECONOMIC PROBLEMS OF AGRICULTURE IN INDUSTRIAL SOCIETIES, Proceedings of a Conference held by the International Economic Association, September 1965, Macmillan, London, and St. Martin's Press, New York, 1969, pp. 606-628.

e. _____ , "Supplement A: Regional Development in a National Setting," THE ROLE OF GROWTH CENTERS IN REGIONAL ECONOMIC DEVELOPMENT (with W.R. Maki, E. Eldridge, M. Julius, and others), in report prepared by the Department of Economics, Iowa State University for the U.S. Department of Commerce, Office of Regional Economic Development, September 1966, 4 volumes (multilithed).

f. _____ , "Strategies for Area Delimitation in a National System of Regional Accounts," paper prepared at the request of C.L. Leven, Director, Institute for Urban and Regional Studies, Washington University, St. Louis, Missouri, November 1967. Most of this material appears in pp. 105-125 and 138-147 of C.L. Leven, J.B. Legler, and P. Shapiro, AN ANALYTICAL FRAMEWORK FOR REGIONAL DEVELOPMENT POLICY, MIT Press, Cambridge, 1970.

g. _____, "Functional Economic Areas and Consolidated Urban Regions of the United States," SOCIAL SCIENCE RESEARCH COUNCIL ITEMS, Vol. 21, No. 4, December 1967, pp. 45-49. (Based on the final report of the SSRC Committee on Areas for Social and Economic Statistics and on research conducted by B.J.L. Berry on behalf of the committee under SSRC and U.S. Census Bureau sponsorship.)

h. _____, "Monopolistic Competition in the Food and Agricultural Sectors," Chap. 16, in R.E. Kuenne (ed.), MONOPOLISTIC COMPETITION THEORY: STUDIES IN IMPACT, Essays in Honor of E.H. Chamberlin, John Wiley and Sons, Inc., New York, 1967, pp. 329-356.

i. _____, A PROGRAM TO PROMOTE MAXIMUM EMPLOYMENT, HUMAN DIGNITY, AND CIVIC RESPONSIBILITY IN THE UNITED STATES, Department of Economics, Iowa State University, April 29, 1968.

j. _____, FUNCTIONAL ECONOMIC AREAS: A STRATEGIC CONCEPT FOR PROMOTING CIVIC RESPONSIBILITY, HUMAN DIGNITY, AND MAXIMUM EMPLOYMENT IN THE UNITED STATES, Department of Economics, Iowa State University, January 10, 1969.

k. _____, "A New Strategy for Urban and Rural America," APPALACHIA, Vol. 2, No. 10, August 1969, pp. 10-13.

l. _____, "Agricultural Policy in an Urban Society," AMERICAN JOURNAL OF AGRICULTURAL ECONOMICS, Vol. 50, No. 5, December 1968, pp. 1135-1148, 1968.

m. _____, "Decentralization or Regionalization of National Economic Policies," Section 8.2.3 in J.K. Sengupta and K.A. Fox, ECONOMIC ANALYSIS AND OPERATIONS RESEARCH: OPTIMIZATION TECHNIQUES IN QUANTITATIVE ECONOMIC MODELS, North-Holland Publishing Company, Amsterdam, 1969, pp. 441-449.

n. _____, "Metamorphosis in America: A New Synthesis of Rural and Urban Society," Chap. 3, W.J. Gore and L.C. Hodapp (eds.), CHANGE IN THE SMALL COMMUNITY: AN INTERDISCIPLINARY SURVEY, Friendship Press, New York, 1967, pp. 62-104.

o. _____, POPULATION REDISTRIBUTION AMONG FUNCTIONAL ECONOMIC AREAS: A NEW STRATEGY FOR URBAN AND RURAL AMERICA, Paper presented at the 137th Meeting of the American Association for the Advancement of Science, Chicago, December 30, 1970. Department of Economics, Iowa State University.

3. Berry, B.J.L., "Approaches to Regional Analysis: A Synthesis," ANNALS, ASSOCIATION OF AMERICAN GEOGRAPHERS, Vol. 54, No. 1, March 1964, pp. 2-11.

4. Berry, B.J.L., P.G. Goheen and H. Goldstein, METROPOLITAN AREA DEFINITION: A REEVALUATION OF CONCEPT AND STATISTICAL PRACTICE, U.S. Bureau of the Census Working Paper 28, June 1968. (Reissued, slightly revised, July 1969.) Contains an extensive bibliography on the definition and delineation of metropolitan areas.

5. Borchert, J.R., and R.B. Adams, TRADE CENTERS AND TRADE AREAS OF THE UPPER MIDWEST, Minneapolis: Upper Midwest Economic Study, Urban Report No. 3, September 1963.

6. Galpin, C.J., THE SOCIAL ANATOMY OF AN AGRICULTURAL COMMUNITY, Agricultural Experiment Station of the University of Wisconsin, Madison, Research Bulletin No. 34, May 1915.

7. Berry, B.J.L. and C.D. Harris, "Central Place," INTERNATIONAL ENCYCLOPEDIA OF THE SOCIAL SCIENCES, Vol. 2, pp. 365-370, Macmillan and Free Press, 1968.

8. Duncan, O.D., et al., METROPOLIS AND REGION, Johns Hopkins Press, Baltimore, 1960.

9. Taaffe, E.J., THE AIR PASSENGER HINTERLAND OF CHICAGO, Research Paper No. 24, Department of Geography, University of Chicago, 1952.

10. Florence, P.S., "Economic Efficiency in the Metropolis," in R.M. Fisher (ed.), THE METROPOLIS IN MODERN LIFE, Doubleday and Company, Garden City, New York, 1955.

11. WHO'S WHO IN AMERICA, Vol. 36, 1970-71, Marquis Who's Who, Inc., Chicago, 1970.

12. Fox, K.A., "Operations Research and Complex Social Systems," Chap. 9 in J.K. Sengupta and K.A. Fox, ECONOMIC ANALYSIS AND OPERATIONS RESEARCH: OPTIMIZATION TECHNIQUES IN QUANTITATIVE ECONOMIC MODELS, North-Holland Publishing Company, Amsterdam, 1969, pp. 452-467.

13. _____ , "Toward a Policy Model of World Economic Development with Special Attention to the Agricultural Sector," pp. 95-126 in E. Thorbecke (ed.), THE ROLE OF AGRICULTURE IN ECONOMIC DEVELOPMENT, Columbia University Press, New York, 1969.

14. _____ , "Combining Economic and Noneconomic Objectives in Development Planning: Problems of Concept and Measurement," in ESSAYS IN HONOR OF JAN TINBERGEN, edited by Willy Sellekaerts. London: Macmillan International, 1972.

3

The Territorial Basis of National Transportation Planning

John Friedmann and Barbara Stuckey,
University of California, Los Angeles

Introduction

After a generation of growing centralization of governmental powers, a process which started in the early days of the New Deal, it is becoming apparent that the system of centralized planning and administration we have evolved is neither as efficient nor as responsive to public needs as we once believed. With an annual budget of more than $200 billion, the Federal Government's present scale of operations is, indeed, unprecedented. Management of a budget this size requires an information-processing capacity of staggering dimensions. Despite heroic efforts to solve this problem, the Federal Government is in some cases acting rapidly but in relative ignorance of the essential facts, and in others with better information but with exasperating slowness.

Partly to overcome this dilemma, federal policies are often formulated and programs conceived and carried out without adequate recognition of the enormous variety of conditions that exist. In a nation of 200 million citizens even small percentages imply impressive absolute numbers. Thus, a policy designed to meet the requirements of a situation in one part of the country may have neutral or even negative effects for substantial numbers of people elsewhere.

These failures, or partial failures, in policy design and program execution have produced a widespread popular demand for bringing governmental operations "closer" to the people. In various ways, and particularly in central cities, people are demanding to be included as active participants in deciding questions concerning their environment. In this way, they hope to bend governmental programs to their specific and local needs as they perceive them.[1]

Finally, the fiscal crisis in state and local governments alike is putting pressures on Washington to share a part of the general revenue and to evolve what has come to be known as a system of "creative federalism." This new relationship between the federal, state, and local governments is beginning to overcome the old antagonism between the states and the central government "whereby the transfer of authority and resources from one legal body to another was deemed to decrease correspondingly the authority and resources of fellow participants . . ."[2] "Creative federalism," says Robert Wood, "grows on the native strength of local institutions."[3]

141

Given this rising awareness of the need to restructure the governmental process, it is easy to understand why a major governmental sector such as the Department of Transportation should look to the regionalization of some of its operations, particularly of its planning, research, and development activities. Assuming that regionalization in this sense is desirable, what regions would best serve the purposes of the Department? This, essentially, was the question assigned to us by the sponsors of this study. But, simple and straightforward as it sounds, the question actually conjures up two contradictory images of regional delimitation. According to the first, one would search for some uniform set of criteria in order to divide the nation into a set of regions exhaustive of the national territory. Each section of the country would be included in one but not more than one region. Appropriate transport planning would subsequently be suited to the contours of these regions. According to the second image, however, the search would be for a complex pattern of regions corresponding to different purposes and needs. This pattern would not have to cover all the territory of the nation, nor would it have to be thought of as being one-dimensional. Rather, it could be imagined as a pattern of overlapping and superimposed regions of different size and composition.

The second image, however, corresponds more precisely to a question other than the one originally posed: How might the planning and related activities of the Department of Transportation be organized in space so as to meet the needs for transport in different parts of the country more effectively?

An answer must be approached through an examination of the existing pattern of spatial organization, including the division of powers among the several levels of government, the pattern of regions established for economic development and general administration, the distribution of population and activities, and the distribution of levels of economic and social wellbeing.

The present chapter will be concerned with these and other questions. It is divided into three sections. In the first, we explore the relationship between transport planning and various regional concepts that have been proposed. In the second section we turn to an analysis of the major transport problems in the country and lay the groundwork for the third section, where we consider the question of spatial organization for transport planning and conclude with our principal recommendations.

The Regional Concept in Transport Planning

Transport's principal impact is "on the ground." By moving goods and people from one place to another, transport facilitates economic growth at these places and along connecting routes. Once the basic pattern has been laid down, however, subsequent economic growth is produced by forces that are largely independent of the character of the transport system. Although transport must continue to increase as demand increases, it has little generative power of its own.

Transport can perform a developmental role, however. Facilities may be built ahead of demand in the hope that the supply of a service will create its own demand. Although the conditions for this "supply strategy" are not always appropriate, the developmental use of transport is particularly frequent in attempts to solve the problem of "lagging" regions, such as Appalachia, or to open frontier areas to development, as in the building of the transcontinental railroad during the last century.

Particularly in their developmental role, transport services may also act as an organizer of relationships in space, such as patterns of settlement, the location of economic activities, and social interaction. The historical progression of transport technology in the United States has been accompanied by a set of decisive shifts in the spatial organization of the nation's economy. The early importance of water routes gave rise to concentrated developments along the Atlantic seaboard, which later were followed by urban and economic developments on both ends of heavily traveled canals. The change from water to rail added the radial pattern of metropolitan areas as well as the linear structure of interregional development. Subsequent reliance on auto transport led to the spreading of metropolitan development on a heretofore unprecedented scale as well as the creation of a complex network of activities along roads and highways between metropolitan centers.

Finally, the introduction of air transport has added to the potential capacity for growth of large centers such as Houston, Dallas, or Atlanta, with many intermetropolitan air connections. Throughout this entire period, some older centers found themselves unable to compete with the new transport technology, became relatively isolated from the mainstream of economic development, and declined in importance.

Although usually thought of in terms of its connective functions, transport may also be a divisive force. The extent of local opposition to the construction of freeways through populated areas is testimony to the real and perceived ability of a large transport line to divide and destroy a community. On a much larger scale, a development such as the proposed Palmdale Intercontinental Airport in Los Angeles County may become a region-forming development. If built, it would in all probability bring about a major reorientation of social and economic relations throughout the Southern California region.

Given these effects of transport services—facilitating, developmental, and space organizing—nothing would appear more logical than to plan the development of transport systems so that these effects are complementary. This raises the question: What sort of area is most suitable for transport planning?

Regional studies have long considered transport links as essential to the definition of regions. The basic spatial patterns in any developed economy can be expressed as the relations between (1) a central city and its surrounding region, and (2) one city region and another.[4] City and region may accordingly be treated as a unit that is characterized by a tight pattern of functional interdependencies and articulated by a system of transport and communication facilities. These interdependencies are centered at the urban core of the region. Metropolitan-centered regions were eventually defined according to the boundaries of market areas for the city's major trade and service functions.

Geographers elaborated this pattern of functional city-region relationships into a theory of "central places."[5] The theory was useful in many ways but deficient in explaining certain types of spatial relations, particularly those arising from manufacturing and certain higher-order services, such as banking and insurance.

Market and service areas often differ substantially in their form and size, so that any given center may be surrounded by as many regions as there are city functions.[6] Although some functional regions may cluster sufficiently to allow one to draw a regional boundary that represents a meaningful average of distance values from the center, other market areas may extend far beyond the immediate localized cluster, even leaping across the contiguous market-service areas of other centers. Moreover, central place theory does not account for the supply areas of urban economic activity, even though the developmental fortunes of two areas may be related "backwards" through the input side as much as "forward" through the pattern of output linkages. In any event, a city may have a close relationship to a region in which it may not be centrally located, if at all.[7]

The question consequently arises of how best to determine the area of influence of any particular urban center in order to construct a set of meaningful urban-centered regions. According to O.D. Duncan, one may take the viewpoint of either the metropolitan center or hinterland. The perspective of the hinterland is reflected in the use of an administrative principle, according to which all land is allocated to the metropolitan area to which it has the closest relationship.[8] Examples of this general procedure are metropolitan regions defined by newspaper circulation (as a surrogate measure for trade area) and Federal Reserve District boundaries (see Figures 3-1 and 3-2).[9] Metro-regions derived in this way take the form of concentric, contiguous areas around the metropolitan center.[10]

If the problem of boundary delimitation is approached from the perspective of the metropolis, however, the relative importance of outlying areas to the functional activities at the center must be considered. Areas nearby may be less important than market or supply areas located large distances away. This approach may therefore lead to sets of discontinuous city-hinterland regions. Moreover, many areas may not be included in any metro-region at all because they are relatively unimportant to metropolitan economies.

The idea of metropolitan-centered regions was officially adopted in 1910, when the Bureau of the Census instituted the concept of the Metropolitan Districts for the purpose of census data collection. A summary of the development and refinement of this concept is contained in the excellent and thorough study by Brian Berry, *Metropolitan Area Definition: A Re-evaluation of Concept*

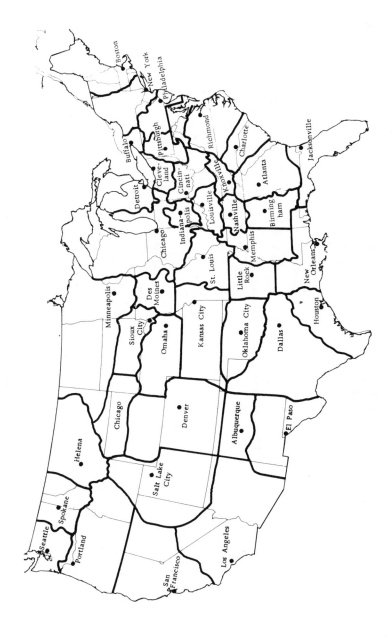

Figure 3-1. Metropolitan Regions in the United States as defined by daily newspaper circulation: 1929.

146

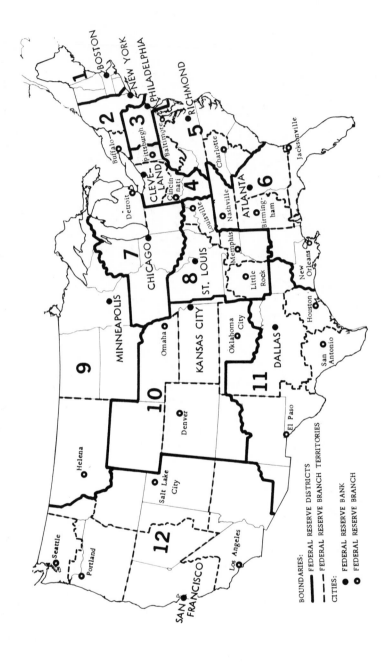

Figure 3-2. Boundaries of Federal Reserve Districts and their branch territories: 1954.

and Statistical Practice.[11] The purpose of this report was to "examine the effect of applying alternative criteria to integration of central cities and their outlying areas . . . and . . . to classify the entire United States into a hierarchy of urban, metropolitan, and consolidated areas using criteria of size and of the linkages between places of work, places of residence, and places of shopping.[12] The project was undertaken to define a more useful set of Standard Metropolitan Statistical Areas than was used in the 1960 Census (see Figure 3-3). Berry succeeded in mapping and analyzing commuter data for the entire country; he then applied the concept of a commuter shed to the delineation of metropolitan-centered regions. Following the lead of Karl Fox, he called them Functional Economic Areas. From an economic standpoint, the FEA is equivalent to the labor market of a city. Since the primary data is obtained from commuting behavior, however, it is easy to see how transport facilities will influence a purely economic variable and give to it a spatial dimension. The significance of FEAs for transport planning is discussed extensively in Karl Fox's contribution to this symposium and needs no further comment at this point.

A third type of metropolitan-centered region has been suggested by Constantine Doxiades who refers to what he calls the "Daily Urban System" (DUS).[13] This is based on a radius of approximately 80 miles around urban centers. Such distances, although covered daily by only a few people, are tending to become normal distances for more and more people.

Doxiades argues that establishment of major transport regions for the United States should be based on the boundaries as defined in his mapping of DUS. His criterion would lead to the construction of fewer regions than are derived from the Berry-Fox analysis of FEAs. Moreover, Berry's mapping leaves out less national territory than Doxiades' (see Figures 3-4 and 3-5).

Yet a fourth metropolitan-centered regional concept has been proposed by Friedmann and Miller in an article entitled "The Urban Field"[14] (see Figure 3-6). The concept is based on the idea of metropolitan core areas and what the authors call the "intermetropolitan periphery." Core areas are identified by their relatively high levels of economic and cultural development. Intermetropolitan peripheral areas, in contrast, show relatively low levels of such development. They are, in effect, the problem areas left over in attempts to divide the entire national territory into metropolitan-centered regions; these peripheral areas stand out primarily for their lack of significant relationship to major core regions. Berry's analysis of metropolitan-centered traverses adds empirical evidence to this concept.[15] It shows economic development indices rising to peaks at metropolitan cores (with small dips in the central areas) and falling off rather steeply into the "troughs" of the intermetropolitan periphery as distance from the core increases.

The Urban Field is seen as an evolving spatial pattern that would tend to weld both metropolitan core and the surrounding peripheries into one integrated unit for planning purposes. The Urban Field may therefore be regarded as an

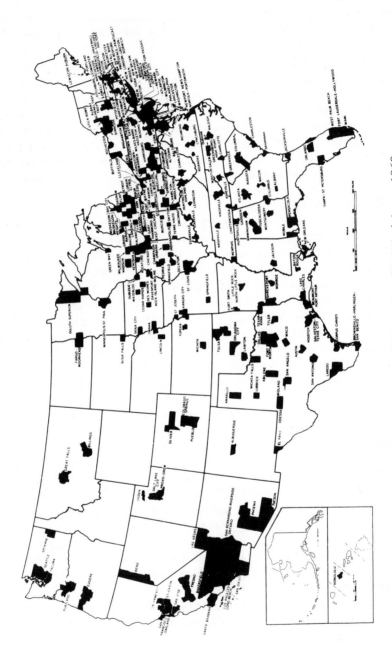

Figure 3-3. Standard Metropolitan Statistical Areas: 1960.

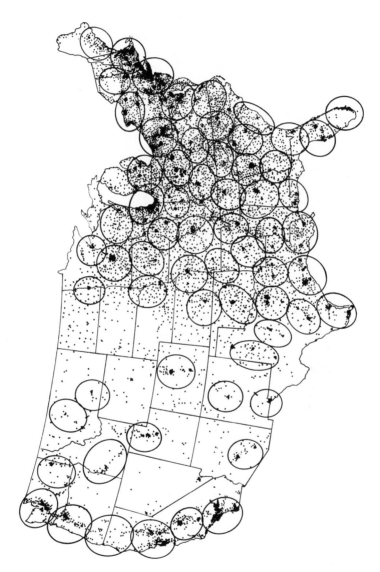

Figure 3-4. Daily Urban Systems.

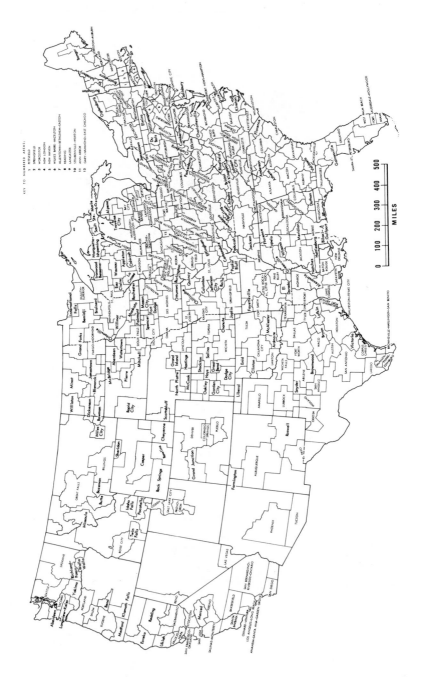

Figure 3-5. Functional Economic Areas.

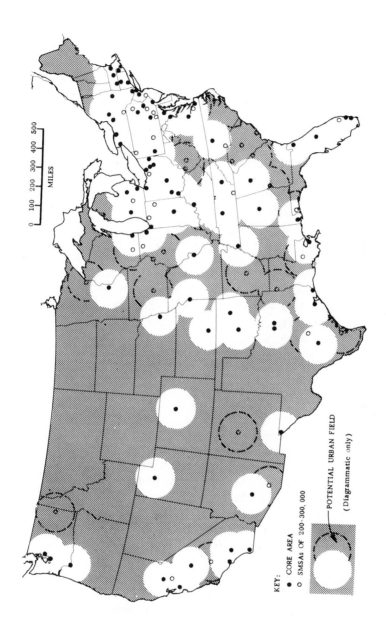

KEY:
● CORE AREA
○ SMSAs OF 200-300,000

POTENTIAL URBAN FIELD
(Diagrammatic only)

MILES
0 100 200 300 400 500

Figure 3-6. Urban Fields.

enlargement of the space for urban living that would extend far beyond the boundaries of FEAs into the open landscape of the periphery. Peripheries would serve as valuable additions of land to densely populated metro-areas, especially for recreation (weekend commuting) and as locations for land-consuming institutions such as schools, hospitals, conference centers, warehouses, and one-story manufacturing units. The authors suggest that Urban Fields be delineated around core areas of at least 300,000 population. Most of the country's population is presently living within the radius of one or another of these fields which occupy approximately one-third of the total land area of the United States.

It is evident from this brief review of regional concepts that the mapping of regional structures will vary with the criterion used. This raises the old question of whether or not regions exist as artifacts or rather as mental constructs that are used to simplify consideration of a complex set of activities. If one could easily delineate regions, one might assert the "real" existence of these regions. On the other hand, no one has ever claimed that regional boundaries can be drawn uniquely and precisely. The relationships that produce a region may exist intuitively or even empirically, but there are great practical difficulties involved in describing the limits of these spatial relationships because, in fact, there are no limits to the spread of interaction. As the authors of a famous public report declared a generation ago:[16]

It seems to be agreed that regional boundaries are usually indefinite, being zones rather than lines. In the majority of instances, therefore, any boundaries which may be drawn will necessarily be arbitrary. It appears, however, that it is desirable to draw boundaries, providing their arbitrary nature be admitted.

Any metropolitan-centered region in the United States is an open region. None of its activities is spatially bounded, even though the intensity of interaction falls off significantly as distance from the central city increases. No matter how carefully regional boundaries may be delimited there is a high degree of overspill into other areas. To trace the boundaries for metropolitan regions, therefore, one must seek the point at which there is the greatest degree of closure for the set of activities considered. Since the choice of activities and their relationships will determine the form of the region, a region is primarily a taxonomical concept.

As we have seen in the development of the Functional Economic Area concept, commuter sheds were the essential element that led to a regional definition. Within each FEA and, to a lesser degree also in the Urban Field, there is a high demand for all forms of ground transport, road and rail, subway and rapid transit. Each of these subsystems must work together in helping to create the spatial pattern of a metropolitan-centered region. Because metropolitan transport systems are tightly integrated and intensively used, there can be little doubt that within each metropolitan region, however defined, there is need for coordinating transport investments of all kinds. Where the transport system at the metropolitan level works poorly, it will hold back economic growth and make the region a less desirable place for living. The particular character of the transport system, influencing urban form and the structure of communities, will inevitably influence the quality of life throughout the region.

Moving from metropolitan-centered regions to the national level, attention must shift to the relationships among these regions. Although transport assumes a major role in defining these relationships, there is little work that adequately describes the nature of interregional interaction.[17] Both Brian Berry and Otis Duncan have done some research in this area, but their work is of limited relevance to our problem. Berry sets forth a method of analyzing cities as elements within a system of cities.[18] His analytical framework is particularly suitable for studying the intraregional relationships of communities within an Urban Field. Built on the precepts of central place theory, it is not especially useful for describing interactions between two metropolitan-centered regions such as New York and Chicago.

Duncan's work, more empirical in nature, focuses on interregional monetary exchanges.[19] Using flow of funds data, easily collected from the Federal Reserve accounting system and therefore current, Duncan analyzes the role of metropolitan centers in articulating the pattern of interregional relationships. But this work, interesting in its own terms, has not been extrapolated to define the nature of interregional contacts. Although the model Duncan developed suggests that interregional interactions could be identified on the basis of a rather simple set of criteria—distance, population, and regional income—this analysis still remains to be done.

In the absence of a formal model, the pattern of interregional relationships may be described in terms of yet another regional concept, the Urban Corridor. The Corridor occupies an intermediate place in the system of spatial relationships important in the planning of transport systems. It may be considered as a linear extension of metropolitan regions. Normally, it is a large, densely populated area containing several urban nuclei. At the same time, it is an expression of intense intermetropolitan interaction.

An Urban Corridor may be defined as a linear system of urban places that, together with the transit facilities connecting them, constitutes a subsystem of the national space economy.[20] Corridor-centered development is the cumulative result of prior transport development.[21] Urban Corridors are, therefore, clear instances of the region-forming character of transportation. The linear nature of early transport developments—along sea coast, lake shore, and valley routes—is reflected in the heavy concentration of urban developments (and intensive agriculture) in such Corridors as Boston-Washington, Milwaukee-Chicago-Detroit-Pittsburgh, Seattle-Portland, and San Fransisco-San Diego. Most of America's urban population lives within the confines of these linear regions.

Since the Urban Corridor is composed of an especially intricate complex of interrelationships, it is a region that requires special solutions to its problems. The transport component of a corridor network of urban activity is, moreover, of special significance, as has been recognized in the Northeast Corridor's approach to intermetropolitan transit.

Nonmetropolitan regions, finally, pose a special problem. In the American context, they are areas that have been by-passed by economic progress. Large in physical area, they are low in population density. They are also poor and subject to large-scale emigration to metropolitan centers and Urban Corridors. As part of the intermetropolitan periphery, they could usefully be considered within the context of the Urban Field. But public policy has preferred to treat them as residual areas, and the Economic Development Administration (EDA) is currently presiding over several Regional Commissions that, established within the major areas of economic depression, are charged with promoting their development. At best, this mission will cushion the shock of continued economic decline.[22] But as long as planning for these regions remains contained within the boundaries of the intermetropolitan periphery—in the Ozarks, the Upper Great Lakes, the Coastal Plains, Appalachia, (Northern) New England, and the Four Corners (comprising parts of Utah, Colorado, Arizona, and New Mexico) —transport planning should be integrated with the general run of developmental planning for these areas. In most cases, however, as in New England, it would be beneficial to think of their development, including transportation, as linked to that of the great metropolitan complexes located outside their boundaries.

In summary, there are three levels at which transport looms as a crucial issue in development policy and planning: the metropolitan-centered region (SMSA, FEA, DUS, or Urban Field); the Urban Corridor; and the Nation. The components of the transport system at subnational levels become articulated and fully integrated at the national level, where concern must focus specifically, though not exclusively, on problems of linkage among Urban Corridors and individual metropolitan regions. Nonmetropolitan areas are best considered as related in development to external core areas. Only where this cannot be done, should they be regarded as yet a fourth level for regional transport planning.

Problems of Transport Planning

The participants in the planning, development, construction, and operation of the national transport system are many. All levels of government—federal, state, metropolitan, and local—perform distinctive roles. Moreover, special transit authorities may have jurisdiction over large metropolitan areas that encompass more than one local government and more than one state. A number of federal agencies, among them the Interstate Commerce Commission, the Federal Aviation Agency, the Interstate Highway Commission, and the Department of

Transportation, have authority to deal with special transport problems. In addition, there are several Congressional committees that deal extensively with transport. The functions of some of these federal participants are represented by counterparts at the state level.

In addition to governmental agencies, there are private participants: railroads, airlines, trucking companies, bus lines, taxi fleets. Although these privately owned systems are publicly regulated by the Federal Government and by scores of agencies at the state and local level, their decisions are seldom made within a common planning framework.[23] Our transport system is therefore managed by a multitude of public and private groups. Although there is a complex pattern of interaction among them, the level of coordination is low. This has led to the development of a transport system that is less than optimal when judged by the multiplicity of needs that it must serve.

The major problems of the national transport system are succinctly stated in the Congressional bill introduced by Senator Magnuson in February 1970.[24] The purpose of the bill is explicit: to provide for the planning and development of a balanced transport system throughout the United States. The bill seeks to encourage "coordinated planning and development of balanced transportation facilities within and between all regions of the United States." Its provisions rest on the explicit assumption that there are, in fact, major geographic and economic regions in the country that, if properly designated, would constitute meaningful areas for planning. Instructions for the delimitation of these regions, however, are brief. According to the authors of the bill, they shall be "major transportation regions," and there must also be geographic, demographic, and economic relationships among the several areas within each region.

In light of the preceding discussion, these apparently simple criteria for regionalization are vague and ambiguous. A clue is perhaps provided in the word "major." Applied to transport regions, it suggests an area of relatively large magnitude, almost certainly larger than that of any single metropolitan-centered region. No constraint, however, is imposed that the relationships of areas *within* such regions must be stronger than relations *among* the regions.

The bill further provides for the establishment by the states, wholly or partially located within such regions, of appropriate multistate regional commissions. Their principal functions are identified as follows:

1. Evaluate transport plans for the region.
2. Initiate and coordinate the preparation of a long-range overall transportation plan for the region.
3. Give due consideration to other federal, state, and local transport planning in the region.
4. Relate transport development to other planning and development activities and needs of the region.
5. Initiate research and development of intercity systems aimed at immediate improvement in intercity passenger service using existing facilities.

6. Initiate research and development of safe and reliable high speed prototype intercity passenger systems.
7. Cooperate with federal, state, and local agencies in conducting or sponsor-
ing research and development programs.
8. Provide a forum for consideration of transportation problems and solutions for the region.
9. Formulate and recommend interregional compacts and other forms of
interstate and interregional cooperation when necessary.

Careful scrutiny of what these functions imply leads to a more precise
definition of criteria for establishing such commissions. Function 3, for instance,
implies that the regional transport commissions are not to have controlling
authority over all forms of transport planning in their areas. The bill also calls
for popular forums to consider their regional transport problems and possible
solutions to them (Function 8). But as a precondition to this "creative"
function, and if it is not to become an empty gesture, certain powers of
coordination, decisionmaking, and financing would have to devolve to the
regions. Although the bill provides for regional funding, it is of prime importance that the funding level be meaningful in terms of the objectives sought.
Provisions are made for regional planning (Functions 1 and 2), but not for
regional control over most transport investments, which are to be undertaken, as
in the past, by a multitude of governmental agencies. By so separating the
planning from the implementing functions, the bill in effect creates an impotent
planning organization that has little or no political muscle and lacks the
economic power to enforce its policies.

Function 4 illustrates the conflict between single-purpose regions (transport
planning) and composite regional organizations where all major aspects of
development may be closely coordinated. The bill does recognize the advantage
of including transport planning in the business of already established regional
commissions in the depressed areas. Unfortunately, these areas are for the most
part excluded from the major metropolitan economies.

Perhaps the most attractive feature of the bill is the concept of intermodal
planning it is seeking to promote. In Senator Magnuson's introduction of the bill
in the Senate, his emphasis was unmistakably and almost exclusively on the
advantage of intermodal planning.[25] The following are excerpts from the
Senator's introductory statement:

It is obvious that we cannot continue building highways in the innocent belief
that more roads will relieve congestion. Already, highways and parking facilities
occupy as much as two-thirds of the land in our major cities.
... we have failed to provide adequate transportation for those millions of
Americans who do not have access to a car.
We must abandon the notion that ... any single mode of transportation can
be relied upon to solve the problems of mobility in a prosperous and populous

society . . . that, left to itself, any single mode can cure our transportation difficulties either within or between cities.

The recent myopic reliance on highway development in all parts of the nation has been partially responsible for the current lack of intermodal planning. The highway industry is now well organized and is combatting, as it has done in the past, attempts at intermodal planning and inclusion of highway planning in comprehensive regional plans.[26] This situation begs for new institutional arrangements to put highway development into a proper perspective. One of the shortcomings of the bill is its failure to deal with this problem in a comprehensive way.

Some of the most vital discussion in the hearings turned on the question of intermodal coordination. The testimony of Robert A. Nelson, Federal Executive Fellow at the Brookings Institute, an institution that has done very excellent and extensive research in the area of transport planning, was particularly to the point. Mr. Nelson testified:[27]

Take the airports. One of the reasons we have noncooperation in airport siting disputes is that in fact they are competing not for passenger service but for freight service. There is a real economic reason not to go ahead and cooperate under these circumstances. The airlines are competing for freight service with the railroads and trucks. The railroads are, of course, in the same position with respect to the trucks and airlines. There is a reason not to go ahead and help make the other modes good. If an airline can connect with a truck line rather than another airline, it wouldn't use the airline. That is why I think some authority must be created to insure cooperation. I don't think the various modes will voluntarily move together.

Where, then, should this coordination take place? Nelson concludes that, since large amounts of intercity transport cross state lines, particularly in the East, transport planning and decisionmaking should occur, not at the state level, but at the level of regional *or* Federal Government.

Senator Edward Kennedy also challenged the bill's authors to put more emphasis on intermodal planning.[28] He went so far as to suggest a reorganization of Congressional jurisdiction over transport programs in order to achieve the desired degree of coordination in the Legislative as well as the Executive Branches of the Government.

Senator Magnuson makes a strong case for the importance of Urban Corridors and cities that three-fourths of the American people will live in cities along such corridors in the near future. He concludes that "satisfying the total transportation needs within and between corridors will involve coordination of different modes and the development of new technology." But his conclusion that "solving the total transportation equation of our transportation regions cannot be the job of a bureaucracy in Washington; the social, environmental, and topographical and demographical factors to be considered will vary too widely from one region to the next" is contradictory to his premises. For there are numerous and important similarities in the problems of the nation's major Urban Corridors. Solutions to these problems are therefore likely to contain many similarities as well.

There is no compelling reason, for example, why research and development programs should be regionally devised as if the situation in each region were unique. It might be better to guide research activities and their priorities from the national center, even though certain development activities could be carried on in the regions where they are most appropriate. The complete decentralization of research and development would be in direct conflict with the search for solutions that may benefit several regions at the same time. It would seem that prototype development, in particular, ought to remain the responsibility of national transport planning (albeit with the close participation of local and regional groups) in order to avoid duplication, unfair regional advantage, and to provide rapid and full information to all the regions on the successes and failures of new technologies and experimental systems.

In his plea for intermodal planning, Senator Magnuson has established an excellent case for establishing new institutional arrangements to allow for more intermodal communication and control in planning, funding, and implementation. His position was reinforced in the hearings on the bill and by current problems encountered in controlling highway development. The failure of the bill, however, lies in jumping indiscriminately to a regional solution. Examination of the problems clearly suggests new emphasis in intermodal planning, but not necessarily and under all circumstances at the multi-state regional level.

In December 1970, the DOT announced plans for Railpax (now Amtrak), a new government corporation designed to reestablish a functioning system of intercity passenger service (see Figure 3-7). This move is a direct reflection of transport policies for interregional and intermetropolitan travel, which, most appropriately, originated at the national, not regional, level. Current transport problems in the United States focus primarily on intrametropolitan and interregional movements. By laying down a basic trunk line system for rail transport, and by opting for the competitive survival of this system as being in the national interest, Amtrak also increases the probability of third-level bus and air service to the non-subsidized portions of intercity transport linkages. This is clearly a matter for national decision that promises to result in a more "balanced" relationship between the public and private sectors in the provision of transport services. Issues of this kind—and the Amtrak proposal is unlikely to be the last such issue—are clearly best decided at some central level; shifting the onus of decision to regional transport authorities would result in less than optimal solutions for the country as a whole.

Spatial Organization for Transport Planning

The regional approach to development planning has an honorable pedigree. In the United States, it may be traced back to the 1930s. During this early period,

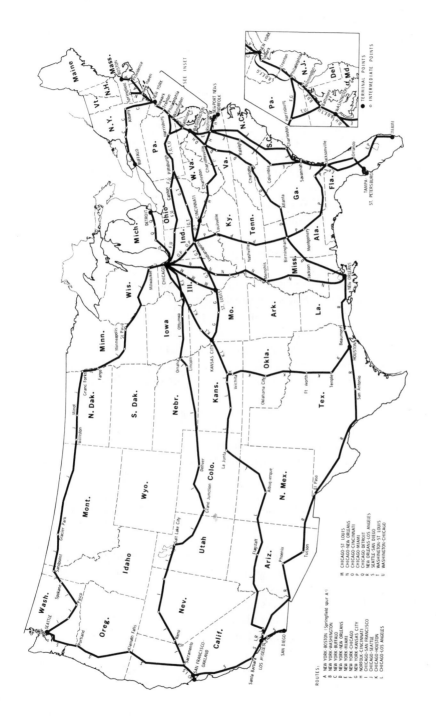

Figure 3-7. AMTRAK Routes.

the river basin was considered the basic unit for planning, and regional policies were aimed at bringing into higher use the water and related land resources of these relatively self-contained physical areas.[29] The most famous example of integrated regional development in this sense was, and still is, the Tennessee Valley Authority. Similar projects, most of them based on the use of water for irrigation, were subsequently undertaken in areas such as the Columbia River Basin. In the light of what has happened since, it is interesting to observe that these early efforts stressed not so much the development of regional economies—which, at the same time, was still a relatively obscure concept—as the "development" of the physical resources and infrastructure of a region. The TVA delighted in the publication of statistics showing the increase in river navigation, the generation of kilowatt hours, the acreage devoted to soil-conserving forage crops, and the number of lake-bound tourists. Integration was to occur in the use of resources, not among the sectors of a regional economy. The Authority did not consider whether its investments would also substantially raise the economic standard of living of the population in the area. This emphasis came only later, after World War II.

Out of this period with its limited vision, however, came a fairly sophisticated and thorough study of regionalization which may still today be read with profit. In 1935, the National Resources Committee presented a report on *Regional Factors in National Planning*. Broad in scope, it includes discussion of the political and organizational implications of regionalization. As its preface announces, "the report deals with important problems of planning and development which overlap state lines or which require the use of combined federal and state powers."[30]

The Committee made an effective case for regionalization in the United States, where existing state boundaries in most cases have little relevance to the problems of area economies. Further, it established a set of principles to guide its search for a solution to the problem of regionalization.[31] These principles retain their validity:

1. There should be a comprehensive view of the policies of all governments in any given area in order to facilitate solutions to problems of public concern.
2. There is a special responsibility of the Federal Government to ensure coordination of its own agencies dealing with any problem of concern to several governments in any area.
3. There must a sharing of powers among all levels of government.
4. There is a need to decentralize planning of development to a subnational level at which there can be a total review of the problems of any given area by all the agencies concerned.
5. The selection of the area and its planning center should be made with reference to the general coincidence of major planning problems.

No great upsurge of regionalism followed publication of the report. World War II so threatened the survival of the nation, that regional problems appeared of small consequence. Vast regional shifts in labor and industry occurred and brought entire new regions, such as Southern California, into the economy of the nation. This created problems for the older regions, many of which found it difficult to adjust to the changing situation and provided much of the labor supply for the new centers of production. The problem of economically lagging regions was finally recognized during the latter part of the 1950s and eventually led to the creation in 1965 of the Appalachian Regional Commission, and the Economic Development Administration in the Department of Commerce. The EDA was established to coordinate the various federal efforts directed at reviving stagnant regional economies (and in some cases declining urban economies as well) in areas throughout the country. A number of distressed areas were designated as Economic Development Regions. With the exception of New England, however, none contained large, dynamic metro-centers through which a self-sustaining process of regional development might be initiated.[32] (see Figure 3-8).

The most recent step in the evolution of regionalism in the United States had its origin in the growing recognition of the inefficiencies inherent in the centralized administration of bulging federal assistance programs. In a move to simplify administrative procedures, President Nixon directed the Bureau of the Budget to designate a uniform set of regions to be worked with by federal agencies and to establish within each region a single city as headquarters for all the agencies.[33] This has been done. The resulting boundaries are clear reflections of the administrative principle of regionalization (see Figure 3-9). The division was made to allow federal agencies to decentralize some of their functions geographically, to improve physical access of the public to these agencies, and to encourage closer collaboration among them. Initial results are reported to be favorable.[34]

The history of the last 35 years has revealed to us some of the main reasons for which the regionalization of government programs may be undertaken. Starting with the most recent experience, regionalization may be promoted *to achieve improved coordination of programs among different sectors of the Federal Government*. In cases of this sort, the region may be looked upon as a substitute for information.[35] By decentralizing government services and programs, the cost of information exchange between the national agency in Washington and local service areas may be reduced.

Where regionalization is undertaken primarily to achieve better coordination among sectors of government activity, program planning and implementation procedures will tend to predominate; it is shortrun considerations that will count. On the other hand, basic policy decisions, resource allocation among sectors and programs, and expenditure controls will remain in the hands of central bureaucrats.

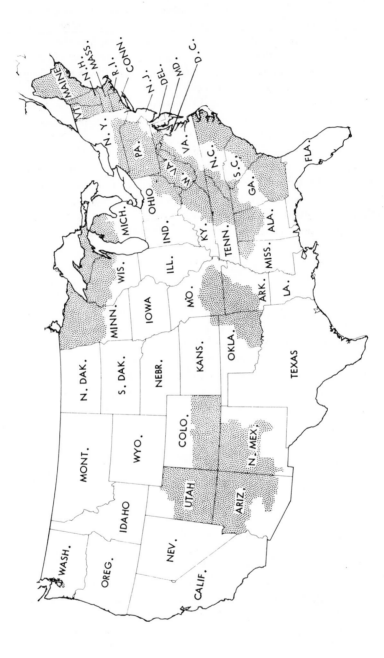

Figure 3-8. Economic Development Regions.

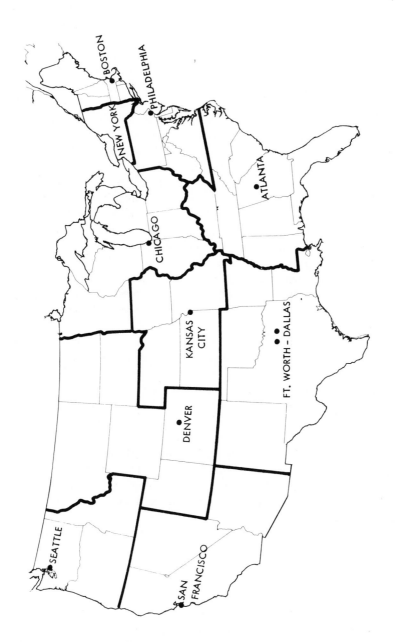

Figure 3-9. Administrative Regional Areas: 1970.

A second reason for regionalization, more ambitious than the first, is *to devolve to regional organizations authority to recommend development policies to the Federal Government*. Such recommendations, which would be evolved in close cooperation with the people of the region through mechanisms such as citizen representation, public hearings, and the like, would have a primarily indicative value for central planners. The Regional Transportation Commissions established under the proposed National Transportation Act (S. 2425, 91st Congress, 1st Session) would be of this sort. As a practical matter, however, such policy-recommending authority is often joined to powers of implementation. A particularly strong policy-program linkage was accomplished with the Tennessee Valley Authority. In this case, authority was devolved to an autonomous agency of the Federal Government, responsible only to the President and to the Congress. This early experiment with the regional administration of development programs was not repeated, however. A looser and politically more responsive arrangement is represented by the five Regional Commissions set up by the Economic Development Administration. In addition to being charged with analyzing the problems of their respective area economies, each Commission is expected to develop an overall strategy for promoting the area's long-term growth and to work with federal, state, and local governments for the implementation of specific programs. To strengthen its bargaining position in the implementation phases of its work, each Commission commands certain invest-ment funds of its own.[36]

Essentially, the devolution of authority over policy matters is yet another attempt—this time at the level of objectives and general instrumentation—to achieve greater coordination among the sectors of government activity. The population living in a region is often thought to have a substantial degree of social cohesion and to be capable of formulating and expressing a mutual interest in the solution of problems specific to their region. Whether this is, in fact, true for every kind of region may be doubted. The traditional broad cultural regions of the United States, such as the Southeast, Northwest, and Northeast, though commonly referred to in everyday conversation, scarcely represent optimal areas for the articulation of a common point of view (see Figure 3-10). This should be borne in mind when considering large multi-state regions for transport planning.

A third reason for undertaking the regionalization of government programs would be *to render such programs more responsive to the wishes of regional populations*. Or, to put it more strongly, it would extend to regional populations a greater measure of political control over the development of their economies. In the extreme case, this would imply some form of regional government. Because of the political structure of the United States, however, the establish-ment of regional governments across state boundaries has never been attempted. There is, nevertheless, a widespread belief that the regionalization (and decen-tralization) of government programs somehow brings government "closer" to the

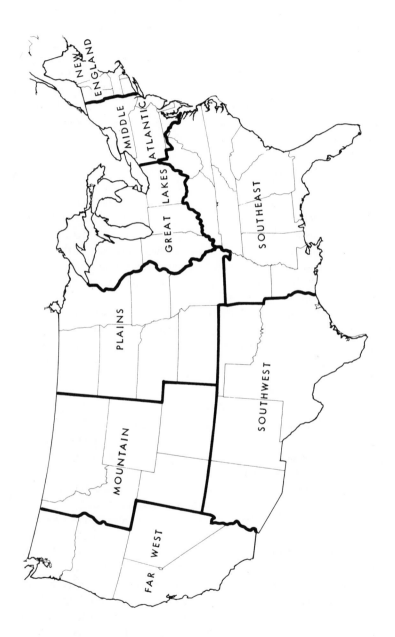

Figure 3-10. Regional grouping of states.

people. As Morton Grodzins has argued in a persuasive essay, this belief may be mistaken.[37] Regional Transportation Commissions, for instance, because of their probable reliance on technical criteria in decisionmaking, their low political profile, the complexity of state-federal negotiations in the context of regionwide bargaining, and their physical location at some central place within a large multi-state region may in fact be less accessible and responsive to the people of the region than Transportation Departments operating within the political framework of a given state. Moreover, even where accountability is built into the structure of such Commissions, it is not clear whether the political will of a regional population group should always prevail in the event of a conflict with national purposes, especially when the funds for implementation come from the Federal Government.

Given this background, the regionalization of transport planning may now be considered in more detail. Earlier in this chapter, we suggested that a useful distinction could be made between the developmental and facilitating functions of transport investments. In case of the former, the extension of transport facilities is regarded as a means for promoting the economic growth of an area and, ultimately, for generating its own demand. The application of this principle is most appropriate in the context of planning for economically depressed regions. The emphasis here would be primarily on relating transport to other kinds of public and private investment in an inter-sectoral or "comprehensive" strategy for regional development. The Economic Development Regions of the country are the logical foci for integrating transport planning with general development planning in this manner. The provision of the proposed National Transportation Act to designate, for purposes of the Act and under certain conditions, an existing Regional Commission as the Regional Transportation Commission is therefore eminently desirable.[38] Its principal shortcoming lies in the fact that nearly all of the depressed areas of the United States are so delimited as to exclude major metropolitan growth centers.

In all other areas of the country, however, transport plays primarily a *facilitating* role in the development process; it is supplied in response to an already existing or projected demand that is generated independently of the provision of transport services. In this case, an inter-sectoral planning approach is needed less than one which emphasizes intermodal coordination.

A further distinction is here required. In many situations, the provision of transport services within a given area does not require repeated and successive decisionmaking. A single project may be planned and actually constructed, but it will be many years before another proposal would make it necessary for this same set of participants to join in a common endeavor. An instance of this would be the joint planning of transport facilities between Southern California and Las Vegas. Cases of this sort can usually be managed quite well through specific *ad hoc* arrangements. They do not require a permanent regional framework for planning and decisionmaking.

In many other situations, however, the complexity of the transport system and its need for adaptability to changing circumstances is such that planning and decisionmaking require continuing attention. This occurs primarily at the level of metropolitan-centered regions, the states, Urban Corridors, and the nation.

In *metropolitan-centered regions*, it would be desirable to integrate transport planning with already existing Metropolitan Associations of Government in order to strengthen coordinating powers at this level. As we have seen, several definitions of metropolitan-centered regions have been proposed, such as the Functional Economic Area, the Urban Daily System, and the Urban Field. Although it is probably true that better planning determinations can be made for larger areas from a strictly technical point of view, administrative convenience may outweigh any advantages of this sort. The jurisdictional area of Metropolitan Government Associations would be a sufficiently good start for achieving greater intermodal coordination in the densely built-up areas of the nation.

For much the same reason, the *states* would appear to be the logical focus for intermodal planning. Less than one-third of the states in the union have to date created departments that might serve as counterparts to the Federal Department of Transportation. Planning and development of each mode is carried on independently by agencies that serve and are supported by special client groups. This arrangement makes it extremely difficult to arrive at a comprehensive transport policy and leads to numerous conflicts that could be avoided or, at least, more readily resolved within the context of a single administrative body. By so bringing the various state transport services together, greater political accountability could be achieved, and tax dollars might be saved on a substantial scale.

A number of *Urban Corridors* fall entirely within the boundaries of a single state (e.g., California, Florida), so that planning for transport facilities could readily be absorbed by the appropriate state agency. In a few instances, however, especially in the Northeast Corridor and in the corridor areas linking Milwaukee with Chicago, Detroit, Buffalo, and Pittsburgh, special transport planning commissions could be established. The transport problems of these corridors are persistent and complex, and intercity problems are particularly critical. Urban corridors could therefore be used to structure and plan for complicated sets of transport problems that are primarily intermodal in character. The provisions of the proposed National Transportation Act are particularly appropriate to corridor planning. In addition to state representatives, members of the Metropolitan Government Associations contained within each corridor could serve on the Regional Transportation Commission to provide for a smoother coordination of all the interests concerned.

Finally, all other problems of inter-metropolitan transport may best be solved at the *national level*. This conclusion should not stand in the way of the decentralization of certain routine administrative functions to the newly established administrative regions of the country. The Bureau of the Budget's recent division of the nation into major administrative areas is perhaps as good as any. The DOT might be well advised to adopt this division for routine purposes, such as grant processing, simply because the advantages of coordination with other agencies might exceed any disadvantages resulting from a possible suboptimal delimitation for the administration of transport programs. In fact, all of the nation's corridor areas, except the Northeast, are included in their entirety within one of the newly established administrative regions. But the formulation of policies, the allocation of resources, and the coordination of rail, highway, and air transit between metropolitan-centered regions and urban corridors are not primarily problems of a regional nature. The recent creation of Railpax (now Amtrak) is a reflection of the national nature of these problems.

Summary of Recommendations

1. The definition of regions for transport planning in the U.S. is best approached through an ordering of specific activities in space.
2. Developmental functions of transport services are best planned in close coordination with other developmental considerations. The Economic Development Regions of the country are logical foci for evolving comprehensive strategies of regional development.
3. The facilitating roles of transport services arise in connection with an already existing of projected demand that is generated independently of the provision of these services. In this case, an intersectoral planning approach may be needed less than one which emphasizes intermodal coordination.
4. Intermodal coordination is called for especially where (a) the provision of transport services within a given area does not require repeated and successive decisionmaking and (b) the complexity of the transport system requires continuing attention. In the first case, planning can generally be accomplished on an *ad hoc* basis, without the designation of special transport regions. In the second case, however, several distinct situations must be considered.
   - at the level of *metropolitan-centered regions*, transport planning should be integrated with already existing Metropolitan Associations of Government in order to strengthen their coordinating powers;
   - at the level of the *states*, improved intermodal coordination may require the creation of Departments of Transportation capable of bringing together the various state transport services, of achieving greater political accountability, and of securing a substantial saving of resources;
   - at the level of interstate *Urban Corridors*, such as the Northeast or the corridor areas linking Milwaukee with Chicago, Detroit, Buffalo, and

Pittsburgh, special transport planning commissions might be established.

5. All other transport planning activities could continue to be carried out centrally at the national level, except certain routine functions, such as grant processing, might be decentralized to the already existing administrative regions for better coordination with other federal programs.

Notes

1. See the papers produced for "Can New York City Be Governed? A Symposium on the Realities of Decentralizing New York City Government," held at the House of the Association of the Bar of the City of New York, December 3-4, 1970.

2. "Intergovernmental Relationships in an Urbanizing America," in D.P. Moynihan (ed.), TOWARD A NATIONAL URBAN POLICY, Basic Books, New York, 1970, p. 47.

3. Ibid., p. 48.

4. J. Friedmann, "The Concept of a Planning Region," LAND ECONOMICS, Vol. 32, 1956, pp. 1-13. Reprinted in Friedmann and Alonso (eds.), REGIONAL DEVELOPMENT AND PLANNING: A READER, The MIT Press, Cambridge, Massachusetts, 1964, pp. 497-518.

5. B.J.L. Berry, GEOGRAPHY OF MARKET CENTERS AND RETAIL DISTRIBUTION, Prentice Hall, Englewood Cliffs, New Jersey, 1967.

6. O.D. Duncan, et al., METROPOLIS AND REGION, The Johns Hopkins Press, Boston, Massachusetts, 1960, p. 39.

7. Ibid., p. 44.

8. Ibid., p. 249.

9. Figure sources listed at end of this chapter.

10. O.D. Duncan, op. cit.

11. U.S. Bureau of the Census (Brian Berry, author), METROPOLITAN AREA DEFINITION: A RE-EVALUATION OF CONCEPT AND STATISTICAL PRACTICE (rev.), Bureau of the Census, Working Paper No. 28, Washington, D.C., 1969.

12. Ibid., p. iii.

13. NATIONAL TRANSPORTATION ACT: HEARINGS BEFORE THE COMMITTEE ON COMMERCE, 91st Cong., Second Sess., S.924 and S.2425, Serial 91-69, U.S. Government Printing Office, Washington, D.C., 1970, p. 195.

14. J. Friedmann and J. Miller, "The Urban Field," JOURNAL OF THE AMERICAN INSTITUTE OF PLANNERS, Vol. 31, No. 4, November 1965, pp. 312-320.

15. U.S. Bureau of the Census, op. cit.

16. National Resources Committee, REGIONAL FACTORS IN NATIONAL

PLANNING, U.S. Government Printing Office, Washington, D.C., 1935, p. 145.

17. J. Friedmann, "The Concept of a Planning Region," op. cit., p. 514.

18. B.J.L. Berry, "Cities as Systems Within Systems of Cities," in Friedmann and Alonso (eds.), REGIONAL DEVELOPMENT AND PLANNING: A READER, The MIT Press, Cambridge, Massachusetts, 1964, pp. 116-137.

19. O.D. Duncan, op. cit., p. 133.

20. C.F.J. Whebell, "Corridors: A Theory of Urban Systems," ANNALS OF THE ASSOCIATION OF AMERICAN GEOGRAPHERS, Vol. 59, No. 1, March 1969, pp. 1-26.

21. Ibid.

22. N. Hansen, RURAL POVERTY AND THE URBAN CRISIS: A STRATEGY FOR REGIONAL DEVELOPMENT, Indiana University Press, Bloomington, Indiana, 1970.

23. NATIONAL TRANSPORTATION ACT: HEARINGS, op. cit., p. 236.

24. NATIONAL TRANSPORTATION ACT OF 1969, S.2425, 91st Cong., U.S. Government Printing Office, Washington, D.C., 1969.

25. "Announcement of Hearings on S.2425, The National Transportation Act," CONGRESSIONAL RECORD - Senate, U.S. Government Printing Office, Washington, D.C., February 20, 1970, pp. S.2127-2129.

26. Witness the recent defeat of Proposition 18 on the November 1970 ballot in California. The measure proposed to divert up to 25 percent of gasoline tax revenue from highway construction to the development of rapid transit systems. Although the proposition had bipartisan support in the legislature, support of the Governor, and widespread citizen support, the members of the highway lobby waged an extensive and expensive campaign based on the false claim that passage of the measure would lead to higher taxes. The role and the extent of monetary outlay by the members of the highway lobby are now being investigated by state officials. See also, T.A. Morehouse, "The 1962 Highway Act: A Study in Artful Interpretation," JOURNAL OF THE AMERICAN INSTITUTE OF PLANNERS, Vol. XXXV, No. 3, May 1969, pp. 160-168.

27. NATIONAL TRANSPORTATION ACT: HEARINGS, op. cit., pp. 112-113.

28. Ibid., pp. 224-228.

29. Friedmann, "The Concept of a Planning Region," op. cit., p. 498.

30. National Resources Committee, op. cit., preface.

31. Ibid., p. vii.

32. J. Friedmann, "Poor Regions and Poor Nations: Perspectives on the Problems of Appalachia," SOUTHERN ECONOMIC JOURNAL, Vol. 32, No. 4, April 1966, pp. 465-473.

33. Bureau of the Budget, SIMPLIFYING FEDERAL AID TO STATES AND COMMUNITIES, (Executive Office of the President), Bureau of the Budget, Washington, D.C., March 1970.

34. Ibid.

35. Walter Stöhr, "The Role of Regions for Development in Latin America," REGIONAL STUDIES, Vol. 3, pp. 81-90.

36. Hansen, op. cit., p. 109.

37. Morton Grodzins, THE AMERICAN SYSTEM, A NEW VIEW OF GOVERNMENT IN THE UNITED STATES, Ch. 7, "Local Is As Local Does," Rand McNally and Co., Chicago, Illinois, 1966.

38. NATIONAL TRANSPORTATION ACT OF 1969, op. cit., Section 5 (b).

Bibliography

Duncan, O.D., et al., METROPOLIS AND REGION, Johns Hopkins Press, Baltimore, 1960. (See especially pp. 26-45 and 90-104.)

Major work done with focus on the role played by metropolitan centers in defining interregional relationships. Also includes some analysis of the economic relationships between metropolitan centers and their surrounding areas.

Dziewonski, Kazimierz, "Economic Regionalization," GEOGRAPHIA POLONICA, Vol. 1, 1964, pp. 171-185.

Brief, comprehensive look at regionalization from economic point of view. Includes specific discussion of delimitation of economic regions.

Friedmann, J., "The Concept of a Planning Region." LAND ECONOMICS, Vol. 32, 1965, pp. 1-13. Reprinted in Friedmann and Alonso (eds.), REGIONAL DEVELOPMENT AND PLANNING: A READER, The MIT Press, Cambridge, Massachusetts, 1964.

An historical summary of the concept of area delimitation for planning purposes in the U.S. Although the focus is on planning activities of a regional rather than city scale, the article concludes with a plea for the integration of city and regional planning within areas that are designated to include both central city and surrounding region.

———, REGIONAL DEVELOPMENT POLICY, The MIT Press, Cambridge, Massachusetts, 1966.

Chapter 3 provides an especially direct discussion of the problems of delimitation.

———, and J. Miller, "The Urban Field," JOURNAL OF THE AMERICAN INSTITUTE OF PLANNERS, Vol. XXXI, No. 4, November 1965, pp. 312-320.

The urban field is an expansion of the metropolitan region. By including the peripheral areas within the concept of urban core region, a new spatial order is proposed which would unify core and periphery into a single matrix.

Fox, K., "The Functional Economic Area: Delineation and Implications for Economic Analysis and Policy," March 1965 (mimeo).

Development of criteria to delimit metropolitan-centered regions, called Functional Economic Areas.

Gajda, R.T., "Research in Methods of Delimitation of Economic Regions in Areas of Extensively-Dispersed Economy: A Case Study of Northern Canada," GEOGRAPHIA POLONICA, Vol. 8, 1965, pp. 27-37.

Specific case study of Northern Canada. Limited possibilities for extrapolation to more common urban centered economies.

Harris, C., "Methods of Research in Economic Regionalization," GEOGRAPHIA POLONICA, Vol. 4, 1965.

Very academic work includes extensive bibliographic work on regionalization, 291 entries. Also includes discussion of types of regions.

Macka, M. (ed.), ECONOMIC REGIONALIZATION, (Proceedings of the 4th General Meeting of the Commission on Methods of Economic Regionalization of the International Geographical Union, September 7-12, 1965, in Brno, Czechoslovakia): Publishing House of the Czechoslovak Academy of Sciences, Prague, 1967.

Collection of papers by variety of nationalities. Includes section on typology and structure of economic regions. Articles are in French or English.

National Resources Committee, REGIONAL FACTORS IN NATIONAL PLANNING, U.S. Government Printing Office, Washington, D.C., 1935.

This report remains the most all-encompassing analysis of the implications of regionalization for the U.S. Although written 35 years ago, the book deals thoroughly with issues that remain frequent topics of debate. Discussion includes spatial, political, and organizational implications of regionalization. See especially Chapter XV.

Stöhr, W., "The Role of Regions for Development in Latin America," REGIONAL STUDIES, Vol. 3, pp. 81-90.

Stress is on relation of regional definition and delimitation to purpose. Although the report deals with developmental situations in Latin America, much of the analysis and observation is appropriate to study of regional policies in the U.S.

U.S. Bureau of the Census (B. Berry, author), METROPOLITAN AREA DEFINITION: A RE-EVALUATION OF CONCEPT AND STATISTICAL PRACTICE (rev.), Bureau of the Census, Working Paper No. 28., Washington, D.C., 1969.

Short, concise summary of the metropolitan area concept from early history (1910) to a critique of the Standard Metropolitan Statistical Area used in the 1960 Census. The report develops alternative criteria to define a more useful statistical reporting area than the SMSA. Berry's work in Functional Economic Areas and core-periphery traverse analysis is included.

Vining, R., "Delimitation of Economic Areas: Statistical Conceptions in the Study of the Spatial Structure of an Economic System," JOURNAL OF THE AMERICAN STATISTICAL ASSOCIATION, Vol. 48, pp. 44-64, 1953.

Early critique of the Bureau of the Census statistical grouping. Argues against idea that there are "natural" units for economic studies.

Whebell, C.F.J., "Corridors: A Theory of Urban Systems," ANNALS OF THE ASSOCIATION OF AMERICAN GEOGRAPHERS, Vol. 59, No. 1, March 1969, pp. 1-26.

Corridor is defined as a linear system of urban places linked by surface transport. The corridor is shown to be a major type of urban system, currently and historically. Builds theory in first part. Empirical work, taken from a study of Southern Ontario, Canada, is used to illustrate theory.

Sources for Figures

1. Adapted from O.D. Duncan, et al., METROPOLIS AND REGION, The Johns Hopkins Press, Baltimore, 1960, p. 94.
2. Adapted. Ibid., p. 97.
3. Adapted from B.J.L. Berry, P.G. Goheen, and H. Goldstein, METROPOLITAN AREA DEFINITION: A RE-EVALUATION OF CONCEPT AND STATISTICAL PRACTICE, (revised), U.S. Department of Commerce, Bureau of the Census, Working Paper 28, p. 22, Figure 11.
4. Adapted from NATIONAL TRANSPORTATION ACT: HEARINGS BEFORE THE COMMITTEE ON COMMERCE, 91st Cong., 2d Sess. on S.924 and S.2425, Serial 91-69, U.S. Government Printing Office, Washington, D.C., 1970, p. 196.
5. Adapted. B.J.L. Berry, et al., op. cit., pp. 28-29, Figure 18.
6. Adapted from John Friedmann and John Miller, "The Urban Field," JOURNAL OF THE AMERICAN INSTITUTE OF PLANNERS, Vol. 31, No. 4, November 1965, p. 314.
7. Adapted from THE NEW YORK TIMES, March 23, 1971, p. 1.
8. Adapted from Niles Hansen, RURAL POVERTY AND THE URBAN CRISIS: A STRATEGY FOR REGIONAL DEVELOPMENT, Indiana University Press, Bloomington, 1970.
9. Adapted from Bureau of the Budget, SIMPLIFYING FEDERAL AID TO STATES AND COMMUNITIES, Executive Office of the President, Bureau of the Budget, Washington, D.C., March 1970, p. 6.
10. H.S. Perloff, et al., REGIONS, RESOURCES AND ECONOMIC GROWTH, The Johns Hopkins Press, Baltimore, 1960, p. 5.

4

Markets and Planning Regions for Transportation

William Alonso,
University of California, Berkeley

Introduction

Transportation differs from most other market goods and services. A market is the forum for transactions between willing buyers and willing sellers, where prices serve as a cybernetic control to determine quantities and distributions. But in the United States, as in other market economies, the transportation activity is thoroughly regulated by public and semi-public institutions that usually set prices and often the supply quantity, frequency, and terms of service. Buyers, and most especially sellers, have little range in which to engage in the processes of bargaining, comparison, and adjustment that are implicit in the paradigm of a market.

The arguments for having transportation operate in a regulated rather than in a free market are well-known. It frequently exhibits many if not all of the conditions that make it difficult or impossible for a conventional market to work: it is the source and the subject of externalities; marginal costs may be lower than average costs; pricing and exclusion are frequently difficult; a lesser or greater degree of local monopoly is commonplace; and so forth. This paper does not discuss these points in detail.[a] Rather it points out that in transporta-

---

[a]During the Rand Conference on Regional Transportation Planning many of the experts present were of the opinion that much current regulation is unnecessary and counterproductive, and that many transportation decisions should be freed to market forces. For instance, it was argued that marginal costs are not lower than average costs for most transportation enterprises, and that intermodal competition greatly lessens the chances of natural monopolies. However, I am not arguing here whether the present degree of regulation of transportation enterprises in this country is either excessive or insufficient, but rather that, for the reasons given, regulation will be greater in this industry than in others. It seemed to me that much of the emphasis by others on the advantages of a self-regulating market came from a narrower definition of the topic and a shorter time perspective than is used in this paper. This narrower view focuses on the economics of carriers operating upon a mature base of infrastructure and a basically stable economic geography, so that most decisions and adjustments are seen as marginal, both for the carriers and for improvements of the infrastructure base. My emphasis derives from a sense that the transportation and communication system is still evolving rapidly, and that many of the decisions involve lumpy investments fraught with externalities, so that transportation changes affect deeply the spatial structure of the society. Among the rapidly changing elements in transportation I would cite aviation, containerization, urban traffic, information transmission, fuel transportation and energy transmission. Among the changes in spatial organization, I would point to the absolute loss in population of half the counties in this country, and to the rapid growth of many urban areas.

tion we are not dealing with a free and competitive market that might be improved through planning. We are dealing instead with markets that are controlled and regulated to a large degree, and therefore only quasi-markets. Yet the paradox is that in spite of such control and regulation, these quasi-markets are essentially unplanned.

Transportation, including communication, is regulated by governmental and quasi-governmental institutions, and much of its actual operation occurs in a penumbra between the private and the public sectors. Mails, telephones, telegraphs, pipelines, railroads, airlines and airports, roads, and ports operate in this ambiguous zone. It is possible that the change would be barely perceptible if some of these were shifted to the public sector, or out of it, since transportation and communication are already effectively a thoroughly socialized sector. But, then, why does there arise the issue of planning what is already controlled? Obviously, because there are some functions, termed "planning," that are different from control and regulation.

Characteristics of Transportation and Regional Development

Before discussing the possible modes and purposes of regional transportation planning, it will be useful to review some of the characteristics of transportation and regional development in some detail, because the difficulties for comprehensive planning in this sector may in their own way be as problematic as the operation of a free market. Just as the regulated transportation sector preserves a number of market characteristics (for instance, demand is fairly free to find its own level), the planning function can only be incorporated into certain strategic junctures and territories; and it would be naive to think that comprehensive regional planning is structurally possible for this sector, even if it were desirable.

Economics, with what Walter Isard has called "the Anglo-Saxon bias," has tended to exclude from its concerns the systematic consideration of space and distance. The world of the economist dances on the head of a geographically dimensionless pin. It is therefore not surprising that traditional economics should fail to deal effectively with the transportation activity, which is spatial in its very essence. Yet an economy functions through exchange as much as by transformation, and transportation and communication are the central processes of exchange in space. Since the main body of economics has assumed them away, it provides little guidance for understanding or for planning in this sector. This is reflected here by my reliance on some ideas outside of the mainstream, many of which are admittedly underdeveloped and confused.

Transportation and Communication:
Instruments for Integration

Economic and social development may be viewed as the process of integrating the society. Integration is the degree to which people and resources are able to move and change so as to achieve their full potential. Lack of integration is the degree to which they are prevented from doing so. Like the cup of tea that is both half full and half empty, transportation and communication are among the principal instruments for integration, together with money and a common body of law and institutions; but to the degree that transportation and communication are costly, they are the principal transaction costs in operating the system, and they prevent its perfect integration. Social integration, of course, involves other considerations, but they do not concern us here.

It is easy to point to instances of lack of integration. Lack of integration in a labor market may face a firm with a labor shortage in a depressed labor-surplus area where the population is dispersed. Vast mineral wealth, such as oil in Alaska or ore in central Australia, may be of no economic value if it cannot be shipped to markets. A colonialized economy, whether a poor country or a poor region, suffers from a lack of internal integration—importing and exporting to the outside, but failing to realize the full advantage of the potential interrelatedness of its own resources. Agricultural regions with poor access to markets suffer from low land values and low incomes and are less productive than land of comparable quality, because the value of the output justifies lower rates of capital investment and fertilizers. The decline in a base industry in an isolated labor market leads to prolonged unemployment because workers do not have access to alternative employment. In some cases, workers are unable to migrate because they are tied down by houses they cannot sell and retirement plans that are not transferrable. Industry may find such an area unattractive because its goods transport system is inadequate, because its salesmen and managers cannot travel easily, and because there is insufficient access to business services.

Although a lack of integration, which keeps factors from their full use, is detrimental to the national system, it can sometimes prove a local boon. Conversely, achieving integration can sometimes spell local disaster. Thus, all ports and transshipment points are a break in the integration of the system and owe their local development to that break. Further integration of the system, such as containerization, lessens the importance of these places and is detrimental to their local economies while benefiting the nation as a whole. Similarly, the improvement of communications and the rapid movement of people can shift activities about, hurting one locality and benefiting another, although resulting in a net national gain. Thus, improvements in telephone and other means of transmitting information, coupled with the use of standardized data in computers and the massive improvement of air connections among major cities, have resulted in the possibility of separation of headquarters from production facilities and have accelerated the concentration of head offices in major cities. On the other hand, improvements in communication and transportation have also permitted the dispersal of many plants from the great capitals to provincial centers. Development and integration manifest themselves in change, including geographic change.

Spatial Integration

We are all familiar with depictions of the national territory in the form of conventional maps and with other types of "maps" of the nation's spatial structure represented as tables of air tariffs, road mileages, freight rates, and so forth. If we were to think of these "maps" in a geometric form, they would not have the familiar geometry of the conventional map's Euclidean plane. Rather, they would be complex surfaces, called hyper-surfaces, which may be imagined as a convoluted crumpling of cellophane over the traditional map. The most direct route from one point to another on the hyper-surface, called the geodesic, would seldom coincide with the most direct route on the conventional map. In a hyper-surface of air accessbility or cost, Los Angeles and New York would lie much closer to each other than would either Portland, Maine, or Portland, Oregon, to Saint Louis. The geodesic path of real access from one mountain town to another may be through a distant larger city, although the two towns may be near neighbors as the crow flies.

In many ways, the spatial integration of the economy may be viewed as the progressive smoothing out of these functional hyper-surfaces, so that they coincide more closely with the shape of conventional geographic space, which is presumably the limiting case.[1] Bridges span rivers or bays and eliminate lengthy detours, cut and fill straightens roads through hilly country, and tunnels shoot through mountains. Pipelines, aircraft, telephones, microwave, and coaxial cables have been added to the traditional modes of roads and ships to facilitate the movement of people, things, and ideas, making it cheaper, easier, and faster for them to relate to each other and thus reducing frictional transaction costs and integrating the national space-economy. Everywhere becomes nearer to everywhere else, and every location becomes more nearly equivalent to every other.

In this respect, the degree of United States integration is striking when compared to other nations. Needless to say, the underdeveloped nations are the most poorly integrated, but even Europe is struggling to catch up. This is true on a continental scale in the European Common Market and in the Comecon of the socialist states, but it also is true within single European nations. The French case is the best known. Communication is easy along the spokes that link other centers to Paris, but it is poor from one of the provincial cities to another. Even cities near to each other must often exchange goods or travellers via Paris. Overall, the degree of spatial integration corresponds closely to the degree of development. This would seem to be the case even within the United States. For instance, the ratio of road distance to air distance from Boston to all other metropolitan areas in the United States is 1.16, with a standard deviation of 0.05. On the other hand, Asheville, North Carolina, (an Appalachian metropolitan area), and Lewiston, Maine, both share an average ratio of road to air distance of 1.21, with a standard deviation of 0.07.

The reduction of functional distances clearly calls for the application of capital and technology but the result is not usually a geographically uniform improvement. The opening of a canal or a pipeline or some other major step cuts a geodesic trench in the functional hyper-surface of that activity. While improving markedly the comparative advantages of locations in that trench, it reduces the comparative advantage of other locations. Thus, overall development is usually accompanied by disruptions and declines in certain localities. There are many present-day equivalents to the obsolescence of road houses when faster vehicles made them unnecessary as overnight stopping places. All over the developed world many urban areas and market centers are declining as a result of overall development.

Gain and Loss

The reason for dwelling on the rather obvious point that an overall gain may be composed of individual losses as well as gains is that this is a central question for the regionalization of transportation planning, and one often ignored under a bland assumption that an overall gain is a gain for all. This effect of transportation development denies to planning in this sector the mild comforts of being guided by the simple-minded version of Pareto optimality, which holds that a desirable improvement leaves some better off and none worse off. Let us consider two examples.

First, as planes become bigger and faster, they become uneconomic for short hops and greatly favor longer-distance trunk lines. These advances in air transportation favor the closer linking and the growth of the nation's major cities but place the smaller centers in a position of comparative disadvantage. On the ground, it is another matter. The airport is a source of localized disadvantages, producing congestion and air and noise pollution, so that within the metropolitan area or the complex of metropolitan areas that a major airport serves the locality that hosts the airport loses rather than gains.

Second, consider that the principal form of national aid and investment in Appalachia has been highway development. The general idea of this investment is to draw Appalachian communities functionally closer to the rest of the country and thus share in its general prosperity. But these roads lead out as well as in. They permit the opening of local markets to distant suppliers who may compete with less efficient local producers. They reduce the pull of raw materials for the location of industry by making it cheaper to ship the resources to outside locations that offer other advantages. Thus, it is not clear that this investment will increase the total amount of economic activity in Appalachia. If it integrates the region with the rest of the country, it will tend to bring per capita incomes into line with those in other regions, but quite possibly at the price of accelerated outmigration of people and activities.

Within Appalachia some of the same questions are repeated. The trouble with Appalachia is that it is under-urbanized, and the strategy of growth centers is based on concentrating dispersed economic activities to get the economies of scale and externalities of larger cities. But clearly this means that within Appalachia some communities will gain while others will lose. In brief, both within Appalachia and for Appalachia vis-à-vis the rest of the country the uneven incidence of costs and benefits raises difficult questions of equity and efficiency. These questions involve conflicts of values and interests that call for political resolution as much as for technical analysis.

The preceding examples raise two important distinctions that must be kept in mind in a discussion of planning regions for transportation. These are the distinctions between adaptive and developmental issues, and the distinction between line and site problems.

Adaptive and Developmental Issues

Adaptive issues in planning have to do with the functioning of an existing system. Instances of this are congestion in a megapolitan corridor; systems for the assembly, storage, processing and marketing of agricultural products; and issues of pollution or ecological balance. Developmental issues have to do with the creation of new activities, or a massive expansion or redirection of existing ones. Instances of this would be the better integration of Appalachia with the rest of America to promote its economic development, or a consideration of the consequences of the Arkansas-Verdigris Navigation System. This distinction is not a hard and fast one. For instance, the adaptive problems of the greater New York region appear to have substantial impact on its attractiveness for people and its economic activity and thus affect its development. Similarly, it has often been the experience in developing countries that major road links initially predicated on the adaptive reason of latent demand for traffic between major cities have in fact had as a major consequence the development of agriculture and primary industry in territories along the route that have been made newly accessible to markets.

Line and Site Issues

The other distinction is between issues of line and issues of site. Commonly, for instance, there will be general agreement on the need for a new airport in the vicinity of a large city, but there will be universal rejection by localities of serving as a host for the facility. However, once a major highway link between distant cities has been decided upon, diverse districts may compete to have it go through their territory. Whether to connect some distant points is an issue of line; where the physical facilities shall actually be placed is an issue of site.

Concentration or Dispersal

The most general question arising from the geographic shifts of people and activities that accompany development and national integration is whether the principal effect will be one of concentration or of dispersal. For instance, in recent years the White House and the principal federal agencies have expressed their territorial policies as some ill-defined "balanced growth." On the one hand, since integration produces a phenomenon of near universal accessibility, transport considerations play a greatly diminished role in the location of economic activity. In terms of location theory, industry loses its transport-orientation and becomes footloose. Being footloose, many have argued that it can and will disperse, seeking local advantages of resources, labor, and amenities. To exaggerate this point slightly, since the locational pulls of transport costs are much diminished, location may become nearly randomized and therefore rather uniform over the territory. Others have argued, I among them, that this locational freedom will manifest itself rather in the freedom to choose locations that provide the advantages of scale and agglomeration. The consequence of this would be increasing spatial concentration.

Although there is clear evidence of increasing spatial concentration in the United States, the process and the resulting patterns are extremely difficult to describe and, in candor, imperfectly understood. That there is concentration there can be no question. Two-thirds of the more than three thousand counties lost population in the last decade, continuing a long-range trend. The great majority of population growth took place in the metropolitan areas. But beyond this the process becomes very complicated. For instance, it was not the largest urban areas that grew most rapidly, but the middle-sized ones. Although the smaller cities and metropolitan areas did very poorly in the aggregate, a far greater proportion of them exhibited rapid growth than in the early decades of the century.[2] Business services and headquarters grew more rapidly in the larger areas (but not in the very largest), but personal services and retailing grew faster in the smaller areas. Manufacturing production plans seem to be moving from larger to smaller centers, but the administrative and sales offices of manufacturing industries appear to be moving in the other direction. Within the vast megapolitan constellations, it was the smaller metropolitan areas that grew rapidly. And nineteen new metropolitan areas have emerged in the last ten years, most of them within the orbit of larger metropolitan centers.

This complex pattern may be pictured as the contrapuntal patterns of the ripples on the surface of a pool into which several heavy rocks have been dropped. The waves from the different rocks crisscross each other and the returning echoes from the shores. The problem of description and interpretation is comparable to that of trying to guess the number, weight, and point of impact of the rocks from periodic and rather fuzzy photographs of a maddeningly complex pattern of ripples. But some generalizations may be hazarded. Economic activity and interaction now take place along a complicated network linking cities, and therefore the transportation system must serve a nation of cities rather than a nation of regions. But this has not meant simply that the problem has been transformed from one of opening and penetrating regional territories by river-like transport systems to one of linking city-dots on the national map by means of a network. Rather the problem is a three-fold one: serving conventional regions devoted primarily to primary activities, linking cities, and serving the vast urban regions that have formed by the joint effect of greatly extended suburbanization and the clustering of metropolitan centers into megapolitan complexes.[3]

Another generalization may be put forth, although very little seems to be known specifically of the matter. This is that the pattern evolves according to the evolving constraints of certain critical distances. For instance, the interlocking commuting fields of metropolitan areas are the effect of some rather yielding maximum commuting range. The location of plants and offices of multi-establishment enterprises are tied together by rubber bands corresponding to the distance and mode that enables managers, salesmen, and technicians to visit these locations easily, often making the round trip within a day.[4] In spite of telephones, picture transmission, and other devices for rapid communication, many activities seem to continue to need face-to-face contact and certain semisocial networks and situations, and these activities will seek locations within the one-square mile area of the true downtown of a metropolis.[5] Traditional economics has done rather poorly with such critical phenomena, having dealt primarily with monotonic relationships. Thus, economic representations of regional structure and linkages tend to ignore the lumpiness and grain that results from such critical distances. Not only is existing theory insufficient to this task, there is also a poverty of systematic data for the phenomena involved, partly because of the delimitation of census territories in which data are gathered and presented. Thus, most of the evidence is anecdotal. But these critical distances are important to the analysis of regional development and transportation because they, in effect, operationally define the geographic extent of a place. They define the territorial extension of a locality and tell us how far away "here" extends to. In these functional terms, the "here" of an urban area may cover considerable territory and be quite different according to the function considered. Further, this territory, being a functional one, may be a complex hyper-surface that cannot be thought of as a conventional contiguous, compact region. Airplanes, computer terminals, warehouse locations, and other components of the functioning system may well result in functional accessibility among dispersed locations, skipping over intervening ones.

Feasibility of Regional Transportation Planning

In light of the views outlined above, the question of regional transportation planning can be seen to be no simple matter of dividing the national territory into some number of multi-state regions and creating an authority for each region charged with comprehensive transportation planning. Transportation planning cannot be administered by such a planning structure and its implied processes, just as it cannot be left to a free market. Transportation and communication are among the principal forms of exchange in any society, and they act as the lubrication of the economic system. But transportation has no purpose in itself. It is preeminently characterized by externalities, and no simple regionalization of information gathering, forecasting, and decision can serve a nation that is so complexly structured. Since transportation is only an instrumental function, its planning structure must be adapted to the structure and needs of the larger system in terms of the hierarchy of spans of decision among modes, sectors, and territories, so that proper account may be taken of the consequences of actions on other elements.

Planning and Closure

Let us return to the question of the meaning of planning for a system that is already regulated. A central, if often implicit, premise for planning is that it deals with a system with a fair degree of closure. That is, it is thought that there is a collection of elements that are so interrelated that their mutual effects must be considered simultaneously, and that these relations and interdependencies are not swamped by outside influences and disturbances or attenuated to triviality by leakages out of the system. To be sure, the difference between planning and regulation is one of degree, but the direction of the difference is that planning tries to look at a broader set of relations and purposes and to consider a longer perspective. Regulation, on the other hand, responds to issues only as they are raised, and thus proceeds step by step, with a narrower agenda of concerns.

Regulation is the steersman, planning the navigator. Regulation exercises greater control but is on a short feedback loop. Planning relies more on predictability, and for this reason it must deal with a fairly closed system.

The Problems of Large-Scale Regions

Large-scale regions are not very good for comprehensive transportation planning for several reasons. First, they are blurred regions that are difficult to bound. They are essentially nodal regions for which it is relatively easy to identify a core or spine, but from this center they diffuse through space so that any bounding is arbitrary. Second, they change considerably over time with changes in technology and the structure of the economy they serve. Thus, any initial regionalization of the country will become obsolete sooner or later. Third, the regionalization that would correspond to one mode would not correspond to another. A regionalization connected by highways would match very poorly a regionalization based on pipelines or on air travel. This will aggravate the first two problems considerably: that of the diffuseness of boundaries and that of changes over time. Fourth, for the three previous reasons, a division of the nation into transportation regions will suffer from the conflict between defining clear jurisdictional boundaries between regions and the tendencies to overlap, interpenetrate, and interlock. A national division into planning regions would have the neatness of a tiled floor, but the reality of the transportation network more closely resembles a complicated overlay of spider webs.

Fifth, a regionalization based on the large-scale regional structure of the transport system would cut across the grain of other bases of regional definition. For instance, the region to be considered to integrate Appalachia with the rest of the economy would obviously have to include the great urban centers of the Atlantic Coast and of the Midwest. Whereas the present Appalachia Region is a north-south valley of economic distress between these two mountain ranges of economic development, transportation regions addressed to the problem of linking the poor to the rich would tend to be east-west slices.

This type of warp and weft will be repeated time and again. Most planning regions are defined by some common characteristic, such as a common economic specialization in some primary industry, a continuing urban spread, economic distress, a common culture, or a commensalistic relation to some major geographic feature such as a valley or a lake. Of course, such regions will contain a transportation element for their own internal functioning. But the role of long distance transportation (and therefore of large multi-state transport systems or regions) is to link and integrate these diverse regions, not on the basis of their similarity but on the basis of their differences and complementarities. Thus, large-scale regionalization for transportation will typically cut across other types of regionalization.

In brief, the division of the nation into large transportation planning regions runs into serious problems because of the difficulty of getting reasonable closure in the system, either within the transport sector or between it and the other sectors of the economy. Lack of sufficient closure would create difficulties for planning that reflect the difficulties of a free market in this sector. Insufficient closure would make it difficult to predict (which is essential to planning) because of the many important elements outside the system. Control and effectuation would suffer for this same reason. But beyond these technical and administrative problems, the lack of closure presents great difficulties for political reasons. Decisions must be made that hurt some while benefiting others, and many of the beneficiaries and the injured will be outside the region's system. Thus the political tradeoffs and bargaining within the region result neither in a full accounting of the pluses and minuses for the most efficient aggregate solution, nor in the most equitable solution from the national point of view, since losing outsiders find it difficult to represent their interests. This consideration is of particular importance because, for reasons argued below, transportation planning is technically weak, and the shortness of technical legitimacy throws most of the burden of decision onto political processes.

One National Region

Of course, it might be argued that if the whole country were viewed as a single region the problems of lack of closure would be overcome. But the trouble with national planning of transportation is that the nation is so big and complicated that no agency has the span or capacity to consider all of the interrelations simultaneously, and that a central planning body is too far away from the problems and the people who are involved in particular decisions. Two traditional approaches have been used to cope with these problems of overload and insufficient feedback. One is sectoral division. The Department of Transportation was created to deal with this sector and divisions within it to deal with particular modes. The other is regional division. The main shortcoming of sectoral division is insufficient consideration of interrelations with other sectors. The shortcoming of regionalization is insufficient consideration of other regions. A sectoral regionalization, such as a transportation planning region, would obviously suffer from shortcomings of both types. The question is whether it would have compensating advantages by being more general than a particular transportation mode and smaller than the nation but big enough to encompass some functional subsystems within its boundaries.

Planning Problems Unique to Transportation Sector

My previous arguments against sectoral regionalization were based on the lack of functional and spatial closure of such transportation planning regions. In addition, general transportation planning regions would run into certain planning problems that are more severe for transportation than for the planning of other sectors. The first of these is that virtually all of the costs and benefits that would arise are external to transportation itself. The consequences internal to transportation of particular rates, regulations, or facilities are probably no harder to predict than comparable projections in other kinds of planning. But the significant effects are outside of the transportation system itself: certain areas may prosper or decline, resources become valuable or worthless, whole industries come into being, and complex ecological chains may be altered. These amplified second- and third-round consequences are much harder to foresee and evaluate than first-round ones, and thus the preponderance of externalities in the case of transportation makes forecasting and planning for it particularly difficult.

The second characteristic is closely related to the first. It is extraordinarily difficult to distinguish between distributional and total effects. For instance, a new road link may bring industry to a given area, and this will conventionally be counted as a gain. But if the road does not create the industry but rather shifts its location from another area, the only gain would be the increased efficiency of the new location over the old one. Similarly, some transportation development may open to development some previously inaccessible resource. But the competition of this new resource may lower the value of some older competing ones. The difficulties here are of three kinds. The first, and closest to our earlier point, is that because of limited data and techniques it is usually extraordinarily difficult to identify all of the subsequent repercussions and thus to distinguish true increments from distributional shifts. Secondly, economic theory is in a state of considerable disarray for the evaluation of some of these effects, there being no general agreement among experts about whether certain changes should be counted as costs or benefits. The example of the new resource is of this kind, which in general includes transportation-induced changes in the value (or rent) of certain human or natural resources based on their relative scarcity and the inaccessibility of substitutes. The third difficulty is political. Costs and benefits of transportation are unevenly distributed, and, even if there were no technical difficulty in prediction, there would be no purely technical means of achieving equity between gainers and losers. This is a matter of conflicting interests, and therefore a political one. Because so many of the consequences of transportation take the form of an uneven incidence of costs and benefits in space, and because our principal mechanisms of government are organized on a territorial basis, the political negotiation will frequently take on a more explicit and vigorous form for transportation than for other forms of planning.

The third characteristic that makes transportation planning particularly difficult is the extraordinary combinatorial complexity of many of the problems encountered. For instance, except in special cases, the problem of the most economic way of linking by highway a given set of cities under a budget constraint cannot be solved by any known method in the sense that one can be confident of having found the best solution.[6] Basically, such problems are solved by trial and error, and the solutions arrived at tend to be satisfactory rather than optimal. This is in part the result of the discreteness or lumpiness of much transport investment that prevents the application of the calculus of variations in the search for solutions. It is also the consequence of the tendency of most planning problems to become explosively complex when territorial considerations are incorporated. Since transportation is spatial, it is particularly subject to this problem, which manifests itself in great technical difficulty in identifying the most promising alternatives toward an optimal solution. Since the technical planning body cannot be too sure of having come up with the "best" solution, it will find itself on technically weak footing and therefore singularly open to criticism and counterproposals.

A fourth characteristic is the high degree of substitutability among transportation and communication modes, and indeed between transportation and other factors. Thus, a firm that must communicate with a distant city may send a representative, or phone, or write a letter, or send a catalogue, or open a branch office. Energy may move by ship, by pipeline, or by electrical lines. Rapid delivery may be substituted for inventories, and, in general, the location of firms will consider the substitution of transportation for other factors. This high degree of substitutability results in a further degree of combinatorial complexity for reasons quite similar to those of the third point above, and similarly opens to question the optimality of any given solution.

A fifth characteristic of transportation is the long period involved between decision and execution, and between execution and the manifestation of consequences. A major transportation improvement takes many years and sometimes decades to decide upon and to carry out, and some further years before its effects can be seen clearly. Long time lags in the feedback loop preclude the possibility of fine-tuning and deny the possibility of experimentation. Indeed, political pressures and the interests of various client groups prevent all but minimal experimentation even for aspects that involve regulation (such as rates and service schedules) rather than major structural changes.

Recommendations

These various transportation characteristics do not deny the need to plan for it, although they do appear to deny the possibility of comprehensive regional master planning of transportation. Technically produced master planning does not make sense for systems that are open, technically indeterminate, politically sensitive, and slow to learn from experience. What seems to be needed is a set of mechanisms that is better adapted to the complex crosscurrents of sectors and areas of the society to be served, that provides forums for diverse viewpoints and information and for the negotiation of costs and benefits set in the context of existing governmental structure, and that provides a framework for making decisions about rather indeterminate projects. In other words, it cannot be a neat hierarchical organization, but rather it must be a flexible, overlapping system.

What seems needed is not the division of the nation into a permanent set of large transportation regions, but rather the better deployment of types of institutions that already exist. Aside from improvements of transportation planning by local and state governments, four general loci of transportation planning activity may be mentioned: (1) transportation planning by the Federal Government, (2) transportation planning by general regional planning authorities, (3) special transportation planning districts, and (4) special mission transportation planning.

Transportation planning at the national level can stand considerable improvement. It should be based to a larger extent on long-range forecasting and on the consistency of transportation policies with other relevant national policies. Perhaps foremost among these is the emerging "national growth policy," which attempts to formulate national goals and procedures to deal with the spatial distribution of the national population. Regardless of the particular objectives that may form the substance of this policy, transportation will undoubtedly be one of the central instrumentalities for carrying it out. At present, transportation, welfare, education, distressed areas and other programs are following narrower objectives and, in so doing, they create a great deal of implicit and largely unintended policy on the larger issues. Attempts by such groups as the Urban Affairs Council to bring about greater clarity and consistency among the various government programs are steps in a continuing struggle that can never be entirely won. Some of the concepts and procedures of the French indicative planning deserve consideration. The problems that these approaches encounter under American anti-trust law, as did the conceptually similar National Recovery Administration of the New Deal, should be less severe within the transportation sector which, as discussed earlier, lies largely in the public and quasi-public domain.

In addition to developing long-range national planning of the transportation sector and coordinating this planning with other areas of national policy within the Executive Branch, some other considerations may be mentioned. First among these is a clear recognition that a great deal, if not most, transportation planning at the national level is done by Congress on an *ad hoc* basis of porkbarrel, pet projects, log-rolling, and sectional interests. It would be unrealistic to think that this would change drastically, but it is entirely possible that planning by the Executive Branch, done in consultation with members of the key congressional committees, would provide a context of well-formulated policies and preliminary specification of projects that would somewhat improve the rationality of the congressional process of decision in this area. Secondly, and similarly, our earlier discussion stressed that a number of intrinsic difficulties in planning and evaluating transportation projects makes it commonly unlikely that a particular project be demonstrably optimal or even beneficial. Planning and evaluation of particular transportation elements would be greatly strengthened if they were formulated in the context of general policy rather than each element having to stand by itself.

Third, as discussed previously, national transportation planning is too large and complex an undertaking to expect total coordination of decisions and centralization of information within the Department of Transportation. Its internal organization might consider the formation of regional desks to serve as clearinghouses for the vertically organized divisions and, to the degree possible, for the independent regulatory boards and those divisions of other Departments that have to do with transportation.

There already exist several broad regional agencies, larger than states but covering only portions of the nation. These agencies, such as the various regional commissions, metropolitan governments or planning agencies, and Councils of Governments, engage in general planning, more or less at a comprehensive, integrated level. Clearly much could be done to improve their performance in transportation planning. Quite often transportation is controlled by powerful agencies that proceed so independently of these regional bodies that the latter are frequently simply uninformed of what is going on. Federal law and administrative practice could be used to enlist the participation of these bodies in the planning of transportation for their regions and to integrate transportation into the other sectors of their consideration.

In some cases, where such general purpose regional bodies do not exist, or where the territory that must be considered for transportation planning differs significantly from the region as defined for other purposes, special transportation planning districts may be indicated. Such a transportation planning district would try to do integrated planning within the transportation sector, including most if not all the various modes of transportation and communication. The roles of such agencies, however, would be extremely complicated since they involve not only planning in the conventional technical sense, but also the function of clearinghouse and brokerage among the various local governments and the powerful state and federal agencies involved.

The fourth type of regional transportation planning agency would have as its mandate a problem or project of special significance, rather than general long-range transportation planning for a region. Instances of this would be agencies concerned with the problems of high-speed intermetropolitan travel within megalopolis or with the developmental aspects of the Arkansas-Verdigris Navigation System. It would seem that such agencies would frequently be as much operational as planning agencies, at least in their mature stages, since such major problems or projects usually involve the expenditure of massive funds. Even in cases such as the Northeast Corridor, where the operational function is viewed as research and development, the R&D function is so lumpy that the costs and the time involved are large.

These four classes of regional transportation planning are probably not exhaustive, but they remind us of some basic issues involved in forming regional transportation planning bodies. The first, and most basic, is the relation of the planning activity to the sources of power and control. Unless this is a functioning link, planning is merely decorative. Therefore any regional transportation planning agency must serve at least two functions. The first is what is commonly meant by planning: collection of information, forecasting, and development and evaluation of alternatives for action. In the presumed absence of autarchic power in the regional agency, the second function is that of clearinghouse and forum for negotiation. Since regional transportation bodies are unlikely to enjoy much autonomous power for action or control, the institutional architecture and location of the agency must be so designed that they can perform this second function. Needless to say, this is extremely difficult.

The second general issue has to do, again, with the definition of the region. At least for some of the types of regional transportation planning mentioned, it is not necessary to define regional boundaries. Rather, the region is defined by its core, and the boundaries are indeterminate zones of diminishing interest. This type of regional definition is impossible where the agency has taxing or quasi-legislative functions, for these functions must have exact territorial bounds, but it is quite possible for some special project agencies, and for organizations whose principal function is to provide intelligence and to serve as negotiation clearinghouses.

The third general issue is temporal rather than territorial. In the case of certain planning organizations defined around a particular issue or problem or based on the territorial extension of a particular activity, it may be expected that there will be enough changes over time that the need for their existence, their structure and the spatial definition of their region should be reconsidered. It would seem prudent, given the tendency of organizations to endure after the basis for their existence is gone, to include a terminal date in the charter of any regional transportation agencies in which the Federal Government played a role. The purpose of this would be not so much to economize on the operating costs of the agencies as to maintain the flexibility necessary to adapt to changing circumstances. Otherwise, any set of regional agencies created for today's needs might become obsolete and, like old generals, end up fighting the last war rather than the current one.

Notes

1. The author is indebted for these ideas to William Warntz, who expressed them in conversation. They are reflected in his "Global Science and the Tyranny of Space," PAPERS OF THE REGIONAL SCIENCE ASSOCIATION, 19, 1967.

2. W. Alonso, and E. Medrich, "Spontaneous Growth Centers in Twentieth

Century American Urbanization," in Niles M. Hansen (ed.), GROWTH CENTERS IN REGIONAL ECONOMIC DEVELOPMENT, New York, The Free Press, 1972.

3. See B.J.L. Berry and E. Neils, "Location, Size, and Shape of Cities as Influenced by Environmental Factors: The Urban Environment Writ Large," in H.S. Perloff (ed.), THE QUALITY OF THE URBAN ENVIRONMENT, The Johns Hopkins Press, Baltimore, 1969, and J.R.P. Friedmann and J. Miller, "The Urban Field," JOURNAL OF THE AMERICAN INSTITUTE OF PLANNERS, November 1965.

4. W.F. Luttrel, FACTORY LOCATION AND INDUSTRIAL MOVEMENT, National Institute of Economic and Social Research, London, 1962.

5. The one-mile critical distance is suggested in Regional Plan Association, THE OFFICE INDUSTRY (prepared by R.B. Armstrong; edited by B. Pushkarev and A. Donheiser), final prepublication draft, March 1970. On this issue the work of Goffman and others on non-verbal communication is very suggestive.

6. Britton Harris has written extensively on this problem. See, for instance, his "Problems in Regional Science," PAPERS OF THE REGIONAL SCIENCE ASSOCIATION, XXI, 1968.

5 Regional Development, Resource Allocation, and Transportation

John H. Cumberland,
University of Maryland

Introduction[a]

Transportation generates important positive and negative economic externalities. Because of the geographic and spatial distribution of these transport-related externalities, regional[b] economic development is significantly affected by transportation, and regional development in turn significantly affects transportation objectives. Recognition of the close interdependence between transportation systems and economic development is indicated by recent proposals to establish regional agencies for the coordination of transportation planning.[1] The purpose of this brief survey is to examine some aspects of the United States experience in regional development in order to assess possibilities of improving performance in both the fields of transportation and economic development.[2]

Some Basic Issues in Regional Development

Historically, conflicts have emerged over unresolved issues in regional development both because of failure to identify objectives clearly, and because of the existence of multiple objectives. These issues have been resolved or compromised in various ways under successive U.S. regional development programs, but many of them remain relevant to current policy debates. While these regional development issues fall far short of exhausting all of the problems involved in transportation planning, they are all sufficiently related to transportation problems to merit examination.

One of the earliest issues to be faced in regional development was the basic question of whether it was even an appropriate objective for federal assistance. Debate has been largely based upon two separate theories of resource allocation and productivity. The competitive national market theory opposes the use of national resources for regional development programs on the basis that national

---

[a]The author is grateful to Alan Carlin of the Environmental Protection Agency and James Stucker of RAND for valuable comments on an earlier version of the paper but bears full responsibility for any remaining shortcomings.

[b]The term *regional* will be used to refer to any sub-national area, such as a county, SMSA, watershed, transport area, or multi-state unit.

market forces allocate the flow of resources to those regions where their application will be most productive. Labor and capital, in seeking their highest return, are assumed to distribute themselves in relation to the geographic endowment of natural resources so that regional and national incomes are maximized. The regional persistence of below-average incomes or above-average unemployment is taken as evidence of excessive population in a region with respect to its resources and productivity. The appropriate policy to follow in the case of lagging regions is then assumed to be to encourage the outmigration of labor, capital, and other mobile resources into growing regions of high productivity. Under this theory, aid to lagging regions can only succeed in delaying necessary productivity adjustments and in depressing total national income.

Opposed to the competitive national market theory is the regional adjustment theory, which is based upon a denial of mobility and other assumptions of the competitive model. The regional adjustment model supports the concept of aid to lagging regions on the basis of labor immobility, capital immobility, and assumed dynamic and cumulative factors in regional development. Its proponents assert that labor is often highly immobile, and indeed that because of high locational preferences, migration should not be a precondition of employment. Aid to regions is also justified because imperfect knowledge and institutional rigidities constrict the free flow of capital into less developed regions. Market factors may also fail to provide the regional development necessary to result in economies of scale and agglomeration which could lead to self-sustaining growth. Proponents of the regional adjustment theory also argue for local assistance to faltering regions on the basis of dynamic processes under which initial economic distress leads to self-reinforcing neglect of public sector expenditures, out-migration of the youngest and most productive members of the labor force, and to other cumulative downward movements that could be arrested by early public assistance.

Of all the issues to be considered in this section, that of whether federal aid should be allocated for regional development and transportation is the least unresolved. Following sections will indicate that the question of whether or not to provide federal aid to lagging and distressed regions has been answered affirmatively, and that transportation has been an important focus for providing aid to regional development.

An issue closely related to the foregoing has been that of what role if any planning should play in determining the form and amount of the aid. In general, the practice has been for the Federal Government to limit its planning role to the establishment of minimal guidelines, leaving the detailed design to state and local governments. While this policy has had the advantage of emphasizing regional objectives and local knowledge of local conditions, it has also largely ignored important questions of resolving conflicts between competing regions and between regional and national objectives. This issue is also inseparable from the problem of optimal transportation planning and remains to be resolved.

Another major issue in regional economic development has been the equity versus efficiency question. It has been difficult to resolve because the regions suffering most from poverty and unemployment are generally those in which productivity is lowest and in which aid is least likely to result in high productivity payoffs from the national point of view. While equity considerations favor investment in the most distressed regions, efficiency objectives favor investment in high productivity regions. This dilemma has resulted in compromise and in acceptance of both objectives with recognition of the nature of the tradeoffs involved, which can only be resolved on a political basis. The equity versus efficiency argument must clearly be faced in transportation planning, as well as in regional development.

A similar but distinct issue in regional development has been that of aid to places versus aid to persons. The well established principle in the United States of providing regional development assistance to lagging regions is usually justified in part, but not exclusively, on equity and humanitarian bases relating to the concentration of poverty and unemployment in such regions. In practice, however, regional development programs have usually resulted in expenditures channeled through established enterprises in the private sector and through existing public sector programs. Rather than emphasizing investment in human capital and raising productivity of the disadvantaged, most regional economic development programs have been based upon investment in physical capital. Consequently, regional development programs have tended to benefit the affluent rather than the indigent. Despite implicit and sometimes explicit assumptions that regional economic development assistance would eventually trickle down to the poor, most of these programs have been designed primarily for economic development of the region rather than for alleviation of poverty. Growing recognition of this fact is becoming a major issue in transportation planning as well, especially in urban ghetto areas.

Closely related is the issue of relocation of jobs versus relocation of persons. The objective of efficiency in resource allocation provides a strong argument for assisting persons in labor surplus areas to migrate to growth areas in order to bring labor into equilibrium with resource endowment and economic opportunity. However, recognition of workers as human beings with strong location preferences rather than simply as factors of production focuses attention upon the human cost of migration and upon the rationality of accepting reduced income as the price of non-migration. Migration as an economic policy also draws objections on obvious political grounds, as well as from the concern that the young and productive are the most likely to migrate, raising the danger of cumulative regional decline.

Relocation of persons is also clearly a factor in transportation planning, not only because efficient transportation can serve as an alternative to relocation of residence, but also because construction of large-scale transportation systems has become a major cause of relocating residences and businesses, especially in urban areas.

A persistent and unresolved issue in U.S. regional development experience has been concentration versus dispersion of development resources. The fact that resources available for regional development programs are necessarily limited forces decisions to be made as to whether to concentrate this aid geographically or to disperse it widely. Arguments based upon equity and political feasibility have been effective in securing broad geographic distribution of most types of regional development programs in the United States. Programs initially designed to meet specific problems in particular regions have often been extended to other regions where these programs are less relevant and less efficient. Constitutional requirements may explain some of the dispersion; the rest may be due to a general tendency toward unselective proliferation of successful programs. Opposing this tendency has been a growing concern for concentrating limited development resources in those areas where they have the greatest probability of success and lasting results. This is seen most clearly in the current emphasis upon limiting aid to growth poles—on the hypothesis that rather than disperse aid so broadly that it is ineffective, development resources should be concentrated where economies of scale and agglomeration offer opportunities for sustained, cumulative, long-run development.

However, the growth pole argument is weakened by limited knowledge about spatial relationships, about interregional linkages, and about interrelationships between regional and national economic development objectives. Although traditional economic analysis has neglected the spatial variable, increasing attention has been given recently to location theory, interregional linkages, urban transformation, and environmental change. In addition to being critical questions in regional development, these problems of concentration, dispersion, and spatial interrelationships are clearly central to transportation analysis and planning.

Finally, among the traditional questions in U.S. regional development planning has been that of small regions versus large, or more generally, the problem of defining the appropriate region for development planning and assistance. Although there exists increasing acceptance for defining a region in terms of the problem to be analyzed, the solution of this problem continues to be impeded by the aforementioned lack of knowledge about spatial interrelationships between economic and other social variables. For operational reasons, a strong case can be made for treating the smallest political decision-making unit, i.e., a county or SMSA, as a building block unit that can be aggregated flexibly into various larger regions that are coterminous with the dimensions of various problems. Conceptually, this approach has much to recommend it for purposes of transportation planning, despite the fact that it places heavy demands upon resources for data collection and analysis. At the other end of the spectrum from the county region is the entire earth. As population densities, urbanization, and industrialization become more widespread and intensive around the globe, and as accelerated communication and interdependencies grow among nations, the

United States and other nations will probably find international coordination of regional development and transportation planning becoming more essential.

Recent experience in regional development suggests that in addition to the traditional issues examined above, a new set of emerging problems is becoming critical both in regional development and transportation planning. The key issue in this new set of development problems is the conflict between economic development and environmental quality. Concerned with the spatial and quali- tative impacts of economic development, students of regional development, resource economics and related fields have drawn attention to the materials balance and residual management problem that had largely been neglected in traditional economic theory.[3] Serious resource allocation problems are created by residual emissions because these wastes are typically discharged into the common property resources of air and water, resulting in divergence between private and social costs. Because transportation systems are among the most prolific emission generators, the issue of environmental protection is inescapable in transportation planning.

Another new issue in regional development and in transportation planning is the question of technology assessment and management. A review of the history of the internal combustion automobile, recognizing both the benefits and costs that it has brought to society, raises the question of whether earlier recognition of the total systems implications of this transportation mode could have increased the benefits and reduced the costs by means of earlier and more extensive research on safety, pollution abatement, alternative power sources, and more balanced integration with mass transit systems. The answer is not clear one way or another as to whether improved performance could have been achieved through advance planning. For the future, however, the total systems implica- tions of vast new proposed systems such as the supersonic transport aircraft make it imperative that technology be carefully assessed before its widespread introduction in order to achieve early specifications of performance character- istics—especially as they relate to pollution, noise, and other environmental and social impacts.

Finally, in planning for regional development and transportation systems, many of the more specific questions discussed above can be summarized in the more general issue of the relationship between economic development and the quality of life. Without question, the development of new transportation systems and the advancement of regional and urban development have con- tributed enormously to efficiency and productivity in U.S. economic develop- ment. The benefits can clearly be identified in aggregate terms in the GNP statistics, and more significantly in welfare terms in the statistics on per capita disposable real personal income. These economic gains have not been achieved without cost, however, and some basic questions have been raised both as to the costs of economic development and the distribution of these costs and benefits of growth.[4] Despite impressive overall performance of the U.S. economy and the spread of affluence, unacceptably large numbers of the population have been bypassed by the general prosperity because of prejudice, neglect, under-investment in health, education, and welfare, and for other reasons. Regional development and transportation planning have typically been designed for the affluent without consulting the most needy and vulnerable, whose homes, livelihoods, and life styles are often sacrificed in the name of development. The distribution of benefits and costs and prior consultation with those affected by these programs have become central issues in planning regional development and transportation for the future.

Following sections survey selected U.S. regional development programs in order to examine how these issues have been addressed historically, and in order to assess their relevance to improvements in future programs for regional development and transportation.

The Era of Internal Improvements

Although not all U.S. programs for regional development have been focused upon transportation, most early regional efforts were based upon transportation as the key to both regional and national economic development. In the Federal Period, major national objectives were to bind the former colonies together politically and to overcome the spatial barriers which constrained access to natural resources. Entrepreneurs and public officials were well aware that improved transportation was essential to permit resource development, regional specialization, and economic growth.

An impressive beginning was made in U.S. transportation planning under Albert Gallatin, Secretary of the Treasury to Thomas Jefferson, in his *Report on Public Roads and Canals* in 1808.[5] Gallatin's *Report* was a systematic, comprehensive study of the nation's transportation needs, and of alternative methods for meeting these needs. This remarkable document compares favorably in quality of analysis and advocacy with many contemporary proposals for federal programs for transportation and regional development. Gallatin began his report with a general proposition that can be broadly interpreted as including an early benefit-cost concept and the idea of indirect benefits:

It is sufficiently evident that, whenever the annual expense of transportation on a certain route in its natural state, exceeds the interest on the capital employed in improving the communication, and the annual expense of transportation (exclusively of tolls) by the improved route, the difference is an annual additional income to the nation. Nor does in that case the general result vary, although the tolls may not have been fixed at a rate sufficient to pay to the undertakers the interest on the capital laid out. They indeed, when that happens, lose; but the community is nevertheless benefited by the undertaking. The general gain is not confined to the difference between the expenses of the transportation of those articles which had been formally conveyed by that route, but many which were brought to market by channels, will then find a new and more advantageous direction; and those which on account of their distance or weight could not be transported in any manner whatever, will acquire a value and become a clear addition to the national wealth.

Gallatin presents cost estimates for each of the projects proposed but does not offer detailed estimates of expected benefits. An appendix by Robert Fulton, however, does present some specific benefit and cost estimates. In fact, Fulton, an ardent advocate of the superiority of canals over turnpikes, provides an excellent early example of two persistent strands in thinking about U.S. regional development. One is the eagerness to adopt new and advanced technologies. Another persistent tendency is to assume that a system that is appropriate in some regions under some circumstances should be universally spread throughout the nation. In fact, Fulton makes proposals for extending canals even over mountain ranges, and concludes his statement with a quotation from his letter to the Governor of Pennsylvania on a complete national system of canals:

Canals should pass through every vale, wind around every hill, and bind the whole country together in the bonds of social intercourse;[6]

Similar enthusiasm and advocacy have been brought to bear subsequently on proposals for railroads, highways, air travel, and mass transit. By contrast, Gallatin's proposals were modest though comprehensive. He offered a specific identification of national objectives, which were to improve communication and to settle the West, and he based this upon a statement of principles:

No other single operation, within the power of government, can more effectually tend to strengthen and perpetuate that union, which secures external independence, domestic peace and internal liberty.[7]

Gallatin based his report upon detailed studies of the geographic and engineering problems involved. He developed his national plan for transportation in relation to the total U.S. budget and other priorities, proposing an annual expenditure rate of $2 million for ten years out of expected surplus.[8] Basing his proposals upon a geographic feasibility study that was impressive for its day, Gallatin recommended a comprehensive system of multiple-mode transportation routes from north to south as well as east to west. The north-south system included both turnpikes and an inland waterway that would make maximum use of existing natural bodies of water efficiently interconnected by canals. The east-west transportation was to be provided by connecting eastern and western rivers by means of a system of canals and turnpikes. The major goal of this program was to overcome the physical barriers to development imposed by the Appalachian mountains. As discussed below, the Appalachian problem in somewhat different form still plays a major role in U.S. thinking about regional development 160 years later.

Gallatin's system, designed on the basis of efficiency, skillful linkage of natural and man-made facilities, and an implicit national benefit-cost analysis, was to be financed by a recommended expenditure of $16.6 million computed upon the requirements of the system rather than upon any particular apportionment among the states involved. In a realistic appraisal of the political factors involved, however, Gallatin proposed that an additional $3.4 million "justice and policy" fund be appropriated in order to aid those states not benefited by the basic plan.

A further contemporary note is provided by the fact that John C. Calhoun, who supported the plan because of the national goals of reducing sectionalism and binding together the nation with a transportation system, also argued that the network was needed for defense purposes. Although work on the program was delayed by the War of 1812, eventually the entire program was completed very much as originally proposed by Gallatin.

The ultimate completion of the elements of Gallatin's proposal demonstrated the high quality of planning in the geographic and engineering aspects of his recommendations. However, his report dealt less thoroughly with the legislative, financial, and administrative aspects of the problem, and eventually the states had to provide much of the financial resources needed. Gallatin recognized the need for pluralistic methods of financing the internal improvements, and this pragmatic approach has become a permanent aspect of the U.S. approach to regional development.

The Gallatin plan is worth citing because implicitly or explicitly it addressed many of the issues that are current in planning transport systems and regional development. The issue of whether or not to provide federal aid for transportation infrastructure was resolved affirmatively because it was recognized that private resources would be underinvested in transportation facilities so long as investors were unable to capture all of the resulting benefits from the spillover effects. Gallatin and his supporters recognized that overcoming the transportation barriers to resource development and regional growth would yield positive net benefits over costs to the nation.

The question of the desirability of detailed economic and physical planning at the federal level was also resolved affirmatively. Gallatin's *Report* proposed a carefully designed national plan based upon investment in those regions where natural features such as water routes, topography, and potential productivity would yield maximum returns. To protect the integrity of the total system, local logrolling and dispersion of resources were specifically limited to the extent of the "justice and policy" fund. The emphasis was upon federal versus local planning, productivity rather than equity, and concentration rather than dispersion of aid, although expedient compromises were included.

The appropriate region defined for transportation planning under the Gallatin proposal was taken as the entire nation, rather than states or smaller geographic units, and national economic objectives were given priority. The emphasis was placed not on assistance to any particular mode of transportation, but on a total national system utilizing natural waterways, canals, and roads, depending upon which was most appropriate to the geography of the region.

Gallatin's program, with its emphasis upon a coordinated national transportation system carefully related to topography and natural features, represented a high point in planning U.S. transportation and regional development that in many ways has not been equalled in the century and a half following it.

After the period of Jefferson and Gallatin, the nation entered upon an age of state supremacy with opposition to the exercise of federal tax powers necessary to continue a strong federal program of internal improvements. The success of Gallatin's transport system, however, led the states to embark upon a variety of transportation experiments with notable examples of both success and failure. Among the most successful examples of a state-supported transportation system was the Erie Canal, which was completed in 1825. Because it made maximum use of existing waterways in order to provide efficient regional linkages between a hinterland and a major industrial port, the economic payoff of this investment in regional infrastructure was dramatic. Transportation rates to the west, which had previously been $0.25 to $0.50 per ton-mile over the National Road, fell on the Erie Canal to $0.005 to $0.01, or about 2 percent of the cost of the overland route.[9]

Although the Erie Canal, which was originally built for $7 million, eventually cost the State of New York a total of $78 million with later improvements, the investment of state resources was a highly profitable one. Not only did the Canal earn high profits until the late 1850s, when railroads began to reduce its long haul advantage, but it also did much to push New York ahead of Boston and Philadelphia as the nation's largest port and city. The enormous economic benefits to the State and to the nation that resulted from the state's investment in the Erie Canal derived from concentration of investment resources in a single transportation system that made maximum use of existing waterways to create a complete linkage of a vast productive hinterland of markets and supply areas with a major industrial processing and trans-shipping port, which in itself became a major market.

The success of the Erie Canal quickly led to an era of competitive canal building in the U.S., characterized by pragmatic experimentation with a wide variety of financial and administrative arrangements among national, state, municipal, and private institutions. However, few of these efforts to emulate the Erie Canal achieved comparable success. The experience of the Chesapeake and Ohio Canal in Maryland illustrates many of the problems involved.

George Washington's Potomac Company (later the Chesapeake and Ohio Canal Company) began by specifying both the engineering and economic objectives that it sought. These were to provide an all-weather route from the

Atlantic coast to Pittsburgh for boats carrying 50 barrels of flour.[10] Although the C & O Canal venture was organized primarily as a private undertaking for profit, the promoters had no ideological bias against acceptance of state assistance, and made strenuous efforts to enlist government support. To justify financial participation, the promoters appealed to the state's rivalry and competition with other coastal states in breaching the barrier of the Appalachian mountains to establish trade routes with the interior. In claims which have a surprisingly contemporary ring, state participation in economic enterprise was rationalized on the basis that it would lower taxes, improve education, and increase land values.

In Maryland and in other states that hastened to repeat the experience of the Erie Canal, however, the results did not reach the level of expectations. A major factor was the emergence of a technologically superior transportation system in the form of railways. Another factor was that most states had no one consistent overall plan and set of priorities for transportation and regional development objectives. Maryland dispersed its aid indiscriminately through the sale of improvement bonds for the support of not only the C & O Canal, but also for the Chesapeake and Delaware Canal, the Western Maryland Railroad, the Baltimore and Ohio Railroad, and for numerous other schemes for internal improvement. This policy not only dispersed scarce resources indiscriminately and failed to add up to a comprehensive transport system, but it actually contained built-in conflicts, such as parallel construction of the C & O Canal and the B & O Railroad. Consequently, while the railway reached Cumberland by 1842, the Canal was not completed that far until 1850, at which point construction ended. This program of aid to transportation was so poorly managed that the state eventually defaulted on the improvement bonds.[11]

In other states, experience with canal building was mixed. Canals did contribute to national and regional economic development by reducing transport costs, opening new markets and supply areas, providing access to natural resources, providing opportunities for regional specialization and by generating regional economic multiplier effects during both the construction and operating phases of the canal systems. As de Tocqueville observed, Americans were no longer condemned to "crawl along the outer shell" of their continent.[12]

However, poorly planned efforts to imitate the Erie Canal resulted in waste and misallocation of resources in states such as Virginia and the Carolinas, where public aid was granted indiscriminately on a political basis in the absence of plans for a comprehensive and efficient system. Even regions as large as states were suboptimal planning units where interstate waterways were involved. Eventually the nation invested an estimated $200 million in canals, of which approximately 70 percent was provided from public sources.[13]

The emergence of railroad technology, with its greater load carrying capacity, speed, and geographic flexibility, quickly made obsolete most of the investment in canals by opening an entirely new set of economic opportunities. For example in Maryland, where great losses had resulted from excessive dispersion of transportation resources at the state level, the Baltimore City promoters of the Baltimore and Ohio Railroad demonstrated that even a unit as small as a city could mobilize federal, state, municipal, and private funds and concentrate them on construction of a single, well-designed system with economic success. Although the B & O was basically a private venture organized for profit, its promoters were eventually able to obtain approximately $12 million in aid from the City of Baltimore. In addition, they exercised great skill in obtaining financial support from federal and state sources as well as from private investors. The planners of the B & O Railroad concentrated upon utilizing the large load-carrying capacity and decreasing cost characteristics of the new railraod technology in order that the Port of Baltimore might specialize in processing and cross-shipping the heavy bulk commodities of the Midwest, especially coal and grain.

They succeeded so well at this objective that by 1852 the rail system had reached Wheeling, West Virginia, and eventually had connections with St. Louis, Chicago, Philadelphia, and New York.[14] Although the construction of the B & O line never did permit Baltimore to achieve a level of performance comparable to that of New York City, it was a primary factor in making Baltimore a major world port and in bringing much of the Midwest into the nation's developing market economy.

The very success of the Port of Baltimore in achieving its initial economic objectives has generated new and unforeseen problems, as must be expected in any developmental process. Maryland, in order to encourage the development of the Port and to aid private firms in related activities, created a Maryland Port Authority with extensive administrative and budgetary authority. Recently a Governor's committee has expressed concern that the Port Authority has used its autonomy to relegate private firms to minor roles in the port and has used its autonomous budget for uneconomic overexpansion without adequate legislative review.

The pressure of the Port Authority to dredge ever deeper channels to accommodate super tankers in competition with other ports has created serious problems of dredge spoil disposal, which is a threat to the seafood industry and ecology of the Chesapeake Bay. One of the unanticipated side effects from the heavy materials processing industries of the Baltimore industrial port complex has been the deposition over the years of metallic residues and other industrial pollutants on the bottom of the Patapsco River, Chesapeake Bay, and its tributaries. Extensive dredging tends to disperse these materials into the water, creating a serious threat to the ecology of the Bay.[15] Oil spills are becoming a major environmental threat to the Bay and its tributaries.

Thus in planning for future regional development of the state, of the Port of Baltimore, and of Chesapeake Bay, it is now becoming apparent that decisions will have to be made concerning alternative courses of action such as:

1. Encourage continued industrial expansion and accept environmental damage to the Chesapeake Bay and tributaries.
2. Retard the rate of industrial expansion to prevent further environmental damage.
3. Find patterns of economic development which are less damaging to the environment.
4. Find improved technologies which cause less environmental damage.

The Port of Baltimore case is significant because it poses transportation problems that will increasingly be encountered in planning for regional development programs throughout the world. Both the impressive economic achievements and the serious environmental damage created by the industrial port affect the large hinterlands from which it draws resources and the extensive estuarial system throughout which it spreads its vast amounts of waste into the air and water and upon the land. The problems which Baltimore and New York are beginning to recognize are rapidly becoming the central problem of regional development in all industrial economies: how to enjoy the benefits of regional industrial development and economic growth without irreversible damage to the very environment upon which the economic activity is based.

The Railroad Era

Just as the Erie Canal initiated an era of canal construction, the success of the Baltimore and Ohio Railroad triggered off a period of intensive investment in railroad construction throughout the United States. Once the B & O had demonstrated that railroads, by linking hinterlands and termini, could, under favorable conditions, accelerate regional economic development and earn large profits, railroads were introduced on a larger scale for the economic development of the West and the rest of the nation.

The policy was to accelerate the economic development of the nation and to achieve political unity by constructing a transcontinental railway system. Reconciliation of the conflicting desires of providing federal financial support and avoiding higher taxes was achieved by making large grants of federal lands to the states. Beyond specifying the termini, the Federal Government left actual detailed physical planning and selection of routes to the states. The states in turn relied upon private investors to promote, design, and operate the systems. Thus national objectives were defined only in the most general form of establishing a transcontinental system without detailed priorities or any cohesive national plan comparable to Gallatin's national system for roads and water routes.

Large-scale federal participation in railroad financing began in 1850 with a grant of 3,750,000 acres of federal lands to the states to support railroad construction. The program of national subsidies to railroads continued through the Civil War. Under additional legislation passed in 1862, promoters were given 10 sections of land (640 acres each) per mile of right-of-way, plus mortgage loans. Another act passed in 1864 raised the grants to 20 sections of land per mile.[16] Estimates of the total amount of subsidy provided for railroad construction range from 129 million acres (plus $62 million in grants)[17] to 223 million acres.[18]

Under this system of generous subsidies, low percentages of risk capital, intense interregional competition, and casual federal supervision, it is not surprising that waste and corruption occurred on a vast scale. Promoters encouraged rival towns to outbid one another on the size of subsidies they would offer for the economic advantage of having the tracks run through their regions. In New York, for example, the New York and Oswego Midland Railroad followed a zig-zag route between towns determined by the size of subsidies offered, but it was not able to earn enough in operating revenues to avoid bankruptcy.

In many instances, the political power of the railroads led to corruption, high speculative profits for the promoters, and losses for the public. For example in promoting construction of the Union Pacific Railroad, the Credit Mobilier distributed shares generously to members of Congress, and with a total investment of approximately $4 million, using federal land subsidies and federal guarantees to attract loan capital, cleared profits conservatively estimated at $14 to $15 million.[19]

Despite the corruption and waste involved, the railroads were built and contributed significantly to the economic development of the nation and of its regions. The importance of attempting to assess the U.S. experience in railway construction is emphasized by the parallels between this earlier experience and more recent transportation issues faced by the nation in debates over the St. Lawrence Seaway, the Ohio Canal, the interstate highway system, the national maritime program, the federal aviation program, and even more recently, proposals for mass transit systems and the supersonic transport plane. As in the era of internal improvements, all of these later proposals have regional development implications and seek federal participation in the absence of adequate private investment. In each case, indirect and secondary benefits, added to the direct benefits, are expected to exceed the costs. The systems implications of the new technologies are found to require new institutional arrangements between federal, state, local, and private agencies in order to promote the public safety and welfare.

The relevance of past U.S. experience with internal improvements and early transport systems to current problems should not be stretched too far, but some tentative conclusions can be advanced. The most successful U.S. efforts in transportation systems and regional development were those where widely accepted but quite specific objectives were identified and resources concentrated upon high priority projects rather than being dispersed. Examples are the Erie

Canal and the Baltimore and Ohio Railroad. The chances of success were improved by planning for interconnected regional systems of productive hinterlands linked to focal points for processing, marketing, and trans-shipping. Large regional systems permitted achievement of regional specialization, economies of scale, and agglomeration. Pragmatic creation of pluralistic partnership institutions of different governmental and private agencies was effective where federal guidelines were specified and performance was closely monitored to prevent abuses. Even where benefits exceeded costs, careful planning and administration of the promotional, construction, and operating phases of the program were necessary in order to regulate the distribution of benefits and costs between the public and the promoters.

By contrast, inefficiency and waste in regional transportation were most likely to occur in those instances where aid was widely dispersed without careful specification of objectives and priorities in an overall plan. Failure to integrate scattered local systems resulted in wasteful interregional competition. Hasty efforts to imitate programs which had been successful in one region by inappropriate application in less suitable areas was a frequent source of losses.

One important result of examining the historical experience of the United States in regional transportation systems is the identification of the urgent need for a national policy for regional development based upon clear identification of goals and priorities and implemented by benefit-cost evaluation of the alternative approaches for achieving those objectives. Following sections examine more recent samples of U.S. experience in regional development for their possible relevance to the design of a U.S. policy for future regional development.

River Basin Development

One specific example of U.S. regional development that has attracted international attention has been river basin management, especially in the Tennessee Valley. TVA is usually evaluated in terms of the extent to which management of water resources can contribute to regional economic development. A more fundamental issue, which is only beginning to be recognized, is to what extent, if any, engineering and management can "improve" a river basin over the long run. This is a basic question, because the history of U.S. river basin development is a testament to the belief that the general interest is served by conquering nature and exploiting water resources for economic development purposes.

Unfortunately, many water development projects have been undertaken for short-run economic purposes based upon an inadequate understanding of the complex interrelationships between the geology, hydrology, and ecology of river basins. Poor farming and construction practices upriver have led to silting of channels and ports, filling in of dams, and flooding. Destruction of soil cover reduces the capacity of watersheds to absorb rainfall and release it slowly, aggravating both flooding and droughts. Instead of adopting an interdisciplinary environmental approach, standard U.S. practice has been to adopt a costly engineering approach to dredging channels and building levees. These river basin programs encourage settlement of flood plains, expose more human life and capital to risk, and generate spiraling demands for ever more protective works. By actually increasing the probability and severity of downstream flooding, the construction of levees can be depended upon to generate self-reinforcing demands for additional construction, with rising benefit-cost ratios to justify them. The less costly alternatives of planning for undeveloped or low density flood plains is seldom adopted.

The issues inherent in regional development decisions have all been evident in river basin planning. The question of whether or not to provide federal assistance has typically been resolved affirmatively—not just because it provides public services on a scale that would not attract private investors, but also because of prospective favorable benefit-cost ratios from combinations of multi-purpose goals including water supply, irrigation, navigation benefits, power generation, flood prevention, low flow augmentation, dilution of pollution, attraction of industry, and creation of recreational opportunities. To a greater extent than in most U.S. regional development programs, the Federal Government has engaged in detailed planning of water management projects, primarily where multi-state regions have been involved. Planning, however, has been primarily of physical engineering details to the neglect of environmental and ecological problems. Emphasis has been placed upon economic development of the region by means of expenditure through established construction activities and federal agencies, rather than upon poverty alleviation or other welfare objectives. Economic development and engineering convenience have generally been assigned higher priority than the rights of the farmers and other persons whose land was taken. Decisions on geographic location of projects have been related to the political situation in the Congress, rather than to equity, need, or environmental impact.

The evolution of these issues in the Tennessee Valley is of particular interest. Here, the traditional U.S. approach of flexible, pragmatic experimentation with new institutions designed for specific purposes was followed with the creation of a highly autonomous authority designed to deal with an entire system of rivers, tributaries, and their drainage basins. Unfortunately, in pursuing its multi-purpose objectives, the issue that received major attention was the relatively insignificant ideological one of public versus private power generation. By concentrating its efforts on reducing internal power costs to establish a yardstick price in competition with private producers, TVA tragically neglected the social costs it was creating on a large scale through poor environmental practices. By emphasizing low contract prices for coal, it encouraged destructive strip mining practices that damaged extensive regions in Appalachia. By failing to install cooling devices, it discharged large quantities of heated water into its water systems. This practice became especially serious when TVA branched out into nuclear power generation, because the lower thermal efficiency of nuclear power combined with the larger scale of operations resulted in an accelerating thermal problem for the TVA system.

It is particularly ironic and unfortunate for the nation that an agency like TVA, established to deal with the interrelated resources of a great river basin system, failed to assign greater significance to the environmental and ecological consequences of its economic development programs.

By 1965 the protests of environmentalists over the consequences of strip mining finally resulted in the inclusion of a proviso in TVA coal contracts for mandatory reclamation of stripped land. The effectiveness of this policy is not yet clear. In the same year, TVA also began to face the implications of its thermal releases on water quality by adding a cooling tower to its Paradise Plant, which was situated on a stream with relatively little cooling capacity. However, it is proceeding to construct a large-scale nuclear plant at Brown's Ferry without cooling towers despite concern that the planned temperature rise of $10°$ F to a level as high as $93°$ F has not been established as a safe level.

The knowledge does not yet exist for making valid comparisons of the gains from reshaping of the river systems with the long-run ecological and environmental costs involved. Until such analyses can be made, no systematic, comprehensive benefit-cost study can be made of the Tennessee Valley experiment, nor can the distribution of benefits and costs be assessed. Until it can be demonstrated that man has achieved sufficient knowledge and capability to make long-range improvements in a river system, the most valuable asset in any regional development plan may well be a natural, unimproved river system.

Development of Urban Regions

Cities are high density nodal regions where society has concentrated both its highest achievements and its most critical problems. The struggle to improve the quality of life will largely be conducted in the urban arena, where approximately three-quarters of the U.S. population live and work. Despite economic growth and rising average per capita real incomes, the nation is faced with the growing intensity of urban problems including social conflict, crime and violence, drug abuse, poverty, unemployment, mental and physical illness, transportation development, housing deterioration, environmental degradation, and fiscal crisis. Accelerated urban economic growth and growing affluence have not only failed to solve this wide range of urban problems, but may even have aggravated them.

Unlike other U.S. regional development efforts, urban growth has been characterized much less by federal assistance and much more by intensive competition between urban areas for economic growth. Early recognition of the role of transportation in creating external economies of scale, aggregation, and linkage resulted in local competition to influence the location of interurban transport systems. In more recent periods, the nature of intraurban transportation systems has become critical to metropolitan development and performance.

Although there have been winners and losers in urban competition for economic development, the overall consequences of interurban competition for growth have been effective in accelerating national growth and in attracting sustained migration from rural to urban areas. However, this undoubted success in growth of urban population and affluence has generated new sets of problems and drastically reordered social priorities.

Many of these urban problems result from the inter-personal and inter-spatial distribution of benefits and costs of urban growth. The technological revolution in agriculture has driven the displaced rural poor into urban areas for which they are often culturally unprepared and where inadequate provision has been made for integrating them into urban life. The counter-migration of affluent commuters into suburban areas meanwhile has been subsidized by low interest federal home mortgage programs and freeway construction. External diseconomies of pollution and congestion result from the divergence of social costs from the private costs of commuting by personal internal combustion vehicles. Freeways are designed for the convenience of the affluent commuter and ignore the need of ghetto dwellers for crosstown transportation and often result in destruction of low income housing. Thus, while urban areas are starved for investment in human capital, affluent commuters are subsidized to move into suburban areas, further depriving cities of needed tax revenue.

In addition to chronic and critical urban ghetto problems, other very serious but less recognized problems result from the relationships between urban centers and their surrounding hinterlands. Cities usually draw their water supplies from distant watersheds and discharge their sewage downstream over large areas. Similarly, cities usually discharge air pollution and solid waste into adjacent regions. While cities provide external economies to their hinterlands in the form of markets, supply areas, job opportunities, and amenities, they create external diseconomies in the form of massive discharges of gaseous, liquid, and solid wastes. Much clearer recognition is needed in the planning and development of urban regions of the environmental, ecological, and economic linkages involved.

Two polar extremes can be suggested as patterns for improving the quality of urban life. One is continuation of current trends toward dependency upon ever more complex technological systems for salvation. With this approach, now being followed, emphasis is given to the creation of small but expanding micro-environments, such as the home, the automobile, and the office, where air quality, temperature, humidity, and noise levels are completely controlled. Extensions of this approach through such developments as geodesic domes like the Houston Astrodome and the gigantic urban machines imagined by Paolo Soleri may make it possible to provide controlled micro-environments for entire cities. Unfortunately, this approach fails to cure environmental problems, since enormous requirements for energy and other inputs merely transfer the environmental impact to the larger macro-environment and to those who cannot afford to live in the affluent micro-environments.

At the other extreme from the technological solution to urban problems is the approach of Lewis Mumford and other environmentalists who urge the necessity of scaling down urban growth and relating it to ecological and environmental relationships. The long-run solution to improvement in the quality of urban life will require both more sophisticated technology, designed to serve human needs, and improved relationships between man and his environment. The problem of urban transportation and development will not be solved in isolation from other critical problems of population size, housing, resource management, land use, regional development, technology assessment, and environmental design. Coordinated national policies are urgently needed in all of these fields. Further sections will examine some of the elements for possible inclusion in such national policies on transportation and related issues.

The Area Redevelopment Administration

While earlier U.S. regional development efforts had been designed to assist the growth of particular areas, by the 1960s it became a matter of national policy to assist all regions that had lagged significantly behind the national market or had suffered from changes in the economy. Largely as the result of a long time effort by one man, economist-Senator Paul Douglas from Illinois, the Area Redevelopment Act was passed in 1961, establishing the Area Redevelopment Administration (ARA).

The basic provision of ARA was that any region should be eligible for economic assistance if its unemployment averaged 6 percent or more for twelve months and was 50 percent or more higher than the national average for two years. Thus, the dispersion versus concentration issue was clearly resolved in favor of wide dispersion. The basic region was the county, but a highly pragmatic approach to the definition of regions also included labor market areas, Indian reservations, and multistate regions.

Aid was provided in the form of technical assistance, grants for public works, and a small manpower program, but primary emphasis was upon business loans. ARA operated essentially by channeling large expenditures through the business community and through other government agencies. Priority was given to investment in business capital, to physical construction of public works, to investment in physical rather than human capital, and aid was directed toward places, not people.

Aside from establishing minimal guidelines, the Federal Government avoided detailed planning or establishment of policy, leaving generous latitude to the administrator of the program. Planning was left to individual communities, which were required to prepare a community Overall Economic Development

Program (OEDP). This was an excellent provision intended to involve representative groups of a community in establishing goals and planning their future. In practice the idea failed badly because of lack of federal guidance and because of the scarcity of competent regional planners. Actual preparation of the OEDP was often left to groups oriented toward engineering, physical design, and business rather than to persons trained in analysis of regional economic development alternatives. Therefore, despite requirements for broad community representation, the OEDPs usually turned out to be shopping lists of projects for "earth moving"[20] and concrete pouring rather than for broad community development.

The most serious deficiency of ARA was its failure to establish an adequate research operation in Washington or in the field. The minimal guidelines of reducing unemployment concentrations were too narrow to permit the establishment of priorities and of a national policy on regional development, or to answer fundamental questions about spatial distribution of economic activity, equity versus efficiency, concentration versus dispersion, or economic development versus general regional development. Little attention was given to establishing goals, evaluating benefits and costs of alternative programs, or to formulating national policy on regional development. The failure to establish research guidance for program development left the agency vulnerable to political pressures and increased the difficulty of rejecting questionable proposals.

ARA did represent a pioneering effort to adopt a comprehensive approach to regional development problems, however, and experience gained under its operation was useful in improving subsequent regional development efforts.

The Economic Development Administration

Once the Area Development Act had established the legitimacy of comprehensive aid to regional development and had demonstrated the possible existence of net economic benefits and positive existence of political benefits from such programs, the predictable next step was to correct obvious deficiencies and extend aid to more regions. Its successor agency, the Economic Development Administration (EDA), undertook these tasks beginning in 1965.

EDA criteria for eligibility of regions for aid included, in addition to the average unemployment criterion, a provision for including regions with median per capita incomes of 50 percent of the national median or less. As in the case of ARA, EDA gave primary emphasis to providing aid to places, not people, though it did include manpower training in its program. The objectives sought were conventional regional economic development by channeling expenditures through the business community and other government agencies, rather than general community development and investment in human capital and alleviation of poverty. The equity versus efficiency issue was compromised by adopting a "worst first" policy of extending aid to the most needy regions, and also by attempting to invest aid in those regions where the payoff in terms of creating jobs and incomes would be greatest. Closely related to this objective was a notable effort to break away from the traditional policy of excessive dispersion of aid by attempting to concentrate aid at growth poles having the potential for sustained, cumulative economic development. Growth pole strategy raises important questions about alternative spatial patterns for the distribution of economic activity, and about optimal relationships between urban, suburban, and rural distribution. Recognizing that adequate data and conceptual models do not yet exist for solving these problems, EDA has begun an ambitious program of internal and external research in order to provide improved information that will be necessary for formulating a national policy on regional development.

The Appalachian Regional Commission

Although many of the counties in Appalachia qualified for EDA regional development assistance under the low income and high unemployment criteria of that program, the new attention focused upon this region during the presidential primaries of 1960 had raised serious doubts as to whether conventional regional assistance approaches would be effective in addressing the intractable Appalachian problem. The seriousness of the issues involved and the size of the region suggested the urgent need for a special, comprehensive program tailored to deal with a complex and interrelated set of problems that had been accumulating for generations.

The problems of Appalachia go far beyond economics and include historical, cultural, sociological, political, institutional, and environmental factors. Many of the Appalachian residents were descended from families that had fled up into the mountain hollows to escape, during different eras, from the English prohibitions against western settlement, from Indian attacks, and from federal revenue agents. Their isolation led to cultural entropy, educational neglect, and lack of participation in governmental processes. By the time the outside world discovered the potential value of natural resources in Appalachia, the owners of these resources were ill prepared to prevent the exploitation of the resources or of themselves.

Agents of corporate developers found it easy to acquire extensive development rights at minimal prices from owners who often could not read the contracts they signed. Developers were careful to obtain rights only to the resources—without land ownership—so that they avoided taxes and responsibility for damages created in removing the timber and coal. The contracts were worded to permit the developers to take any action they wished in order to remove the resources without regard to the effects upon the residents or their environment.[21] Timber operators clear cut the hillsides, damaging the land cover, and leaving the soil to be washed from the slopes into streams. In the short run it was more profitable to cut the timber and leave the land to erode than to acquire land, pay taxes, and reforest.

Even greater destruction was caused by coal operators whose mineral rights were written to permit them to do whatever was necessary to extract the coal, including pushing the land cover onto houses and farms and into streams. The timber and coal operators found it profitable to avoid taxes and starve public education in order to assure a continuing supply of cheap, docile labor. Neglect of the public sector reduced the capability of local people to protect themselves or participate in government, so that the timber and coal companies dominated the local courts and legislatures.

The timber and coal of the region were regarded as individual economic resources for exploitation. Little or no recognition was given to the interrelated nature of the land, water, mineral, and human resources of the area. Stripping of the timber cover caused the hillsides and farm lands to erode, silting the streams. Coal mining further stripped the hills of cover and caused acid mine drainage into the water, killing fish and damaging downstream water quality.

In the short run, the developers and the rest of the nation benefitted from the apparent low cost of timber and coal from Appalachia. However, the external diseconomies imposed upon the people of the region, and upon the environment of a large part of the nation are only partially measured by the cost of the Appalachian program, which was designed to correct a small fraction of the damage done to the natural and human resources of this region.

In many ways, the Appalachian Regional Commission (ARC) represents an advanced stage in the evolution of U.S. regional development efforts. The Appalachian effort is based firmly upon rejection of the national market hypothesis of regional development and acceptance of the need for massive economic intervention in regional adjustment in order to compensate for the immobilities of labor and capital and to correct adverse dynamic factors. The region for management has been defined in terms of the multi-state area where a common set of problems exists. To a greater extent than previous programs, the ARC is concerned not only with developing a lagging region, but also with alleviating the poverty of people within the region by addressing the causes of their poverty. Heavy expenditures have been made on education, training, nutrition, and health. Backed up by a central research effort, the Federal Government has engaged in far-reaching detailed planning, which in previous efforts had typically been left to the local level. The Appalachian program also innovates in the environmental area by attempting to correct some of the damage resulting from extractive activities. ARC has financed programs for reforestation, soil conservation, reduction of acid mine seepage, rehabilitating mine spoil banks, extinguishing underground mine fires, arresting the subsidence of surface areas from mining activities, and reducing water pollution.

One of the most important innovations by ARC has been its creation of new institutional approaches in joint administration of regional programs between federal, state, and local agencies. Federal guidelines have been established to insure the priority of national objectives, but state governments have been given large measures of autonomy to express local priorities within these guidelines. Within ARC, the Federal Government supports a common research effort to provide consistent data sources and avoid conflicts between state programs. State governments are insured against unwelcome federal intervention by requirements that states approve all programs proposed for their areas, giving them an effective veto power. Efficiency in the use of scarce resources has been sought by limiting investment to areas that states have identified as having growth potential.

The major criticism of the Appalachian program has been directed at the fact that despite its highly appropriate emphasis upon poverty alleviation, human capital, and environmental objectives, disproportionately large amounts of the total funds involved have been allocated to highway construction. Although comparisons are difficult because of differing periods for appropriations and expenditures, out of total appropriations of $769 million for fiscal years 1965 through 1969, $470.0 million or more than 60 percent of the total funds available for Appalachia were appropriated for highway construction.[22] Additional amendments authorize more than $1 billion for eventual highway construction. Another $93.5 million was authorized for airport construction.

Although many persuasive arguments have been advanced to justify the weight given highway construction—emphasizing the need to reduce isolation, encourage migration, and permit the delivery of services to rural people—the supporters of highway construction have not demonstrated that these massive expenditures represent the most efficient approach to the basic human problems of Appalachia. Highway construction aids those from other regions wishing to cross through Appalachia, and aids the highway construction industry more than it does most of the impoverished Appalachians. The traditional concept of regional development as a process of channeling federal funds through the business community for construction of physical capital has dominated the Appalachian effort, as it has most previous U.S. efforts at regional development. However, the fact that some funds have been used to deal with the neglected human problems of the region and to restore environmental damage indicates a growing recognition of the systems relationships between the people, the resources, and the institutions of a region.

Other Multi-State Regional Commissions

As would be expected from previous U.S. regional development efforts, the successful funding of the Appalachian Regional Commission quickly led to the proliferation of other multi-state regional commissions. Those established to date are:

The Ozarks Regional Commission (parts of Arkansas, Kansas, Missouri, and Oklahoma)

The New England Regional Commission (all of Connecticut, Maine, Massachusetts, New Hampshire, Rhode Island, and Vermont)

The Upper Great Lakes Regional Commission (parts of Michigan, Minnesota, and Wisconsin)

The Four Corners Regional Commission (parts of Arizona, Colorado, New Mexico, and Utah)

The Coastal Plains Regional Commission (parts of Georgia, North Carolina, and South Carolina)

Although funding constraints have limited the programs of these multi-state commissions, it is possible that their diverse regional orientations will result in significant innovations. An impressive research contribution by Brian Berry supported by the Great Lakes Regional Commission has reemphasized the importance of spatial relationships, regional linkages, and interregional flows of goods and services in regional development.[23] Berry's analysis of economic space identifies potential growth areas, peripheral zones, slow growth areas, and lagging regions. His work on the linkages and spread effects of these regions can be used as the basis for a detailed spatial plan for the location of specific primary growth centers, secondary growth centers, service centers, and zones of influence of these concentrations. The significance of this research is that it helps identify regions where investment of scarce resources is more likely to yield lasting developmental benefits than unselective dispersion of funds into areas with weaker economic linkages.

A similar concern with selectivity in managing economic growth has been demonstrated by the New England Regional Commission. In a significant departure from the universal growth syndrome, and recognizing more explicitly than most public documents the issue of conflict between economic growth and environmental quality, the Commission draws attention to air and water pollution, traffic congestion, and other urban problems caused by dense urban population growth. The Commission has recommended a policy of controlling growth in the congested urban areas of southern New England and encouraging growth in the less developed northern states, with the objective of achieving a clean and livable environment.[24]

One problem that has not been solved by the multi-state regional commissions is that of defining the appropriate region. All of the commissions, except that for New England, include parts of states, and the Four Corners Commission even includes part of a complete county. For purposes of administration and decision-making, inclusion of complete counties, states, and their SMSAs in these planning regions would be more functional. Also, there is no reason to expect that one set of regional planning areas would be ideal for all purposes. The relevant airshed for a region is often geographically distinct from its watershed. An optimal air and water transportation region could well diverge from a reasonable highway planning or economic development region. These considerations argue for a building block approach, in which the smallest administrative and data collection region, usually a county, would be combined flexibly with other sets of counties for different analytic, planning, and administrative purposes.

The multi-state regional commissions have raised one issue that is relatively new in regional development. The Coastal Plains and Great Lakes Regional Commissions have argued the case that lagging regions should be assisted by relaxing federal regulations. Historically, most regional aid has been in the form of added subsidies. This new proposal is that lagging regions should be aided by relaxing federal tax regulations, reducing national interest rate regulations, relaxing regulatory requirements, and by selective adjustments in policies relating to reserve requirements, transportation licensing, inspection procedures, labor practice, and planning and zoning regulations.

Logically, there is no reason why relaxation of national regulations should not be considered as an alternative to the traditional policy of adding subsidies to aid lagging regions. However, some possible policy problems are raised by these proposals. The commissions argue that national inflation would not be increased by freeing from anti-inflation policies those regions that have unemployed resources. This argument overlooks interregional linkages. Most regions are far from self-sufficient, and expansionary expenditures from within regions leak to other regions, and vice versa. Also, proposals to relax regulatory practices in lagging regions raise the problem of externalities affecting other regions. Competitive relaxation of air and water quality standards, for example, could adversely affect other regions and the nation.

Administratively, it might prove difficult ever to restore regulations that had been modified to assist the developing region, especially if the region developed a dependence upon special treatment. In respect to resource allocation, subsidies have the advantage that they are more visible and measurable than would be the cost to the nation of selective modification of national standards. It should also be recognized that historically any special privileges granted to one region tend to be proliferated to other regions. The important issue raised by this proposal is what types of regional assistance and what types of interregional competition are most likely to yield the desired outcomes in terms of both regional and national objectives. This question is considered in the following section.

Findings and Recommendations

In summarizing what has been a highly critical review of U.S. regional development experience, it must be emphasized that this experience has been, on the average, outstandingly successful in terms of the generally accepted economic variables. Real per capita personal incomes even in the poorest regions of the nation, are higher than in most of the developed nations of the world. The ideal of self-sustaining growth of affluence has been achieved in all of the states in the U.S. The highly developed market economy of the U.S. offers large incomes to most of those whose productivity, mobility, and motivation permit them to function effectively in this economy. Interregional competition has contributed to regional specialization and national economic productivity.

However, limiting the evaluation of regional economic performance to the income variable, as traditionally defined, and measuring this performance by averages over large regions masks some basic problems of serious magnitude in U.S. society. Concealed by the aggregative data is the plight of large numbers of Americans who have not participated fully in the national economy primarily because of low productivity resulting from inadequate education and training, racial prejudice, poor mental and physical health, excessive family size, broken homes, cultural differences, and related problems that are often cumulative from generation to generation. Extensive pockets of poverty remain in rural backwaters and in urban ghettos.

In addition to the failures of the market economy to eliminate poverty and unemployment and to achieve distributive goals, the success of the market economy has created other problems of pollution, congestion, urban deterioration, and damage to the quality of life. Pollution, which formerly was regarded as an isolated and exceptional phenomenon, is now recognized as being a direct function of the level and composition of economic activity and growth.[25] Continuing increases in agricultural productivity and rapid economic growth of urban areas have attracted massive migrations of displaced rural populations into hostile urban environments for which they have been culturally unprepared, and where no adequate provision has been made for their reception and assimilation.

The resulting failures of the market economy to deal with the problems of the minorities and the disadvantaged, the breakdown of urban society, the accelerating environmental crises, the general deterioration of the quality of life at a time when vast resources are allocated to aerospace and military programs rather than to the solution of human problems have alienated many of the most able and idealistic in society. It is highly unrealistic to suppose that these deep and fundamental problems can be fully explained by evaluating regional economic development experience, or that they can all be solved by improving regional development and transportation policies. However, there are lessons to be learned from the U.S. regional development experience that have possible relevance for future improvement.

Market competition between regions, as between individuals and firms, has resulted in great productivity and economic growth for the nation, but this market performance has been nurtured and improved by government intervention at many points. In the early period of independence, the Federal

Government acted to provide a transportation infrastructure when it was not clear that private investment would emerge on a scale justified by the potential gain to be achieved from regional specialization and expansion of market size. Later, states and local governments took similar steps to provide public services, often in cooperation with private investors. This flexible, pragmatic, pluralistic U.S. approach to the creation of new institutions for meeting regional economic development and transportation objectives has been an important factor in achieving development objectives.

Efforts to achieve regional development in the United States have been most successful when they have been based upon a systematic, comprehensive plan for concentrating available resources on the execution of a well-designed system with specific objectives. The Gallatin plan for a national transportation system, the New York State plan for the Erie Canal system, and the Baltimore City plan for the Baltimore and Ohio Railroad are good examples. The welfare payoff of U.S. regional development programs has been significant in those programs where direct steps have been taken outside the market economy to correct market deficiencies. Examples are the direct grants of homesteads to actual settlers, use of federal lands to establish land grant universities, and current efforts in Appalachia to overcome the effects of generations of underinvestment in human capital.

Failures in U.S. regional development policies can be traced to some well-defined patterns. The most serious of these deficiencies in development patterns has been a general tendency to neglect and override the rights of minority groups and the disadvantaged. This tendency began with the conquest of the continent from the Indians, and has continued with the exploitation of slave labor, discrimination against successive waves of immigrants, down to contemporary neglect of urban and rural groups, and the virtual exclusion of the Eskimos from the development process in Alaska.[26]

Another shortcoming in U.S. regional development policy has been a general reluctance, except in the notable exceptions discussed above, to undertake the necessary detailed identification of objectives, evaluation of benefits and costs of alternative programs, and specific comprehensive planning required to assure that both national and regional goals are reconciled and achieved through a total systems approach. Much of the U.S. economic development policy has been determined on the basis of narrow engineering approaches that depend upon unevaluated technologies. Massive new technologies are typically introduced without prior evaluation of their full direct and indirect consequences. Too often these are single-purpose engineering technologies that are inappropriate for the complex human and social problems they are designed to address. Examples include irrigation of western lands, the impact of the internal combustion automobile and city freeways on the quality of urban life, use of agricultural chemicals, and premature introduction of nuclear energy before achievement of concensus among scientists upon adequate controls for safety and management of thermal and radioactive wastes.

Another persistent problem in U.S. regional development has been the basic tendency to emphasize the quantitative, aggregative aspects of development, rather than the qualitative aspects and the tendency towards unselective proliferation of programs. Programs carefully designed to yield a high level of social benefits over costs in one region tend to create a demand for extension of these programs into less appropriate regions where net social benefits over costs are low or even negative. Examples are the early construction of unprofitable canals and railroads, extension of irrigation to production of crops in surplus supply, indiscriminate dispersion of regional development funds to areas without capability for sustained growth, extension of interstate highways into downtown areas, overemphasis on highway construction in Appalachia, promotion of waste-generating industry in resource-conservation areas, and numerous other regional economic development excesses. In the irrigation of western lands, the establishment of a trust fund contributed toward excessive investment in this particular type of investment, extension of irrigation into inappropriate areas, and the overproduction of crops in surplus supply.[c]

One of the most serious defects in U.S. regional economic development has been the failure to protect the nation's environment. Planning for economic development has consistently been based upon the assumption that man could and should conquer nature and reshape it to serve his wants. This tendency has been most obvious in the construction of dams and irrigation projects, massive transfers of water supplies, large-scale use of agricultural chemicals, stripping of forest cover, and extraction of minerals without provision for the restoration of the damage or protection of ecological relationships. The market incentives for discharging wastes, residuals, and pollutants directly into the common property resources of air, land, and water have created external diseconomies on a scale which threatens the quality not only of the national, but also the global environment.[27] This factor is particularly important for transportation planning, because transportation systems are among the most serious of all pollution emitters.

An excellent current example and test case for all of these unresolved problems is that of regional economic development in Alaska. Discoveries of petroleum on the north slope have resulted in proposals to pipe the oil overland. The rights of the Eskimos who live in the area have been given low priority. The possible impacts of the pipeline and oil spills on the ecology of the permafrost region have not been fully evaluated. An untested engineering technology is being developed for a single-purpose objective, without comprehensive evaluation of its effect upon the ecology and environment of the state. No comprehensive regional development policy or program has been prepared at the federal or state level for Alaska. Unless at least a small fraction of the revenue received for the oil rights is used to design an overall development plan for Alaska with examination of the benefits and costs of development alternatives, protection of

---

[c]This persistent tendency toward unselective proliferation raises serious doubts about whether any initial restrictions on flight patterns for the SST would be enforced.

the rights of the Eskimos, and assurance of ecological and environmental safeguards, the regional economic development of Alaska may repeat all of the traditional mistakes of the past on a monumental scale.

A very compelling case can be advanced that the nation urgently needs to formulate a national transportation policy based upon a clear identification of objectives, and an appraisal of the benefits and costs of alternative programs for achieving these objectives. However, a basic principle is that no formulation of national transportation policy can be satisfactorily achieved in isolation from other major policy areas. Transportation is, after all, a means to various ends and not an end in itself, except to the transportation industries and for recreational travel. Therefore, rational design of transportation policy must be related to national policies in the associated areas of regional and urban development, land use, natural resource management, technology assessment, and environmental protection. Unfortunately, while the nation has numerous programs in each of these areas, it has no detailed, comprehensive, coordinated national policy in any of them. This concluding section attempts to suggest some of the elements that might be included in a coherent set of national policies in these overlapping fields.

The major need in regional development policy is to abandon the concept of ubiquitous acceleration of economic growth in all regions in favor of moving toward improvement in the quality of regional and urban life through resource allocation according to the priority of objectives. The unselective spatial proliferation of growth has resulted in inefficient dispersion of funds and in extensive damage to natural and environmental resources. Improved performance requires the establishment of federal guidelines for improving the quality of development and for identifying those areas where intensive economic growth is not in the national interest. Of the two, identification of non-growth regions will be the more difficult. Suggested candidates for non-growth areas are all seashores, river and stream banks, flood plains, highest peaks and deepest valleys, wilderness areas, areas of unique geological, ecological, environmental, recreational and historic significance, regions with potentially hazardous soil, seismic, drought, storm, meteorological, and brush fire conditions.

Current pressures exerted on all regions to pursue economic development could be reduced by revenue sharing, by federal guidelines for development priorities, by more detailed federal and state physical planning, and by requirements that local authorities refer their plans to higher levels of government for coordination of regional and national interests.

However, regional policy should provide that just as no region should be forced to develop in order to raise revenue for public services, no region should suffer economically from economic response to changes in national priorities. For example, an important argument advanced for continuing work on the supersonic transport plane was the possible economic distress that termination would cause for some of those working on the project, as well as for those who would be affected by resulting regional multiplier effects. The debate over the future of the SST is of far too great national importance to be biased by regional economic factors. A rational and humane national policy on regional development would give top priority to human welfare problems and provide generous assistance to people and to regions that experience economic distress as the result of changes in national goals, technology, or market forces. Easing the process of economic adjustment to external changes can be justified on grounds of both humanity and efficiency.

In the areas of land use and natural resource management, one concept that could reduce irreversible damage and misallocation of investment is life cycle resource planning. This concept would require that, prior to beginning of operations, a comprehensive plan was submitted for all phases of operation, including development, exploration, and eventual restoration of the area. As applied to strip mining, for example, this concept would require that the developer submit a detailed proposal indicating the steps to be taken at every stage to prevent environmental damage of resource systems during operations, together with responsible bonding for eventual restoration of the area. The damage suffered by the region and the nation from the exploitation of Appalachia indicates the need to profit from this experience as the nation moves on to the development of other major resource systems, such as petroleum on the continental shelf and in Alaska, oil shales in the West, and the many resources of the oceans. Past failures to consider the full consequences of natural resource exploitation schemes raise serious questions about the adequacy of the current state of human knowledge and wisdom in undertaking large-scale weather modification, discharge of radioactive wastes into underground areas, and uses of nuclear explosions for mining and engineering projects.

A major problem in planning future development and transportation policies will be reconciling economic growth with environmental protection and technology management. The growing recognition of direct relationships between levels and composition of economic activity and the emission of pollutants has emphasized the need for improved treatment of pollutants, but more importantly, for reducing emissions at the source, for finding additional opportunities for recycling of wastes, for limiting population size, for changing consumption patterns, and for developing more emission-free technological processes. Economic incentives to achieve environmental quality can be provided by national policies of taxation, subsidy, and regulation to encourage recycling, prevent discharges into common property resources, and by developing environmentally neutral technologies.

Improved performance in regional development and transportation will require better methods for dealing with new technologies as their size and frequency of introduction accelerate.[28] Important lessons can be learned from experience with the internal combustion automobile, agricultural chemicals, and nuclear energy, all of which were applied on a large scale before adequate assessment of their indirect, environmental and ecological effects. The responsibility and potential control over these systems that the Federal Government could exercise through its research and development, regulatory, and other functions could be used to spell out in advance the performance characteristics of these systems before they are introduced. Experience gained in the space program and elsewhere suggests that science, systems analysis, and applications of research and development resources can be effectively used to shape technology to human requirements, rather than requiring people and society to adapt to immature, destructive technologies. The delay and waste involved in the SST controversy indicate the importance of comprehensive, cooperative, advanced specification of performance standards by physical scientists, social scientists, environmental scientists, and systems analysts in the early stages of large-scale R & D efforts.[29]

In designing a national transportation policy and coordinating it with objectives in related areas of regional and urban planning, land use, resource management, environmental quality, and technology assessment, a first requirement is that transportation systems be planned to give priority to improvement in the quality of life, rather than merely to accelerate economic growth. Therefore, the planning of transportation systems should involve the active participation not only of those groups that would produce and use them, but also all those who would be affected by them. In the urban transportation area, it is becoming vital that systems be planned not only for commuters, but also for ghetto dwellers whose homes and jobs are at stake, and who have specialized transportation needs. In the case of massive transportation systems like the SST, equal voice in the planning process should be given not only to engineers and industry, but also to ecologists, environmentalists, social scientists, and the general public that would bear the costs of the sonic booms and environmental change.

In the development of transportation systems, the need for participation at all levels of government is clear. During the era of "internal improvements," before the worst excesses of the industrial revolution, most viable forms of regional economic development could be assumed to result in improved total social welfare with few accompanying external diseconomies. The appropriate role of government was then to avoid underinvestment in infrastructure and to guide interregional competition into productive channels. Currently, events have reordered priorities in regional development and transportation planning. The high growth rates that are now operating upon an already extensive economic structure generate an accompanying waste burden which is massive in relationship to the common property environmental resources of air and water into which these wastes are typically discharged. Consequently an emerging responsibility of government must be to regulate the quantity and quality of regional and national economic growth with greater attention both to social priorities and to environmental quality. More detailed planning, physical design, and specification of guidelines will be necessary by federal and state agencies, in contrast to the latitude which was previously left to local and private planning.

Rather than establish a single set of regions for transportation planning, flexible systems of regions should be established from small-area building blocks that can be combined in various ways to represent all of the governmental levels and units, including international, that are affected by the systems involved. Transportation planning is more likely to serve general social goals if, instead of setting up separate transportation planning regions, it is carried on in conjunction with established regional planning units. The traditional economic planning emphasis should be broadened to include overall regional planning serving social and environmental as well as economic goals.

To assure shifting of emphasis away from quantitative development toward qualitative improvement, and in order to avoid over-allocation of scarce resources to specific transportation modes, consideration should be given to phasing out of trust funds, so that every transport mode and every transportation program and project could be considered on its merits and in relationship to total transportation systems with net social benefits and costs compared with those of alternative programs. Growing dissatisfaction with the use of gasoline tax trust funds for overinvestment in highways should not of course be used as justification for converting the use of trust funds for overinvestment in mass transit or any other transportation systems, all of which should be closely examined with respect to economic efficiency, social priorities, environmental impact, and alternative programs.

Opposition to the development of transportation systems could be reduced by requirements that they pay their full social costs and internalize external diseconomies. This would mean, for example, that in the case of urban transport systems of all kinds, before any construction took place, the transportation systems would bear the full costs of replacing with satisfactory alternatives the housing, parks, business and any other public or private assets that were affected. Also, transportation systems should be planned from the design stage not only to eliminate congestion, noise, fumes, and other environmentally damaging emissions, but also to make transportation not an unpleasant ordeal, but to the extent possible an enjoyable human experience.

In earlier periods of the U.S. experience in transportation and regional development, transportation programs that met minimal criteria for systems planning and economic efficiency could generally be assumed to improve the quality of life. Most wastes were assimilated by the absorptive capacity of common property resources, as social problems were alleviated by the availability of free land on the frontier. Now that many of the nation's narrowly economic objectives have been achieved, the task of designing transportation systems with a high probability of improving the quality of life requires a broadening of guidelines to include national goals for technology assessment, population management, social welfare, and environmental quality. Transportation planners alone cannot formulate national policies in all of these areas, but they can and should emphasize the dependence of improved transportation planning on the development of coherent national goals in these related areas.

Notes

1. See, for example, the proposed National Transportation Act, S.2425, 91st Congress, 1st Session; and "Statement of John A. Volpe, Secretary of Transportation, Before the Senate Commerce Committee Regarding S.2425, the Proposed 'National Transportation Act,' "Wednesday, April 15, 1970.

2. Rather than providing fully documented case studies, this paper is intended to present a limited set of hypotheses drawn from the author's REGIONAL DEVELOPMENT EXPERIENCES AND PROSPECTS IN THE UNITED STATES OF AMERICA (United Nations Institute For Social Development, Mouton, Paris 1971).

3. J.H. Cumberland, "A Regional Interindustry Model for the Analysis of Development Objectives," REGIONAL SCIENCE ASSOCIATION PAPERS, Vol. 16, Philadelphia meeting, 1965, published 1966, pp. 64-95; and R.U. Ayres and A.V. Kneese, "Production Consumption and Externalities," AMERICAN ECONOMIC REVIEW, Volume 59, No. 7, June 1969, pp. 282-297.

4. See especially, E.J. Mishan, THE COST OF ECONOMIC GROWTH, London, Staples Press, 1967.

5. Albert Gallatin, REPORT OF THE SECRETARY OF THE TREASURY ON THE SUBJECT OF PUBLIC ROADS AND CANALS, Washington, 1808, reprinted by A.M. Kelly, New York, 1968.

6. Ibid., p. 123.

7. Ibid., p. 8.

8. Carter Goodrich (ed.), THE GOVERNMENT AND THE ECONOMY, 1783-1811, New York, Bobbs-Merill Co., 1967.

9. Dudley Dillard, ECONOMIC DEVELOPMENT OF THE NORTH ATLANTIC COMMUNITY, Englewood Cliffs, New Jersey, Prentice Hall, 1967, p. 323.

10. Carter Goodrich, GOVERNMENT PROMOTION OF AMERICAN CANALS AND RAILROADS, 1800-1890, New York, Columbia University Press, 1960, Chapter 3.

11. Ibid., p. 273.

12. Carter Goodrich (ed.), with Julius Rubin, H. Jerome Cranmer, and Harvey H. Siegel, CANALS AND AMERICAN ECONOMIC DEVELOPMENT, New York, Columbia University Press, 1961.

13. Goodrich, GOVERNMENT PROMOTION OF AMERICAN CANALS AND RAILROADS, op. cit.

14. Ibid., p. 186-190.

15. J.B. Coulter, "Marine Shipping Industry—Effects and Impacts on the Chesapeake Bay," PROCEEDINGS OF THE GOVERNOR'S CONFERENCE ON CHESAPEAKE BAY, September 12-13, 1968, Annapolis, Maryland. See other sections of the PROCEEDINGS for discussions of conflicts between industrial use of Chesapeake Bay and preservation of environmental quality.

16. Goodrich, GOVERNMENT PROMOTION OF AMERICAN CANALS AND RAILROADS, 1800-1890, op. cit.

17. Ibid.

18. David M. Ellis, "The Railroads and Their Land Grants," in Gerald D. Nash (ed.), ISSUES IN AMERICAN ECONOMIC HISTORY, D.C. Heath & Co., Boston, 1964.

19. Goodrich, GOVERNMENT PROMOTION OF AMERICAN CANALS AND RAILROADS, pp. 186-189.

20. Sar A. Levitan, FEDERAL AID TO DEPRESSED AREAS, Baltimore, Johns Hopkins Press, 1964, p. 219.

21. For an excellent appraisal of these problems, see Harry M. Caudill, NIGHT COMES TO THE CUMBERLANDS, Little, Brown, Boston, 1963.

22. Appalachian Regional Commission, ANNUAL REPORT, 1968, pp. 30-31.

23. B.J.L. Berry, GROWTH CENTERS AND THEIR POTENTIALS IN THE UPPER GREAT LAKES REGION, Upper Great Lakes Regional Commission, Washington, D.C., May 1969.

24. New England Regional Commission, REGIONAL DEVELOPMENT PLAN, Draft, July 10, 1969, p. 4.

25. John H. Cumberland, "A Regional Interindustry Model for the Analysis of Development Objectives," op. cit.

26. See, for example, MAN'S IMPACT ON THE GLOBAL ENVIRONMENT, Report of the Study of Critical Environmental Problems (SCEP), The M.I.T. Press, Cambridge, Massachusetts, 1970.

27. John H. Cumberland, "Application of Input-Output Techniques to the Analysis of Environmental Problems," paper presented before the Fifth International Conference on Input-Output Techniques, Geneva, January 11-15, 1971.

28. See, for example, National Academy of Public Administration, A TECHNOLOGY ASSESSMENT SYSTEM FOR THE EXECUTIVE BRANCH, U.S. Congress, Committee on Science and Astronautics, July 1970.

29. See the CONGRESSIONAL RECORD, 91st Congress, Second Session, Vol. 116, No. 160, September 15, 1970, pp. S-15397-S-15405, statement of sixteen eminent economists, all of whom except one opposed continuation of work on the SST.

A Critique of Governmental Intervention in Transport

James C. Nelson,
Washington State University

Government in the United States has intervened in transport in two fundamental ways. First, all through its almost 200 years of existence, financial and other public aids have been granted to encourage development of new and more efficient transport facilities. Since 1920, governments have invested heavily to provide highways, inland waterways, and airways and airports under government enterprise conditions. This type of intervention can be termed promotional or developmental action. Second, for about 100 years, state and Federal governments have intervened to regulate common carriers (and more recently, contract carriers) on various economic grounds. These include the failure of the market under monopoly or partial monopoly conditions to limit rate and service discrimination or the markets' assumed failure under conditions of excessive, or "destructive," competition to yield normal competitive returns to carriers, stable services and rates, and efficient divisions of traffic and allocations of resources.

Both of those forms of governmental intervention have powerfully influenced the development of transport systems and the rates and services rendered to the national, regional, and state economies. This paper will review whether governmental regulatory and promotional policies have primarily been directed toward national economic development or regional, state, and urban area development. To the extent possible, it will also discuss the sense in which national, regional or local planning was involved either in regulating carriers or in aiding and developing private or public transport facilities. As a major task, however, the paper states the general economic effects of government regulation and promotion, placing emphasis on the modern period of revolutionary change in the transport structure, 1920 to 1970. Additionally, it draws attention to how those effects have shaped the serious national, regional, state, and local transport problems of today. Finally, the paper comments on the directions that regulatory and promotional policy should take to solve the outstanding issues of the day. At this point, the paper focuses more closely on how changes in government interventional policies can help to solve the great urban and regional transport development needs of the future.

General Nature of the Influences of Government Intervention in Transport

In terms of transport's role in influencing economic development, perhaps the promotional policies of governments have been more significant than their regulatory activities. Thus, state entrepreneurship in building the Erie Canal and other canals in the first half of the last century made possible the exchange of large volumes of goods between the Atlantic Seaboard and the rich but underdeveloped lands west of the Allegheny Mountains along the Great Lakes. Governments' free-entry, eminent-domain and other encouragements to railway building and linkage in the last century, especially the Federal land grants to selected railways to hasten development of long lines along the Mississippi River, to the Southwest, and along the three transcontinental routes to the Pacific Coast, had an even wider geographical impact on population settlement, development of resource-orientated industries, growth of new cities, and rapid economic and political integration of the continental and highly specialized economy of the United States. The early state investments in canals, the Federal land grants to a number of key railways, and the policy of private railway development under free entry conditions were important factors in the rapid installation of modern kinds of efficient transport systems for the first time and in the national and regional economic development that took place in response to efficient and faster transport.

In the last 50 years, the role of government promotion has been even more prominent in transport development than in the nineteenth century, and it has had a greater impact on the transport supply system. Most significantly, the state and Federal governments have cooperatively engaged in the greatest long-term investment program in U.S. transport history, the development of the Federal-aid highway systems. Starting with the paving of the principal intercity and interstate routes in the 1920s and the 1930s, that program has continued since World War II with great enlargements in the capacity of the primary highways, including the Interstate System and urban highways. With almost continually rising Federal financial support in huge annual volumes since 1956, this government enterprise has revolutionized the relative transport roles of the major modes; substituted pervasive competition for monopoly as the most prevailing natural condition of transport markets; added greatly to decentralization of cities and the decline of villages and small towns; and has made highway transport overwhelmingly dominant in the transport of persons and in short-haul transport of goods.

Likewise, the growing role of the inland waterways in both short-haul and long-distance transport of raw materials, liquid products, and heavy semi-manufactures has been based on Federal enterprise and investment in inland waterway channels and locks built by the Corps of Engineers. Federal enterprise and investment in the civil airways and in some large airports and growing Federal aid to major airports under local control made possible the great growth of long-distance passenger travel by air at speeds unattainable in surface transport. As a consequence of the gigantic Federal and state investments and aids to the new modes, however, a sharp decline in the railroads' role in intercity passenger travel, small-shipment traffic, and in short- and medium-distance freight markets has taken place.[1]

Government economic regulation was the second principal form of governmental intervention in transport. Originally, it came in response to marked monopoly or cartel conditions in many transport markets after the railroads, by their cost and service efficiencies, superseded the canals and restricted wagon road transport to gathering and distribution functions to and from rail stations. Early state commissions (1870s) and the Interstate Commerce Commission (1887) were organized to give small shippers, communities served only by rail transport, and producing areas far from markets assurance of more equal access to their markets. This principally involved elimination of discrimination in rates and services that could not reasonably be justified.

Until 1920, regulatory intervention controlled the excesses of monopoly power and discriminating rates. It did not rationalize the competitive structure of railroads between major centers or producing areas, nor did it break up rate cartels that had long managed more or less successfully to establish monopoly rates and returns. Regulation affirmatively influenced the economic organization of the railroads only after the Transportation Act of 1920 became law, and regulation's marked influence on the economic structure of regulated trucking and on the intermodal division of traffic and revenues came only after passage of the Motor Carrier Act of 1935. However, regulation of the conditions for airmail contracts by the Post Office Department and of entry and mergers by the Civil Aeronautics Board beginning in 1938 markedly influenced the market structure of air transport almost from the beginning.

The promotional and allocative functions of economic regulation, which came late and are highly controversial today, were based on entirely new concepts of transport regulation. The promotion of air transport, including airline profitability, by the Civil Aeronautics Act of 1938 best exemplifies the new promotional or developmental objective of regulation. Minimum rate control by the ICC after 1935 and 1940 to prevent price competition on relative unit costs from allocating traffic and revenues between the railroads and their closest intermodal competitors furnishes the best example of the exercise of the allocative function between modes of transport.

Using economic regulation in recent decades for transport industry promotional and allocative purposes has much in common with promotional policy in transport. Whether or not designed to be complementary, both types of governmental intervention have emphasized rapid development of air, highway, and inland waterway transport through a variety of governmental controls and continuing aids or subsidies. In addition to contributing flexible schedules, higher speeds, and comfortable or protective services and some gains in economy, these government-promoted changes were important factors in the long and gradual decline in the railroads' role, in their low profitability, and in their lessening financial ability to introduce technological innovations, to replace capital, and to continue customary services.

In view of the mixed results of governmental intervention in transport during the modern period, several questions seem pertinent. Has using promotional and regulatory intervention to foster rapid development of the newer modes of transport in recent decades—with significant and some long-continuing subsidies—been fully economic? Have those policies made the best use of the scarce private and public resources invested in transport? Have the impacts on national, regional, and urban development been wholly desirable and entirely economic? Or can some of the most urgent transport problems of the day, such as enormous traffic congestion, lack of modal alternatives in urban communities, inadequate investment in and modernization of railways, and the common external diseconomies of rubber-tired and above-the-surface transport be ascribed significantly to those promotional and regulatory policies? Can today's urban, regional, and national development and resource-use problems be satisfactorily solved without major changes in current transport policies?

Regulatory Intervention in Transport by Government

Criticism of the effects of transport regulation by economists and many others, including leading Congressmen, has mounted and become widespread in recent years. This has brought the role and accomplishments or defects of economic regulation of carriers into sharp controversy within transport circles and even among other public groups. Consequently, discussion will focus first on the changing nature of economic regulation, the effects of regulatory policies, and on the changes essential to promote a more efficient use of the resources committed to transport. Emphasis will be on the regulation of surface carriers of freight—the area of almost all ICC regulation and the one in which the economic costs of misallocated traffic are the greatest. Although resource misallocation in the sense of inefficient market structures and excess capacity from service competition exist in the airline field, airline regulation will be treated only briefly, as it primarily is concerned with intercity passenger travel and contributes only slightly to misallocations of freight traffic.

Effects of Railroad Regulation to 1935

The prime period of Federal regulation of the railroads was between 1887 and 1935. During the early years of that period, a well-known criticism was that the ICC was ineffective in controlling rate discriminations and high rates. The courts had declared that the ICC lacked the power to prescribe maximum rates and to deal effectively with long-short haul discrimination. The explicit grant of those powers to the ICC by the Hepburn and Mann-Elkins Acts in 1906 and 1910, respectively, started regulation on a path toward some alleviation of discriminatory conditions and excessive rates.

Soon, however, World War I intervened to disrupt transport conditions and to necessitate government operation of the railroads from 1917 to 1920. By the time the railroads regained private ownership in 1920, the rise of new modes was changing intercity transport from an industry of many monopoly markets and cartel rate-making into one of pervasive competition, with monopoly markets gradually becoming exceptional.

Nevertheless, some generalizations on the nature and effects of early regulation are tenable. First, although some recent historians have reinterpreted regulatory history in finding that ICC regulation strengthened the railroad cartels in price fixing,[2] it remains clear that the *public tasks* assigned by the Act to Regulate Commerce were those of limiting monopoly and discriminating rates and of encouraging as much competition between railroads and between rail and water carriers as possible. Regulation was distinctly shipper- or consumer-motivated in its rationale. To the extent it was effective, it substituted for competitive forces that were not strong or pervasive enough to limit rates to costs and to prevent uneconomic discrimination. Second, after the Mann-Elkins amendment, the ICC greatly limited long- and short-haul discrimination. This gave intermediate cities such as Spokane, Washington, and Salt Lake City, Utah, better relative rate opportunities with which to develop their wholesaling and manufacturing industries in competition with Pacific coastal cities differentially enjoying the competition between intercoastal water carriers and the transcontinental rail carriers.[3] Third, the ICC often gave some relief from rate discrimination to particular shippers, distant producing areas, and low-grade commodities unable to stand high rates.[4]

Long before regulation became tolerably effective in terms of its original purposes, the discriminating freight rate structure of the railroads had been fashioned by the forces of railroad monopoly at intermediate points, route competition, market competition, and the carriers' profit interest in increasing utilization by quoting low rates on agricultural and extractive commodities over long distances and assessing high rates on short-haul movements and on high-value commodities. The ICC basically accepted that rate structure as fitting the railroads' economic characteristics and as promotive of national and regional economic development, changing it only as to details.[5] In times of rising prices, the ICC limited general rate increases and the profitability of the railroads, but the ICC seldom reduced the general level of rates, even during the Great Depression. By controlling personal, long-short haul, commodity, and place discrimination to an extent, the ICC widened the competitive opportunity of particular shippers, communities, and regions, especially for shippers of agricultural and extractive products located far from their markets.

Unquestionably, the railroad discriminating rate structure facilitated the economic integration of the continental United States. It fostered much regional specialization, afforded wide markets for both extractive and manufactured products, and stimulated large-scale production in industry. Consequently, it promoted the national and regional development that already was taking place on the basis of other economic factors. Under the influence of low rates on foods and raw materials from western and southern origins and its early start in manufacturing, the Northeast developed as the core economic region of the country, having most of its manufacturing, its largest cities, and about half of the population. And the value-of-service rate structure assisted the South, Southwest, and West to develop basically as agricultural and extractive regions.

This national economic structure, with large-volume movements of extractive products eastward and northward to the Northeast and reverse large flows of manufactured products to the outlying southern, southwestern, and western regions, came about without comprehensive economic planning. Rather, it happened in response to the profit stimulus for development strengthened by the right to homestead on public lands, sale of the public domain at low prices, the availability of excellent natural resources in the West, and the policies that hastened railroad development (such as free entry) until 1920, the right of eminent domain, and Federal land grants and other aids. Thus, last century's predominant transport policy consisted of encouraging the development of as many competitive rail routes and lines as would be attractive to private capital, the supply of efficient transport in advance of the traffic demand, and a rate structure that would stimulate a maximum flow of commodities and a more efficient utilization of railroad facilities.

As a broad generalization, then, regulation until the 1930s was basically consistent both with the economic and cost characteristics of the railroads and the requirements of national and regional economic development.[6] The economic development to which the scheme of regulation contributed yielded marked national economic growth, vast regional specialization and division of labor, the maximum exchange of products between regions, wide markets for large-scale production of industrial products in the Northeast, and a rapidly growing population enjoying ever-increasing per capita real incomes.

Ultimately, however, significant economic development problems emerged, especially as the outlying regions began to engage in manufacturing and to press for government investments and policies designed to promote balanced regional economies. In addition, some of the perplexing and unsolved urban problems of today eventually emerged from the great concentrations of population and industry fostered by efficient transport and the value-of-service rate structure accepted by the ICC.

New Concepts in Transport Regulation and
Rising Criticism

In the decade of the 1930s, however, transport regulation took a highly paradoxical direction. Even though transport markets were becoming more competitive and the railroads were experiencing a sharp diversion of traffic and revenues to new modes, economic regulation by the ICC shifted from the task of controlling monopoly power and maintaining competition in transport to that of limiting intramodal and intermodal competition. This was accomplished by extending regulation to new competitive modes (not practicing obnoxious discrimination in rates and services or fixing extortionate rate levels) and by shifting to the regulatory tools of controlled entry and minimum rate regulation from long-standing dependence on control of discrimination and prescription of maximum rates.

At the time, a few economists and some shipper groups cautioned that a logical basis for this extension of regulation to restrict competition in transport was largely lacking. They argued that the new regulatory controls would ultimately produce inefficiencies in transport. The Congress largely ignored those cautions, however, except in granting regulatory exemptions for agricultural and bulk commodities and for private carriage.

Gradually, however, the paradox became better understood of expanding regulation when competition increasingly enables the transport markets to function as efficiently as in many unregulated industries. Even the railroads, the original sponsors of extended regulation, began to voice criticisms of particular regulatory policies as their market shares and profitability rates declined after World War II. And in a series of reports to the Congress, the Executive Branch of the Federal Government recommended some relaxation of the new restrictive regulation to permit the forces of competition to divide the traffic more efficiently among the modes. Moreover, the long delays in getting substantial change in regulation and the accumulating evidence that regulation has been misallocating resources in intercity freight traffic have promoted a widening demand for drastic regulatory policy revision, including even abolition of the ICC.[7] Because the ICC's regulation touches the pocketbooks of shippers and influences industrial location and the availability of markets, most criticism of transport regulation has focused on the ICC. Though not free of criticism by any means, the CAB has operated under favorable conditions of demand growth and with aircraft innovations improving service, thus escaping the harsh criticism that has been leveled against ICC regulation.

The earliest criticism of extended ICC regulation came from a few transport economists in the late 1930s.[8] Agricultural industries opted early for the free market in truck and water carriage, strongly preferring exempt carriers to regulated carriers on grounds of more flexible services and competitive rates. Since the 1950s, the railroads have increasingly blamed ICC regulation of minimum rates for their declining market shares—as preventing them from making their low-cost advantage effective. Moreover, many shippers have turned to private trucking and have criticized the deficiencies in regulated trucking service and the generous rate and profit levels allowed by the ICC. The most serious strictures, however, have been those of a number of economists, whose studies have repetitively shown that ICC regulation has been making freight transport inefficient and has been contributing to unnecessary railroad decline.[9] Even CAB regulation of airline travel has not escaped criticism that it has contributed to cost-increasing excess capacity by emphasizing service competition and resisting competitive fares.[10]

These growing criticisms have raised the fundamental question of whether the benefits of economic regulation of surface modes are any longer worth the costs imposed on consumers, governments, shippers, and carriers. Thus, the basic issue stated in the 1942 report of the National Resources Planning Board on *Transportation and National Policy* has surfaced for active consideration and legislative action in the 1970s.[11] Should this nation continue to implement the policy of restricting competition in domestic transport by the brand of protective regulation adopted in the heart of the Great Depression and continue to move in the direction of monopoly organization and cartel pricing in transport? Or should it turn regulatory policy toward increasing the widespread competitive forces that now naturally exist in transport, and toward allowing the free market to determine the relative economic roles of the competing modes?

Underlying those critical questions, of course, are the transport requirements for national, regional, urban and rural economic development. Would the national and regional economies be more productive if transport supply and rates were determined more by the forces of a free market? Would urban areas benefit from a more balanced supply of transport?

The Specific Effects of the New Regulation
after 1935

A staff paper appearing in *Transportation and National Policy* in 1942 questioned the economic rationale advanced for extending minimum rate and entry controls to interstate motor and water carriers.[12] The alleged destructiveness of competition, the financial demoralization attributed to competition, the supposed excessive contribution of competition to excess capacity, and the rate and service instability at the time were traced to the low general level of aggregate demand and employment during the Great Depression rather than to the growing competition in transport. Thus, excessive competition could not be a logical economic basis for restricting transport competition in full-employment economies for modes not evidencing long-run decreasing costs to scale.[13]

Structural, rate, and service effects in the early years of the new regulation. The NRPB paper found that entry control and minimum rate regulation were having significant impacts on the market structures of transport and on rates and service. These included strong tendencies toward fewer and larger firms in regulated trucking, attributable to the highly restrictive "Grandfather" and new-service entry policies of the ICC and to the incentives that closed entry gave to mergers.[14]

A most important structural change that occurred was the rapid organization of many new rate bureaus in the trucking industry. Stimulated by ICC insistence on uniform rates and rate bureau influences, the regulated truckers (except in New England) adopted the rail value-of-service rate structure, adjusted to discourage types of traffic that the truckers could not haul profitably at rates based on low rail costs.[15] Without this institutional structure for rate agreements, discriminating prices had not been viable in trucking because of the atomistic competitive conditions in that field. Hence, the ability of the regulated truckers to establish value-of-service rates revealed that regulation had converted the industry from a highly competitive field into a cartelized one.

Regulated truck rates were found to prevail at higher levels than the rates in unregulated trucking markets. The higher regulated rates were brought about by agreements on rates, ICC prescription for large territories of minimum rates that individual carriers could not cut without permission, protests by rate bureaus against independent rate actions, and frequent ICC suspensions of rate reductions. High minimum rate levels were prescribed on the industry's view that emergency conditions of financial demoralization existed in depressed years, on limited cost information, and on samples of revenue-cost relationships for the large carriers in the unprofitable first quarter of the year. The ICC's standard of historical average costs prevented many rate reductions even in back-haul situations where back-haul rates below average cost would have efficiently stimulated traffic to utilize excess capacity in the return direction. Rate competition between road and rail carriers was often hindered and service competition was frequently substituted by regulatory encouragement of competition on the basis of the rail value-of-service rates.[16]

The quality of trucking service was also affected by regulation. Even when regulated truckers held extensive "Grandfather" rights, there was a straitjacketing of service into rigid molds. Commodity, return-haul, route, point, and service restrictions in certificates and permits reduced the inherent flexibility of trucking services. Denials of entries and division of markets between noncompeting groups by means of service restrictions reduced the number of carriers permitted to carry particular commodities between city-pair markets. Back-haul restrictions often reduced the opportunities of shippers to utilize private trucking efficiently. The regulatory discouragement of carriers offering lower rates for lesser service greatly limited shippers' choice between low rates for inferior service or high rates for superior service. The enhanced service competition under the requirement that all carriers assess the same rates increased the unit costs of regulated service and the level of regulated rates.[17]

Continuing structural, rate, and service effects of the new regulation. Subsequent studies of the new protective regulation confirm both the structural and final effects noted above. With few exceptions, the ICC has continued its restrictive entry policies to the present time.[18] And the ICC has also continued to authorize many mergers involving large truckers each year, though these have not been supported by evidence of economies of scale in size of firm.

Significant market structural changes in regulated trucking have taken place. The number of ICC-regulated truckers has fallen from an estimated 26,167 in 1939 to about 15,100 carriers in 1971. This reduction took place in spite of an enormous growth in total trucking traffic and revenues.

Of greater significance is the decrease in the number of regulated truckers *with like authority* to operate in particular city-pair markets. Today there are numerous routes, including dense-traffic routes, that are served by only two or three up to six or ten general-commodity motor carriers authorized to give single-line service. While large numbers of regulated carriers still operate in a region or the nation, between specific city-pair markets over particular routes and for particular groups of authorized commodities the typical situation has become one of oligopoly, even of a small number of firms.[19]

As a consequence of the declining number of regulated truckers due to restrictive regulation and the rapid growth in truck traffic and revenues, numerous very large firms have evolved. In 1968, one hundred Class I regulated truckers had annual revenues of more than $18.8 million; fifty had more than $38.5 million; and nine had more than $100 million. Some are approaching $300 million or more.[20] This condition obviously increases the dominance of the large firms in particular markets of few firms and in the affairs of rate bureaus. And since no or negligible economies of scale in size of the trucking firm have been found, the market power of dominant firms has been increased without bringing cost and rate reductions to justify monopoly or oligopoly of a few firms.[21]

Evidence has multiplied that regulated trucking rates have been maintained at levels substantially higher than competitive rates. On agricultural products, the U.S. Department of Agriculture has shown that regulated trucking rates have exceeded the unregulated rates to a marked extent. For example, after removal from regulation, the USDA field studies found that the 1957 truck rates on frozen fruits and vegetables had declined to levels 11 to 29 percent below the regulated rates in 1955. The exempt trucking rates were relatively stable and sufficiently high to attract capital for growth in capacity and employment of modern equipment.[22]

The higher regulated trucking rates can be explained by the higher costs of regulated truckers and by monopoly influences. Regulated carriers bear the regulatory and court costs of attending hearings, of submitting and protesting entry applications, and of giving evidence in regulatory proceedings. Higher cost levels also reflect commodity, return-haul, route, and service restrictions that bring about poorer utilization and excessive supplies of trucks and labor.[23] However, the higher costs of the regulated truckers of general commodities also reflect their undertaking to transport more less-truckload shipments in regular services than exempt truckers. Notwithstanding, the high rates of return earned by regulated truckers comprise strong evidence of cartel influences in rate making.

High rates of return to regulated truckers. Evidence of the U.S. Department of Transportation in ICC rate cases reveals that regulated truckers have earned relatively high rates of return. Class I regulated truckers earned a return on net investment after income taxes averaging 11.78 percent in the 1957-1966 decade, with a range between 7.21 percent in 1960 and 13.86 percent in 1964. The ratio of net income after taxes to shareholders' and proprietors' equity for Class I motor carriers was 15.7 percent in 1966. This placed regulated trucking among the leading industries in high returns to equity, being exceeded only by the automotive-vehicle and scientific-instrument industries. The average return on net investment after income taxes greatly exceeded the typical fair return rates prescribed for electric utilities and even the 10.5 percent that the CAB generously authorized in 1960 to enable the trunk airlines to attract capital for financing jet planes.[24]

Regulated truckers would have a case for such high returns if the risk to capital were actually higher because of low revenue margins or other factors. However, since they have been protected from additional entries and extensions, have legally fixed rates by agreement, and have had rate cutting limited by minimum rate orders, their rates have most likely exceeded marginal costs, an indication that monopoly explains part of their high returns.[25]

Significant misallocation of traffic and revenues away from railways. Misallocation of traffic and resources traces to several regulatory factors. First, regulations holding truck rates and profits above competitive levels has encouraged private carrier transport, often when common carrier transport could be conducted more efficiently. Second, regulatory encouragement of trucker adoption of rail value-of-service rates and of railroad dependence on restrictive regulation to cure their ills contributed to a false sense of security—i.e., that the existing rail market shares would continue without aggressive rate and service competition by the railroads against other modes. Third, when the railroads later discovered that rate parity with trucking was not dividing the traffic according to relative costs, their attempts to reduce many rates above fully distributed costs or above out-of-pocket costs became difficult to achieve because of the full-cost and fair-sharing standards of the ICC in intermodal minimum rate cases.[26] Finally, technological improvements in railroading have been retarded by regulatory processes or disapproval of the necessary rate and service adjustments because of the competitive impacts on competing modes.[27]

No estimates are available on the economic cost of misallocation of traffic to private motor carriers. But highway studies have revealed that common motor carriers operate with a higher percentage of full-load round trips, a lower incidence of empty returns, and with higher average loads than private carriers. Consequently, a misallocation occurs at higher total cost because regulated conditions prevent common carrier economies from lowering regulated rates to efficient competitive levels.[28]

Evidence has multiplied that the static costs of misallocation of road-rail traffic are substantial. Thus in a Brookings Institution study, *Railroad Transportation and Public Policy*, James C. Nelson found that total transport costs would be minimized if more of the aggregate traffic were to move by rail. That study showed that the relative outputs of rail and highway freight carriers with equal inputs of labor, fuel, and comparable capital favored the railroads by ratios of approximately 3 to 1, making the railroads the low-cost mode except for small shipments and very short hauls. While the added costs to shippers for utilizing rail service were not measured, the resource-cost advantage of the railroads was so marked that the extra cost to shippers of using rail service would not completely offset the strong low-cost advantage of the railroads. With truck and rail rates held at the same level in spite of the markedly lower rail costs, changes in the actual division of the traffic do not prove that traffic has moved by the most efficient mode.[29]

The Harvard study by Meyer and Associates, *The Economics of Competition in the Transportation Industries*, also found a misallocation of traffic between road and rail. Here the added costs of rail services to shippers in view of the service advantages of trucks were taken into account. For the same social cost of $5.5 billion expended either on intercity rail freight or on intercity truck freight, the Meyer study found that railroads would produce 567 billion revenue ton-miles while the trucks would produce only 414 billion revenue ton-miles. Thus if expended for rail service, that amount would yield a 37-percent greater output for the same social cost.[30] As the analysis consistently sought to estimate truck costs on the low side, the economic cost of misallocation was greater than stated.

The report by Ernest W. Williams, Jr., and David W. Bluestone, *Rationale of Federal Transportation Policy*, accompanying the Mueller Report of 1960, made general estimates of misallocation. Restrictive regulation played a large part in their finding that some forms of transport have extended into the handling of traffic for which other forms have a comparative advantage; and that if all traffic had been allocated in accordance with the true comparative advantage of the several modes, several billions of dollars could be saved annually on freight alone.[31]

In his book, *The Transportation Act of 1968*, George W. Hilton estimated the economic cost of the regulatory cartel that he contends the ICC administers. Using USDA's studies showing that regulated truck rates on chicken and frozen foods were about 20 percent higher than competitive rates, Hilton calculated that ICC regulation increases the common carrier freight bill to annual levels some $4 billion to $5 billion higher than it would be under full competition. This increased cost was then adjusted downward to an amount greater than $2 billion each year, to which Hilton would add the Commission's annual budget, the costs of litigation, and other costs.[32]

In an article in *The Journal of Law and Economics*, Robert W. Harbeson found that an impressive economic loss takes place because of the misallocation of traffic between rail and for-hire intercity truck transport. Harbeson also considered the extra costs of shippers in using rail service, but he took no account of the savings in highway construction and maintenance costs or in traffic congestion costs that elimination of uneconomical intercity for-hire trucking would yield. Notwithstanding, for only 24 groups of manufacturers, Harbeson found an economic loss from the use of for-hire trucks instead of rail transport to amount to between $1.1 billion and $2.9 billion per annum.[33]

In her recent Brookings Institution book, *The Dilemma of Freight Transport Regulation*, Ann F. Friedlaender also found that a considerable amount of high-density traffic goes by truck that could go more cheaply by rail. This was attributed to the fact that the ICC has not allowed railroads and trucks to compete for high-density traffic by cutting rates, an area in which the railroads have an advantage; and to the regulatory channeling of road-rail competition along service lines, an area in which the trucks have the advantage. After calculating the added costs to shippers of shipping by rail in a manner generous to the trucks, Friedlaender estimated the direct social losses of the road-rail misallocation have amounted to about $500 million per year, an amount sufficient to distort locational, consumption, and production decisions. Moreover, she found that the dynamic consequences of ICC regulation—including maintaining unnecessary excess capacity, failing to weed out the less efficient producers, and regulatory stifling of incentives for technological change and innovation—might be more important than the short-run allocation losses. Friedlaender attributed the considerable economic costs of ICC regulation to maintenance of value-of-service pricing.[34]

Finally, in a study done for the Brookings Institution *The Feasibility of Deregulating Surface Freight Transportation*, T.G. Moore estimated the economic loss from traffic carried by trucks instead of by railroads due to ICC regulation to range between $450 million and $900 million per year.[35]

Regulatory signals toward overinvestment in highways and inland waterways and misallocation of resources. Regulation restricting intermodal competition has long transferred considerable freight traffic from low-cost modes to high-cost modes. The resulting higher traffic volumes over the highways have exerted additional demands for expanding highway capacity and for stronger highways and bridges. Anticipated and actual diversions of traffic to inland waterways, including those that greater competitive freedom for the railways might have avoided, have stimulated greater investments in channels and locks. Thus, the investment signals given in the transport markets call for more highway and inland waterway investment by the Federal and state governments and less railway investment by the privately-owned railroads than otherwise would occur. Hence, the large misallocations of traffic and revenues resulting from regulation have also affected resource allocation uneconomically over the long run.

The economic effects of regulation have made railroads inefficient and unable to play their full economic role in development. To the extent that increasing returns exist, the traffic lost to railroads because of regulation has raised their average costs. And the revenues lost on high-value traffic have lowered railroad returns to capital, and this has limited the capital railroads could raise for modernization of way and for modern freight cars.[36] As low long-haul rates by rail have contributed importantly to regional specialization, regulatory influences actually impair the railroads' ability to render long-haul service at low rates. This tends to decentralize industry and to promote regional self-sufficiency. And the low profitability of the railroads under regulation restricting intermodal competition has contributed to declining suburban and intercity passenger train services and thus to air pollution, noise, and excessive congestion, the principal concerns of advocates of regional planning in transport today.[37]

Airline regulation by the CAB also appears to have changed the market structure of the U.S. airline industry toward an imperfect cartel of fewer and larger firms, to have encouraged high levels of excess capacity and less intensive resource utilization, and to have raised airline service levels, average costs, fare levels, and profit rates over what they would be under more workable competition. Thus, on the basis of his comparison of the economic performance of CAB-regulated airlines with that of the relatively unregulated intrastate air carriers operating wholly within California under state jurisdiction between 1946 and 1965, William A. Jordan concluded in his book, *Airline Regulation in America, Effects and Imperfections* (1970), as follows:[38]

The overall findings are that the economic effects of the CAB's regulation of the certificated carriers have been to limit entry and control exit, to reduce the number of firms in existence, to promote service quality, to raise price levels and encourage price discrimination (yielding a complicated fare structure), to decrease the intensity of resource utilization (thereby increasing average costs), and to benefit aircraft manufacturers and other suppliers of resources as well as the regulated airlines themselves. All of these results are consistent with the implications of cartel theory, where the cartel is not perfectly organized. Without regulation, the U.S. airline industry would have, it appears, an oligopolistic market structure with a significant degree of price rivalry, limited price discrimination, and relatively large numbers of specialized airlines providing services whose average quality would be lower than that existing under regulation. In total, the social costs of air transportation seem to have been significantly increased by the CAB's regulatory activities.

Clearly, except for the oil pipelines, fully competitive transport with a minimum of economic regulation would be more efficient than today's regulated transport, in which intramodal and intermodal competition are limited.[39] As the lowest real transport costs are conducive to maximum travel and economic development, the uneconomic effects of regulation restrictive of competition are adverse to maximum growth and productivity in the national and regional economies over the long run.[40]

Adjustment of Economic Regulation to an Efficient Role

If regulatory reform is to be effective, changes will have to be made in the key provisions, standards, and policies that have molded transport regulation into uneconomic channels in the past four decades.

Statutory standards and regulatory policies in the uneconomic role of the new regulation. Of prime importance is the wording of the National Transportation Policy. While the ICC was directed "to recognize and preserve the inherent advantages of each" mode, the Policy also called for ruling out "unfair or destructive competitive practices" and for fostering "sound economic conditions in transportation and among the several carriers." The latter standards have been the statutory basis for the Commission's protective minimum rate and entry control policies and its full-cost standards in intermodal minimum rate cases. Even an effort by the Congress to correct the overemphasis on protecting high-cost modes in the 1958 Act failed because of the linking of the new rate control standard in Section 15a(3) to those influential policy standards.[41]

The many rate and entry decisions of the ICC that shore up the traditional value-of-service rate structure and continue high rates on high-value motor-rail traffic have been influential in the misallocative effects that have taken place and also in the decline of the railroads.[42] Specifically, these effects resulted from the ICC's application of full-cost standards in intermodal competitive rate cases, often preventing the low-cost railroads from taking traffic from competing modes.

As most ICC entry policies started before the National Transportation Policy was enacted in 1940, they must either be traced to standards in the Motor Carrier Act of 1935 or to deliberate protective standards adopted by the ICC itself.[43] The ICC clearly could have adopted liberal policies that would have avoided uneconomic service restrictions and was urged to do so by Commissioner William E. Lee, the great dissenter in motor carrier entry cases.[44] Notwithstanding, the Commission adopted the restrictive standards that fragmented regulated trucking markets, reduced particular markets to a few competitors, and created unnecessary regulatory costs and the substantial inefficiencies associated with protecting high-cost carriers and encouraging service competition. The ICC also authorized many mergers creating large-scale trucking firms, even though the Commission was fully aware that growing traffic and revenue in trucking would have supported more firms and had testified in Congressional hearings in 1955 that it did not have studies to indicate whether larger trucking firms would attain significant economies of scale in size of firm.[45] Consequently, the ICC's large-firm emphasis can be traced largely to its own policies.[46]

Again the ICC itself adopted loose standards for determining the earnings levels for the regulated truckers.[47] Under carrier pressures, the ICC utilized the operating ratio as a standard for rate-level and profits control despite the fact that regulatory practice and economic theory had long validated the rate of return on necessary capital as the appropriate return standard for regulated enterprise. Hence, the Commission's own policies must be held accountable for the generous rates of return on depreciated capital investment that many regulated truckers have earned.

Both the Congress, in enacting the 1935, 1940, 1942, and 1958 Acts and the ICC must therefore be held accountable for the substantial inefficiencies in transport that regulation restrictive of competition has produced. Even so, many actual economic effects could have been avoided or minimized if the ICC had interpreted the mandates of the Congress differently and had utilized the tools of minimum rate regulation and entry control less restrictively of competition.

Alternatives for an economic role for transport regulation. Two basic alternatives exist for modifying ICC regulation so that it can play an efficient role. The most drastic one would abandon most or all regulation and the ICC itself. The other one would selectively change the statutory mandates to direct the ICC to modify its entry, merger, and minimum rate policies so as not to be in conflict with an economic organization of the transport industries, efficient competitive pricing, and economic competition between the modes. In between those poles various schemes of partial deregulation are possible.

In dealing with the long-term effects of the newer modes on maintaining an adequate supply of efficient railroad service, several European countries have deregulated surface transport. Great Britain and the Netherlands now have almost no special economic regulation for railroads and motor carriers, and Sweden has largely deregulated both rail and road goods transport. Canada has adopted a combination of deregulation and changed regulatory standards to allow far more competition in transport. In 1967, Canada freed her railroads from control of the rate level and from maximum rate regulation except where a shipper can prove that he is served by a monopoly; and Canada permitted the railroads to compete in rates with other modes down to variable costs, thereby avoiding the "fair-sharing" of traffic that has taken place under the full-cost standards of the ICC. Generally, the state-owned European railroads are given much commercial freedom in competing with other modes and are allowed to use marginal costs as the floor to competitive rates.[48]

Until the Nixon Administration in February 1971 moved toward a comprehensive scheme of deregulation of transport over a period of several years, most officially suggested revisions of regulation have called for modest regulatory change.[49] Thus, President Eisenhower's Cabinet Committee Report in 1955 recommended the use of out-of-pocket costs as the standard for minimum rate control, some relaxation in maximum rate and discrimination controls, but no substantial change in entry control or in merger policy except for relaxing restrictions on intermodal ownership.[50] President Kennedy's Transportation Message in 1962 chiefly sought to remove minimum rate regulation from agricultural and bulk commodities for all modes, a policy that would have lifted minimum rate regulation from commodities comprising 44 percent of rail revenue and 70 percent of rail tonnage, 47 percent of ICC-regulated water revenue and 84 percent of the tonnage, and 22 percent of ICC-regulated truck revenue and 55 percent of the tonnage.[51] However, the Cabinet Committee also called for a new National Transportation Policy to provide a wholly coherent emphasis on encouraging transport competition and a competitive allocation of traffic. And leading scholars have long recommended complete deregulation of the competitive modes and considerable deregulation of air transport.

Two realistic alternatives exist for modifying ICC regulation toward performance of an efficient role. These are (1) the introduction of change in ICC entry, merger, and minimum rate policies to minimize their uneconomic effects, continuing the present structure of regulation largely intact; and (2) partial deregulation by eliminating some important parts of the existing regulatory structure and the questionable mandates in the regulatory statutes.

If politically practicable, the second alternative would be the preferable one because it would remove the root causes of the principal inefficiencies and misallocative effects of the new regulation. As recommended three decades ago in a staff study on "New Concepts in Transportation Regulation" done by this writer for the NRPB, this course would abolish minimum rate regulation and entry control for motor and water carriers, restrict the ICC to control of rate and service discrimination and maximum rates, and reapply the relevant antitrust laws to common carriers. The only minimum rate control retained would be applicable to the railroads to prevent true impairment of competition.[52] This amount of deregulation would eliminate totally the fallacious new concepts in surface transport regulation introduced in 1935; that is, the idea that ordinary competition in the naturally competitive modes requires regulation as much as monopoly power in a monopoly mode, and the associated notion that regulation can allocate traffic between the modes more efficiently than competition.

Short of altering the present structure of regulation in this drastic fashion, several lesser, but yet significant, legislative actions could be taken. For example, the "unfair or destructive competitive practices" and the "sound economic conditions in transportation and among the several carriers' " standards of the National Transportation Policy could be abandoned. Or a new policy with coherent emphasis on maintaining workable competition within and between modes could be substituted. Either would go a long way to reduce the misallocative effects of minimum rate regulation, since the ICC would be constrained to apply the logic of economic theory by utilizing the long-run variable or marginal costs as the relevant standard for competitive rates.

Deletion of the questionable standards in the present National Transportation Policy or a new policy declaration emphasizing competition would also motivate the ICC to move faster to remove the cost-increasing and service-deteriorating service restrictions now found in motor carrier certificates and permits. However, the desirable liberalization of operating authorities could be brought about far more quickly if the Congress enacted the special legislation recommended in 1945 by the Board of Investigation and Research (BIR). On the basis of a comprehensive sample study of certificate and permit restrictions on interstate motor carriers in 1942 and of their evolving economic effects, the BIR recommended that all commodity restrictions be abolished except those based on specialized equipment; that route restrictions that involve unnecessary circuitous movements be abandoned; that all restrictions on the points within authorized territories or through which vehicles pass be eliminated; and that the only service restrictions retained be those confining carriers to common or contract carriage. Elimination of return-haul restrictions was also recommended.[53]

An obvious first step in making existing regulations efficient would be a legislative directive to the ICC to abandon all restrictions on commodities, return-hauls, routes and points served, and types of service in motor carrier certificates and permits. Such restrictions result in higher average costs of service and in service less than the flexible capabilities of trucks are capable of rendering. But at least the minimum changes outlined above for the National Transportation Policy are also essential. They are needed to redirect the ICC's energies toward implementation of workable competition and efficient divisions of traffic. But if the ICC should fail to adopt fully economic cost criteria for measuring the low-cost mode and for setting floors on competitive rates, legislation would also be needed to clarify Section 15a(3) by specifying that the standard of variable or relevant marginal cost should be used in minimum rate cases.[54]

Past experience has shown that enactment of even small fundamental changes in the Interstate Commerce Act have been politically difficult to achieve because of the opposition of the carrier groups benefiting from protective regulation. This was true of the 1972 Congressional consideration of the partial deregulation proposed by the DOT's Transportation Regulatory Modernization Act of 1971, even though great difficulties are being experienced in reorganizing the bankrupt Penn Central Railroad and other railroads have recently entered bankruptcy. Thus, the possibility that the ICC might be induced to change its own administrative standards to yield a more efficient role for regulation might be considered.

Obviously, the Commission cannot abandon minimum rate regulation or entry control under present statutory law. What the Commission could do, however, is to make a far more minimal—and a more *economic*—use of the minimum rate and entry control powers than in the past. The statute does not require the Commission to use its rate control powers to raise the profits of motor carriers above competitive or fair-return levels. The ICC could refuse to allow earnings higher than necessary to attract capital. Furthermore, the Commission could refuse to suspend independently-filed rate reductions by carriers whose costs and service might be more efficient than those of the protesting carriers. Also, a greater burden could be placed on the protesting carriers to prove that proposed rate reductions might be unlawful.

Present law requires the elimination of "unfair or destructive competitive practices," but it does not define those practices. The Commission has much discretion and could apply the logic of relevant economic theory in determining the cost standards for judging whether competition is economic or "destructive" in each situation. In the *Ingot Molds* case, the Supreme Court held that determination of the cost criteria in intermodal competitive cases was within the special expertise of the ICC.[55] Hence, if the Commission resolves this issue in the *Cost Standards in Intermodal Rate Proceedings* case by finding that the variable or long-run marginal cost standard is the relevant one for establishing limits for minimum competitive rates, the Commission could remove the protective coloring and fair-sharing traffic allocations that its past full-cost standards have introduced.

Moreover, even without legislation the Commission could remove many of the uneconomic service restrictions in certificates and permits. Shipper complaints of inadequate through service for less-truck-load shipments and of the cost-raising service practices under certificate restrictions recently prompted the ICC to move modestly toward some liberalization. For example, in *Removal of Truckload Lot Restrictions*, the ICC in 1968 ordered deletion of truckload restrictions in common carrier certificates, on a blanket basis as recommended by the BIR.[56] This blanket removal of truckload restrictions was a forward step in freeing competition to work toward greater efficiency. Clearly, the Commission could order additional blanket liberalizations of certificate restrictions limiting efficiency.

The question of income losses to the protected regulated carriers and some shippers. A policy of allowing competitive forces more sway in motor-rail and water-rail markets would bring about appreciable income losses to regulated truckers and possibly some adverse income changes for long-distance shippers of agricultural and extractive products. Shippers located in small centers might also be affected. On the other hand, more competitive markets would mean greater traffic and revenues for the railroads, fuller utilization of their facilities, and higher returns. And there would be widespread but varying gains in consumers' surplus as the real prices of goods fell in reflection of lower costs for essential inputs of transport service.

The adverse income distributional effects from deregulation can be exaggerated. First, the offsets to income losses would include lessened regulatory expenses and the avoidance of the cost-raising effects of restricted operations and costly service competition. Highly restricted motor carriers would gain new markets and greater revenues. Second, many overextended trucking operations could shift from long-haul and volume transport to short-haul and gathering and distributional services just as the automobile truckers shifted to such types of operations after the introduction of efficient rail tri-level rack cars returned the medium- and long-haul automobile traffic to the railroads. Third, much truck-type traffic now moved by private and exempt carriers could be attracted to the regulated truckers. Even if not avoidable in those ways, the income losses to protected truckers represent monopoly gains from regulation lessening competition, gains of a type that are not justifiable as economic returns.

Some income losses to long-distance shippers of agricultural and extractive products might occur as relaxed regulation allowed the railroads to raise numerous rail rates that do not yield revenues sufficient to cover out-of-pocket costs. With greater competition lowering the high value-of-service rates on manufactured commodities, the railroads would be under financial pressure to raise their low rates. The railroads, however, are already pressed by their low returns to take such pricing action. And they might take even more drastic action to raise below-cost and marginal rates if the diversion of profitable high-value traffic to trucking continues. On the other hand, since larger shares of the profitable traffic will increase the profitability of the railroads over the long run, the need for raising the true-loss rates on agricultural and extractive goods can be limited to avoidance of the real losses from such traffic.

The question arises regarding why income changes from deregulation or limiting regulation to an economic role should be considered a barrier to change at all. Traffic frequently has been diverted from one regulated mode to another in response to technological developments and rate and service changes in the market. The income losses to inefficient carriers in such cases are seldom compensated. For example, no compensation was granted to the automobile carriers by truck, many of whom lost their entire business or large parts of it to the railroads a decade or so ago. The shift to efficient rail tri-level cars was regarded merely as a beneficial technical change and the working of competition toward efficiency. In some cases, however, it might be better to compensate some income losses from deregulation than to continue indefinitely the uneconomic effects of regulation restrictive of competition. Or, in the alternative, deregulation of rate and entry control could be phased over some years to permit regulated carriers more easily to adjust to greater intramodal and intermodal competition. This was the amelioration for possible income effects on regulated truckers proposed by the Nixon Administration's Transportation Regulatory Modernization Act of 1971.

Some benefits of regulatory revision toward greater competition in transport.
Giving freer rein to competitive forces in transport would make freight
transport more efficient and raise the output of the economy. First, the lower
rates resulting for most firms would extend the market, promote further
exploitation of resources, and increase regional specialization. Secondly, more
rapid introduction of technical advances would take place because the associated
service and rate designs for making them profitable would not be limited. Third,
efficient intermodal transport combining the economies of large efficient
container ships, mass land carriers for long container hauls, and the flexible
trucks for the short gathering and distribution hauls would be encouraged.[57]
Finally, the savings in resources of up to several billions of dollars each year
from ending misallocations of traffic could be employed to enlarge the output of
other goods and services.

The modern railroad problem traces both to the long-term displacement by
new modes operating in their efficient market areas and to the railroads'
progressive loss of high-value traffic for which their costs have been lowest.
Deregulation or relaxation by the ICC of its restrictive standards would enable
the railroads to command more of the profitable traffic, utilize some facilities
more fully, and increase their returns while reducing costs and improving
services. Hence, such a policy, together with some relaxation of maximum rate
and discrimination controls to enable the railroads to eliminate their below-true
cost rates more easily, offers the best inducement for railroad self-help measures
capable of improving their economic performance.

Lessened regulation will be conducive to achieving a more balanced transport
development and greater economic progress in transport in the future. By
revealing the true relative economic demands for each mode's services more
accurately, competitive transport markets will assist government planners to
correct the large imbalances in transport investment and development since 1920
in the United States. And by freeing the railroads to compete, those carriers can
earn higher returns with which to acquire the capital for modernization,
innovation, and selective expansion of their capacity. Removal of the truck
regulatory restrictions will enable the regulated truckers to make the adjustments in routes, services, and rates required for highway transport to perform its
most economic role.

Finally, society will benefit in yet another way. Enlarging the efficient role of
rail transport should reduce the social costs of current transport and assist urban
areas to solve their congestion and passenger transport problems. A direct
minimization of accidents, congestion, noise, and smog would come from
transference of long-distance freight to the railroads, with fewer large truck
combinations on the highways. Indirectly, by reducing the needs expressed for
costly investment in additional high-capacity highways such as another Interstate
System, more capital funds can become available for investments in socially

efficient rapid transit and intercity high-speed trains in corridors while remaining sufficient to improve highways for their best uses, including greater employment of trucks in short-haul transport, in gathering and distribution, in special services, and in services to rural communities.

Promotion of Transport by Government Investments and Subsidies

In the last half century, the role of Government as a public entrepreneur in ownership and operation of transport facilities and in giving financial aids and subsidies for transport investment has been the controlling factor in shaping the development of the entire transport system. Thus, state and Federal investment in highways and airports and Federal investment in airways and inland waterways have provided the vast highway, airway and airport, and inland waterway systems of the United States. Without those facilities, the great growth of highway, air, and inland water carrier transport could not have taken place. Likewise, the significant and continuing effects of those modes on the role and problems of the railroads could not have occurred. Although many of the basic way, terminal, and navigational facilities for highway, air, and inland water carriers would have been developed either by private enterprise or toll-financing authorities if they had not been provided directly as government enterprises, the development of those facilities would have been on a smaller scale overall and with far less subsidy than has actually been involved.[58] Consequently, the adverse impacts on the role of the railways would have been far less.

National, Regional, and Local Emphasis in Transport Promotional Policy

Regions of the country, states, and municipalities have long been active in promoting public transport development. The example of New York State's construction of the Erie Canal has been cited. Inland waterways require deeper channels, locks, and navigation aids to become navigable by efficient ships, barges, and tows, and the promotional pressures for public investment usually come from cities, states, and regions contiguous to or nearby the rivers and lakes on which they are located. Thus, though most improved inland waterways today are planned and financed on the Federal level and are operated by the Corps of Engineers, regional and local planning for economic development from construction activities and enlargement of the industrial base is inherently involved.

This is especially true of the marginal or submarginal waterways, as they do not necessarily make a contribution to development of the national economy. As the efficient *central* waterways of the Mississippi River System and the Great

Lakes have obviously contributed to national economic development in a manner much like the railways, they command wider support and are planned with more attention to national development objectives. Their role in supplying efficient transport would continue even though user fees were assessed. The situation is different with the marginal and submarginal waterways that are not well utilized—full user fees on those waterways might contract the traffic and raise the question of whether they should be closed to save annual maintenance and operation costs. Therefore, the significant wastes from overinvestment in waterways are principally associated with marginal and submarginal waterway projects. It follows that their development raises the question for the Federal Government of whether extractive and industrial development at locations along such heavily subsidized waterways can promote the most productive national economic development. The regional and local economic benefits gained might well come at the expense of the loss of far greater economic gains from investment in another mode of transport or from industrial development elsewhere in the nation.

The case of promotion of modern highways is considerably different from that of inland waterways, yet it has common features. A major difference is that the state governments and their subdivisions own and operate the highways and streets, and until recent years, have largely planned and financed them as well. The Federal Bureau of Public Roads has granted matching aid from general funds up to 1956 and from Federal user fees since that time toward financing the construction costs of the state systems having general and interstate, or national, economic significance. The process of state and Federal planning and development has been a cooperative one. State and local development was the primary objective for road improvement in the early period of modern highways and Federal aid. But during post World War II years, national economic development and planning of highways have come increasingly to the fore with the planning, authorization, and implementation of the Interstate System, financed largely by gigantic annual grants of Federal aid to the states. From Federal user fees going into the Federal Highway Trust Fund, the BPR finances 90 percent of the construction costs of that system and the states only 10 percent. However, although state user fees were inadequate to cover the entire cost of highway modernization in the early years, and although a long period existed in which Federal user fees were not assessed to raise funds for the Federal investments in federal-aid systems, highway users, unlike waterway users, have had to pay significantly toward the economic costs of their highway use almost from the beginning.

There can be little question concerning the ways highway modernization by state and federal investment have affected local, regional, and national economies. In addition to being the largest factor in the revolutionary changes in the transport system and in the division of passenger and freight traffic among the modes since 1920, highway development has radically changed the location and style of living of urban populations, the configuration and functions of cities, the role of the small town in rural areas, and the location and relocation of many industries. Unfortunately, however, it has also produced the lion's share of the most discouraging of the social costs from transport. These include excessive noise, health-damaging smog, and a high accident toll of fatalities, personal injuries, and property damage each year.[59] To be included also are some social problems associated with the decline of central cities. Some examples are inadequate urban transport alternatives for urban residents and job-seekers; and the decline of the railroads in a situation in which highway transport cannot match the low unit costs of rail transport or entirely substitute for rail service, even in the passenger field.

As the growing use of highways attest, most effects of the vast highway development during the last 50 years have been beneficial and probably economic. The flexibility of the automobile has rendered both urban and rural life much more social and livable in terms of alternative recreational and educational pursuits and of greater contact with other people. The automobile has increased the range of living opportunities and locations available to people having good incomes, and it has greatly decentralized and suburbanized cities, both large and small. The motor bus has often improved the common carrier schedules available to travelers within large cities and between them and rural towns, and school buses have made consolidated schools feasible, together with their advantages of a wider range of curricula and more qualified teachers. The truck, too, has improved rural transport for the farmer; has facilitated delivery of goods within city, town, and rural areas; has economized the short-haul transport of almost all goods and improved the service; has widened the alternatives available to shippers of high-value goods and special shipments over medium and long distances; and has brought far greater competition into transport than ever before. In addition, smaller towns and suburban areas have become more advantageous locations for some types of industrial plants.[60] On the other hand, highway transport carrying traffic for which the railroads are distinctly more efficient, in scarce resources required, has been the prime cause of the uneconomic part of the railroad decline and of the huge annual costs from misallocations of traffic.

The current problems that arise from highway development for passenger transport have their most serious impacts in urban communities and in densely populated regions. Although urban goods movements by truck have become an area of transport in which significant economic problems have arisen, the most serious urban problems associated with urban highway development and use have been in the sphere of personal travel. One of these is the congestion at times of peak use of streets and freeways and of parking facilities. Another is the decline and inadequacies of public transit services in recent decades that has seriously affected some classes of urban residents. A third is growing social costs, to which the highway-only or highway-mostly solution for passenger travel definitely contributes. The difficulty of finding effective long-run solutions for those problems has stimulated large and small cities to make studies, to engage in planning for transport development with state and Federal aid, and in instances to establish metropolitan or regional planning or operating agencies.[61]

On the other hand, overdeveloped truck transport of goods over medium and long distances has had a far more general impact on the nation as a whole. First, if regulatory and promotional policies do not change and if improved management and pricing by the railroads do not take place, the nation will face permanent government ownership of some or all railroads instead of temporary takeovers as during wartime or labor emergencies. This would create widespread demands from cities, counties, and school districts for the Federal Government to continue payments to them equal to the huge local property taxes now paid annually by the railroads in support of schools and local roads. General Federal tax revenues or highway user revenues might also be drawn upon to support the subsidization of some essential rail services and even to raise capital for railroad investment. Alternatively, significant restrictions might be placed on the development and use of highways and other public transport facilities. Second, railway passenger services have already been greatly curtailed and even the National Railroad Passenger Corporation plan of government aid enacted by the Congress in 1970 will save only a moderate mileage and quantity of intercity rail passenger service.[62] Third, low railroad profitability will turn the railroads more actively in the direction of abandoning unprofitable lines and freight services, particularly in rural areas. Finally, the higher total cost of overland transport, because of the huge misallocations of medium- and long-distance traffic between road and rail, already increases the cost of goods for all consumers to a greater or lesser extent.

The Federal role in the development of air transport has been predominant, although local authorities have been prominent in planning, managing, and financing the airport terminals. Thus, the U.S. Post Office Department started the first commercial airlines and long regulated and subsidized the trunk airlines through its airmail contracts. At first, this policy sought to improve mail service and later it also aimed to stimulate provision of high-speed passenger service. Municipalities, counties, and special public authorities provided most large airport terminals with large amounts of Federal aid. The competitive positions and economic opportunities of large cities came to depend heavily on their having adequate and competitive domestic and international airline services. From the beginning, the Federal Government provided and operated the civil airways. The CAB, guided by the promotional guidelines in the 1938 Act, regulated the trunk airlines to promote a rapid development of air transport and aircraft manufacturing.[63] The CAB has also given the smaller cities and towns scheduled air service that would not have developed without continuing airmail subsidies, at least until the fairly recent organization of the third-level airlines employing small but speedy and safe aircraft afforded an alternative.[64]

In view of the differential speed of air transport that makes it particularly efficient in long-distance travel, national planning for national transport improvement and objectives has always been predominant in air transport. Although large subsidies have been involved in airmail payments, in the long-time lack and present inadequacy of user fees for airways, and in insufficient landing fees for airport services, there can be little question about the economic contribution of air transport to national, regional, and local development. The only questionable area would concern the economic contribution of the local service airlines that depend on large subsidies in an attempt to equalize the travel opportunities of rural and small communities with those of large cities.[65]

In many ways, the people, enterprises and institutions of the entire nation have been made more productive by the speed and efficiency of air transport. They have also been given travel, educational, and recreational opportunities that could not have arisen otherwise. The economic advantages of airline travel, however, probably have gone largely to the huge cities and population clusters, as the very large cities have been in the best position to generate the traffic volumes required to support competitive services, frequent and nonstop services, and thus to attract the brain-type industries into their orbits. The fact that the demand for air cargo of very high-value goods is concentrated on the routes between large centers has also attracted most of the air cargo services to the large metropolitan areas. Air cargo, however, has yet to attain a significant role in freight transport or in the location of many industries. And though the air services available at rural communities and small towns still receive heavy airmail subsidies, they are distinctly inferior to those available at large cities in frequency of schedules, in comfort of aircraft, in conveniences and interconnections, and in fare cost to the travelers. Moreover, even with Federal aid the efforts of rural communities to provide ever-larger and more modern airport facilities to accommodate the larger aircraft that the airlines seek to employ are costly in airport tax subsidies that rural and town taxpayers have to pay.[66]

Although most benefits from air travel go to the large metropolises, these urban communities also experience the great bulk of its disbenefits. These are in the form of uncompensated social costs. Large airports are in the large cities or near them, so the residents of those communities must necessarily experience the noise of aircraft in terminal operations and the smog contributed by jet planes and bear much of the tax subsidy costs for local airports that are not self-sustaining. Additionally, they experience the street and highway congestion from large flows of persons to and from airports. Rural residents largely escape these disbenefits. In terms of reducing the net benefits of air travel to the travelers, the congestion to, from, and at airports is probably the major disbenefit.

From this discussion certain things are evident. First, the supply of public transport facilities has been planned to bring about national economic gains and development as well as to satisfy regional objectives for development of state, urban, and local needs. Necessarily, some transport systems, such as the railroads and the trunk airlines, have been planned primarily with national needs in mind, and others, such as the local service airlines and many inland waterways, have been planned largely to satisfy regional needs. And rail rapid transit systems, such as the ones under construction in Atlanta, San Francisco, and Washington, D.C., have been planned to provide improved home-to-work and other travel for the population of localized urban areas. Second, in the highly mobile and integrated American economy, the beneficial and disbeneficial impacts of development of public transport facilities can affect almost all citizens, although their incidence is concentrated in the large urban centers and corridors. In passenger transport especially, the disbenefits of the promotional solutions of past years largely fall on the great urban clusters of population. Thus, the urban and corridor person transport problems are among the most difficult remaining to be solved, and these will very likely command the greatest attention in future regional planning of transport development and in the regional considerations of national transport planning. Thirdly, viable solutions for the inefficiencies and inadequacies of the nation's promotional and regulatory policies will require attention to national, regional, and local problems. Planning and action, though not organization for planning, will necessarily have to be as comprehensive as are the elements of the transport problem to be solved.

Deficiencies in Developmental Policies for Transport and Their Economic Effects

In several ways, state and Federal promotional policies for transport have been deficient from an economic point of view. First, investments in highways, airways and airports, and inland waterways have recurrently been undertaken in response to political as well as economic demands. Political demands can be congruent with economic demands, but often they are not, reflecting as they do the log-rolling process, the organized interests of strong pressure groups, and an acquisitive motivation of communities and areas for regional or local development. Second, the investment planning process for public transport facilities usually does not consider whether the most productive investment might be in another mode of transport. Instead, emphasis is placed on ascertaining which of the several investments possible in one mode, for example in highway transport, will be given priority among such projects. That process inevitably leads to some investments in other modes being ruled out, even though the benefit-to-cost ratios and net benefits might be higher than for the projects actually chosen. Third, the investment decisions in the case of highways, airports and airways, and inland waterways are not made under the same economic constraints that railway and pipeline investments are. Even today, there are no user fees on domestic inland waterways that would aid the markets for rail and barge freight services to ascertain the true economic demand for barge services and for waterway development to accommodate barge operations. User fees have only recently been assessed in support of airway services and those to finance airways and airports have not in the past covered all the costs.[67] Highway user fees have not been finely adjusted to the differential investment and maintenance costs of the demands of the different classes of motor vehicles for special highway features and services.[68] Fourth, the cost-benefit studies made to test whether particular public transport projects are economic are often not rigorous enough to give assurance that a positive net benefit actually confirms that a given proposed investment would be economic. In the inland waterway projects, the overestimation of benefits and underestimation of costs have been chronic.[69] Fifth, until recently, none of the indirect or social costs of a public transport facility investment have been counted, although the indirect or social benefits have often been taken into account.

In addition, the tradition that user fee revenues going into state and federal highway trust funds must be spent on highways is another source of misallocation of capital among the alternative modes of transport. Billions of dollars of user revenues flow into those trust funds each year from the inelastic demands for motor fuels and highway services. Those funds provide an automatic source of capital for reinvestment and new investment in highways of gigantic annual magnitude. The necessity of spending almost all highway user revenues collected from national or statewide levies only for highway purposes and the fact that the Federal Government or a state is in a monopoly position in imposing such levies result in financing many highway investments that otherwise would fall by the wayside. Under those conditions, what can be collected from user charges provides no sufficient economic test of what outlays are justified for specific highway projects or systems. Overall, highway investment has been greater than it would have been if each project had to compete in the capital markets for capital funds and if the requirement to fix user fees or tolls generally to pay its full long-run costs had been imposed. According to Ann F. Friedlaender's study of the economics of public investment, the traffic in rural areas traversed by the Interstate System is too small to support an entire network with the planned capital intensity, and a somewhat smaller urban Interstate System in conjunction with mass transit would probably have been closer to the optimal investment for the urban component of the Interstate System.[70]

In addition to other factors that expand highways, airways and airports, and inland waterways at an unduly rapid rate and result in excessive investment in low-traffic systems and insufficient investment in high-traffic systems, railways and pipelines have to pay ordinary property taxes on their ways and terminal facilities as well as on their equipment. Moreover, if net income is earned, including that earned in way operations, they must pay state and Federal income taxes on all such income. Of course, carriers in the three modes using public transport facilities pay equivalent property taxes on their equipment and owned terminals. They also must pay income taxes on the net income earned in the carrier enterprises. But the government agencies owning and operating the public way or channel and public terminal facilities do not pay property taxes on those immense fixed facilities. And they do not pay income taxes on any net income earned or which could be earned from their operation. In justifying investments in public transport facilities, government agencies do not have to include in the total costs to be covered by the total revenues or total benefits any increments for such taxes as do the railways and the pipelines.[71]

The total effect of all those differential factors is that the annual public investments for highways, airways and airports, and inland waterways have probably been considerably larger than otherwise would be the case. In other words, more capacity is installed in such facilities than would be economically justifiable if the same pricing conditions and criteria of investment applied to both the private and public investments in basic transport facilities.

This situation leads to several effects favorable to rapid growth of the newer modes dependent on public transport facilities and to growth in excess of the true economic demands for their services. First, it generally affords the motor, air, and inland water carriers ample and riskless capacity in ways, channels and locks, and terminals to accommodate rapid expansion of carrier facilities and services. Second, the high rate of development of the public transport facilities promotes high rates of innovation and modernization in such facilities. In turn, the operating cost savings from vehicular use of improved ways, channels and terminals stimulate a rapid innovation and modernization of carrier-owned power units and carrying units and the attainment of the economies of scale in size of such equipment. Third, rapid public way, terminal, and channel modernization usually facilitate higher speed in service and more dependable schedules by the air, motor, and inland water carriers. Fourth, the ability to use larger power and carrying units lowers the unit costs of those modes and enables them to extend their markets against the railroads. Fifth, the lack of user fees on inland water carriers and the assessment of inadequate user fees to cover all relevant public costs for heavy and large motor vehicles powered by diesel fuel further lower the unit costs of the barge lines and the motor carriers, again enabling them to penetrate into railroad markets more deeply and extensively. Finally, the unit costs of those modes and the airlines have not been increased by addition of property and other tax equivalents or by addition of the social costs of noise, smog, congestion, and of a reduced capacity in public carrier facilities and higher-cost travel for people dependent on such alternative transport.

In sharp contrast to the rapid growth of the demand for the services of the highway, air, and inland water carriers, their growing shares of the market, and their comparatively attractive rates of return over many years, the railroads have been relatively stagnant in postwar traffic and revenue growth until the 1960s, and their overall shares of the market have continued to decline. Although the railroads have resumed growth in bulk traffic in the last decade, they have continued to lose the profitable high-value, but over-priced, traffic over medium and long distances to the highway and air carriers. As those conditions have been adverse to good rates of return for the railroads, their overall rates of capital investment have been low, their efficient cars and locomotives in short supply, and their technical innovations and modernization rates slowed.

It remains impossible to state exactly how much of the continuing large-scale diversions of traffic, revenue, and earnings from the railroads to the other modes accompanying public transport promotional activities has been uneconomic. Furthermore, it is not possible to indicate how much of the vast diversion that occurred could have been prevented if the railroads had been more aggressive in improving their services and in lowering many of their high discriminating rates and in raising their unprofitably low rates. And it would be almost as difficult to determine how much of the uneconomic diversion that occurred has been specifically attributable to regulation and how much to public promotional policies. Nevertheless, there can be little question that the promotional policies of the state and Federal governments have contributed to considerable uneconomic diversion of traffic and revenues from the railways and to the economic decline of the railways over the decades. Those public policies have worked hand in hand with regulatory policies in lowering the market shares of the railroads, in hastening their withdrawal of many passenger services, in contributing to their low rates of return, and in bringing about underinvestment and too little modernization, particularly in ways and terminals.

Notwithstanding the uncertainties with respect to precise measurement of economic versus uneconomic diversion from the railways as a result of public policies, it can be concluded that public promotional policies have contributed to large-scale inefficiencies in the supply of transport services to the nation. As noted above, the new regulation introduced monopoly discriminating rate structures in regulated trucking and in this and other ways interfered with economic rate and service competition by the low-cost mode. It thereby created inefficient utilization of the railroads, and by misallocating traffic, added billions of dollars a year to transport costs for shippers and consumers. To this must be added the large additional cost of trucking in its efficient markets occasioned by restrictive entry and operating authority control, and the $100 million or higher costs each year to the governments, carriers, and shippers for the regulatory process itself.

Moreover, enormous waste in the expenditure of public funds from taxpayer sources has occurred from overinvestment in public transport projects and systems. This excessive cost to taxpayers has resulted from political demands for marginal inland waterways, the rural Interstate System, quality and scale of county roads beyond those justified by traffic requirements or the support of benefited landowners, and airports not justified by prospective traffic. Other sources of waste of public funds are the premature breakup and excessive maintenance of highway surfaces and the premature obsolescence of bridges because of growing volumes of heavy-axle and heavy gross-load truck movements over many highway sections not constructed for such vehicles.[72] The application of nonrigorous and nonuniform investment criteria and preferential tax and user fee treatment for the modes using public ways and terminals are factors in overinvestment in those public facilities, specifically by adding to the benefits and the traffic demands advanced to justify public investment and by not counting the future social costs from the operation of motor vehicles, aircraft, and even subsidized barges.

Altogether, those wastes in use of resources could possibly match the huge annual costs from the misallocations of traffic on account of regulatory policy and uneconomic pricing of freight services. But the precise total annual costs of misallocation of resources from regulation as distinct from promotional policies are not known. Additional research to measure them more closely would be well justified.

An important implication of the immense and continuing government promotion of public way, channel, and terminal facilities is that regulatory reform alone would be incapable of achieving an efficient allocation of resources in transport. As noted above, regulatory reform restoring intramodal competition in the naturally competitive modes and changing the basis for intermodal competition can do much to reduce the wastes from misallocations of traffic. However, correction of overinvestment in public transport facilities and underinvestment in the railroads will also require major change in the promotional and investment policies of the state and Federal governments, and substantial adjustment of the state and Federal user fee policies in the direction of greater economy.

Visible Crises in Transport Supply Requiring
Transport Policy Change

Several real crisis situations have arisen in transport due to longstanding public transport policies. These suggest drastic changes in both regulatory policy and in transport promotional policies.

The first crisis involves the future of private ownership and operation of the American railroads. This is more seriously threatened than ever before. Several large and small railroads are in bankruptcy and a number of other bankruptcies may occur in spite of industry and ICC faith in railway mergers as a solution for the railroad problem. This situation came about, not in deep depression as in the 1930s, but under almost full employment conditions. Furthermore, the rates of return of many other railroads have sunk to extremely low levels. And again the railroads and the ICC are trying to improve the rate-of-return situation with increases in the general level of rates, action that does not solve fundamental pricing problems and can ultimately lessen the market share of the railroads in profitable high-value traffic. The implications of a do-nothing policy with respect to the railroads since World War II have now become evident. They reveal themselves in the Federal Government's decision to share in financing a minimum quantity of intercity rail passenger service; in the threatened abandonment of up to 100,000 miles or more of railway routes for freight traffic; and in the possible nationalization of the Penn-Central and other roads.[73] Those conditions are in addition to the long-standing freight car shortages and the low rate of improvement in way facilities such as tunnels, track curvature, and gradient. The latter conditions have reflected the railroads' long-continuing capital shortages for adequate railway modernization to improve services and reduce operating costs.[74]

Second, a crisis situation has been developing in urban transportation. The rail rapid transit and other mass transit systems of large cities and the bus systems of many small cities have typically deteriorated as to equipment, and the latter in extent and frequency of service. And public transit, except for taxicabs, is nonexistent in many American communities. Even in the great metropolises that have long had rail rapid transit, some extensions appear to be needed and service has deteriorated though fare levels have risen markedly. Several other large American cities may have sufficient traffic densities now or in the future to warrant developing a rapid transit system to handle a large part of the home-to-work traffic loads to and from the core areas, to reduce excessive congestion on the streets and highways, and to lessen the need for expansion of urban freeways. But only one, San Francisco, will soon have an entirely new and modern rapid transit system. Construction on the one authorized for Washington, D.C. is taking place after many delays because of the political opposition of highway interests to funding by the Congress; and Atlanta recently voted to build a rapid transit system. Boston, New York, Chicago, Cleveland, and Philadelphia have extended their rapid transit systems in recent years: Chicago with the innovation of rapid transit on median strips of expressways; Cleveland with the first rapid transit system connected to a major airport in the United States; and Philadelphia with extensions into another state and a unique demonstration of intergovernmental planning.

Los Angeles, Seattle, St. Louis and some other cities planned for rail rapid transit facilities, but Los Angeles and Seattle have not undertaken their construction because the voters voted not to approve raising capital by the sale of bonds supported by property or other taxes. Even the many cities too small for rapid transit, for example, Spokane, Washington, have been having extreme difficulty in maintaining adequate bus transit under public ownership or financial responsibility.

In spite of the declining or static customer patronage of public transit systems since 1945, many people believe that rail rapid transit or possibly bus mass transit on separate lanes or ways is the desirable long-term solution for airport access and airport location problems as well as for home-to-work travel in the great cities. They recognize that capital subsidies and Federal aid will be required to finance rail rapid transit, but point out that the economic demand for transit has been lower than it would be if satisfactory alternatives to automobiles and the ordinary frequent-stop bus services were in existence and if freeway and expressway users paid peak-use fees and full congestion prices for use of such facilities. They look to rail rapid's capacity to lessen smog and noise levels in addition to its speed of service as unique advantages. On the other hand, Wilfred Owen, as well as Meyer, Kain, and Wohl, contend that rail rapid transit will seldom be a viable solution except in the great cities already having such systems. They argue that automobiles and bus systems serve the decentralizing urban areas better and develop lower unit costs except where traffic densities are extremely high. Before new capital-intense rail rapid systems are undertaken, they argue, vigorous effort should be made to improve the efficiency of mass bus systems on reserved lanes, to explore new transit technology further, and to regulate highway use more effectively.[75]

Third, vehicle congestion has limited the speed and increased the cost of transport service in the growing corridors of urban communities having a linear structure along the Atlantic Seaboard, the Great Lakes, the coastal area of California between San Diego and San Francisco, and along the Puget Sound to Portland, Oregon. Some of these megalopolises may eventually require high-speed train service similar to that between Tokyo and Osaka in Japan. In the United States, only a small beginning has been made to test the future market for the type of high-speed intercity train service now operating in Japan and Europe, namely, by the Metroliner service between New York and Washington, D.C., and the Turbo-Train service between New York and Boston. Both run on existing tracks in contrast to the entirely new trackage in Japan. Quite possibly, a massive investment of capital might be desirable to test the market for high-speed train service more definitively and its possibilities for reducing the high social costs of excessive congestion.[76]

The effects of not allocating the capital funds for better solutions for the urban and megalopolitan passenger transport problems and of not solving the railroad problem by fundamental policy reform are becoming obvious to a great many people. Though freeways and automobiles have improved urban mobility in great cities such as Los Angeles and Seattle compared to what it had been before, and though mass transit by bus on reserved lanes might further improve urban mobility, traffic congestion at peak periods becomes ever more harassing, often more costly in time and expense for travel and parking, and always more fraught with noise and air pollution. Numerous classes of urban residents do not have a means of travel alternative to public transit, as they either do not own automobiles or hesitate to drive under congested traffic and accident-hazard conditions. Some low-income groups find their employment and educational opportunities limited to areas having public transit services because they do not own automobiles. In the megalopolitan or corridor regions, congestion is growing and public transport alternatives are becoming more limited or are often of poor quality despite development of expressways, toll roads, and commuter airline services. Thus, many people wonder why this country cannot afford at least one high-speed train on the Japanese model and why they cannot travel in passenger trains between cities as easily and comfortably as in Europe.

In truth, the underlying crisis in United States transport, both city and intercity, is in the automatic investment standards and political motivation that dominate public investment in transport facilities. Highway investments automatically reach ever higher levels as user revenues pour into state and Federal highway trust funds, enlarged partly because of the deteriorating alternatives that the unbalanced transport investment policy makes available. And even as the Interstate System nears completion, new highway user pressures have been exerted for another interstate system of 60,000 to 100,000 miles or more. Moreover, strong pressures from truckers, highway users, and the manufacturers of large vehicles have continuously been exerted at the state capitals and the Congress for heavier axle and gross loads and wider and longer vehicle-trains. Bills to provide nationwide Federal standards allowing use of such motor vehicles were defeated in the Congress during 1968, to a large extent because of opposition from automobile groups and the general public.[77]

If further crisis in transport is to be avoided, the effects of adopting another vast national highway program and of relaxing the size and weight limitations on the multiple-use highways should be given extremely close attention. Wider trucks, longer vehicle-trains and heavier axle and gross loads, in addition to raising the public costs of highway construction, maintenance, and operation, will divert still more medium- and long-distance traffic from the railroads, further induce the railroads to reduce their capacities and services, and further increase the noise and smog pollution and the serious accident toll.[78] If the proposed changes in sizes and weights are authorized without greatly increased user fees on heavy vehicles and upward adjustments to assess user charges more in accordance with mileage and weight use of highways and the long-run marginal construction and maintenance costs, the lowered ton-mile cost by truck would be uneconomic. Therefore, such relaxation of size and weight regulations would increase the existing traffic misallocations and their huge annual waste of scarce resources.

But as the immediate prospects are not bright for enactment of fully economic user fees for large and heavy trucks and buses, or for requiring their owners to finance their own highways, a further deterioration of the financial condition of the railways can be anticipated from relaxation of highway restrictions. Thus, the substitution of highway carriage for rail carriage would be promoted without any assurance of net social gains and in face of good prospects for social losses.

The continuing community and political pressures exerted for development of highly marginal inland waterways for regional advantage, such as navigation on the Columbia River between Pasco and Wenatchee, Washington, are another example of the crisis in public investment standards for transport development.[79] At a time when the capacity of alternative highways and railways is ample for additional freight traffic, marginal but expensive inland waterway projects are still being promoted and transport projects promising greater social returns continue to be neglected.

Adjustment of Transport Promotion to
an Efficient Role

The obvious first step toward more efficient investment in public transport facilities is to subject all state and Federal transport projects, whatever the mode, to far more rigorous economic analysis than heretofore. This requires the uniform and competent application of fully economic investment criteria to all modes in which public investments occur in the manner originally contemplated when legislation to create the U.S. Department of Transportation was under consideration.

Priority lists of individual transport development projects should be established in such a manner as to differentiate those with high net benefits from those with low or negative net benefits. Then, investments in specific transport development projects should be undertaken in the order that will bring the largest real net benefits and make the best use of scarce capital and other resources. To assure that result, it would be essential to arrange that investments in a single mode cannot automatically and excessively be made just because user funds or other capital funds have become available to the authorities. Another essential is an arrangement to insure that the best net-benefit producing projects in each mode will be undertaken only to the extent that those projects can meet their opportunity costs by out-producing investment projects in alternative modes in real net benefits to society.

Selection of the best investment analysis tests or standards for the different modes would be something of a problem. This arises from the necessity, if transport development is to be fully efficient, of comparing the net benefits of particular public transport projects against those to be realized from alternative investment projects in privately-owned transport facilities. There is an excellent and growing literature in economic writings, however, on the criteria and procedures for making efficient public project investments, some of which also examine the problem of evaluating public investments against private investments in terms of social efficiency.[80] Suffice it to say that productive and unproductive public projects must be differentiated as expertly as this is done among projects of private firms having the advantage of operating in highly developed markets and under complete, though often imperfect, price systems for final goods, factors of production, and capital funds. Already benefit-cost ratios are commonly used in appraising inland waterway and other public transport investments; and for many significant highway projects, revenue-cost or rate-of-return tests similar to those used in private enterprise have been used. The urgent need is for more rigor in avoiding double-counting of benefits; in subjecting the indirect or social benefits to tests equivalent to the willingness of particular consumers to pay for the services of the project under consideration; in avoiding underestimation of the future costs of the carriers using public transport facilities and overestimation of the future costs of the closest alternative mode; and in expending far more effort to count explicitly all of the social costs of a public transport project as well as the indirect or social benefits. A requirement of special importance is that realistic interest and discount rates be employed to represent the real and considerable social cost of capital raised from taxpayers. The assumption that such capital is costless or relatively without cost really begs the question and often prevents public investment analysis from finding truly efficient public investments.

The second step toward improving the economy in investment in public transport facilities is for the Congress to act quickly to close the gaps in user charges for such facilities. Primarily, this means enactment of suitable and sufficient user fees or tolls for the inland waterways to recover at least all annual maintenance and operating costs of keeping individual waterways navigable and open and all annual costs, including capital costs, of new waterways not yet constructed. A number of Federal studies have been made of the economic case for and against user charging for waterways and to ascertain the user fee structure best designed for that mode. Hence, the intelligence essential for this final step in bringing about uniform application of user fees for public transport facilities is clearly available. Only the strong opposition of the barge lines, the large corporate users of their services at uneconomically low rates or private barge costs, and the nearby communities benefiting from subsidized transport—often at the expense of the nation as a whole—prevent this return to the toll-pricing policies for inland waterways such as the Erie Canal in the nineteenth century. Inland waterways are not free even after they have been constructed, as they continue to utilize scarce resources for operation and maintenance. Hence, the myth should be ended that inland waterways are free goods to their users and that their services need not be priced as are other transport services, including highway services, airport services, and the services of international canals such as the Panama Canal and the St. Lawrence Seaway.

In addition, however, existing state and Federal user fees for highway services require adjustment to increase the payments from the large and heavy vehicles, especially the diesel-powered vehicles, so that they correspond with the long-run marginal construction, maintenance, and operation costs occasioned by those vehicles. Although finding the differential cost of highway services for each class of motor vehicle is complicated by the existence of fixed and common costs in the highway function, a great deal of Federal-state test-road and other research has been done on that problem. Sufficient differential cost and user payment information is available and has been reported to the state legislatures and the Congress in the state studies and those of the BPR to enable immediate action to be taken by the state legislatures and the Congress that would go far toward eliminating the underpayments of large and heavy vehicles.[81]

By enacting state and Federal diesel motor fuel fees, approximately 50 percent above the fee levels for gasoline used for motor fuel (because diesel-powered vehicles obtain about 50 percent more miles per gallon), the states and the Federal Government could approximately exact the amounts required to raise the payments of the large and heavy over-the-road vehicles to cover most of their differential costs. This step has been recommended in many state and Federal highway user fee studies on both equity and economic grounds and by several Presidents of the United States.[82] But the opposition of the organized truckers and other highway interests have prevented enactment of diesel differentials except in a few states. As most of the truck combinations that are employed in medium- and long-distance carriage are powered with diesel fuel and are the combinations carrying traffic in high-value goods that have uneconomically been misallocated away from the railroads by regulatory policy, parity pricing on value-of-service criteria, and promotional policy, enactment of the diesel differential would to an extent lessen the wastes of traffic misallocations.

In view of the attention being given environmental influences today, much more consideration than in the past should be given to the social costs of highway use, including the differential social costs of highway use by the large and heavy vehicles. Because of the social costs of air and noise pollution, displacement of residences and business units, displacement of alternative forms of travel without substituting entirely and efficiently for the displaced modes, user prices for highway use should raise the social marginal cost of highway use above the highway-service (or private) marginal cost.[83] Hence, user fees should be higher than levels just sufficient to cover the long-run marginal costs of highway services whenever those social costs are tangible and significant, and especially when they can be at least roughly measured. Moreover, when congestion exists on urban streets and highways and on intercity highways, the social marginal cost of highway use rises steeply above the levels during uncongested periods of highway use (and above private marginal costs). Peak-period user fees or tolls should be high in those periods to equate with the high social marginal costs occasioned by congestion, with lower off-peak charges when there is no congestion to raise the private marginal vehicular cost to all users or to lower highway capacity.[84]

Such pricing policies for street and highway use would reduce the expressway and high-capacity highway investments needed to accommodate the traffic that moves most efficiently by highway carriers and would reallocate intercity traffic to the low-cost railroads contributing little to the social costs of modern transport. In addition, by raising the cost of automobile use for driving to and from work, most of which travel occurs in peak periods, specific expressway user charges in urban areas to assess the social and peak costs attributable to that use of automobiles would enlarge the effective demand for ordinary bus services, express bus services, suburban rail services, and for rail rapid transit services. Thus, such peak pricing would make it easier to finance much needed mass transit systems from revenues from users collected through the fare box.

A third step toward improving transport promotional policy involves some pooling of the trust fund revenues earmarked for highway or airway and airport development with other revenues available for financing public transport investments such as rapid transit. Then from the pooled financial resources, Federal and state aid would be granted so as to bring about the most efficient investments in whatever mode of transport the high priority projects happened to appear.

It should be recognized that the case for earmarking user funds for expenditure only for the particular way or terminal facilities desired by those who pay the user fees is subject to some limitations. First, as indicated above, expending all highway user funds automatically for highway purposes can lead to overinvestment in highways. Second, the need for trust funds to be totally reinvested in a particular mode's basic facilities is greater in the developmental period for a new transport technology than after it has matured and the required basic facilities have been developed. Thus, in the early days of the new motor transport technology and in view of its evident potential for improving transport service in many ways, it made good economic sense to utilize all revenues collected from highway user fees for investment in the necessary improved road system to test and improve the new technology and rapidly establish a new mode of transport. However, now that the motor transport technology has become well established, and an excellent and extensive highway, road, and street network has come into being, the *excess* user revenues over the annual maintenance and operating costs and the necessary replacements of capital required by continuing traffic flows should be considered as a free pool of capital funds. Capital funds in such pools should be invested in whatever projects in whatever modes, including highways, that happen to have the potential of producing the maximum net benefits to society. This suggests that highway trust funds should be partially opened, or partially pooled with other user fee revenues in trust funds, for financing investments in rapid transit or in other modes when they qualify by that investment test.[85]

Various objections have been raised to opening highway and other trust funds partially or wholly for investments in other modes. Some fear that lower rates of return might be realized from alternative modal investments than in highway or airway projects, or that diversion of trust fund revenues could make it easier for politically-inspired allocations of capital to finance low-productivity investments such as in marginal waterways or railroad passenger facilities. The argument is made that benefit-cost studies do not necessarily give assurance that uneconomic public investments will not take place, as questionable investments in inland waterways have been made on the basis of extensive benefit-cost justifications that exaggerate the benefits in relation to the costs. Additionally, it has been argued that it would be inequitable to ask highway users to subsidize users of rail rapid transit in addition to paying for highways.

The possibility exists that a partial opening of highway trust funds for investment in other modes would occasionally provide funds for investments in rapid transit or in politically-inspired transport facilities that are not economically justified, all factors considered. The remedy for this, however, is to arrange for an unbiased planning organization to make rigorous benefit-cost analyses for alternative projects. Moreover, there is evidence that the process of automatic reinvestment of highway trust funds in highway projects has far from eliminated all politically-inspired road investments. And since the social costs from air and noise pollution and relocations are far from being fully counted as highway costs to be covered by user payments, it cannot be assumed that highway users always fully pay for their highway services. If those social costs were assessed and peak charges were levied to reduce both congestion and otherwise required highway expansion, the excess revenues that would accumulate in trust funds could more logically be employed to compensate all persons disadvantaged by highways or to provide alternative transport facilities to lessen the social costs of highways than to expand the highway facilities more or less automatically.[86] With user fees lacking for waterways and inadequate to cover all relevant public costs of highway use, the derived demands for waterways and highways can be exaggerated by the market, and the demand for alternative transport facilities, such as rapid transit, can be understated. In any case, the problems that have arisen from relying only or mostly on highways for urban travel seem so obvious and difficult to solve by building more freeways that some partial opening of highway user funds appears to be justified for investment in appropriate transit systems for which good benefit-cost justifications exist.

With the allocation of trust fund revenues for investment in alternative transport limited to the excess user revenues from peak charges and the user charge increments to cover the social costs of highways and highway use, the highway users would not be subsidizing the riders of rapid transit systems. Highway users would be paying fully for the social marginal costs of their use of highways, but they would not be overpaying as implied in the subsidy argument. These and other excess revenues would be a capital pool, available for investment in any mode yielding the largest net benefits, all factors considered. To the extent that geographical inequities might arise from diversion of highway trust funds for rapid transit, these can be mitigated or eliminated by utilizing the excess user revenues collected from urban areas whose rapid transit systems are to receive aids from the trust funds. Again, the apportionment of state highway user funds among road systems has long created significant inequities, mainly to the disadvantage of the urban populations and in favor of those who live on and use county roads.[87] In light of this widespread situation, the complete avoidance of some inequities can be considered far less important than financing balanced transport systems in urban areas to avoid the excessive congestion, social costs, and other inadequacies of highway-only or highway-mostly solutions.

Since the 1930s, highway and other public transport investments have at times been justified primarily as a counter-depression device to increase employment and stimulate business, as the best way to utilize public expenditures to deal with depressed areas, such as the Appalachian Region, or as a fruitful way of insuring real economic growth over the long run. But experience has indicated that highway programs take too long to plan and to organize to be of much aid in increasing employment during recession periods; that often it takes far more than a program of building roads in rural areas to stimulate industrial development in a depressed region;[88] and that the 1956 Federal policy of utilizing the Interstate System and higher levels of Federal-state highway expenditures to stimulate a rapid rate of real economic growth has several limitations.[89] One of these drawbacks is the huge annual cost of misallocation of traffic away from the low-cost mode to which that policy has contributed. Another is the threat of general bankruptcy of the railroads and their nationalization. Hence, the time has come to reevaluate the gains of using highway and other public transport development for general economic development purposes against losses, failures, and wastes of public funds that heavy reliance on that public expenditure policy occasions.

Government ownership and operation of the rights-of-way of the privately-owned railroads has received increased attention in the United States in recent years as a policy element in rationalizing intercity transport within the current regulatory setting. Such a policy would continue the privately-owned railroads as operating companies which would utilize government-owned tracks and ways on cost-related user fees. This would reduce the fixed costs of the railroad companies by converting the fixed costs of ways into variable cost user charges just as the fixed costs of highways have long been converted into variable costs for auto, bus, and truck operators. Governments would bear the fixed costs of rail rights-of-way just as of highways and other public transport facilities. As the railroad rights-of-ways become public property, property taxes would no longer necessarily be assessed, though general fund payments in lieu of current property taxes on such ways would doubtless have to be substituted. Thus, the carriers of the competing modes would be placed on an equal footing in expenditures for the maintenance-of-way facilities, nonpayment of property taxes on way properties, and the claims for public investment expenditures for essential way facilities. In addition, such a policy would greatly facilitate application of the same investment criteria for the railroads and alternative modes, simplify the opening of trust funds for economic investments in all modes, and reduce the differences in the extent of variability in the service costs of the competing modes. The latter effect would facilitate adoption of cost-based freight rate structures that would lessen the economic cost of misallocated freight traffic. If the Federal Government took over responsibility for railroad rights-of-way and adopted a much needed long-range investment program emphasizing way, track, and tunnel improvement of the main-traffic railway lines and discontinuance of the very light-traffic railway lines, a policy of nationalization of rail rights-of-way, in addition to achieving sizeable resource cost equalization between the modes, could bring about modern and efficient railroad ways and trackage, more long tunnels under mountains and hills as in Europe, and new railways for fast, efficient, and environmentally-adapted transport as in Japan.

A nationalization of railroad rights-of-way policy, with or without the recommended regulatory reform, appears an attractive policy in solving some longstanding transport problems. Many complications arise as to its implementation, however. Among these are the difficulties for rail managements that might arise in operation of trains over ways whose maintenance and investments are determined by government agencies or public corporations. The original reasons for not operating railroad way and track facilities generally as public highways doubtless still have some validity. Moreover, abandonment of redundant railways might take place *less rapidly* under government ownership than under private ownership, as political pressures probably would have greater weight in abandonment decisions than in the past. Political standards, as with highways, waterways and airports, might require unneeded investments in improving some railroad way facilities or unnecessary expenditures in overmaintaining them. Finally, without adjusting the ownership of ways, other policy alternatives exist that might raise fewer operational complications and might go far toward equalizing the cost conditions between the modes. Government payments could be made, as in France, to the railroads to compensate them for bearing way and social costs not borne by the highway and other modal competitors. This, too, would equalize the competitive conditions between the modes. And government investment aids could be extended to the railways in order to obtain more rapid progress in basic modernization of the main freight and passenger way and track facilities where economically justified. Hence, unless government ownership of the railways comes about by default, as a result of continued inaction by the Congress to solve the basic problems of transport policy herein discussed, a general policy of government take-overs of railroad rights-of-way seems premature. Before adopting such a policy, the subject should be accorded far greater study and public discussion. And in such research and discussion, the experience of other countries in solving the track question in transport should be thoroughly studied.[90]

Implications for National, Regional, State, and Local Planning

As stated in the section on regulatory policy, adjustments of economic regulation of transport industries to perform an efficient role will require a substantial reduction in restrictive regulation by the ICC and the CAB or enactment of partial or complete deregulation by the Congress. The purpose of such reform would be to permit competition in transport markets to operate more fully; to bring about a readjustment of pricing and service structures; and to produce a more efficient allocation of resources within transport and between transport and other sectors.

In such a setting, the only planning required is that designed to determine the precise extent to which deregulation should be enacted, to fix the timing of deregulation actions to minimize the transitional effects of moving toward freer transport markets, and to reexamine the regulatory standards and policies to be changed by the regulatory bodies to allow competition in transport to work more productively than in the past. The U.S. Department of Transportation is the principal agency to plan deregulation and the series of steps to be taken in that direction, although the Antitrust Division of the Department of Justice and other departments also have roles to play. If the regulatory bodies are to be entrusted to relax regulatory policies restrictive of competition under minimal statutory changes, they would have the leading role in reforming regulatory policy. But even here, the Department of Transportation and other departments would have significant inputs of research and advice to offer and would serve as public advocates of desirable changes in the key regulatory cases.

Obviously, since the important regulatory policies affecting air and surface transport are determined at the Federal level and the need is to arrange for transport markets to work more freely, regional planning could contribute little, if anything, toward adjusting regulation to an efficient role. However, the states that regulate wholly intrastate transportation would have a role to play in planning regulatory reform within their jurisdictions. As some states, for example, New York, have already transferred transport regulation from independent commissions to state departments of transportation in an effort to improve policy and to coordinate regulatory and promotional policies, it can be expected that many states would follow the Federal Government if the latter should substantially deregulate transportation. However, since transport can serve its most efficient role in development if it is allowed to operate more competitively, regulation of carrier rates, services, and returns seems an unworkable and blunt tool for promoting regional economic development.

The application of rigorous and more uniform investment criteria for public transport facilities and more efficient user pricing will obviously require centralized planning of the public transport development function at whatever level is appropriate under the circumstances. At the Federal level, the U.S.

Department of Transportation already has general jurisdiction over Federal highway investment and aids, civil airway development and operations, and the grant of aids for construction of civil airports. However, the DOT does not have jurisdiction over inland waterway investments and merchant marine investments, and the DOT has limited statutory power to coordinate economically the investment planning and project reporting by the action agencies under its general supervision. The DOT jurisdiction should at least be extended over the investment planning activities for inland waterways and for the merchant marine; and its power to subject Federal public investment planning for all modes to common and relevant economic investment criteria and to coordinate the investment recommendations of all action agencies should be increased.

The potential benefits of utilizing the DOT as an effective coordinating body in transport investment planning would be considerable over the long run. The Congressional Committees and the Congress would then have full knowledge of the benefits and costs of the alternative transport development plans or transport projects that would come before them for consideration. Overall, this would more surely lead to rejection of the least beneficial projects in each mode and to a more balanced transport development program than in the past. Though the Congress might still vote to undertake some public transport projects not having a high priority on the lists supplied by the DOT in terms of net benefits and ability to meet all opportunity costs, the number of such cases undoubtedly would be significantly reduced. If such investment priority information were available, public opinion could be marshalled to exercise more restraint on political log-rolling in connection with acquisitive projects of no or limited value to the economy as a whole. Regions and communities would be less able to press successfully for projects that create benefits to them during the construction stage but have no real promise of stimulating economic growth afterwards. But since such venal projects would not be economically justified, other more effective means can be found to aid the disadvantaged regions and communities without creating an oversupply of expensive fixed transport facilities.

At the state level, too, an urgent need exists for state departments of transportation to be established with power to plan and to integrate statewide transport development for all modes in which state investments are made or to which state aid is given. Like the Federal DOT, such agencies should rigorously apply economic investment standards as uniformly as possible over all modes under their jurisdiction and work out more efficient user fee structures. As in the case of the Federal-state cooperation in planning the highway and airport functions, the state DOTs and the Federal DOT would often work closely together in analysis and priority evaluation of particular public transport investment projects. Such cooperation would increase the Federal Government's awareness of state, urban, and corridor transport needs that press for attention. The process would not only further inject the expertise of the Federal DOT's economists and engineers into state and local planning, but it would reciprocally contribute to the knowledge and expertise of the Federal planners. Already, at least 15 state DOTs have been established; and additional ones will be organized to centralize planning for statewide and local transport development and to provide greater staff resources for planning efficient transport investments and user fee structures.[91]

The transport problems of large metropolitan areas are of sufficient magnitude and complexity as to require those urban regions to engage in transport investment analysis essential to selection of the best economic projects within their orbits. Urban regions require organizations for planning, investing in, and operating transport facilities such as airports, transit systems, suburban trains, and bridges and highways.[92] However, as illustrated by the Port of New York Authority, a compact or other interstate type of regional planning organization will be essential when projects extend into or affect two or more states. This might also be true of regional airports in rural areas serving two or more states. As both Federal and state financial aids for metropolitan or corridor transport development will likely be on a vaster scale in the future, cooperative planning and investment analysis between the Federal DOT and metropolitan or urban regional authorities and between the state DOTs and those authorities will also become more essential.

On the other hand, far less need exists for regional transportation authorities beyond the urban or corridor-type regional organizations to plan transport development, to make investment analyses, and to undertake transport investments. An exception might exist in the case of underdeveloped or disadvantaged regions (such as the Appalachian Region), which do not show evidence of full participation in a growth economy. Even in such cases, however, there can be considerable doubt that large-scale transport development programs, such as building rural roads to a higher level, will transform a region quickly or at all into a diversified and growing regional economy. Often, there will be other measures that will succeed better than furnishing additional public transport facilities. In any case, by cooperative planning efforts the state departments of transportation and the Federal DOT can discover the good opportunities for providing additional public transport facilities that will contribute to diversification and development of disadvantaged regions. Only if the urban, state, and Federal planning agencies that already exist or that could be established on the pattern of the leading states did not sufficiently take into account the legitimate transport development needs of disadvantaged or less-developed regions would a good case exist for establishing a new set of regional planning organizations intermediate between the states and the Federal Government.

Summary and Conclusions

Government in the United States has intervened in transport by granting aids to and investing in transport development and by regulating carriers as to rates, services, entry and withdrawal, consolidations and mergers, and rates of return. These interventions are long-standing and both types have powerfully influenced the development of transport systems and the rates and services rendered to the national, regional and state economies.

Probably the promotional policies of American governments have been of greater long-term significance in influencing transport and economic development than regulation. State canal building in the early nineteenth century, specifically New York's construction and operation of the Erie Canal as a toll facility, contributed efficient transport between the Great Lakes and the Atlantic Seaboard for the first time. Encouraged by government's free entry and eminent domain policies and Federal land grants, private enterprise contributed the nation's large network of railroads, which greatly facilitated and stimulated national and regional economic development in the last half of that century. State and Federal enterprise after 1916 and 1921 provided the country's vast system of modern highways, roads, and streets, financed largely from user revenues. Federal enterprise started the trunk airlines; turned them over to private enterprise in 1925 with airmail subsidies; constructed and operated the Federal civil airways; gave both emergency and regular grants to local authorities for construction of airports; and ended airmail subsidies to the airlines in the 1950s, except to local service airlines. Finally, the Federal Government, through the Corps of Engineers, planned, constructed, and operated most inland waterways developed during the current century.

Government regulation of the railroads, starting in the 1870s on the state level and in 1887 with establishment of the ICC to control interstate transportation, came in response to marked monopoly or cartel conditions and until 1920 sought to limit excessively high and discriminating rates. Except for the Panama Canal Act policy of keeping rail and water industries separate and competitive and for an early prohibition of railroad pools, regulation did not attempt to rationalize transport industries until 1920 and particularly until after passage of the Motor Carrier Act of 1935. Prior to 1935, the principal regulatory tools were the maximum rate power and the controls over discrimination. These tools were obviously designed for shipper or consumer benefits. But with extension of regulation to interstate motor and water carriers in 1935 and 1940, regulation fundamentally changed character from early emphasis on control of monopoly price and service practices and the encouragement of intermodal competition to the present-day emphasis on restricting both intramodal and intermodal competition. Under this scheme, primary reliance has been on entry controls and minimum rate regulation to eliminate "destructive" competition. In view of the growing competitive areas in transport after 1920, however, this change was paradoxical and obviously was mostly motivated toward producing benefits for carriers rather than for consumers.

Although it is popular in some circles today to impute that ICC policies were intended to strengthen the railroad cartels in the early period of regulation, early

ICC regulation was generally shipper and consumer motivated. To the extent that it was effective, it substituted for competitive forces that were not strong or pervasive enough to limit rates to cost and prevent uneconomic discrimination. Thus, after the 1906 and 1910 amendments to the Act to Regulate Commerce, early ICC regulation eliminated much long-short haul discrimination and often gave relief from rate discriminations to particular shippers, distant producing areas, and low-grade commodities unable to stand high rates. The ICC basically accepted the value-of-service, or discriminating, rate structure that the railroads had already adopted, finding that it well suited the railroads' economic characteristics and promoted national and regional economic development. This rate structure unquestionably facilitated the economic integration of the continental United States; fostered wide regional specialization and wide markets; and stimulated efficient large-scale production in industry. Consequently, up to the 1930s, ICC regulation promoted national and regional development that was already taking place on the basis of other economic factors. Dissatisfaction arose over the lack of progress toward consolidation of the railroads, however; and the outlying regions seeking to diversify their economies in the 1930s complained that the rail rate structure handicapped them by continuing to promote industrialization of the Northeast and agricultural and extractive economies in the South and West.

The new regulation, which was never accepted by agricultural shippers and whose economic bases came under early attack by discerning economists, gradually produced economic effects that have stimulated widespread dissatisfaction and growing demands for deregulation and a policy of allowing competition to work in transport. Competent studies have shown that the highly competitive trucking industry has been cartelized under regulation and that the motor carriers have adopted a discriminating rate structure, the railroad value-of-service rates, with modifications. Restrictive entry control has fragmented trucking markets; reduced the number of competing firms to a few in many markets; increased the size of trucking firms' far beyond the economies of scale; and together with minimum rate regulation has encouraged costly service competition, excess capacity due to certificate restrictions, higher costs and rates, and high rates of return.

Moreover, the rate parity policy of the motor carriers and the railroads on high value-of-service rates for goods of high value, encouraged by ICC minimum rate regulation and limited entry, has diverted vast volumes of high-value freight over medium- and long-distance hauls and billions of dollars of revenue annually from the low-cost railroads to the high-cost truckers. While this has been very profitable for the trucking industry, it has impoverished the railroads. Their rates of return have fallen to very low levels and many are in bankruptcy or are facing that condition. Of perhaps greater consequence to the economy are the huge costs of misallocation of traffic and resources found by economists to range up to several billions of dollars each year. Additionally, the dynamic consequences of restrictive regulation, including maintaining unnecessary excess capacity, failing to weed out inefficient carriers, and stifling the incentives for technical change and innovation, are possibly even more costly.

Curiously, the new regulation that was originally designed to help the railroads continue their common carrier services and rate equalization responsibilities, has turned out to provide incentives for more rapid expansion of trucking and barge transport than otherwise would have occurred. Moreover, it stimulated greater investment in public highway and waterway facilities. Thus, the new regulation has gone hand in hand with the promotional policies of government in the last several decades in encouraging overdevelopment of the modes dependent on public facilities and underdevelopment of the part of the railroad network that the economy highly depends on as the most efficient mode for medium- and long-distance traffic except for liquids through large-diameter pipelines and the hauling of bulk commodities on efficient waterways. Even airline regulation by the CAB is increasingly coming under attack as creating imperfect cartel conditions restricting rate competition and as leading to high rate levels, overencouraging service competition and vast excess seat capacity, and allowing carriers to become too large to be efficient and to adjust profitably to changing market conditions.

Without the vast highway, airway and airport, and inland waterway systems provided by state and Federal investment and subsidies in the last half century, the great growth of highway, air, and barge transport could not have taken place. However, the most needed and highly used of those facilities would have been provided by private enterprise or by toll-financing authorities, as was demonstrated by the rapid expansion of modern toll roads soon after World War II. Beyond doubt, government promotion has expanded those types of public facilities beyond the capacities that the market would have provided.

A number of factors explain this conclusion. First, political demands have been important in building roads to higher quality than otherwise would occur, in improving many waterways, and in constructing some airports. Second, the investment planning process for public transport facilities does not consider whether the most productive investment might be in another mode of transport. Thus, under the trust fund concept, almost all highway user revenues, amounting to many billions of dollars each year, are automatically reinvested in highways, a process that can lead to overinvestment, especially when coupled with political apportionments of user funds among the road systems. Third, the economic demands for waterways are not limited by any user fees even to cover the annual operation and maintenance costs, and those for highways, airways, and airports have not been limited by user fees sufficient to cover the long-run marginal costs of the way and terminal services rendered to the carriers in close competition with the railroads. Fourth, the carriers depending on public transport facilities have not been assessed user fee increments for property taxes on public facilities that are not subject to taxation. Fifth, benefit-cost analyses for public facilities often count the indirect or social benefits but not the indirect or social costs and hence exaggerate the need for additional investment. Sixth, highway users have not ordinarily been assessed the full social marginal costs traceable to use of expressways at peak periods and to smog, noise, relocations, and the deterioration in public transport facilities that cannot completely be eliminated.

The total effect of all those differential factors is that the annual public investments for highways, airways and airports, and inland waterways have been considerably larger than would be economically justified if the same pricing conditions and criteria for investment applied to both private and public investments in transport facilities. In a number of ways, this situation has led to a rapid growth of the newer modes of transport and to growth in excess of the true economic demands for their services. Motor, barge, and air carriers have ample and riskless capacity in ways, channels and locks, and terminals to accommodate rapid expansion. In addition, they can more quickly take advantage of technological improvements that lower their costs and make their services faster. Their rates can be lower than otherwise to the extent that user fees are not assessed or are insufficient to cover the long-run public and social costs of public transport facilities. The effects on the railroads, however, have been adverse and far from wholly economic. To what extent uneconomic promotional policies for the modes dependent on public facilities have contributed to uneconomic diversion of traffic and revenues from the railroads is unknown. Nevertheless, there can be little question that the promotional policies of the state and Federal governments have contributed to considerable uneconomic diversion and to the economic decline of the railways over several decades.

Promotional and regulatory policy have both contributed to the present crises that are visible in transport, including the threat of permanent government ownership and operation of the railroads, the unbalanced transport supply situations in both large and small cities, and the growing problem of providing access to airports, relief from the social costs of air and highway transport, and adequate passenger transport in corridor regions. Adjusting government regulatory and promotional policies to more efficient roles will make significant contributions to solving both the intercity and urban transport problems.

With respect to regulation, the fact that transport industries, except for the oil pipelines, have become essentially and pervasively competitive should be accepted, and regulatory policy should be made to conform to this market condition. Thus, either the ICC and the CAB should change their entry and exit, minimum rate, and merger policies to allow competition, especially rate competition, to work more freely, or substantial deregulation by legislative means should take place. In the case of freight transport, control of entry and prescription of minimum rates for truck and barge carriers could well be eliminated, although some discrimination and maximum rate control of the railroads might still be essential with respect to their remaining monopoly markets. At the minimum, the standards in the National Transportation Policy that provide the legal basis for protective, cartel-like regulation restrictive of competition should be eliminated; the variable cost standard for minimum competitive rates should be adopted; and the wasteful restrictions on commodities, return hauls, routes, and points should be removed from certificates and permits, by legislation, if necessary. Substantial change in CAB regulation, too, is probably desirable to permit competition to work more fully in determining fare levels, to reduce excess capacity, and to eliminate inefficient carriers.

The obvious first step toward more efficient investment in public transport facilities is to subject all state and Federal transport projects, whatever the mode, to far more rigorous economic analysis than heretofore. This will require uniform application of fully economic investment criteria to all modes in which public investments occur in the manner originally contemplated for the U.S. Department of Transportation. It will also require the drawing up of priority lists of individual transport projects to differentiate those with high net benefits from those with low or negative net benefits. Finally, investments in specific transport projects should be undertaken in the order that will bring the largest real net benefits and make the best use of scarce resources. The ability of a proposed transport investment in one mode to meet the full opportunity cost of an alternative project in an alternative mode should be proven. In other words, selection of the top-priority investment projects should not be limited to those in a given mode.

As it will be difficult to make efficient public transport investments and to avoid some misallocations of traffic without user fees for all modes, the gaps in user fee requirements should be closed. In addition, the existing user fees for highway, airway, and airport services should be more closely adjusted to the long-run marginal costs for each class of user. Thus, user fees or tolls should be enacted for the inland waterways. Diesel differentials in motor fuel taxes should be enacted at the state and Federal levels to raise the user contributions of the large and heavy vehicles that have been shown by the BPR and state studies to be below their differential costs. Property tax equivalents and increments to compensate for the social costs of smog, noise, relocations, and displacement of essential public services, including peak-use charges, should be assessed on motor vehicles, barges, and aircraft to the extent feasible.

A final step toward improving transport promotional policy involves opening up trust fund revenues earmarked for highway or airway and airport development for financing other public transport investments such as bus or rail rapid transit in cases where good benefit-cost justifications exist for such investments. Automatic investment of the user revenues going into trust funds has been a cause of overinvestment in highways, at least in the sense of overinvesting in systems carrying light traffic loads. It has also contributed to the unbalanced transport development trends in urban areas and throughout transport in recent decades. Now that the airways and airports, the highways, and the inland waterways have been developed to make air, motor, and barge transport viable and mature parts of the transport system, the case that once existed for reinvesting all user revenues in the same mode is far less persuasive than it was in the 1920s. Consequently, the excess user revenues over the annual maintenance and operating costs and the necessary replacements of capital required by continuing traffic flows should be considered as a free pool of capital funds for investment in whatever mode, including highways, in which the projects of highest priority in terms of net benefits actually occur.

Obviously, since the regulatory policies affecting air and surface transport are determined at the Federal and state levels and the need is to arrange for transport markets to work more competitively, regional planning could contribute little, if anything, toward adjusting regulation to an efficient role. This will have to be done either by the regulatory bodies themselves under legislative directives to act or by specific legislation to deregulate transport to the extent desirable. In adjusting transport promotional policy to a more economic role, the principal planning and analytical tasks will be done by the U.S. Department of Transportation, the state departments of transportation, and the municipal or interstate compact authorities that presently exist or are being formed. The power of the Federal DOT to coordinate Federal transport investments should be strengthened. More state DOTs should be established to plan and coordinate public transport development within the states. Federal, state, and municipal planning groups should cooperate fully and give close attention to regional development needs. A case for special regional authorities may exist in a very few cases where special problems exist, such as corridor transport, but not for general establishment of such authorities for transport planning.

Notes

1. For the history, magnitude, problems and effects of the promotional role of government in transport development in this period, see C.L. Dearing and Wilfred Owen, NATIONAL TRANSPORTATION POLICY, The Brookings Institution, Washington, 1949, Chapters 1-8; James C. Nelson, RAILROAD TRANSPORTATION AND PUBLIC POLICY, The Brookings Institution, Washington, 1959, Chapters 2-4, and "Policy Issues and Economic Effects of Public Aids to Domestic Transport," LAW AND CONTEMPORARY PROBLEMS, Autumn 1959, pp. 531-556; and Association of American Railroads, GOVERNMENT EXPENDITURES FOR HIGHWAY, WATERWAY, AND AIR FACILITIES AND PRIVATE EXPENDITURES FOR RAILROAD FACILITIES, Washington, D.C., May 1971.

2. For example, see Gabriel Kolko, RAILROADS AND REGULATION, 1877-1916, Princeton University Press, Princeton, 1965. But see the review-article on that book by R.W. Harbeson, in THE JOURNAL OF ECONOMIC HISTORY, June 1967, pp. 230-242; and C.L. Dearing, "Transportation," in

Lyon and Associates, GOVERNMENT AND ECONOMIC LIFE, The Brookings Institution, Washington, 1940, Vol. II, Chap. 22, pp. 753-770.

3. See J.C. Nelson, SOME ECONOMIC EFFECTS OF LIMITATION ON LONG-AND-SHORT-HAUL DISCRIMINATION ON THE INTERMOUNTAIN REGION OF THE UNITED STATES, a study prepared for the Province of Alberta and presented as Exhibit 160 in testimony before the Royal Commission on Transportation, Ottawa, Canada, October 13-14, 1960 (Hearings Volume Nos.: 99, pp. 16774-16844, and 100, pp. 16846-16916).

4. For case details and ICC policies in cases involving particular rates on particular commodities and between particular points and several types of discrimination issues, see D.P. Locklin, ECONOMICS OF TRANSPORTATION, 6th ed., Richard D. Irwin, Inc., Homewood, 1966, Chapters 19-23. In general, the Commission has denied the railroads the right to maintain high rates to offset natural advantages of location of particular shippers or communities, although the carriers may at times maintain less than normal rates to offset the disadvantages of location.

5. K.T. Healy, THE ECONOMICS OF TRANSPORTATION IN AMERICA, The Ronald Press Company, New York, 1940, pp. 202-232, 237, 240-250, 285-286, 462, 464, 488, and 501.

6. Compare R.W. Fogel, RAILROADS AND AMERICAN ECONOMIC GROWTH: ESSAYS IN ECONOMETRIC HISTORY, The Johns Hopkins Press, Baltimore, 1964.

7. This widening public interest in the reform or abolition of ICC regulation apparently prompted The Ralph Nader Study Group Report on the Interstate Commerce Commission and Transportation, THE INTERSTATE COMMERCE OMISSION by Robert C. Fellmeth and Associates, Grossman Publishers, Inc., New York, 1970. See pp. 324-325 for the Nader Group's recommendation to abolish the ICC. Also see the statement of Senator Robert Taft, Jr., to the U.S. Senate in CONGRESSIONAL RECORD, 92nd Congress, 1st session, March 3, 1971 (reprint).

8. C.L. Dearing, "Transportation," op. cit., pp. 842-853 and 857-863; R.L. Dewey, "Transport Coordination," TRANSPORTATION AND NATIONAL POLICY, National Resources Planning Board, Washington, D.C., May 1942, pp. 154-160; and J.C. Nelson, "The Motor Carrier Act of 1935," THE JOURNAL OF POLITICAL ECONOMY, August 1936, pp. 464-504, especially pp. 497-504, and "New Concepts in Transportation Regulation," TRANSPORTATION AND NATIONAL POLICY, op. cit., pp. 197-237.

9. J.C. Nelson, RAILROAD TRANSPORTATION AND PUBLIC POLICY, op. cit., pp. 171-179, 184-186 and 191-192; J.R. Meyer, M.J. Peck, John Stenason and Charles Zwick, THE ECONOMICS OF COMPETITION IN THE TRANSPORTATION INDUSTRIES, Harvard University Press, Cambridge, 1959, pp. 145-167, 184-186 and 189-196; E.W. Williams, Jr., and D.W. Bluestone, RATIONALE OF FEDERAL TRANSPORTATION POLICY, U.S.

Department of Commerce, Washington, D.C., April 1960, pp. 4-7; G.W. Hilton, THE TRANSPORTATION ACT OF 1958, Indiana University Press, Bloomington, 1969, pp. 205-207; R.W. Harbeson, "Toward Better Resource Allocation in Transport," THE JOURNAL OF LAW AND ECONOMICS, October 1969, pp. 321-338; and A.F. Friedlaender, THE DILEMMA OF FREIGHT TRANSPORT REGULATION, The Brookings Institution, Washington, D.C., 1969, pp. 65-99.

10. W.A. Jordan, AIRLINE REGULATION IN AMERICA, EFFECTS AND IMPERFECTIONS, The Johns Hopkins Press, Baltimore, 1970, pp. 13, 53-56, 70-72, 131-133, 143, 155-157, 175-177, and 223-244.

11. J.C. Nelson, "New Concepts in Transportation Regulation," op. cit., pp. 204 and 232-233. This basic issue of regulatory policy earlier surfaced in 1955 and 1962 in Congressional discussion of the Cabinet Committee's Report and President Kennedy's Message, but it was not fully presented to the Congress by any Administration until the Nixon Administration sent to the Congress the Transportation Regulatory Modernization Act of 1971 on November 8, 1971. See U.S. Department of Transportation, EXECUTIVE BRIEFING, Transportation Regulatory Modernization and Assistance Legislation, January 1972.

12. J.C. Nelson, "New Concepts in Transportation Regulation," op.cit., pp. 204-216, 230, and 233-237.

13. For an extensive treatment of the economic theory rationale for motor carrier regulation, to the extent one exists, see the recent work by C.J. Oort, THE ECONOMIC REGULATION OF THE ROAD TRANSPORT INDUSTRY, International Bank for Reconstruction and Development, Washington, D.C., Report No. EC-177, September 1970.

14. J.C. Nelson, "New Concepts in Transportation Regulation," op. cit., pp. 216-219.

15. Ibid., pp. 219-224 and 226-227.

16. Ibid., pp. 224-230.

17. Ibid., pp. 230-232.

18. Board of Investigation and Research, FEDERAL REGULATORY RESTRICTIONS UPON MOTOR AND WATER CARRIERS, S. Doc. 78, 79th Cong., 1st sess., 1945; ICC ADMINISTRATION OF THE MOTOR CARRIER ACT, Hearings before the Senate Select Committee on Small Business, 84th Cong., 1st sess., 1955; COMPETITION, REGULATION AND THE PUBLIC INTEREST IN THE MOTOR CARRIER INDUSTRY, Report of the Senate Select Committee on Small Business, March 19, 1956; J.C. Nelson, CONTROLS OF ENTRY INTO DOMESTIC SURFACE TRANSPORTATION UNDER THE INTERSTATE COMMERCE ACT, U.S. Department of Commerce (multilithed), October 1959; and J.C. Nelson, "The Effects of Entry Control in Surface Transport," TRANSPORTATION ECONOMICS, National Bureau of Economic Research, New York, distributed by Columbia University Press, 1965, pp. 381-422. See also the Nader Study, THE INTERSTATE COMMERCE OMISSION, op. cit., pp. 120-131.

19. J.C. Nelson, "The Effects of Entry Control in Surface Transport," op.

cit., pp. 401-407, and "Coming Organizational Changes in Transportation," TRANSPORTATION PROBLEMS AND POLICIES IN THE TRANS-MISSOURI WEST, University of Nebraska Press, Lincoln, Nebraska, 1967, pp. 319-323; 82ND ANNUAL REPORT, 1968, ICC, pp. 64-67, 137 and 149; and 81ST ANNUAL REPORT, 1967, pp. 44-46 and 108-110.

20. "The Top 100 Carriers, ICC Class I Motor Freight Carriers Ranked by 1968 Gross Operating Revenue," COMMERCIAL CAR JOURNAL, July 1969, pp. 79-85. Preliminary data for 1969 revealed the top 100 regulated truckers had revenues of more than $20.2 million; 50, more than $41.2 million; and 11, more than $100 million, with United Parcel Service with $327 million, 1969 REVENUES, LARGEST REGULATED CARRIERS, Carrier Reports, Old Saybrook, Connecticut.

21. For a critical review of British studies on economies of scale in trucking and his conclusion that "no convincing evidence of economies of scale" exist in road haulage, see A.A. Walters, INTEGRATION IN FREIGHT TRANSPORT, The Institute of Economic Affairs, Research Monograph 15, London, England, 1968, pp. 28-33. Also see Brian T. Bayliss, THE SMALL FIRM IN THE ROAD HAULAGE INDUSTRY, Committee of Inquiry on Small Firms, Research Report No. 1, Her Majesty's Stationery Office, London, 1971, pp. 1 and 43-49; and S.L. Edwards and B.T. Bayliss, OPERATING COSTS IN ROAD FREIGHT TRANSPORT, Department of the Environment, London, 1971.

22. J.C. Nelson, "The Effects of Entry Control in Surface Transport," op. cit., pp. 414-415; and Walter Miklius, ECONOMIC PERFORMANCE OF MOTOR CARRIERS OPERATING UNDER THE AGRICULTURAL EXEMPTION IN INTERSTATE TRUCKING, U.S. Department of Agriculture, Marketing Research Report No. 838, Washington, D.C., January 1969, pp. 1, 3-5.

23. T.G. Moore has estimated that the higher cost per year due to ICC's restrictions on the operating authority of common motor carriers and other regulatory influences amounted to from $1,400 million to $1,890 million. THE FEASIBILITY OF DEREGULATING SURFACE FREIGHT TRANSPORTATION, CONGRESSIONAL RECORD-Senate, September 28, 1971, pp. S15159-S15170, particularly pp. S15160 and S15162.

24. Protest and Petition for Suspension of the Department of Transportation against Increased Rates and Charges in Tariffs Published by the Pacific Inland Tariff Bureau, the Middle Atlantic Conference, the New England Motor Rate Bureau, Inc., and the Middlewest Motor Freight Bureau, Cases Nos. 47280, 47374, 47375, 47376 and 47380, ICC Suspension Board, March 20, 1968, pp. 13-16; and 84TH ANNUAL REPORT, 1970, ICC, pp. 67 and 142, where Class I intercity motor carriers of property were shown to average 18.4 percent as the rate of return from transportation service and 11.4 percent as the ratio of net income to shareholders' and proprietors' equity for the decade of the 1960s. For CAB fair rates of return, see Richard E. Caves, AIR TRANSPORT AND ITS REGULATORS, Harvard University Press, Cambridge, 1962, pp. 149-154. For

the status of the CAB's Docket 21866, the current DOMESTIC PASSENGER-FARE INVESTIGATION, see CAB REPORTS TO CONGRESS, Fiscal year 1971, p. 48. In this case, the CAB found the fair rate of return to be 12 percent for the trunk airlines and 12.35 percent for the local service carriers. J.C. Miller III, "The Domestic Passenger Fare Investigation and the Future of CAB Regulation," paper given at Dartmouth College, Hanover, N.H., August 30, 1971, pp. 78-88.

25. G.W. Wilson, "The I.C.C. Profit Criteria-Rail vs. Truck," TRANSPORTATION JOURNAL, Fall 1966, pp. 17-19; and R. Nevel and W. Miklius, "The Operating Ratio as a Regulatory Standard," ibid., Winter 1968, pp. 15-18. Also see ANNUAL REPORTS OF MOTOR CARRIERS OF PROPERTY, 335 I.C.C. 707(1969). T.G. Moore estimated the monopoly profits for Class I and II common carrier truckers due to regulation to range between $26.2 million and $229 million in 1968, the latter amounting to almost half of the net operating income of $499 million. THE FEASIBILITY OF DEREGULATING SURFACE FREIGHT TRANSPORTATION, CONGRESSIONAL RECORD-Senate, September 28, 1971, p. S15160.

26. J.R. Rose, "Regulation of Rates and Intermodal Transport Competition," I.C.C. PRACTITIONERS' JOURNAL, October 1965, pp. 11-26.

27. E.A. Nightingale, "Some Effects of Recent Changes in the Railway Grain-Rate Structure on Interregional Competition and Regional Development," TRANSPORTATION PROBLEMS AND POLICIES IN THE TRANS-MISSOURI WEST, op. cit., pp. 105-168, especially pp. 109-131; and G.E. McCallum, NEW TECHNIQUES IN RAILROAD RATEMAKING, Bureau of Economic and Business Research, Washington State University, February 1968, pp. 115-127.

28. A.F. Friedlaender, THE DILEMMA OF FREIGHT TRANSPORT REGULATION, op. cit., pp. 115-120. The author relied on the findings of W.Y. Oi and A.P. Hurter, Jr., ECONOMICS OF PRIVATE TRUCK TRANSPORTATION, William C. Brown Company Publishers (for the Transportation Center at Northwestern University), Dubuque, 1965. See also Meyer and Associates, THE ECONOMICS OF COMPETITION IN THE TRANSPORTATION INDUSTRIES, op. cit., pp. 97-100. Restrictive regulation, specifically the prohibition by the ICC against private truckers soliciting backhaul traffic for compensation, has been estimated by T.G. Moore to impose an uneconomic cost of from $100 million to $1 billion per year on private trucking by requiring additional vehicle-miles to transport the volume of traffic transported by private trucking. THE FEASIBILITY OF DEREGULATING SURFACE FREIGHT TRANSPORTATION, CONGRESSIONAL RECORD—Senate, September 28, 1971, pp. S15160-16162.

29. RAILROAD TRANSPORTATION AND PUBLIC POLICY, pp. 171-179, 186-188 and 191-192.

30. THE ECONOMICS OF COMPETITION IN THE TRANSPORTATION INDUSTRIES, pp. 159-165. Before the Subcommittee on Transportation and

Aeronautics, House Committee on Interstate and Foreign Commerce on April 27, 1972, A.C. Flott, Director, Department of Research and Transport Economics, American Trucking Associations, Inc., criticized the analyses of misallocation of traffic by Meyer and Associates, T.G. Moore and A.F. Friedlaender, and those of several other economists. See the Flott testimony and the ATA Review Statements B-1, B-3 and B-4 submitted for the record along with Statements B-2, B-5 and B-6, the latter three dealing with other works bearing on the cost of regulation. It is very doubtful, however, that the ATA criticisms effectively questioned the accumulating logical and factual evidence of the huge annual cost of misallocation due to restrictive regulation by the ICC.

31. RATIONALE OF FEDERAL TRANSPORTATION POLICY, op. cit., pp. 4-7.

32. THE TRANSPORTATION ACT OF 1958, op. cit., pp. 205-206.

33. "Toward Better Resource Allocation in Transport," op. cit., pp. 332 and 334.

34. THE DILEMMA OF FREIGHT TRANSPORT REGULATION, pp. 98-99. Also see pp. 65-98 and a paper by A.F. Friedlaender, "The Social Costs of Regulating the Railroads," presented at the Meetings of the American Economic Association, December 28, 1970, and published in THE AMERICAN ECONOMIC REVIEW, May 1971, pp. 226-234. She found that the deadweight loss from value-of-service pricing amounted to about $300 million in 1969 while the costs of excess capacity in the railroad industry ranged between $2.4 billion and $3.8 billion. In terms of policy prescriptions, this implies that relaxation of regulatory restraints on abandonments and rate competition by the railroads would yield considerable social savings. For another estimate of the net savings from reduction of inefficiencies in transport of about $4 billion per year and a nominal estimate of the cost of the transport regulatory process itself, see G.W. Wilson, "Transportation and Price Stability," THE AMERICAN ECONOMIC REVIEW, May 1969, pp. 263-265.

35. CONGRESSIONAL RECORD-Senate, September 28, 1971, p. S15162.

36. RAILROAD TRANSPORTATION AND PUBLIC POLICY, Chapters 2-3, 5-7, 9, and 11.

37. NATIONAL TRANSPORTATION ACT, Hearings before the Senate Committee on Commerce, 91st Cong., 2d Sess., on S.924 and S.2425, "To Develop a Comprehensive National Transportation System," Serial 91-69, February, April and May, 1970.

38. W.A. Jordan, AIRLINE REGULATION IN AMERICA, EFFECTS AND IMPERFECTIONS, The Johns Hopkins Press, Baltimore, 1970, p. 13.

39. G.W. Wilson, "Transportation and Price Stability," op. cit., pp. 261-269.

40. Ibid.

41. Hilton, THE TRANSPORTATION ACT OF 1958, pp. 28-34, 47-78, and 186-193.

42. M.J. Peck, "Competitive Policy for Transportation?," in THE CRISIS OF

THE REGULATORY COMMISSIONS, P.W. MacAvoy (ed.), W.W. Norton & Company, Inc., New York, 1970, pp. 74-78; and E.W. Williams, Jr., THE REGULATION OF RAIL-MOTOR RATE COMPETITION, Harper & Brothers, New York, 1958, pp. 220-222.

43. J.C. Nelson, "The Motor Carrier Act of 1935," op. cit., pp. 471-475, 499-500, and 502-503.

44. FEDERAL REGULATORY RESTRICTIONS UPON MOTOR AND WATER CARRIERS, op. cit., pp. 218-221, 223, 229, and 239.

45. ICC ADMINISTRATION OF THE MOTOR CARRIER ACT, op. cit., pp. 188-195, and 333-334; and Nelson, "The Effects of Entry Control in Surface Transport," op. cit., pp. 406-407 and 409.

46. See the Commission's defense of its trucking merger policies in TRUCK-ING MERGERS AND CONCENTRATION, Hearings before the Senate Select Committee on Small Business, 85th Cong., 1st Sess., July 1-12, 1957, pp. 40-123 and 154-157; and the Appendix, a reprint of the study by Dr. Walter Adams and Dr. James B. Hendry, TRUCKING MERGERS, CONCENTRATION, AND SMALL BUSINESS: AN ANALYSIS OF INTERSTATE COMMERCE COMMIS-SION POLICY, 1950-56, pp. 211-384.

47. See H.A. Levine, A CRITICAL EVALUATION OF THE CRITERIA TO DETERMINE THE REVENUE NEED OF MOTOR COMMON CARRIERS, unpublished Ph.D. thesis in Business Administration, The American University, Washington, D.C., 1972; and Larry J. Dobesh, "Earnings Control Standards for Regulated Motor Carriers," unpublished Ph.D. Thesis in Economics, Washington State University, Pullman, Washington, 1973.

48. Appendix C, REPLY STATEMENT OF JAMES C. NELSON, in Rail-roads' Reply to Submission of Other Parties, Docket No. 34013 (Sub. No. 1), COST STANDARDS IN INTERMODAL RATE PROCEEDINGS, before the Interstate Commerce Commission, April 30, 1970. See NEW GUIDE LINES FOR SWEDISH TRANSPORT POLICY (Stockholm: AB Bilstatistik, 1964) and SWEDISH TRANSPORT POLICY—A NEW APPROACH (Stockholm: AB Bil-statistik, 1962), both in the English Language. The U.S. Department of Transportation has developed some papers on experience with deregulation in Australia, Canada, Great Britain and Sweden for the Congressional hearings on the Transportation Regulatory Modernization Act of 1971.

49. ECONOMIC REPORT OF THE PRESIDENT, Transmitted to the Con-gress, February 1971, U.S. Government Printing Office, Washington, D.C., 1971, pp. 8-9 and 122-130, (and the January 1972 ECONOMIC REPORT OF THE PRESIDENT, pp. 130-135). See also R.F. Morison, "Deregulation Concept Gets New Support—Nixon Economic Adviser Supports Plan to Relax Transport Regulation," NEW YORK JOURNAL OF COMMERCE, March 25, 1971, pp. 1 and 8, a report on the speech of H.S. Houthakker, member of President Nixon's Council of Economic Advisers, before a forum sponsored by the Transportation Association of America.

50. REVISION OF FEDERAL TRANSPORTATION POLICY, A Report to the President, prepared by the Presidential Advisory Committee on Transport

Policy and Organization, Sinclair Weeks, Chairman, April 1955. Inconsistently, this Report recommended repeal of the bulk commodity exemption applicable to water carriers and a clarification by the Congress of the agricultural commodity exemptions for motor carriers.

51. Peck, "Competitive Policy for Transportation?," op. cit., pp. 72-73 and 78-79.

52. J.C. Nelson, "New Concepts in Transportation Regulation," op. cit., pp. 236-237.

53. FEDERAL REGULATORY RESTRICTIONS UPON MOTOR AND WATER CARRIERS, op. cit., p. 1.

54. Hilton, THE TRANSPORTATION ACT OF 1958, op. cit., pp. 47-48, 186-193 and 204-207; and D.J. Oswald, COST STANDARDS FOR RAIL-BARGE COMPETITION, M.A. Thesis, Washington State University, 1969, pp. 186-189, 191-194, and 208-224.

55. Oswald, ibid., pp. 77-79. See reprint of the Supreme Court decision in AMERICAN LINES V. L. & N.R. CO., Nos. 797, 804, 808, and 809, October Term 1967, decided by Mr. Justice Marshall on June 17, 1968, with Mr. Justice Douglas dissenting and Mr. Justice Harlan concurring in the result, pp. 13-16 and 18-19, particularly footnote 16. Case cited as 392 U.S. 571 (1968). The Commission appears very hesitant to follow the plain implications of economic theory in resolving this issue and seems to be dragging its feet, as several years have elapsed without a decision on this vital regulatory issue concerning control of minimum rates and intermodal competition.

56. 106 M.C.C. 455, 490 (1968). But see MOTOR COMMON CARRIERS OF PROPERTY—ROUTES AND SERVICE, 88 M.C.C. 415 (1961); and Nelson, "The Effects of Entry Control in Surface Transport," op.cit., pp. 408-409.

57. J.C. Nelson, "The Economics of Intermodal Transport," INTERMODAL TRANSPORT: ITS EFFECT ON RATES AND SERVICE, Proceedings of a Conference at Oregon State University, School of Business and Technology, March 20, 1969, pp. 1-40, especially pp. 16-21.

58. For evidence of the viability of toll authorities, see Ed Henry, "Recession Detours Nation's Big Tollways; Leading Roads Had Record Earnings in '70," THE WALL STREET JOURNAL, March 24, 1971, p. 10.

59. For estimates of huge social costs of those types and their special incidence in highway transport, see A STATEMENT ON NATIONAL TRANS-PORTATION POLICY, Department of Transportation, September 8, 1971, pp. 14-16 and Figure 7, Emissions Inventory, All Sources of Pollution, 1969. See J.C. Nelson, "A Critique of DOT Transport Policy," TRANSPORTATION JOURNAL, Spring 1972, pp. 5-22.

60. "Main Street, Mass." THE ECONOMIST, February 27, 1971, p. 50.

61. For the Chicago area problem of organization for transport development, see "Illinois Wants to Help—But How?," RAILWAY AGE, March 8, 1971, pp. 38-39.

62. "ICC Adds Plea for Rail-Passenger Network Less Skimpy Than One Proposed by Volpe," THE WALL STREET JOURNAL, December 30, 1970, p. 4; and W.D. Grampp, "Railpax Key: Avoiding the ICC," ibid., March 25, 1971, p. 12. See AMTRAK-STATE OF RAIL PASSENGER SERVICE, EFFECTIVE-NESS OF THE ACT, Interstate Commerce Commission, Oct. 30, 1971; and the ANNUAL REPORT OF NATIONAL RAILROAD PASSENGER CORPORA-TION, covering the period October 30, 1970-October 29, 1971, Washington, D.C.

63. AIR TRANSPORT AND ITS REGULATORS, op. cit., pp. 125-127; and AIRLINE REGULATION IN AMERICA, EFFECTS, AND IMPERFECTIONS, op. cit., pp. 55-56, 224-225, 230-233, and 238-243.

64. SERVICE TO SMALL COMMUNITIES, A Staff Study of the Bureau of Operating Rights, Civil Aeronautics Board, Washington, D.C., Parts I, II and III, March 1972; also see the Press Release of July 19, 1972, announcing that the CAB had "replaced the existing 12,500 pound takeoff weight limitation for commuter and air taxi aircraft with a 30-seat and 7,500-pound payload carrying capacity restriction." This should improve rural air service and lessen subsidy.

65. See George C. Eads, THE LOCAL SERVICE AIRLINE EXPERIMENT, The Brookings Institution, Washington, D.C., 1972.

66. See Jeremy J. Warford, PUBLIC POLICY TOWARD GENERAL AVIA-TION, The Brookings Institution, Washington, D.C., 1971.

67. GOVERNMENT EXPENDITURES FOR HIGHWAY, WATERWAY, AND AIR FACILITIES AND PRIVATE EXPENDITURES FOR RAILROAD FACILITIES, op. cit., p. 4; RAILROAD TRANSPORTATION AND PUBLIC POLICY, op. cit., pp. 93-107; and the Airport and Airway Development Act of 1970, Public Law 91-258, 91st Cong., approved by the President May 21, 1970, Title II—Airport and Airway Revenue Act of 1970 contains the user charges and provides in Sec. 208 for an Airport and Airway Trust Fund.

68. THE DILEMMA OF FREIGHT TRANSPORT REGULATION, op. cit., pp. 37-38 and 103-107; and the U.S. Bureau of Public Road's report, SUPPLE-MENTARY REPORT OF THE HIGHWAY COST ALLOCATION STUDY, Letter from the Secretary of Commerce, H. Doc. 124, 89th Cong., 1st Sess., 1965, Table 2, p. 4.

69. For example, see J.R. Cannon, AN ECONOMIC EVALUATION OF THE PROPOSAL TO EXTEND COLUMBIA RIVER NAVIGATION FROM PASCO TO WENATCHEE, M.A. Thesis, Washington State University, Pullman, Washington, pp. 77-121 and 129-133; and Edward P. Renshaw, TOWARD RESPONSI-BLE GOVERNMENT, Idyia Press, Chicago, 1957. For a discussion of the effect of adoption of realistic discount rates on waterway projects, see John A. Creedy, "Toward a Resolution of the Controversy over Criteria for Water Resource Development," paper before the Transportation Research Forum, Denver, November 8-10, 1972.

70. A.F. Friedlaender, THE INTERSTATE HIGHWAY SYSTEM, A STUDY IN PUBLIC INVESTMENT, North-Holland Publishing Company, Amsterdam, 1965, pp. 2-4, 34-36, 51-55, 73-78, 113-115, 133-134, and especially pp.

136-138. See Shorey Peterson, "The Highway from the Point of View of the Economist," in J. Labatut and W.J. Lane (eds.), HIGHWAYS IN OUR NATIONAL LIFE, Princeton University Press, Princeton, New Jersey, 1950, p. 195.

71. Compare THE DILEMMA OF FREIGHT TRANSPORT REGULATION, op. cit., pp. 37 and 110-111, and THE INTERSTATE HIGHWAY SYSTEM, op. cit., p. 126, footnote 17.

72. THE INTERSTATE HIGHWAY SYSTEM, pp. 3 and 136-137; Dearing and Owen, NATIONAL TRANSPORTATION POLICY, op. cit., pp. 86-87, 351, and 353-354; J.C. Nelson, FINANCING WASHINGTON'S HIGHWAYS, ROADS AND STREETS, Joint Fact-Finding Committee on Highways, Streets and Bridges of the State of Washington, Olympia, 1948, pp. xii and 94-104; and John W. Fuller, CURRENT ISSUES IN THE REGULATION OF MOTOR VEHICLE SIZES AND WEIGHTS, Ph.D. Thesis, Washington State University, 1968; and CONGRESSIONAL RECORD, Vol. 114, No. 124, 90th Cong., 2d Sess., July 18-29, 1968, pp. H7608-H7617 and H7773-H7774.

73. According to ICC Chairman G.M. Stafford, as many as eighteen of the country's 71 major railroads are in precarious financial condition and could be candidates for bankruptcy. See W.A. Martin, "Stafford Says Financial Status of 18 Major Rails 'Precarious,' " NEW YORK JOURNAL OF COMMERCE, March 11, 1971, p. 1. See also "Collapse of Nation's Rails Predicted," ibid., August 11, 1970, pp. 1 and 5; W.A. Martin, "Nationalization of Rails Urged," ibid., November 11, 1970, pp. 1 and 24; and Alan Goldsand, "Railroad Financing May Pose Major Problem in Early 1971," ibid., December 17, 1970, pp. 1 and 17; T.E. Fandell, "End of the Line," WALL STREET JOURNAL, September 30, 1970, pp. 1 and 14; W.A. Martin, "Rails 'Bid to Retire Track' Stirs Debate," NEW YORK JOURNAL OF COMMERCE, October 19, 1970, pp. 1, 4 and 7; J.H. Morris, "A Freight Trip Shows Penn Central Faces Long Recovery Route," WALL STREET JOURNAL, March 29, 1971, pp. 1 and 14; "Will Big Brother Ride the Rails," FORBES, April 1, 1971, pp. 22-23; and Reid Beddow, "RAILPAX: 16 basic 'city pairs'—but many alternative routes," RAILWAY AGE, December 14, 1970, pp. 26-29 and 58.

74. RAILROAD TRANSPORTATION AND PUBLIC POLICY, op. cit., Chap. 11, pp. 374-411.

75. For views recognizing some need for extension of rail rapid transit, see Williams and Bluestone, RATIONALE OF FEDERAL TRANSPORTATION POLICY, op. cit., pp. 52-54; Friedlaender, THE INTERSTATE HIGHWAY SYSTEM, op. cit., pp. 137-138; Lyle C. Fitch and Associates, URBAN TRANSPORTATION AND PUBLIC POLICY, Chandler Publishing Company, San Francisco, 1964, pp. 5-6 and 206; G.M. Smerk, URBAN TRANSPORTATION: THE FEDERAL ROLE, Indiana University Press, Bloomington, 1965, pp. 79-81 and 186-193. On the other hand, a very limited efficient role is found for rail rapid transit in J.R. Meyer, J.F. Kain, and M. Wohl, THE URBAN TRANSPORTATION PROBLEM, Harvard University Press, Cambridge, 1965,

pp. 364-367; and by Wilfred Owen, THE METROPOLITAN TRANSPORTA-
TION PROBLEM, rev. ed., The Brookings Institution, Washington, 1966, pp.
133-141. Wilfred Owen appears to support a relatively greater role than in earlier
writings for rail rapid transit in THE ACCESSIBLE CITY, The Brookings
Institution, Washington, D.C., 1972. See also J.R. Meyer and M.R. Straszheim,
PRICING AND PROJECT EVALUATION, The Brookings Institution, Washington, 1971, pp. 131-133. For a critical analysis of the benefit-cost analysis in
support of the proposed rail rapid transit system for Los Angeles, see Alan Carlin
and Martin Wohl, AN ECONOMIC RE-EVALUATION OF THE PROPOSED
LOS ANGELES RAPID TRANSIT SYSTEM, The Rand Corporation, Santa
Monica, California, P-3918, September 1968.

76. The costs of renovating, expanding, or constructing new rapid transit
systems have been estimated to total $34 billion by 1980 by the supporters of
public transit. The Mass Transportation Assistance Act of 1970, approved by
President Nixon on October 15, 1970, sets a 12-year goal of $10 billion in
Federal aid, with $5 billion in state and local aid, or $15 billion for rapid transit
systems, plus $2.5 billion for the Washington, D.C. Metro System, funded under
a different Federal appropriation, RAILWAY AGE, November 9, 1970, p. 12. If
feasible in the United States, the investment requirements for corridor high-
speed trains on new rights-of-way would add several billions to the total. See
Japanese National Railways, THE NEW TOKAIDO LINE, March 1969, and
TECHNICAL ASPECTS OF THE NEW TOKAIDO LINE, 1966.

77. J.W. Fuller, CURRENT ISSUES IN THE REGULATION OF MOTOR
VEHICLE SIZES AND WEIGHTS, op. cit. This work was published in the
CONGRESSIONAL RECORD, 90th Cong., 2nd Sess., Vol. 114, No. 124, July
18, 23-25, 27, and 29, 1968. The Fuller study, which found that the public and
social costs of the proposed relaxation of sizes and weights greatly exceeded the
savings in applicable truck operating costs and rates, contributed to the defeat of
the 1968 proposals.

78. Ibid., Chapter VII, pp. 341-367.

79. N.C. Yucel, "The Transportation Requirements of the Columbia Basin
Project Area," Ph.D. Thesis (unpublished), Washington State University, 1967,
pp. 192-209 and 214-216. See J.R. Cannon, AN ECONOMIC EVALUATION
OF THE PROPOSAL TO EXTEND COLUMBIA RIVER NAVIGATION FROM
PASCO TO WENATCHEE, op. cit.

80. C.D. Foster, "Investment Policy and Pricing in Transport," paper before
the International Symposium on Transportation Pricing, The American University, Washington, D.C., June 17, 1969, and THE TRANSPORTATION PROB-
LEM, Blackie & Son Limited, London, 1963, Chaps. 5, 6, 11, and 13; Meyer
and Straszheim, PRICING AND PROJECT EVALUATION, op. cit., Chaps.
11-16 and Appendix B; and Conrad J. Oort, "Criteria for Investment in the
Infrastructure of Inland Transport," SECOND INTERNATIONAL SYMPOSIUM
ON THEORY AND PRACTICE IN TRANSPORT ECONOMICS, European Conference of Ministers of Transport, 1967, pp. 13-114.

81. THE DILEMMA OF FREIGHT TRANSPORT REGULATION, op. cit., pp. 37-38. As noted in a previous footnote, user fees for public air facilities have recently been raised by Public Law 91-258, and another study of appropriate user contributions for the airport/airway system is now being conducted within the U.S. Department of Transportation. Hence, encouraging steps are being taken to evaluate and to adjust user pricing in terms of user cost responsibility.

82. For example, see J.C. Nelson and W.H. Dodge, FINANCING NORTH DAKOTA'S HIGHWAYS, ROADS, AND STREETS, The Legislative Research Committee, State of North Dakota, Bismarck, North Dakota, September 15, 1952, pp. xxvi and 243-250.

83. A.A. Walters, THE ECONOMICS OF ROAD USER CHARGES, International Bank for Reconstruction and Development, Washington, D.C., January 11, 1968. Compare with J.C. Nelson, "The Pricing of Highway, Waterway, and Airway Facilities," THE AMERICAN ECONOMIC REVIEW, May 1962, pp. 426-435.

84. Fitch and Associates, URBAN TRANSPORTATION AND PUBLIC POLICY, op. cit., pp. 122-161; and Meyer, Kain, and Wohl, THE URBAN TRANSPORTATION PROBLEM, op. cit., pp. 69-74. See J.C. Nelson, "Toward Rational Price Policies," in THE FUTURE OF AMERICAN TRANSPORTATION, edited by E.W. Williams, Jr., Prentice-Hall, Inc., Englewood Cliffs, N.J., for the American Assembly, 1971, pp. 115-154; and the editorial, "Pricing Transportation," in the WALL STREET JOURNAL, November 8, 1971, p. 10.

85. The State of California, with the highest number of motor vehicle registrations in any state, narrowly defeated Proposition 18, a proposed amendment to the California Constitution, at the General Election, November 3, 1970. The vote was 3,161,611 against and 2,648,283 for. Proposition 18 would have permitted revenues from California highway user fees, after apportionment to the state, counties, and cities in the usual manner, to be redistributed "for control of environmental pollution caused by motor vehicles, and for public transportation, including mass transit systems, upon approval of electorate in the area affected, such expenditure limited to 25 percent of revenues generated in area, also 25 percent of revenues apportioned to city or county may be used for such purpose." PROPOSED AMENDMENTS TO CONSTITUTION, PROPOSITIONS 18, 19, AND 20, together with Arguments, to be submitted to the Electors of the State of California at the General Election, Tuesday, Nov. 3, 1970, distributed by H.P. Sullivan, Secretary of State; and TRANSPORT TOPICS, November 16, 1970, pp. 1 and 34, editorial, p. 14. A term paper done in Econ. 364, "Proposition 18: A Design for Defeat," January 5, 1971, by Thomas J. Sweetman, a graduate student in Political Science at Washington State University, who conducted interviews and gathered information in San Francisco in December 1970, revealed that Proposition 18 was defeated largely by a massive advertising campaign that associated the measure with public resistance to higher taxation. That campaign was financed largely by the oil companies and highway user interests. However, the size of the vote for the use of highway user

revenues for controlling the social costs of pollution and for development of adequate public and mass transit may well be a harbinger of the future. For confirmation of Sweetman's findings on the forces that defeated the measure, see Lloyd Shearer, "The Nation's Worst Scandal," PARADE, March 21, 1971, pp. 4-5. Also see PUBLIC TRANSIT IN CALIFORNIA, A Report on Interim Hearings to the California State Senate by the Senate Select Committee on Rapid Transit, January 4, 1971.

86. J.C. Spychalski, "The Diversion of Motor Vehicle-Related Tax Revenues to Urban Mass Transport: A Critique of Its Economic Tenability," TRANS-PORTATION JOURNAL, Spring 1970, pp. 44-50, in particular pp. 46-48.

87. R.W. Harbeson, "Some Allocational Problems in Highway Finance," in TRANSPORTATION ECONOMICS, National Bureau of Economic Research, New York, 1965, pp. 139-160, especially pp. 144-153.

88. J.M. Munro, "Planning the Appalachian Development Highway System: Some Critical Questions," LAND ECONOMICS, May 1969, pp. 149-161.

89. Friedlaender, THE INTERSTATE HIGHWAY SYSTEM, op. cit., pp. 36, 51-58, 64-67, 113-115, and 136-138.

90. See John P. Carter, "A Railway Proposal," paper presented at the Annual Meeting of the Western Economic Association, August 21-22, 1969, 7 pp., abstracted in the WESTERN ECONOMIC JOURNAL, September 1969, p. 275; and John L. Weller, "Access to Capital Markets," in THE FUTURE OF AMERICAN TRANSPORTATION, op. cit., pp. 107-111.

91. "NARUC Eyes Emerging State Departments of Transportation," TRANSPORT TOPICS, September 7, 1970; J.W. Bennett, Jr., and W.J. DeWitt, III, "The Development of State Departments of Transportation—A Recent Organizational Phenomenon," TRANSPORTATION JOURNAL, Fall 1972, pp. 5-14.

92. For a comparison of the activities of the New York Metropolitan Transportation Authority with those of the Port of New York Authority, see J.D. Williams, "The People Mover: MTA's Ronan Pushes to Improve Mass Transit," THE WALL STREET JOURNAL, April 2, 1971, pp. 1 and 29.

7

Regional Transportation Planning Experience in the United States: A Critical Review of Selected Cases

Ralph Gakenheimer with G.M. Croan,
D.S. Greenbaum, W.W. Hill, J.O. Litten,
and P. Messeri,[a]
Massachusetts Institute of Technology

The Study Approach

Regional transportation planning offers, unfortunately, only a lean body of experience to evaluate when considering steps toward its further development. Nevertheless, it shows characteristics that suggest its strength of analytic grasp on the relevant phenomena at the present time and the possibilities of successfully administering and implementing transportation development programs within given frameworks. These in turn suggest the feasibility of planning under related but different circumstances in the future. The study facilitates the proposition of a series of regions and approaches for regional transportation planning that emerge as apt from the experience it reviews.

The Functionality Versus Implementation Debate

The characteristics of the spatial domain of a "regional transportation problem" are crucial to an understanding of its viability for planning. There are two fundamental kinds of issues at stake when considering particular cases:

1. *Functional relationships*: The extent to which the uses of a single system (e.g., the Northeast Corridor Metroliner) and its competing alternatives are significant enough to define a transportation region surrounding them.

[a]This paper is the product of a survey project under the leadership of Ralph Gakenheimer, Associate Professor of Urban Studies and Planning, MIT. The other participants are MIT students: Gerald M. Croan, majoring in urban studies and operations research, Daniel S. Greenbaum, majoring in urban studies with emphasis on urban political systems; Wayne Wesley Hill, a master's student in urban design, with studies directed toward policy and implementation strategies in urban and regional transportation; Joe C. Litten, majoring in urban studies and economics; and Peter Messeri, majoring in urban studies with a specialization in systems analysis. Special thanks are extended for the generous assistance of our MIT colleagues: H.W. Bruck, Marvin Manheim, Nigel Wilson, Arlee Reno, Robert Simpson, Ernest G. Frankel, Wayne Pecknold, Ata Safai, and Anthony Yezer. We also appreciate the help of Jack Cairl of the New England Regional Commission.

291

Whether the connectedness of transportation systems (in the sense of the loads they transfer to one another—e.g., between an airport and its highway access) warrants circumscribing them within a single planning region. The measure to which the specific, planable effects of such systems on their surroundings (e.g., highways on land development) are of such magnitude as to require planning the systems' effects as a single pattern. These matters will be incorporated in the term "functionality" with respect to a region.

2. *Implementation issues*: The extent to which there is a sufficient level of public authority and interagency collaboration to make the planning of such unified systems or patterns possible.

The relative importance of these matters can be seen in any general debate on regional transportation planning, such as the hearings on the National Transportation Act. Some may feel, at one extreme, that virtually all the technology included under the term "transportation" in the English language is *a priori* related, and that transportation planning therefore should be integrated, with consideration for its ultimately far-reaching effects on surrounding phenomena. They typically assume that the necessary analytic grasp of interrelationships exists or will be created, and that public authority and interagency collaboration to a substantial degree can be secured. Those more conservative about the prospects, on the other hand, typically insist upon closer system relationships of type 1 above, and interpret the possibilities of public authority and interagency collaboration more conservatively.[1]

In most cases, ironically, there is a tradeoff between the goodness of a region with respect to function on one hand and implementation quality on the other. In the present experience of transportation planning, when one is high, the other is inclined to be low. This is due mainly to the poor functionality of the states as spatial units.

This paper relates the characteristics of transportation problems to a series of aspects of the planning processes that deal with them in the U.S. experience. These characteristics include: (a) the region, its form of demarcation and comprehensiveness; (b) the amplitude of transportation and other considerations included within the planning framework; (c) the stated or *de facto* purpose of planning; and (d) the analytical strategies and techniques chosen for study of the problem. The matters we broadly refer to as implementation issues above are investigated in the agencies reviewed by means of looking at (e) the administrative arrangements by which the agencies function; and (f) the forms they have at their disposal for implementing plans.

Not being considered here is the use of regions for decentralized administration. That is, the use of the region for managing the allocation of manpower and resources to such matters as engineering design, construction supervision, maintenance, and relationships with client local governments and populations.

The detailed criteria by which regions are established for this purpose must be largely internal to the national agencies involved and cannot be dealt with effectively in this paper.

The Regions Considered

Consider here regions that are normally larger than a state, or that lap state boundaries in some important cases. Clearly the political unity of the states makes them by far the superior means of handling problems they normally encompass. We include them here only to display the obvious alternative to any multistate regionalization.

Five types of experience in regional transportation planning are reviewed in this study. The types were chosen on the basis of the amount of planning effort they account for, or their apparent potential to disclose guiding criteria for establishing future transportation regions. As such, they are not coordinate in any sense; they do not represent different options within the same criteria for transportation planning, nor even different criteria for approaching the same problems. They are established for different purposes. What they do have in common is a concern for the design and regulation of transportation infrastructure and related phenomena over multistate space.

The *metropolitan regions* are the type that includes the most cases. After decades of concern about the influence of transportation on land development in cities, a methodology emerged in the middle 1950s for its measurement.[2] Appropriations for the Interstate Highway System, beginning in 1956, provided the impulse for extensive planning. It was an era when transportation was typically considered the highest priority urban problem. These circumstances gave rise to an explosive proliferation of metropolitan transportation studies during the following years.[3]

Though the practice of the field was in some respects steadily improved through experience and research, it was unable to adapt from its fairly narrow methodological orientation to accommodate the reformulated demands that were increasingly made of it. It failed to achieve some of its aspirations; others were superseded by the rapidly rising concerns for social welfare in a form it could not deal with and concerns for small-scale community problems to which it was also largely insensitive.[4] Metropolitan transportation planning methodology, then, is left to us as a partly fossilized approach likely soon to be used only for specialized purposes, and with few heirs apparent to a new form of the art.

It is included in this study because the metropolitan areas account for a substantial concentration of expenditures on transportation facilities in what are sometimes interstate regions, since technological and social change is extending these regions to scales that may soon have multistate significance in many more cases,[5] and because reformulations of methodology may result in the use of larger regions at least for part of the planning function.

The cases chosen for this review are the National Capital Region, the Penn-Jersey Region of Philadelphia, and the Tri-State Region of New York City. These are the principal multistate cases, and are handily, for our purposes, staged in time through the periods of development of the field. Since the metropolitan approach is fairly standardized, relative to that of the other kinds of regions under discussion, it is possible to generalize our conclusions.

Corridor regions are the type with only one active example: The Northeast Corridor. The study was begun in 1963, received project status in the Department of Commerce in 1964, and was moved to the Department of Transportation three years later. After an initial stage of broad methodological research on corridor planning possibilities, it developed alternative line haul plans and has moved into the study of implementation. The high functionality of the region—that is, the relative simplicity with which its functions could be interpreted—attracted, in the final stages, a definitively technological approach to the problem and a fairly rigorous systems analytic form of methodology. Its facility for implementation has yet to be demonstrated.

The justification for including the region here rests on the prospects for establishing other corridors. There have been such proposals. In considering the case, however, it is necessary to be constantly aware that the Northeast Corridor is certainly the best corridor we will ever have. With its conveniently linear arrangement of population concentrations, natural isolation, its 42.7 million population, and 25 percent of the gross national product on 1½ percent of the nation's land area, it is a far more apt region for corridor treatment than any of the others suggested, with the exception of the Southern Great Lakes Region.

The *states* as domains for regional transportation planning of a comprehensive sort are of relatively recent origin, but are sure to gain importance rapidly. At present, there are nineteen state transportation planning programs, most of them in their infancy.

There are two variations principal among their approaches: On the side of amplitude of functions, the state agencies extend from those which do relatively straightforward highway planning, built upon the standard responsibilities of state highway departments, on one hand, to those with more comprehensive, multimodal responsibilities associated with additional sectors of planning on the other. With respect to their authority, they extend from purely advisory bodies to cases in which their plans have legislative designation (cf. Wisconsin), or in which they are implemented by a state secretary of transportation (cf. New Jersey, Connecticut and other states). Their basic methodologies of planning show strong legacy from the metropolitan planning approach, but in the best of agencies extend to broader planning considerations.

The Connecticut Planning Program, one of the strongest and most mature of them, received the greatest attention here as a case. The California and Wisconsin programs are more briefly reviewed as examples of strong agencies. The program in Wyoming is reviewed as an example of work by a mostly rural state with somewhat different problems.

The states serve as examples of regions that show very poor functionality, since state boundaries for historical reasons seldom define useful problem regions, but they have superior means for the unified implementation of plans and inter-sectoral coordination.

It is important to include them, since the states are the obvious competition to any other system or regionalization, and since their political strength will require that responsibilities be divided satisfactorily between them and any multistate region if the latter is to survive.

The *economic development regions* as transportation planning regions are perhaps the most interesting and the most complex type. They are defined, of course, by criteria that do not include the functionality of the area for transportation planning purposes. Since transportation is included as an auxiliary sector to other development activities, the issue for present purposes becomes whether transportation planning to serve their objectives can be most profitably done within these regions.

Discussion in the paper relies principally on two cases, those of the Appalachia and New England Regional Commissions. Appalachia was the Federal Government's first entry into this form of planning (leaving New Deal and river basin cases aside). The Appalachian region, or at least a good part of the area that presently composes it, has long been understood as an area of poverty, exhibiting widespread forms of social and economic underdevelopment. In 1960, a group of nine Appalachian governors convened a conference that resulted in a study requesting that President Kennedy establish a federal-states commission to prepare plans for dealing with the problems confronting the region. Kennedy established a Presidential Commission which reported a year later to President Johnson that the magnitude and uniqueness of the region's problems were such that only sustained collaboration between federal and state governments could approach the need. The Appalachian Regional Development Act, passed in 1965, established the Appalachian Regional Commission, and a large sum of money was appropriated for investment in infrastructure and social services for the area. These were based on specific plans for the region that were prepared prior to the existence of the Regional Commission.

Shortly thereafter the Public Works and Economic Development Act of 1965 created the Economic Development Administration, under an Assistant Secretary of Commerce, an office also created by the legislation. Its purpose is to provide technical assistance and a focus of federal investment in geographical areas that meet the criteria of the Act as being economically depressed. Areas that can qualify for aid and technical assistance are indicated in a hierarchical form, starting with regions as small as a county or large municipality and including as the largest scale a multistate economic development region. The five multistate regional development commissions founded under this Act have since been released from the EDA and report directly to the Department. Among them we deal here with New England, because of its accessibility to this study and its convenient contrast with the problems of Appalachia.

The New England Regional Commission was formed at the request of its six constitutent governors in 1966. Their initiative followed decades of close collaboration among governors and many other public and private authorities of New England.

These two regions show an important contrast: Appalachia is a classical case of underdevelopment, where the nature of the problems invites some parallels with a developing country. New England, on the other hand, is hardly an underdeveloped area in any general sense. The establishment of its Commission, while largely suspending the Administration's criteria, was clearly based on its tradition of unity and collaboration, its promise of success.

The important fact to remember, then, while examining these cases as economic development regions is that they are sure to be the most successful of them. Appalachia's initial funding of more than a billion dollars (most of it for roads) assured sustained political strength, budgetary immunity, and local support. It can count on strong support from the states in which it operates, much as the TVA did among the relatively conservative states in which it operated, in spite of criticism from elements elsewhere in the country that it was an overly liberal institution. The strong tradition of collaboration in New England, as shown through the activities of the previous New England Govern- ors' Conference and many other cooperative ventures, reflects a strong historical association among the states because of their relative spatial isolation from the rest of the country, a historical pride, and a social unity that some might define even as culturally unique in the United States. These facts are some assurance against the porkbarreling, stalemates, tenuous agreements, and lack of strong joint advocacy that otherwise threaten to afflict such bodies.

The strategic and methodologic approaches of these commissions are largely accumulated from attention to various relatively isolated problems and sectors, and are resistant to generalization, but the overarching concern for economic development as a framework for planning activities may be generating a unified basis for comprehensive approaches.

The *focal region* is an obvious choice for this review on account of the obviousness of the widespread impacts of certain major facilities on substantial surrounding areas. There have been cases in which the need for regional highway planning has been claimed on account of a large projected airport. The far-reaching effects of major ports have often been discussed in the context of the need for planning their regional effects, an interest that has increased in recent years by the movement toward the centralization of containerized port equipment in the United States.

The only regional administrative form that can be easily associated with this region type is the port authority, whose jurisdiction, of course, does not extend beyond the impact stimulating infrastructure itself. Nonetheless, it seemed important to qualify the applicability of the focal region, looking at such experiences as that of the Port of New York Authority, in order to suggest its competitive chances among the other region types mentioned.

We have purposely omitted the study of certain distinguished historical cases, such as the NPRB and the TVA, assuming that their methodological heritage should be represented among the active cases, and that their relevance to current problem priorities and political conditions must be held in serious question. Any discussion of transportation planning at present that calls upon knowledge of its institutionalization and methodology from even the recent past must constantly remind the reader that transportation is a much different problem now; it is a lower priority problem than it was just a few years ago, and its contribution is sure to be valued in the future on the basis of its known effect on the social and economic conditions of families, rather than on the general faith that high investments in publicly or privately owned infrastructure (which permits high speeds and ample ranges of access) is beneficial to us all. These changes, in fact, are the greatest threat to the value of this study in general. Some speculations that attempt to reach beyond the limitations of our format are attempted at appropriate points.

These remarks also explain our disinclination to emphasize natural resource regions. The river basins would be the foremost candidates among them, and are attractive from the point of view of their substantial functionality as transportation and economic regions within a certain kind of framework. But, at present, their prospects of engaging problems considered central to the nation's concerns seem, as suggested by Melvin Levin, very questionable. Nor have we considered highly specialized region types, such as conservation regions. These, aside from falling into the resource category as well, function better as subregions of a larger pattern.

The following discussion deals with particular aspects across regional agency types, rather than with each kind of agency integrally, because the generic differences among the region types makes them impossible to compare as such. Indeed, there would be little purpose in doing so, since we are clearly not preparing to advocate one or more among them as superior for all purposes. The aspects of a single agency's form, duties, plight, and performance, furthermore, are the elements that may include substantial strengths and weaknesses within a single case.

The Regions of Agency Jurisdiction

In looking at the regions identified as the domains of the transportation planning activities under study, the issues are (1) the criteria by which they were established, (2) the validity of the regions for the operational purposes of the agency's mission, and (3) their usefulness for likely future work. The task will require calling forth the conclusions of sections further on and providing a partial summary of the findings.

Metropolitan Regions

The metropolitan regions are limited in their applicability to the present task because they are established mostly to constitute areas where urban densities presently exist, or where they are expected to appear within the term of the plan. There is a necessary distinction between the planning that needs to be done in such areas, as opposed to planning that can take place in the larger spheres of metropolitan influence beyond the urbanized areas. The most frequent bases for establishing such regions are the metropolitan SMSA or the expanse of space defined by some criterion relating to the proportion of commuter trips made from the outlying areas to the central city, modified by informal judgments.

The Tri-State Transportation Commission plans for 22 counties in the states of New York, New Jersey and Connecticut. It includes an area of 8,000 square miles, of which 32 percent is presently considered urbanized, and a population of almost 20 million people. The initial criterion was based on the commuting field of New York City, with the assumption that commuting trips are such an important proportion of the total traffic load that they set the capacity requirements for the infrastructure and that their economic significance forms a measure of the region's cohesiveness. In addition to the area so defined, other counties were added in the belief that future urbanization might be dispersed into them as a matter of policy. An internal boundary was drawn, separating an inner urbanized region from an outer one, where the most active future urbanization was expected to take place. It is, by far, the largest of the metropolitan transportation regions.

The Philadelphia region of the Penn-Jersey Transportation Study (now the Delaware Valley Regional Planning Commission) includes nine counties and two cities in Pennsylvania and New Jersey. It covers 3,800 square miles and had a population of 4,600,000 in 1960. The region was defined by the counties that make up the SMSAs of Philadelphia and Trenton-Camden. Penn-Jersey defined an inner region intended to enclose the presently urbanized part of the region as well as the part that would be urbanized within the term of the plan, including over 80 percent of the region's population, and a smaller outer region regarded as the horizon of urbanization beyond the term of the plan.

The National Capital Region encompasses the District of Columbia, six counties in Maryland and Virginia, and three independent cities in Virginia. It had a population of 2,600,000 in 1966. The regional boundaries were set by Congress, rather than by the participating jurisdictions. The original National Capital Transportation Act of 1960 included Loudon County, Virginia, which later removed itself from the region by not participating in the interstate compact that was executed for the other member jurisdictions. The region was later amended to include Dulles Airport in Loudon County as one of the important access demand generators in the area.

The matter of the extent to which regions of this sort are satisfactory for planning purposes has been subject to some discussion, but not a great deal of serious concern, over the past several years. The study by Boyce et al., however, partly congealed the position that some parts of the metropolitan planning study should be addressed to the problem at the subregional local level.[6] Taking this view a step further, it is possible that a substantial part of the planning might be done at that level. This is congruent with an emphatic movement at present in urban planning toward greater attention to community level problems and less to metropolitan scale concerns. It would also meet needs to overcome community resistance to urban highway construction more effectively. It is conceivable that this trend, a very likely one for the near future, might remove the need to describe metropolitan boundaries in the manner of the studies reviewed and invite the establishment of larger regions. These larger metropolitan-centered regions, unencumbered by the need for detailed urban analysis and planning, could consider the role of metropolitan-oriented transportation and its hinterland determinants in the fuller perspective of resources, technology, economic functions, environmental effects, and so forth. Speculations about the operational use of such larger regions are difficult to make at present, but the region could easily precede the methodology.

Rising mobility may well distribute urban populations over much larger areas than at present, as suggested by the well reasoned work of Friedmann and Miller.[7] To the extent that it is possible for families to live at increasing distances from central cities (or to have two residences, urban and fringe) because of higher speed transportation technology, increased affluence, and less reason to be present at workplaces on account of improved communications systems, urban domains may grow rapidly into much larger areas in which the transportation problems are essentially urban in nature. This is an effect that might be accelerated by the innovation of new systems providing connections in town from well out of the centrally urbanized areas, such as rails for dual mode vehicles. It could also be stimulated by a sustained preference for socially homogeneous neighborhoods—with the affluent retreating from the increasingly egalitarian city. While it is most unlikely that these regions will grow in the foreseeable future to scales represented by Constandinos Doxiadis' Daily Urban Systems,[8] the prospects for the appearance of much larger urbanized areas deserves further research based on specific assumptions about the coming years. They could substantially increase the number of interstate metropolitan areas.

It should be mentioned that this discussion is generically different from the proposal of National Metropolitan Areas in Karl Fox's paper in this series, which deals with the issues of social and economic influence of central metropolitan areas, not with regions defined by the spread of urban land development. The difference is crucial as long as transportation infrastructure remains a central matter in the planning.

Corridor Regions

Prospects for corridor regions are found by examining the currently existing Northeast Corridor, the possibilities of other linear corridors in the United States that would be amenable to the planning of high volume line haul transportation along a string of cities, and the viability of proposed "cluster corridors," groups of interrelated cities that are not in a linear configuration. ("Cluster" and "linear" are our words and cause a certain contradiction in terms, but they are necessary to follow the discussions that have been presented on the subject.)

The Northeast Corridor includes five entire states and the District of Columbia, plus portions of five other states extending from southern Maine to the Virginia-North Carolina border. According to recent estimates, the population of the region's 165 counties and cities was 42.7 million. Its strong natural boundaries, including the Atlantic Ocean and the Great Lakes, and the political border with Canada give it a more peninsular form than any other possible corridor. The area was basically defined to accommodate the planning of line haul systems of innovative transportation technology between Boston and Washington, or extending as far south as the Hampton Roads area (or to points outside those cities, to avoid high cost and congestion problems in the central cities). There is a generous expanse of hinterland for the study of anticipated economic and land development effects and, presumably, the planning of policies appropriate for the management of these effects and auxiliary transportation. Since the planning work to date has emphasized the development of the line haul systems, the region can so far be regarded as substantially excessive in coverage to what would have been necessary.

Toward the possibility of defining other corridors that could be similarly organized, it is useful to cite some thinking on the subject. A composite list of possibilities follows, in order of rank in urban population size:

1. Northeast
2. Southern Great Lakes
3. Texas
4. Ohio-Indiana
5. Northern California
6. Central Southwest
7. Missouri
8. Upstate New York
9. Florida
10. Northwest
11. Oklahoma
12. Southern California
13. Gulf of Mexico
14. Arizona
15. New Mexico

Nine of the fifteen are interstate regions. Their specific elements will be brought up as the occasion demands. Additional combinations, such as a Chicago-St.

Louis corridor, have also been proposed. They have been based on the aggregation of 1960 SMSAs in patterns with sufficient distance between to avoid including commuters in corridor traffic, but sufficient proximity to suggest close interrelationship. These criteria are broader than those of the simple linearity that provides for line haul technology, but they should show the viable cases of linearity.

Among these candidates, the only clear possibility as a linear corridor is the Southern Great Lakes Region, extending from Pittsburgh and/or Erie, Pennsylvania, on the east through Chicago to Milwaukee on the West. Attention to the megalopolitan nature of this region began shortly after the publication of Gottman's book on the Eastern Seaboard; its social and economic potentials were studies by Meier and his associates.[9]

Following the Southern Great Lakes Region in the rank hierarchy above there is a break in population size by a factor of five, the Great Lakes Region including about 18 million people, and the Texas (Ft. Worth and Dallas to Galveston) Region encompassing less than 4 million. Further, most of the other regions listed present serious problems of linearity. Some that are linear are relatively simple and contain few urban places (e.g., Northern California from San Francisco to Sacramento).

The question of "linear" versus "cluster" configuration is crucial to the kind of planning done. The linear corridor can propose a single, strong, line haul system that involves its full jurisdictional constituency, aggregates its population to the level of maximum efficiency for innovative technology, and constitutes a politically imageable proposal. The cluster, alternatively, is forced either to propose a central trunk with many costly spurs or, inevitably in most of the cases suggested, to deal with its constituent urban places by pairs or threes, with a concomitant loss of aggregation, imageability, and force. To the extent that corridor planning might emphasize economic and land development effects, a binding is added to the cluster concept. But the Northeast Corridor's disinclination to follow up the sophisticated models they had prepared on this subject suggests the weakness of corresponding quantifiable relationships and the problems of managing that kind of policy for a regional agency of this type. Also, there would be an encouraging relation between the two corridor forms if a series of local interstate linkages were assembled for joint study as corridor links; for example, a chain including the proposed bridge from Connecticut to Long Island, the New Jersey/New York tunnel crossings, the Lindenwold Line from Philadelphia across the Delaware River, proposed subway penetrations out of the District of Columbia into Maryland and Virginia, and so on. But there is little reason to anticipate this, since the linkages mentioned are far more important as intrametropolitan features than as parts of a corridor.

As a final caveat against excessive expectations from corridors, it must be recalled that the natural features defining them are disregarded by increasingly important air trips, except to the extent that previous and current land transport patterns can keep them knit.[10] This effect of reducing corridor-like character is likely to be the most important in the presently weaker cases.

Still, the good functionality of the linear corridor and the simplicity of proposals that can emerge from it makes it a desirable region form whenever it is possible.

The States

The states as regions for transportation planning comprise a set with no alternatives for demarcation and offer little reason for discussion under this heading. They are the ideal regions for administrative purposes and are quite arbitrary by functional criteria. The only sense in which they encompass a homogeneous or functionally exclusive set of activities is the extent to which these characteristics have been created by a history of unified administration, or by boundaries that originally reflected functional facts which remain significant. With the exception of a few of the states, these effects are not very important. Their purpose is administrative, and their boundaries correspond.

Economic Development Regions

The economic development regions are defined by criteria in the Public Works and Economic Development Act of 1965. The legislation requires that the regions be internally related geographically, culturally, historically, and economically. The region selected must be lagging behind the rest of the nation economically. Particular criteria mentioned in the act are based on: (1) rate of unemployment; (2) median level of family income; (3) conditions of housing, health services, and education; (4) extent of domination of the area by a few industries that are on the decline; (5) rate of outmigration; (6) effects of changing industrial technology; (7) effect of national defense facility or production locations, and (8) indices of the level of regional product.

The Appalachian Commission precedes the establishment of these standards but shares the same motivations. The region consists of a set of counties, not coterminus with state boundaries, that extends from the Southern Tier of New York on the north to the northern counties of Mississippi and Alabama on the south. Some attention was given to defining the region by the use of SEAs (State Economic Areas), a designation by the Bureau of the Census that unites counties of similar social and economic nature. The region is not fully explained by this criterion, however, and changes were made (to include additional counties in Mississippi and New York) after passage of the Act, which originally prohibited further expansion of the region. The region has two basic parts, the southern mountains, showing the characteristics of classic underdevelopment and tenuous association with the rest of the national economy, and the northern part, where social services may be equally poor but where unemployment has been cyclical, showing an unfortunate relation to the surrounding economy rather than isolation from it. The north also has a less traditional or otherwise distinguishable cultural form. The unity of the region may be most convincing if one considers the similar personal problems of the Southern mountain dweller and the Pennsylvania coal miner. Still, the economic distinction will show up in different styles of transportation planning, the Southern part being the one that mainly suffers from the problem of low internal connectivity.

The New England Region consists simply of the six New England states, with no application of criteria to marginal spatial units. Its boundaries fail to include possibly deserving counties in Northeastern New York, and yet include prosperous Fairfield County, Connecticut, a commuting area of New York City. Though some pockets of poverty do exist in the region, especially in the three northern states, the only EDA criterion that seems to apply is that of outmigrating labor.[11] As a region, it is not among the less prosperous of the country. It is clear that it was chosen for its cohesion and likelihood of success.

Cohesion it has, except for some independence in the case of Connecticut, which is more inclined to value its relationship to New York and whose relative wealth leaves it less to gain than the others from an economic development effort. Collaboration in the form of the Governors' Conference, and groups of federal agency heads, railroad owners, airport managers, and representatives of many other regional functional interests can be called upon to suggest its workability. New England has a Federal Regional Council in which the local representatives of DOT, HUD, HEW, OEO, and the Labor Department meet regularly to coordinate programs.

There is, in addition, some cause for claiming a set of common functional problems as a basis for the region's viability. It is a region somewhat isolated from the rest of the nation's producing and consuming areas. Large proportions of its food, animal feed, fuel, building supplies, and industrial raw materials must therefore be imported at costs that make it difficult to compete with the rest of the country. A relatively complete but aging highway system in the context of intensive urbanization in a good part of the region constitutes another uniformity of context. New England has twice the national average of total highway mileage in urban areas (41.5 percent). It has the lowest proportion of total surfaced mileage on the Federal Aid System (20.6 percent). The equipment in its trucking fleets is more obsolete than the average for the rest of the country.

Within the region it is useful to distinguish between the more developed southern part, affected by the end of the Northeast Corridor and problems of congestion, and the northern part, where development-oriented planning is more appropriate.

Discussion in later sections further substantiates our summary here of the applicability of these two regions to various kinds of transportation planning. In spite of Appalachia's strength in highway development, based on large initial federal funding, it would appear that the regions are not inherently very suitable for this purpose. This is because highways are a well-handled responsibility of the states, which are not likely to tolerate such invasion of their authority in the matter, except in the case of major, clearly regional projects, such as the West-East highway across northern New England. Also, to the extent that the purpose of highways is to link a depressed area with its sourrounding more favored areas, the regions' jurisdictions are inconvenient. Railroads are the most natural objects of regional economic development attention because of the inclination of the companies' interests to fall within. But this usefulness is, of course, confined to the bounds of manageability of the current railroad situation. Airports and waterways can also be approached profitably at this scale.

The most important attraction of transportation planning in the economic development regions is the opportunity of planning in concert with a wide variety of issues in social and economic development. The linkage is surely there in the present cases, but its significance escapes analytical grasp for the time being and is subject to many opinions. This, of course, is the classic enigma of transportation and development, which remains largely unsolved.

Focal Regions

The concept of focal region has no present interpretation in the form of active planning agencies, so we are left to test the possibilities.

From time to time a major airport is proposed, and it is claimed that the surrounding region ought to be planned for fast land access to facilitate its use. Examples include the one proposed for Ozarkia, one near Otis Air Force Base in Massachusetts, and one in the New Jersey Pine Barrens. While the need for such a plan is often mentioned, to our knowledge no such plan has ever been prepared. The prospects of a region defined by the effects of such a facility, even in a context of relatively little competition from other criteria, must be taken as minimal. The environmental effects of an airport will seldom be a multistate regional problem. The question of air traffic control is definitely a large-scale problem (New York City traffic controls reach as far away as Harrisburg, Pennsylvania), but its lack of association with other problems of the same scale make it easily isolated for attention by a specialized agency.

The greatest prospect for the use of airports to define regions would appear to be on the basis of ground access needs, but this criterion fails also. The ground traffic seeking access to an airport remote from a major metropolitan area is likely to be small, as discovered even by the Port of New York Authority when testing possible outlying locations for a new airport in that area. Even the intensity of traffic to an airport within a metropolitan area is not likely to reach a volume requiring more than some planning attention in the immediate vicinity of the facility.[1][2]

The other possible case is that of the water ports. It is presently difficult to envision the impacts a strong switch to containerization might have on the traffic load they put on surrounding systems, but evidence suggests that the problem would not require the attention of a multistate regional authority. In a study of the National Academy of Sciences-National Research Council, it was estimated that the average distance a ton of cargo was hauled from the Port of New York was 220 miles by truck and 370 miles by rail.

Litten calculated that the average daily load out of the Port of New York in 1960 required approximately 11,000 trucks and 4,000 railroad cars. The calculation arbitrarily assumed that each mode carried half the load. Granted that these figures are not up to date, result from some artificial assumptions, and do not deal with the phenomenon of containerization, they do deal with the nation's largest port complex. Because the number of trucks mentioned could easily be carried on a single highway, and the railroad load could not approach the capacious line haul capacity of that industry, there seems little basis for claiming the need for infrastructural planning of transportation for ports on any but a local level. The traffic loadings quickly disappear into the networks' general demand at a relatively short distance from origin.

Since the economic effects of ports are obviously significant, there are grounds for claiming the existence of very widespread effects on that basis. In fact, they may justify dealing with the planning of ports on a national basis as development generators and confluences of transport networks. But such effects with reference to limited regions are ordinarily buried in the larger role of the central metropolis containing the port.

Conclusions

Concluding the issue of region types, it is useful to summarize their basic characteristics. We have dealt with those whose strength of transport functionality (linear corridors and metropolitan areas) suggests a relatively strong grasp on the problems, no matter how well or poorly they may be interpreted. There are the states, whose administrative unity guarantees effect in dealing with the problems, and finally the economic development regions, whose association with the high priority problems of the nation and whose force as platforms for joint advocacy (at least for the strong cases studied) creates the hope that the contribution of transportation will be substantial. Notwithstanding the vagaries of the association between transportation and development, and other arguments set forth above, it seems reasonable that the economic development regions be the frames for the transportation planning that takes place in their areas, with arrangements for sufficient complementarity from the state level to insure an adequate role for both, and with the hope that further work by the commissions (such as is planned by the New England Regional Commission—see section on Strategies) will provide increasingly systematic means of doing so.

Administrative Forms

The administrative forms by which the regional agencies function are, in some measure, creators and reflectors of their performance. In this brief review, we attempt to summarize the administrative structure within which the agencies' work is guided, their sources of legitimacy as planning bodies, their relationship to other planning and implementation groups, and the interests they effectively represent and engage. The investigation does not permit analysis of important informal factors, so we have unquestionably missed points resulting from personalized authority and indirect influence. Still, this aspect of the study offers useful indications toward the workability of future agencies, depending on their structure, ranges of collaboration, and interests represented.

Metropolitan Agencies

The metropolitan agencies have typically had large directive boards with representation of elected officials from all the constituent cities and counties, as well as several federal and state agencies. This is particularly true of the earlier agencies. The unwieldiness of the boards' size, as well as the various natural conflicts of interests they typically represent in the face of planning problems that are very resistant to consensus, have been major obstacles in the production of strong metropolitan plans. Many have functioned with an executive committee of some strength, but the underlying difficulties of technical and jurisdictional representation have been extremely difficult to resolve. There is no evidence at hand to suggest that this is more complex at the multistate level than otherwise, provided interstate operating compacts are not involved.

The effective incorporation of local citizen interests has been an even greater difficulty, as the many widely publicized confrontations between highway planners and neighborhood groups testify. In the operation of the studies, standard public hearings have been the only means of incorporating such interests in most cases; a few have attempted brief preference surveys and limited experiments in community participation. This problem emerges mainly from the firm methodology of the process, which has no easy manner of incorporating other interests. It results from the insistence on judgments based upon the demand for system continuity for the whole metropolitan area—that analytically convenient but invisible region which corresponds to no one's personal interest. There are also problems presented by the coercions of federal subsidies which favor highway construction, controversies about means of serving the interests of the poor, and a "direct solution" ethos in the transport planning professions which, at least until recently, has been resistant to dealing with more subtle requirements.[13] It is unlikely that these problems will be substantially resolved in the near future.

From this discussion, incidentally, it appears more likely that metropolitan transportation planning will soon take place in smaller subregions of the metropolis, with general directives extracted from consideration of factors in a larger one, enabling the planners better to engage neighborhood concerns at the one level and to turn to larger matters at the other.

The other forms of regional planning have generally not approached, nor been beset by, the concerns of citizen clients. It is a topic requiring more attention. Whether these issues will continue to beset transportation planning at a larger metropolitan-oriented regional level, and whether they will confront the activities of other regional bodies is not clear. In any case, it is questionable that regional bodies should continue to derive their full legitimacy from associations with line state agencies that are presumably controlled by legislatures. In the present social mood of the nation, this is neither a strong position nor a morally justified one for many of their activities.

The Penn-Jersey Transportation Study exemplifies some of the problems pointed out above. Just after its founding in 1959 it had a very large policy committee, which was eventually worked down to 13 members, including one representative of each of the constituent local governmental jurisdictions, one from each of the state highway departments, and one from the Bureau of Public Roads. It had, as did several of the major studies, a supplementary technical advisory committee composed of professionals from the transport-related agencies within the local jurisdictions serving as counterparts to the elected officials on the policy committee. Powers of the agency leadership were only advisory; it counted on voluntary compliance to agreements by the participating local officials and on most of the funding from the Bureau of Public Roads.

The NCTA (National Capital Transportation Agency) was established in 1960, primarily to prepare detailed plans for the Washington, D.C. area based on a series of transportation studies completed in the years before. It extended its work far beyond this charge, mostly on the grounds that increased concern for public transportation by the Federal Government in the intervening years effectively changed the possibilities for planning. The Agency was succeeded by the Washington Metropolitan Area Transit Authority as an implementation agency upon the passage of an interstate compact enabling the construction of a metropolitan transit system in 1966.

The NCTA board was composed of five members appointed by the President as advisors to the agency administrator, another Presidential appointee. The Agency was able to operate, ultimately, only with the approval of Congress and its constituencies in Maryland and Virginia. The NCTA had the relation of sponsorship by the National Capital Planning Commission, the planning agency for Washington, D.C., and a close relationship with the weaker National Capital Regional Planning Council.

An interstate compact for establishing the Tri-State Transportation Commission was passed in 1963 by New York and Connecticut. New Jersey did not enter into the agreement until a provision for the possible operation of a transit system by the Commission was removed in 1965. It had been preceded by the Tri-State Transportation Committee, which had operated as a collaborative transportation planning group for the three states since 1961. The Commission is made up of five representatives appointed by the governors of each of the three states. Members from the Bureau of Public Roads, the Department of Housing and Urban Development, and the Federal Aviation Agency all serve without vote. As in the cases of most metropolitan planning agencies, collaboration with other bodies is mainly through the representation of them in its Commission, one of whom by law must be the Chairman of the New York City Planning Commission. The Chairman of the Metropolitan Transit Authority is also a member. There has, in addition, been some collaboration with the Regional Plan Association of New York, a distinguished private organization that has given attention to transportation on a regional scale, but differences in professional style between the two agencies has limited the effectiveness of the relationship.

These are fairly representative cases. The metropolitan transportation agencies are primarily advisory offices (with rare exceptions such as Southeastern Wisconsin, whose plans receive legislative designation, or the Twin Cities Metropolitan Planning Council, which has both planning and operating qualities). The advice is primarily directed to the usually unified judgment of the Bureau of Public Roads and the constituent state highway departments, whose representation on the policy committees is both essential and highly influential. Their secondary objective of advice is the land planning process in member jurisdictions by way of the elected representatives on their policy committees. Other collaborations are miscellaneous and typically tenuous, partly because of the difficulties of obtaining strength and flexibility in agreements within the commissions themselves.

Some hope more widely collaborative processes may emerge from the experiments with joint development or the recent "integrated funding packages," which are combination grants to local authorities in which HUD, DOT, HEW, and OEO participate together.[14] Further, recent informally reported knowledge of Tri-State and Delaware Valley Regional Planning Commission (DVRPC) strategies suggest that the agencies are entering upon broader collaboration and less internal methodological closure. The DVRPC is said to be consulting some 2,000 people in related agencies and interest groups. But joint development results thus far have not been entirely encouraging, the integrated funding packages are too recent to judge, and the results of the extended agency collaborations mentioned are not yet evident.

Northeast Corridor

The corridor region, as exemplified by the Northeast Corridor Project, is our simplest example of regional transportation development administration. Set up basically to determine the means of solving the corridor's line haul requirements up to the year 1980, the study began in 1963. It has always been administered directly by the Federal Government, eventually coming to reside in the office of the Assistant Secretary for Policy and International Affairs of the Department of Transportation, which has a project director who reports directly to the Assistant Secretary. Government expectations from the functional simplicity of the region are reflected by this administrative form.

The project incorporates no implementation authority; a form for the latter is currently being chosen. It has no direct contact with client users and very little with the myriad local governments constituent to its region. The expectation of using only airways and existing line haul rights of way, together with minimizing attention to relationships with surrounding development except to the extent of measuring the demand likely to emerge from it, have increased the simplicity of the operation to the point that operating line haul interests are virtually the only ones with which it has to deal.

State Agencies

The states, at another extreme of administrative identity, are the regions with a possible maximum of intermodal and intersectoral coherence because they include planning in the context of fully unified administrative systems. This facilitates coordination of elements up to the limits of known relationships and the normal obstacles to interagency collaboration within the same government. Further, since state agencies in the various sectors have long histories of collaboration with their federal counterparts, of which they are often just differently scaled staffs of the same professional makeup, their ability to work with the federal agencies is usually very good. Indeed, perhaps the greatest problem with comprehensive state planning is the strong preference for sectoral agencies at federal and state levels to deal with each other, rather than with a more comprehensive body.

The viability of this arrangement as a means of planning is further enhanced by the incorporation of planning and executive powers under the same structure. This produces continuity and tends to evoke concern for citizen interests; state planning must respond to them on account of the proximity of fully responsible government authority to the process, and finds it easier to do so because the fuller structure is known to be comprehensively responsible and to have the implementation bite to respond significantly to articulated interests. Therefore, while the states have not yet responded widely to such concerns, there are good indications that means for doing so are being developed (or thrust upon them). The recent highway building moratorium in Boston proclaimed by Governor Sargent of Massachusetts may be a significant bellwether. Task Force recommendations (June 1970) for the creation of a state DOT in Massachusetts have proposed a series of means for public involvement, including open memorandum files, forms of access to government by interest groups, and funds for the development of alternative plans by community interest groups. A system of response to public initiatives is being designed for Puerto Rico by Chandler Stevens and others at MIT's Sloan School.

Connecticut's transportation program is the most formally imbedded in the breadth of planning considerations of which the states are capable. The Connecticut Interregional Planning Program, established in 1961, was a joint venture of the Connecticut Development Commission, Department of Agriculture and Natural Resources, Department of Finance and Control, and the Highway Department (since succeeded by a State Department of Transportation) to integrate the efforts of state and federal agencies in the planning of the state's regions. There is evidence of collaboration among these participants in many of the program's activities, though the perennial problem of the sophisticated separateness of transportation planning is also manifest. The program involves also the participation of six intrastate regional agencies and the Tri-State (New York City region) Commission. In particular, much of its basic data come from these already existing groups.

The California approach is quite different from the others mentioned; it primarily pieces together transportation plans from the proposals of local transportation districts of that state.[b] The process is handled by the Division of Highways and is one of collecting designs of systems prepared by the subregional (district) transportation planning groups, conducting studies of these juxtaposed plans so that the result will be compatible, and applying priorities to system elements for state-supported development.

The decentralized approach is further validated by the California highway financing system, which assures a minimum expenditure to each of the 58 counties of the State.

The uniqueness of this planning system is based on its decentralization, its reliance on subregional planning. In some respects, the system resembles an elaborated form of the *de facto* status of planning in less advanced states. But the full effect of this format is not easily transferable to many other states, since it requires the relative affluence and the extraordinary number of subregional planning agencies found in California.

The Wisconsin Planning Program is carried out by the State Department of Transportation, Division of Planning, as part of the State Planning Program. The

---

[b]We wish to acknowledge help on this topic from Arlee Reno, who has worked with the state of California for the Highways and Communities Values Project of the MIT Urban Systems Laboratory.

process receives inputs from the Bureau of State Planning, the Department of Natural Resources, and other agencies. The preparation of statewide plans is a centralized process, as in Connecticut. In Wisconsin, however, a state transportation plan was recently formally ratified by the legislature, like the plans of the Southeastern Wisconsin (Milwaukee) Commission. In reality, the ratification of a transportation plan by a legislature is a gesture of unclear significance, since these are investment plans, rather than being primarily plans of controls whose implementation would be assured by legislative approval. In any case, surely the commitment of ratification adds some strength to the planning process.

The Wyoming transportation planning procedure is quite new and untried, like those of many of the other states that have recently entered the area. It was initiated in early 1969. Since Wyoming is a rural state, the growth of concentrated centers of travel demand and competition for land resources are not as serious as in the others reviewed. The process is confined to the planning of highways. For this purpose, however, the collaboration of a substantial series of related agencies has been secured. Involved groups include the Department of Economic Planning and Development, the Wyoming Recreation Commission, the University of Wyoming, the County Commissioners' Association, and the Association of Municipalities of Wyoming. Strong motivation has been developed on the basis of the conviction that highway development is closely associated with economic development.

The states, then, show the potential strength of planning closely backed by direct implementation powers, close collaboration within a unified comprehensive governmental structure, responsiveness to user interests, and strong ties with the appropriate federal agencies. These advantages are sure to increase with time, possibly with the creation of intermodal state transportation trust funds, as advocated by Senator Kennedy in Massachusetts, former Federal Highway Administrator Lowell K. Bridwell, and others. The creation of state departments of transportation, headed by strong secretaries, constitutes another force behind the development of yet greater significance for the activity.[15]

These realities serve warning to our inclination to "re-import" regional planning from the developing countries, where the establishment of useful functional regions is typically facilitated by the fact that state-like political subdivisions are very weak.

Economic Development Regions

The economic development regions' administrative form is the most important to investigate if we are to hope for the viability of functionally determined multistate regions. The primary issues are the extent to which they can secure strong federal commitment to the regions and deal with the states in a way that encourages aggressive development activity within a regional framework, without threatening the existence of the regional commission as monitor of that framework. Again, it must be recalled that we are dealing with the most promising of the economic development regions.

The members of a Title 5 regional commission include the governors, or their appointed representatives, of the states within the region, and a federal co-chairman appointed by the President. A state co-chairman is selected on a rotating basis among the governors. There is a small Washington staff to the operation, a regional staff under the direction of an executive director, and in most cases, small complementary state staffs. Decisions of the commission are carried by a majority of the states and the federal co-chairman (who officially has a veto power over decisions). The legislation lists a number of responsibilities of the commissions, including the preparation of long-range economic development programs, collecting data, assisting states in the designation of economic development districts, promoting increased private investment, conducting research and demonstrations, preparing studies for federal and state governments, and encouraging interstate and state-federal cooperation.

Two additions to the legislation in the amendment of 1969 are of special interest here. One was the authorization of supplemental grants-in-aid to the regions. Under the original act, the commissions were limited to an advisory capacity. Proponents of the commissions argued that planning powers were insufficient. There were no means of assuring implementation, since the regions' conditions of economic underdevelopment made them unable to contribute the necessary matching funds to federal grants under standard programs. The result was an inadequate dispersal to the regions with the greatest need. During Congressional hearings Appalachia was cited as a successful prototype in the use of grants-in-aid. The other addition to the legislation was a provision authorizing funds for a program in cooperation with the Secretary of Transportation to conduct regional transportation studies. A report on this program was due for submission to Congress on January 10, 1971.

The form of organization of the regional commissions is of considerable interest to the analysis, since it is virtually the same as the one suggested subsequently in the legislation for multistate transportation regions.

The Appalachian Regional Commission, also in this sense serving as prototype for the Title 5 regions, has an administrative structure of the type described above. The states have added a full time regional representative who is continuously in contact with the federal co-chairman.

There are two broad working groups under the Executive Director, the Divisions of Planning and of Technical Services. The planning division is further subdivided into six areas of concern, of which one is transportation. The Commission accomplishes regional transportation planning primarily by coordinating the participating state agencies, which are the instrumental comprehensive planning agencies.

It is important to understand the extent to which the states are in control of the planning process, both in plan preparation and implementation. They have the basic control over investment priorities. All requests must originate from the state representatives for approval of the Commission and technical review by the applicable federal agency. Localities cannot bypass state government in requests for aid. The federal co-chairman theoretically holds a veto power on behalf of the federal establishment, but as Commission members happily pointed out during the 1967 hearing, he had never used the power. The limited six year life of the Appalachia Commission may also suggest the states' reluctance to permit an activity that stands to exist indefinitely and, perhaps, increasingly circumscribe their authority.

The New England Commission is organized along exactly the same lines. It may be indicative that the annual reports refer to the regional Commission's activity as the preparation of a "comprehensive economic plan," and that of the states as presenting "state investment plans." The terminology again suggests the inclination for the Commission to concern itself with overall guidance, leaving to the states the job of programming the development. The format was summarized by the federal co-chairman to a Senate Subcommittee in 1967 as beginning with the communities submissions to the states of development requests for examination on the basis of state criteria, and afterwards the approval of the Commission in accordance with more general criteria.[16] The participation of the states in the planning, however, is not as dominant as in Appalachia.

There is no doubt that the New England Commission has been successful in sustaining interstate collaboration. The governors meet in person quarterly to discuss principal decision issues, and their interim representatives are in most cases officials who are close to the governors. The Commission has sponsored the Geo-Transport Foundation as a non-profit organization for the study of the region's transportation problems. The Foundation is now working on the possibilities for the revival of rail passenger transportation in the region, and other subjects.

Both Commissions secure the temporary services of technical personnel from various federal departments to work on special problems raised by the Commissions' interests.

In summary, it can be said that the Commissions have four sources of strength: (1) federal funds, (2) federal agency staff assistance, (3) facilitating joint advocacy of objectives held in common by the included states, and (4) as planning and development entities with permanent staffs to conduct programs for the multistate regions. The fourth function is of great importance, especially in the cases of the more economically depressed states, and was a frank objective of the legislation that created the Commissions. The third is clearly of great importance in focusing attention on the serious problems of these areas at the national level. However, the concern here polarizes around the extent to which these forces tend to create region-wide planning on the part of the Commissions. While suspending discussion of actual performance for the time being, it is clear at this point that the regional planning function must certainly be conceived as a limited one.

Focal Regions

The focal regions are not represented by an active example of regional administration. The only relevant institution type in play is the port authority which, while concerned about regional economic impacts, has little direct effect beyond the construction and maintenance of its own facilities. These may span something up to the 20-mile radius jurisdiction of the Port of New York Authority.

Conclusions

In concluding these summary statements on administrative forms, it is important to separate regional bodies that are constituted to solve what is envisioned to be a clearly stated problem (as was the Northeast Corridor) on one hand, or which are created to conduct an open search for problem definition (e.g., the economic development region). It is reasonable to assume that our task is more concerned with the latter than with the former. This is important, since the "open search" agencies have much greater requirements of administrative strength and collaboration in the course of their work.

The agencies are also divided among those that are part of unified sources of implementation (e.g., the state planning agencies), those that are more removed from implementation authorities or that must deal with them as a highly decentralized set of interests (e.g., the metropolitan agencies), and those for which unusual special access to implementation means has been provided (the economic development regions). The experience suggests that only when good access to implementation means is a forceful component of administrative endowment can a regional agency have a chance to maintain useful leadership among its constituent states. A possible exception may be the corridor case, in which the simplism of proposals makes the lapping into state jurisdictions limited and more easily negotiable. The experience has yet to produce definite evidence.

The arguments above are the primary ones that condition the possibilities for collaboration with the necessary variety of modes and sectors, extending from the limited involvements of the corridor study to the more integrated position of the state agency.

The most important generalization is the irreducible administrative importance of the states in any interesting regional transportation planning effort. Their agencies are by far in the best position to represent implementation authority, build constructive on-going collaborative relationships, and therefore to conduct constructive open searches for problem interpretations and to deal with the client public. Indeed, they appear to be the only groups really capable of dealing directly with client user interests.

Purposes, Strategies, and Techniques

We move now from regional transportation planning as an administrative construct to its nature as a technical process. For the present it is convenient to characterize the process as proceeding from a statement of initial purposes, likely to be very general and possibly specified with little attention to real potentialities for accomplishment. These purposes are then subject to a variety of interpretations. Some of them are underlying concerns that development hopes to serve in a general way, but that are subject to little further attention in the actual planning and development process. Others are interpreted into strategies that show some level of operationalization of the purposes toward forms of specific accomplishment with their intent. At the next level techniques are employed for the more direct specification of solutions.

As a matter of fact, very few original purposes ever reach the end of this reduction process. Some important purposes cannot be well articulated in the more definite forms and are set aside to the "general intent" category as a matter of priority in favor of the more clearly operational ones. Further, new purposes are invariably imposed by the techniques themselves, which are generated by some standard conceptualization of the problems that assumes purposes of its own. Meanwhile, indirect pressures, sources of money, and other outside influences constantly bear on the formation of the solution process.

It is not possible to complete a description of this process for the various types of regional planning in any detail here, but certain prominent characteristics of it for each type of planning can be identified and juxtaposed with those of the other types in the interest of checking the capabilities of the planning systems investigated.

Metropolitan Transportation Planning

The metropolitan case is the classic one for interpreting purposes by a highly operational technical model that effectively defines the problem, the more subtle and thoughtful objectives of the directive committees notwithstanding. Statements of purposes are typically general and discursive. An orderly procedure is followed that begins with the collection of an immense amount of data toward their use in a series of mathematical models. These models proceed from the concept of the generation of trips by activities taking place at fixed locations in the city and extend into a series of analyses to forecast traffic loadings in proposed transportation systems. Land use proposals are developed simultaneously, by hand or model methods, in order to analyze their compatibility with the transportation systems proposed. Further elaboration of technical detail is unnecessary here; it is covered adequately in the textbooks. The problems encountered in obtaining useful results at the evaluation stage, where an effort is made to choose among land use and transportation network alternatives by loading the implications of one onto a model of the other, have been extensively discussed by David E. Boyce, et al.[17] These are serious problems that have badly damaged the confidence in metropolitan transportation planning to the extent that new studies are rarely commissioned at the present time.

Over the past ten years, virtually all the studies accomplished have adhered closely to this format. The best known exception was the study of the San Francisco area, which set out explicitly to generate the BART rapid transit system and did short-cut many of the conventional procedures on the way.

One special characteristic of this procedure is that it is particularly amenable to a study that sets out to produce a single plan and nothing more. While there has been much discussion of continuing transportation studies that would detail, adjust, and update the original job, the duties of continuation are mostly tied to maintaining the original plan and are seldom those of continuous problem searching and solving in any general sense.

Another characteristic of the procedure, as of most highly standardized methodologies, is that it is rather resistant to relationships with sectors other than those systematically included and to innovations in such forms as new technology. The proposal for innovative technology posits such discontinuities with the status of the urban systems, as registered by the methods, as to make use of the methods very difficult.

Consideration of these purposes and methods here is particularly important, notwithstanding the possibilities that metropolitan areas may grow to region-like scale. The methods of this field are the first to develop a really persuasive, policy-oriented set of cross-sectoral relationships (between traffic and land use), and as such are extremely compelling, their problems notwithstanding. As we discuss later, they serve important roles in corridor and state transportation planning, and are likely to infiltrate the activity at any scale, though somewhat decreasingly as the scale grows larger.

The purposes of metropolitan transportation planning, as presented by the early studies (late 1950s) were rather simple but highly general, typically mentioning the need for increased access to all parts of the region with greater safety, in a context of greater compatibility with land uses and increased efficiency in the use of public funds. As time went on the idiom of social benefits increasingly entered the concerns of the agencies in preparing such statements.

The studies reviewed show this sequence. The early NCTA's objectives as received in the charge from Congress stated (1) there would be planning on a regional basis of major transportation facilities, (2) the Agency should evaluate the 1959 plan (in fact a series of consultants' plans which they went considerably beyond), and (3) the Agency should prepare for the construction and development of a transit development program. With this the Agency set out to "provide for the movement of people throughout the National Capital Region at a minimum cost through a balanced transportation system."[18] The nature of the charge is further clarified by the legislation, which provided that the Agency could deal only with (1) the routes of carriers (surface, water, and airborne) within the region, and (2) the locations of related facilities (e.g., stations and terminals).

The Penn-Jersey Transportation Study released informal prospectuses of that study in 1959, 1960, and later, which amplified the conceptualization of purposes a bit more and introduced their ill-fated intent to rely heavily on an activities allocation model to evaluate the alternative plans to be designed.[19]

The Boston study (EMRPP) made use of the terms "choice, freedom, amenity, and stability" in explaining the objectives of the work.

Statement of intent for the later Tri-State study, perhaps indicatively, did not appear in published form until 1968, though it had been preceded by less formal statements. It presents goals in almost poetic terms, mentioning the need to "harness natural forces," to encourage an "equitable society," to build an "interesting environment," provide for "wider opportunities for full participation," and so forth.[20] The publication tends to discuss these goals in a context within poor reach of the contributions from any transportation system, and no really operational statements are made.

The *de facto* purpose of these studies was to allocate investments to transportation infrastructure in accordance with effective demand for it as measured by the methodology mentioned, and to consider the efficiency of these investments in the context of limited alternatives of modal choice and land use configurations.

The exposition of these statements serves only to emphasize the effort at response to increasing demands for social relevance made of the metropolitan transportation studies; the problems of technique show the constraints which fetter the reality of that response.

The *strategies and techniques* employed in these three studies are congruent with the summary at the beginning of this section. The NCTA study released its methodological memoranda for very limited distribution in 1962. Most of the technical emphasis was given to development of the traffic models; attention to land development was in the form of simpler planning. Since the charge to the agency included the proposal of a transit system and preparation for its implementation, considerable effort was given to the study of financing and implementing that system. The work included study of the interstate compact and public bond financing for the purpose.

At Penn-Jersey, events with considerable formative influence on the field took place. The great attention given to the activities allocation model during the study as a means of generating and evaluating land development plans gave its interpretation of the format of urban transportation planning a specially developmental character. This model was an important contribution to the science of the field, but sensitivity problems and other obstacles to its successful use caused its failure to evaluate the six proposed land development alternatives in time for the 1965 deadline by which the plan needed to be completed so that the region's federal highway aid not be compromised.[21] The model was dropped and the study was completed by methods of greatest expediency. The successor agency, the DVRPC (Delaware Valley Regional Planning Commission), has turned to less formal evaluation methods, described by the author of the case study cited as "muddling through." The failure of Penn-Jersey's ambitious effort caused a pall of reactionism to descend on subsequent efforts.

The Tri-State Transportation Commission, laboring under this post-Penn-Jersey effect and also under the problems of the immense scale of New York, has not established an altogether clear role among the studies about the nature of its approach. The study has published a substantial amount of information, but it tends not to clarify the central methodology being used. An interim plan was presented in 1968; the final report is not yet completed. The agency has conducted a series of demonstrations to test the possibilities of increased viability of transit for the region, but the usefulness of these to the central concerns of the planning process is not clear.

This brief analysis serves to unify some of the symptoms attached to the brittleness of metropolitan transportation planning methodology at the present time. It is a practice whose *de facto* purpose is to achieve aggregate compatibility between a designed transportation system and a desired pattern of human activities over space. The quest is worthy, even if it does not live up to the ambitious requirements typically mentioned in the studies' objectives. But the exasperation of Penn-Jersey has led to Seidman's position that it is time to call research *research*. The basic problems in evaluating transportation plans have been that (1) the various policies tested exhibit similarly high levels of service when compared to present conditions, so that the differences between them are not perceived as significant, (2) zones used as the units for measuring trip generation and land development are too large to account properly for impacts, (3) the land development-transportation relationship takes too long to come to equilibrium, such that the term of the plan would have to be longer than the usual maximum of 20 years, and (4) most new highways are planned for the urban periphery, where traffic volumes are low, such that alternative land development assumptions make little difference to the proposed traffic networks. This last criticism is particularly important. It is congruent with the position often taken by Aaron Fleisher: urban transportation planning, by this formulation, is a matter either of increasing the connectivity between points in space or expanding channel capacity. Connectivity is, in general, not a problem in metropolitan areas; their present networks are so ubiquitous that marginal increases are not likely to much repay the effort. So the objective becomes relief for congestion (though it makes inefficient use of the elaborate methodology), and in low density areas where this is not a problem the techniques lose interest.

Considering these limitations in the context of an enlarged metropolitan region, one that would attract interest in the sphere of this study leads to an obvious and unencouraging conclusion. All four limitations mentioned apply at least equally to this kind of region, and the fourth would present particularly great difficulties. It is for these reasons that positions suggesting the immiscibility between urban and regional transportation planning were taken at certain points above.

Hope for a closer analytic relationship from the metropolis outward toward its hinterland, however, may be implicit in the recent strategies of the DVRPC and Tri-State. Their apparent tendencies (not yet fully reported) to deal with the problems in a much looser, more informal analytic context and to expose, therefore, their plans to more outside recommendations may open a new metropolitan approach that is more apt for large region planning.

New kinds of emphasis in the planning of mobility may further enhance these possibilities. Out of the current concern for the mobility of the poor is sure to emerge a style for part of the process that focuses on the transportation problems of the particular urban (or regional) family. We might speculate that starting with techniques which more amply reflect the mobility potential and needs of small groups of people, new methods might emerge that would be unencumbered by the problems cited above. Some suggestions toward the possibilities for approaches of this sort are appearing from the work in differential pricing of transportation. Much interest has been shown lately in the possibility of subsidizing the ownership of automobiles by the poor.[c] This is a suggestion that could be applied equally to urban ghettos and to lagging urban hinterlands.

We are not suggesting that such approaches will replace the more standard ones toward accomplishing the same purposes. Rather they represent a new ordering of priorities, a redefinition of the job from emphasis on structural compatibility to emphasis on social benefit. This process of introducing a new method and objective to replace an older method whose objective has been lowered in priority and weakened by a lack of impressive success at the job it was intended to achieve is typical in planning history.

---

[c]This suggestion was made by Lloyd Rodwin and various others in the Workshop on Transportation for New Towns and Communities, sponsored by the Institute of Public Administration, December 1969. It was a conclusion of a study made by Aaron Fleisher and Philip Herr on the mobility of the poor in Boston (unpublished).

The Northeast Corridor Project

As an example of purposiveness and methodology that is as direct as its streamlined administrative orientation, the Northeast Corridor is among the studies reviewed an extreme case. When Senator Pell introduced the original resolution that would have created the Project in 1962, he called on the region to enter "into a compact to establish a multi-state authority to construct and operate a rail passenger transportation system within the area...." Though later consideration broadened the charge of the study to include all modes and impacts, the issue of linear interconnection has remained central to the job. It was possible for Earl Ruiter to prototype fairly adequately an elemental statement of the final procedure in a systems analytic statement that appears in a textbook for university instruction.[22]

The level and scope of the Project are difficult to fully summarize, since its emphasis changed in course. The effort, as defined by a White House Task Force in 1962 and again in 1964, was directed toward determining a methodology for transportation planning at the corridor level. In the years that followed, substantial contributions of a methodological type were made by the Search and Choice Project at MIT, the Northwestern University Transportation Center, The Rand Corporation, and other consulted groups. This productive stage of the Project is poorly represented in our review, which gives more attention to the regional plan emphasis that emerged during the Project's more recent years, and that made only partial use of the foregoing work. The earlier stage, for example, gave serious consideration to the problems of the Corridor's freight movements that did not survive into the highly directed approach characterizing its later stages. The technological aspects increased in emphasis during these stages because of the research and development and demonstration activities authorized by the High Speed Ground Transportation Act of 1965. The Project's incorporation into the Federal Railroad Administration upon the establishment of DOT in 1967 had the effect of truncating many of its other ambitions.

The Project was generated by a sense that the modes providing for corridor movement in the Northeast were overcrowded, unable to expand their capacities adequately, and subject to decision-making that was not sufficiently centralized to yield solutions. Particular aspects of the problem that were cited included (1) rail capacities that are under-utilized; (2) potentialities for short and intermediate haul air transport that may not be otherwise exploited; (3) downtown to downtown regional traffic that is contributing to the congestion of urban transportation facilities; (4) the tendency for the modes creating the greatest personal hazard, the most pollution, and the greatest demand for space (highways) to be the most rapidly expanding; (5) the trend for the less populated parts of the corridor to lose intercity service; and (6) lack of coordination among existing intercity modes. The weakness of the railroads, the congested air terminals, and the proliferation of highways seemed the main components of the syndrome.

The purposes, then, are relatively straightforward. Little effort is made in the documentation to stretch the significance of the work on the nebulous topic of personal benefits (most intercity travel is by middle income people anyway), or to address the gargantuan task of impacts on activities' locations in a region of almost 50 million people. Indeed, it might have been more concerned with this latter topic, even though in a highly aggregated form. The more novel among the final alternative technologies proposed would generate more than twice the present corridor traffic volumes. These volumes, concentrating origins and destinations at or near city centers on route, suggest important changes that merit further study.

The final general strategy of the study was to develop means for measuring travel demand, conduct technological research toward establishing the viability of the various possible modes of transportation, design a series of alternative corridor systems, test these in terms of their practical and financial feasibility, and find means of implementing them through satisfactory institutionalization.

The basic set of models for the analysis of the problem included six components:

1. An econometric model for the projection of population, income, employment, and land use for the 131 districts.
2. A demand model to forecast intercity transportation by modes. This model included a model split submodel.
3. A supply model for air and high speed ground modes, sensitive to the output levels of these technologies.
4. Models of the costs of mode and system elements.
5. Impact models for the study of effects of transportation on population locations, employment, income and land use.
6. Balancing techniques to make possible the simulation of supply-demand equilibrium.

The approach represented by this set of models is a kind of mixture between a supply-demand analysis of the transportation problem and the methodology of the metropolitan transportation studies discussed above. It is of interest to notice that the results of the impact models have not been a significant part of the results. These models were prepared some years ago by a competent consultant. It is likely that he ran into exaggerated forms of the problems mentioned above in connection with them under metropolitan planning. No evidence is available. In any case, the study as presented is basically a discussion of the problem of new technology on the basis of supply-demand equilibrium.

The study produced nine alternative systems for consideration. They include superimposition upon the present modes of various combinations of high-speed rail transport on existing rights-of-way, high speed rail on new rights-of-way, STOL, VTOL, and air cushion vehicles. The evaluative problem is stated primarily in terms of cost and implementation feasibilities. The basic distinctions drawn among the alternatives were (1) degree of technological innovation required; (2) an emphasis on landing people in central cities or at urban peripheries (e.g., airport locations); (3) magnitude of the capital costs involved; (4) flexibility of the mode, in the sense of whether the rights-of-way serve other purposes, etc.; (5) relative amounts of private and public expenditures required; (6) extent of institutional change required; and (7) the extent to which federal intervention would be implied.

In fact, some brief examinations of the less central issues were undertaken. An effort was made, for example, to learn whether a system change would create a shift in economic activity from the fringe of the region toward the cores of the urban areas. The results reported were that no such shift would be expected. In view of the substantial traffic volume changes, this result is suspiciously counterintuitive, but adequate methods to measure impacts for a region of this magnitude are difficult to come by.

The studies were supplemented by the metroliner demonstration, which is relevant to the purposes as a means of testing demand. VTOL and the metroliner turned out to be the alternatives considered the most feasible. The Project is now working toward the possibilities of implementation.

In concluding about the potentialities of corridor studies, it is necessary to keep in mind the caveat resulting from our analysis of the other possible corridors as regions; few other candidates are likely. Even in the case of the Northeast Corridor, the position has been taken that it is an insufficiently homogeneous region of two major areas split at New York City. There is, of course, no reason in principal that the methods summarized above could not be profitably applied to what we were calling a "cluster corridor," but the scale of use of the technology in these cases would be smaller, easily to the extent of a qualitative difference in the result. Certainly the more advanced modes investigated in this study, many of them rejected from the Northeast Corridor on grounds of high cost, could not even be considered for the other regions. In the case of all of them but the Mid-West Corridor, there is serious question that warrant for any technological innovation could be developed.

The smaller scale of operation would impose a number of other qualitative differences in operation too. Whereas the gigantic scale of this region has enabled the situation to be analyzed in a highly aggregated form mostly isolated from local interests, study of smaller corridors—and especially the urban pair-wise associations of the cluster corridors—would give their study a much more local flavor. The studies would have to take smaller scale phenomena into account, be concerned with who is to receive the benefits of development, confront more directly the local government representatives who are concerned about the indirect effects of the plan, and probably deal with client publics. In other words, as the corridor becomes smaller, the study of it increasingly resembles a metropolitan transportation study, with all the complicating effects we have already reviewed in that connection.

On the side of commendation, we must admit that the form of the Northeast Corridor Project study is probably the most (perhaps only) effective means of approaching the solution it intends. Further, it was reasonably sincere in not extending the reach of its claims further than the grasp of its work. Finally, it has has systematically considered new technology as the solution to transportation problems of a complex geographical region—for the first time in history, to our knowledge. As the demand grows for solutions of this type in other kinds of regions, the methods used in this study may be found basic to the planning process.

State Transportation Planning

As the most widespread form of truly regional transportation planning in the United States, state transportation planning deserves careful attention in regard to purposes and strategies. More than any other type, the state regions include planning for various modes of transportation and related activities within the same structure, and their important role as subregions to whatever multi-state regions may appear qualifies them as significant experiences.

To the extent that it can be penetrated by a review of this type, the purposes and methodological approaches of state planning appear to be rather uniform among the strongest participants. In fact, the appearance of the *National Transportation Planning Manuals* (DOT) serves, to some extent, to confirm their resemblance at present (manuals only appear on well settled issues), and promises to further create uniformity in the future.[23] The kinds of information that will be required from the states include estimated levels of federal expenditures required, the mix of expenditures by modes, the method of allocating federal funds by the state, availability of the funds used to match federal contributions, and expected changes in transportation technology, economy and life styles in the state.

As suggested even by the titles of the DOT manuals (each one addresses a different mode), state transportation planning methodology has little capacity for integrating modes beyond the most general gestures. The planning processes are generally accumulations of problems, each handled by means separately applicable to it.

In view of the similarities mentioned, we chose to dwell mainly on the mature Connecticut program, and remark on the other cases only in regard to the limited ways they differ.

As an urbanized state, Connecticut views the purpose of transportation as being to minimize the time-distance disadvantage between all elements of its ubiquitous pattern of urban places, while preserving natural features and the amenities of the state. Hence, transportation is seen primarily as a service to this pattern, but it is also of interest as a means of facilitating planned development. The planning of highways is considered to be both constrained by, and to facilitate, proposed uses of land. With respect to the highway mode, then, the only one effectively addressed by these statements, the direction of state transportation planning is unmistakably influenced by the metropolitan approach, but without the blatant conflict with social problems more evident at the smaller scale. The methodology will follow the expectations suggested by this orientation fairly closely.

While the objectives of the process, and ultimately the work, reflect wide concern for various transport modes, the sophisticated methodology is applied to highway planning and the other modes dealt with in briefer ways.

The office maintains a statewide origin-destination file with trips broken down into standard classifications of trip purpose. Unlike the metropolitan studies, it also surveys the movement of goods in order to deal with the performance characteristics of these trips. This comprehensive data file is important. It offers a quantity of base information that gives the Connecticut program special possibilities relative to other states.

The projected demand for tripmaking is based on forecasted future patterns of state economic and social development that have been previously prepared by other components of the State Planning Program. These projections are developed by means of an economic growth model, which primarily estimates state population and employment by categories for each decade to the year 2000, followed by a growth distribution model that locates the growth in a state-wide set of traffic zones. In addition, there is a recreational activities model with estimates by geographical area. The three variables—population, employment, and recreation—are the key ones, then, for trip projection.

Having in this manner estimated the location of future activities and demand for trips, traffic volumes are distributed over the state and considered as loadings on present, committed, or proposed highway networks. It is then possible to consider the quality of transportation and resulting impacts on land development patterns.

The planning program is now considering alternative patterns of concentration for planned new development. The forms include a linear concentration scheme, a multiple urban centers scheme, and a "regional plans composite" scheme. The linear scheme proposes a considerable concentration of development in the Central Valley and along the southwest coast toward New York; the multiple urban centers are designed to distribute development widely over the state, but in a pattern that contains it within large-scale complexes; "plans composite" is the scheme that makes no regional pattern assumption but merely integrates the local region plans of the state into a consolidated pattern. The tripmaking patterns implied by these schemes are examined.

The development of these schemes is methodologically important, since they assume a certain functional integrity of the state as a geographical region. Present sources do not permit the evaluation of these options for ordering development within such a functionally arbitrary area as a state, so no judgment can be passed on the matter here. One is inclined to suspect, however, that this kind of planning would be better undertaken at a scale that permits some kind of systematic closure on a system of cities, such as a multi-state region.

Planning for other modes of transportation is considered separately, and not nearly so completely. Railroads, for example, are more important to Connecticut than they are to most states. Their significance is particularly great in the southwestern part of the state, where they form a vital component of Connecticut's close association with New York City. Fifty-four percent of all personal travel to New York is by rail, and 32 percent of personal travel to Boston. The activities of the planning program seem limited to measuring the characteristics and usage of service and commenting on proposals made elsewhere for improved service or additional railroad financing. Demands for service are projected in much the same manner as for highways. There is a sense of hopelessness in the efforts being made. This is no doubt due in part to the fact that the railroads are privately owned and not easily susceptible to control by state government and to their precarious financial situation. These factors are surely in some good measure responsible, though, for the fact that railroads are organized on the basis of regions considerably larger than states. With respect to almost all states, the railroads are means by which trips are interacted with external places, the internal portions of the routing being too limited for consideration as a unified problem. Here we may have the most reasonable case for multi-state planning.

Planning for air travel suffers from similar problems, except that the routing is less amenable to circumscription even by a larger region. As an expanding mode, however, the planning of its terminals is a means of building development. Demand projections are made by the Connecticut program, based on growth in the centers of trip origins. The variables considered include population, declining real air fares, price and income elasticities, and improved service. The construction and expansion of airport facilities is planned on the basis of these projections, but availability of funds for the purpose is a serious limitation. Municipalities are encouraged to consider VSTOL aircraft in their local planning, but there have been no investigations in depth concerning the potentialities of these modes. Air cargo transport receives little attention; it accounts for less than one percent of total commodity ton-miles in Connecticut.

Water and pipeline transportation are given some attention. Waterborne cargo is forecast to the year 2000 on the basis of projected rates of consumption, manufacturing employment, and population. Preliminary recommendations for expansion of port facilities are based on these forecasts. The matter of pipelines is dealt with very briefly.

Looking more briefly at the California system, its style is essentially a simplified form of the Connecticut strategy. Trends are analyzed to project future trip volumes and relate them to the 12,410-mile California Freeway and Expressway System, which was enacted by the state legislature in 1959 to meet the needs of the growing population and economy through 1980 (though it is not likely to be completed by then).

Air and rail transportation receive similarly brief and separate treatment as in Connecticut. Data on these topics are not as complete, but studies of airport adequacy and air access to geographic areas are currently being undertaken by the California Division of Aeronautics. The railroads are relatively less important than in the East and receive less attention in the planning process.

It is of interest to note that although the California planning system is administratively different from that of Connecticut, being concerned more with the compatibility of subregional plans than with the development of a single state plan by centralized consideration, the structural thought going into the process is nevertheless very similar. Means sufficiently systematic to build a full state planning approach out of the process of integrating subregional plans seems not to be within reach.

The Wisconsin system is similar again, except that rail and port facilities are in this case handled outside the state DOT. Intermodal concern is shown by an effort to check the adequacy with which the Highway Plan serves present and projected airport and lakeport facilities. It is also systematically tested for the service it provides to various point demands, including population centers, trade centers, state offices, and educational and health facilities, as well as recreational sites. Wisconsin planning is done also in a unified, centralized form, with the exception of the metropolitanized Southeast Region, for which planning is done independently by its respective Commission, coordinated by the state agency, with plans ratified by the State Legislature.

The Wyoming Statewide Highway Transportation Planning Process was, by last reports, in too early a stage for consideration of its methodology in terms that would relate its approach to the cases mentioned.

In concluding the brief review of state transportation planning approaches, several points can be tentatively suggested, subject to more thorough investigation. The purposes guiding the process of planning for transportation in the states, aside from some statements of generic faith in its economic development effects, are congruent with the methods used to approach the problems. In no case, however, is a highly integrated strategy involved. The problems are handled separately by mode, with some unity to the data underlying the projections upon which modal plans are based. There is no doubt that the use of common data sources is efficient for the development of plans, and facilitates whatever cross-modal thought may be given to judgments between alternative modes by funding priorities. The extent to which it may add greater compatibility to the performance of the modes, on the otherhand, is questionable and must be subject to closer investigation. It is clear that as cross-modal analytic methods are established, perhaps departing from the pioneering work of the Northeast Corridor Study, the states are the obvious places to use them first.

With respect to the viability of the states as geographic regions for the kinds of planning they are doing, our most interesting symptom for further investigation arises from the case of Connecticut's consideration of alternative urban pattern plans. This approach is likely to spread, since Connecticut is distinguished from the other cases more by the maturity of its process than by the nature of its style. Its relatively unified form of planning is facilitated by the availability of copious transportation data and the existence of a state plan for land development. As other states' transportation planning matures to the same level, they will also be developing frameworks that intentionally or inadvertently assume that the state boundaries enclose some kind of functionally coherent region, probably most typically to be characterized as a "system of cities" of some type. There is good reason to be suspicious of this tendency, and to consider it grounds for suggesting the more comprehensive guidance that might be found in a multi-state region.

The clear domination of highway considerations in state transportation planning partly results from the derivation of their planning systems from state highway departments, and partly results from the fact that intensive attention to the analytics of this mode over the past fifteen years makes it easier to deal with systematically. It also surely results, however, from the fact that highway systems are more functionally contained within state boundaries than any other form of transportation. The larger dimensions of air, water, and pipeline networks tend to leave only their terminal facilities easily within the grasp of state policy. The railroads, with the exception of certain short-run commutation activities, are in the same category. The break in system scale betweeen these different types of transportation suggests a corresponding delegation of responsibilities between state and large regional planning authorities. Such a division of responsibility might be regarded as counterproductive to their eventual coordination, but coordination is sure to be almost the exclusive role of multi-state regions anyway. In view of the present impenetrability of the problems in relating the modes and the poor cross elasticities typically found among them, there might be far more gained than lost.

The Economic Development Regions

The Title 5 Commissions have a very different style of transportation planning than the other agencies reviewed. They are charged to plan for economic and social development—that elusive objective whose attainment requires highly intuitive strategies and techniques that have little application to transportation problems as such. As a natural consequence, development objective. Then the performance of planning is a separated set of various of thoughtful statements that attempt to apply the resources available to the development objective. Then the performance of planning is a separated set of various activities designed to find the weak points in the regional networks and to compose solutions that take those networks themselves as the primary frameworks for solution. The strategy is very much one of open search, rather than being one imposed by a specific problem concept or set of techniques. The urge to bring the whole regional system into some kind of operational coherence, which is explicit in metropolitan planning, precisely formulated in corridor planning, and at least latent in state planning, makes only fleeting appearance here.

Within this very general orientation, however, the Appalachian and New England Commissions are rather different in their approaches. Appalachia, with its huge prior allocation of funds to highways, has dedicated its thrust primarily to a "development highway system" to yield new access and more connections between points in the region as the instrument for development, with secondary attention to other modes. New England, on the other hand, has mostly concentrated on railroads and has a strategy more evenly spread over the various modes; it is the more prototypic case of the orientation mentioned above.

The reasons for this, even aside from prior fund allocation, are apparent. Appalachia can claim the condition of a classical underdeveloped region, where, as in all such regions, the isolation of localities from the whole on account of poor connections can be cited as a basic problem. This is a problem at least partly served by substantial highway investments. New England, on the other hand, does not suffer from poor connections, with the possible exception of the northern part of the region. The basis of its claim to aid is the age and obsolescence of its infrastructure and its need for better connections with the rest of the country. As the earliest industrialized part of the country, its infrastructural endowment is complete; problems have emerged from the introduction of new technologies and economies that leave this endowment insufficient to the region's needs. The incidence of these problems has been spotty, and the strategies useful for their solution cannot be easily unified. Appalachia emerges, then, as a region with an emphasis on aggressive forward motion trying to break a bad equilibrium, while New England is attempting to restore equilibrium to an outworn system.

The purpose of the Appalachian Commission is to stimulate the region's economy and contribute to its social welfare. Objectives are set out in the *Annual Report* of 1968: "... to set in motion a large and comprehensive effort to narrow the wide economic and social gap between Appalachia and the rest of the country and to make it unnecessary for so many millions to move out of the region in search of economic opportunity." Existing programs, both state and federal, had not been achieving this objective.[24] To achieve these objectives, the Commission was assigned the following functions as enumerated in the legislation:

1. Develop, on a continuing basis, comprehensive and coordinated plans and programs and establish priorities thereunder, giving due consideration to other Federal, State, and local planning in the region;

2. Conduct and sponsor investigations, research, and studies, including an inventory and analysis of the resources of the region, and, in cooperation with Federal, State, and local agencies, sponsor demonstration projects designed to foster regional productivity and growth;

3. Review and study, in cooperation with the agency involved, Federal, State, and local public and private programs and where appropriate, recommend modifications or additions which will increase their effectiveness in the region;

4. Formulate and recommend, where appropriate, interstate compacts and other forms of interstate cooperation and work with State and local agencies in developing appropriate model legislation;

5. Encourage the formation of local development districts;

6. Encourage private investment in industrial, commercial, and recreational programs;

7. Serve as a focal point and coordinating unit for Appalachian programs;

8. Provide a forum for consideration of problems of the region and proposed solutions and establish and utilize, as appropriate, citizens and special advisory councils and public conferences; and

9. Advise the Secretary of Commerce on applications for grants for administrative expenses to local development districts. (This item repealed in 1967.)[25]

From the Commission's point of view, analysis of the problems puts great stress on external factors as causing the depressed state of the region. Planning seems to rely heavily on the concept that high unemployment, low wages, and outmigration are attributable to the lack of good job opportunities, which in turn can be traced to the unwillingness of industry, especially manufacturers, to locate in Appalachia due to the unfavorable transportation costs. Thus a primary objective becomes the need to link the region with healthier external places.

This analysis is compatible with the highway development policy to:

1. Make it possible for the people of Appalachia to commute to new opportunities in the region which the program develops;

2. Link key centers in the region to national markets, so that they can take advantage of their development potential on a competitive basis, and

3. Open up sites for new development in the region by providing additional access advantage.[26]

The interest in internal linkage is evident in the plan that resulted from the efforts. Due attention is given to secondary roads, which are an important aspect of the campaign to bring currently isolated localities into the network. The plan claims that when the system is fully completed, all the populated parts of the region will be within an hour of a high-speed highway. There is an internal-external corridors aspect to the plan, including a Cincinnati to Baltimore corridor and the Appalachian Throughway from Keyser, West Virginia, to Cortland, N.Y., combined with policies to encourage development to accompany the highway trajectories.

These are complemented by a series of state highway plans, intended to include and extend the network proposed by the Regional Commission. There is a particular tendency for the states to develop their plans on the basis of corridor concepts that are compatible with the network superstructure provided by the regional plan. As would be expected, the greatest commitment to the extension of highways is found in the plans of the poorer deep Southern states, with the Northern ones giving greater emphasis to airports and auxiliary facilities.[27]

Compared with the highway effort, attention to the problems of air transportation and navigation is very limited. Patterns of regional airports, especially with a view toward making areas more acceptable for industrial location, have been proposed by many of the states in the region. The Office of Appalachian Studies of the U.S. Corps of Engineers has been studying the navigation needs of the region and the best use of its regional railroads.

New England's planning objectives are stated similarly. Analysis of the problems and derivation of approaches are based on an immense backlog of regional research sponsored by a number of groups preceding the Commission.[28]

In good measure, the consensus arising from the various treatments of the problem is contained in the statement by Rudolph W. Hardy that the region suffers from "an infrastructure inherited from an older industrial economy and characterized by a rapid evolution from older and slower growing industries such as textiles to advanced products and services such as electronics and research."[29] The issues of consolidating the railroads and securing better rate situations for New England have been subject to recurrent intensive study since the early 1920s, receiving particular emphasis by the New England Governors' Conference during the late 1950s. The problems of the motor freight industry, complicated by its obsolete equipment, have also received substantial study, as well as intercity bus transportation, airports (primarily by the Governors' Conference), and water transportation.

While a few of these reports recommend the creation of new institutions (e.g., local, and sometimes interstate airport authorities), and the rhetoric of intermodal balance occasionally appears among them, they are oriented toward the study of modal systems as independent industries and given only cursory attention to the relevance of circumstances surrounding them.

Until recently, the approach in New England has been based firmly on the economic role of transportation infrastructure. Appalachia, in contrast, has emphasized the use of its planned infrastructure in the more contemporary idiom of carrying people, and has claimed the economic importance of the improvements as emanating from that function.

Moving into the domain of the New England Commission itself, the first comprehensive report it received on transportation was in 1968.[30] This report, which primarily expands the format of previous studies, deals at length with the railroads, suggesting consolidation once again to ameliorate the region's disproportionately high transport costs. Aviation is considered and recommendations made based on studies of origins and destinations, mileage distances, and costs; recommendations are also made for the consideration of a region wide system of airports for stimulating selective local development. There are also brief reviews of port capacities, especially with a view to the possibilities for containerization and pipeline transportation.

In general, then, the background of consideration of the region's transportation systems in isolation from the social and economic systems they serve is a posture maintained in this report. The only substantive regional project proposed is an East-West Highway across the northern part of the region.

At the present time, the New England Commission is noticeably changing strategies. It is apparent that it has sensed the confinement of considering regional transportation in the context only of the health of a set of industries, especially given the political and social mood of the nation at present. Concentrated efforts among its current activities include study of the proposed East-West Highway through the less developed, northern part of the region. Consultants are attempting to derive estimates of the developmental impacts of this proposed highway from Amsterdam, N.Y., to Calais, Maine, and to choose among the three proposed locations for it based on those criteria.

There is also a project under study to revive rail passenger service within the region. This is a courageous effort (present rail passenger service within New England is nil) undertaken by the Geo-Transport Foundation in the expectation of support from the new National Railroad Passenger Corporation. This will be the main emphasis in railroad planning, although the Commission has begun to study freight movement also. It is undertaken with the assumption that if the scheme will not work in the densely urbanized New England region, there will be little hope for it as a non-corridor scheme anywhere. Early stages of the project will attempt service improvements as a matter of encouraging use. In later stages effort will be made to introduce new rail technology on an experimental basis.

These new initiatives by the New England Regional Commission are elemental, but seem the beginning of a focus that is the interesting one for a regional development agency. If we assume, as concluded in the section on state planning, that highway planning is a practically inalienable domain of the states, except in cases where highly cohesive interstate corridor linkages are involved, then the development of a relationship between larger scale networks and the social/economic development of regions is more properly the problem of regional agencies.

One of the Commission's recent interests most closely related to transportation has been its studies on the decentralization of economic development away from the metropolitan cities of the region and into selected smaller towns that seem to have good growth potential. Consultant reports, however, were not encouraging about this general strategy, since, among other reasons, it counter-vails prevalent trends and thrusts on the smaller cities development requirements that they are unlikely to be able to handle.[31] Thus, this strategy, which might have been related to transportation development, is likely to be confined just to special cases, such as balancing the seasonality of activity in resort towns.

The problem is a difficult one. There has as yet emerged no means of systematically relating these modes to each other in New England (or anywhere else), much less to the other enterprises of the Commission in industrial development, human resources, and environmental management. With respect to modes represented regionally only by terminals—air and water—the problems of gauging impact and controlling performance are limiting. Consideration of the railroads in this manner has been limited by their moribund condition. As long as substantial service increases (outside of commuting services) cannot be managed, and in view of the fact that surely no one is thinking of building new trackage, there is no way to get a clear view of their economic and social significance. The experimental intraregional passenger service could reveal new possibilities.

Concluding Remarks

The role of transportation in political and professional thinking is in a bewildering state of change. We are emerging from the period in which it was the natural noncontroversial sector for the expenditure of large amounts of money in visible infrastructure believed to be beneficial to all, an era in which it was backed by powerful and largely unopposed industrial lobbies, and considered to be—ironically—both the foremost problem of the cities and the foremost accomplishment of the nation. Attachments to the almost mystic value of transportation have appeared even in interpretations of national history, which can be traced by the development of colonial trade routes, the appearance of great canals, the conquest of the frontier by rails and of national isolation by airways, and finally the attainment of international supremacy by space travel.

We are at an end of this. Geographical mobility is, in general, no longer a high priority problem. Intraurban access and land development compatibilities have been subordinated to more urgent problems. The belief is waning that highways will cause development and prosperity to spring up in their path wherever they go. The proposition of supersonic transport creates more concern for noise than anticipation of swift arrivals.

This situation leaves difficult problems for the interpretation of even recent experience in regional transportation policymaking as to its application to the future.

During our review we have suspended the normative question of what kind of transportation planning we want. We did discover that the desires that generated the kinds of agencies discussed were rarely realized by their performance. National legislation has typically used the terms "balanced" and "comprehensive," but the contexts invariably show them to be faint ambitions rather than real objectives. Use of the terms again in the multi-state region bill notwithstanding, we are in no position at present "to develop a comprehensive national transportation system." The states are too strong and mediation of their interests is difficult. The intermodal and intersectoral problems remain largely unsolved, both analytically and institutionally.

The review does, however, indicate a series of key options in the development of regional transportation planning. A summary of them suggests opportunities and constraints for future attempts.

Administrative coherence versus functionality. Regions that are highly coherent from the administrative point of view (e.g., the states) offer much better means of implementation, more responsiveness to client users, and better opportunities for intersectoral collaboration. The functional regions (corridors and metropolitan areas) provide greater leverage on analytic solution and may be the only means of solving the more important problems, but they suffer unfortunate implementation disadvantages.

This situation suggests two points. First, the states are preferable as planning and implementation regions for the problems they can encompass. All the planning that can be done at the state level should surely be left there, even when inviting but elusive social and economic relationships suggest some kind of completeness on a larger scale. This has emerged at various points from our review. If the planning authority of the states is to be limited by a multistate agency, it must be done for very good reason, and even then probably with limited effectiveness and tenuous permanence. In particular, it seems clear that highways must be planned at the state level, except in cases of extraordinary development opportunity (e.g., possibly the East-West Highway in Northern New England). The definition of such opportunities deserves further investigation. On the other hand, it is clear that the stronger network closure offered at a larger scale by the railroads makes them a multistate problem, the management of which causes little imposition on the domain of the states. The break points in scale for other transportation modes—air terminals and pipelines, for example—require systematic investigation that the topic, to our knowledge, has not received.

The second point is that it is probably better for a region to be very functional or very coherent administratively, than to occupy a compromise position between the two criteria. Our cases most closely representing this compromise position are the economic development regions, which are good attempts to encompass relevant problems, but which from the transportation point of view suffer from the lack of both administrative and functional unity.

Problem orientation versus open search for solution. The option of identifying a concrete, necessarily simplistic problem in a region for the purpose of policy-making (e.g., metropolitan areas and corridors), as opposed to creating a general purpose agency that conducts an open search for regional policies (e.g., the economic development agencies) is another important alternative. It is unfortunate that we have no good case of a problem-oriented agency in a context of unified administrative possibilities; it appears that the lack of the latter is an important generative factor in the creation of problem orientation.

There seems no alternative for the open search agencies but to have very strong special implementation powers. Only the states among current experiences of this type show really good signs of successfully developing this kind of approach, though it is not yet very far advanced. More time is needed to evaluate how well the economic development regions perform this activity, but their difficulties to date, and the fact that the most promising of them were reviewed, create little confidence that an expanded number of such regions could successfully pursue open search for solutions. Experimentation at the metropolitan level, as described in the review, may show some possibilities, but the situation at present is not encouraging.

These circumstances suggest the possibility of creating short-term and well-funded special agencies to solve specific regional problems. These would be agencies created, say, to deal with a specific problem such as railroad service in a multistate region by quickly extracting the analytic information necessary to solve the problem in concert with conditions initially specified in a problem statement, designing a solution, and leaving the implementation responsibilities to regular operating agencies. After implementation has indicated the effect of this solution on the region, a new temporary agency could be created for the same multistate region, or an otherwise-defined overlapping one, to take a new clearly-oriented cut at a problem.

It is not appropriate to attempt further elaboration of the short term agency idea here. It emerges logically from our analysis because problem orientation seems to insure the strongest contribution and greatest likelihood of success, but over time a number of different problems must be engaged to provide comprehensive treatment. Thus, a sequence of such short-term, sharply focused efforts, possibly under the aegis of a general open search agency, might create the effect of comprehensiveness over the long term. The Appalachian Commission seems to be following this pattern with its emphasis on transportation as a means of development, particularly during its early years, and its limited term of existence. The creation of the Geo-Transport Foundation by the New England Commission to investigate certain problems of regional transportation might be taken as one model of the intent expressed here.

As a general organizational method, the short term agency clearly imposes a series of problems. It could result in piecemeal approaches to problems that exacerbate current problems of collaboration. Special means would have to be developed to avoid the tendency for self-perpetuation of successful short-term agencies. But means should be found of taking advantage of the special coherence of problem orientation without imposing a narrow perspective on the development of a complex region for a long period of time.

Change orientation versus allocation orientation. We define change orientation as a process that strives for a qualitatively different form for the involved social or physical situations, such as the Northeast Corridor intent to introduce new technology, or the Appalachian intent to change an existing social pattern more desirable or the Appalachian intent to change an existing social pattern among the standard channels and attempts, in terms of transportation, to lubricate the existing system by removing impediments and raising its efficiency without altering major system characteristics. The cases of metropolitan planning and the work of most state agencies serve as examples of the latter approach among the experiences reviewed. No agency, of course, is a pure case of either of these orientations, and the distinctions between them are blurred with regard to many specific policies.

Most of the influences that generate change-oriented efforts have to do with the commitments of the society and its politics, and as such are beyond the scope of this paper. It is difficult to say whether a national commitment to social problems is growing and what implications it might have for transportation. We shall only say that, if it is growing, change orientation becomes the more possible; whereas problem orientation, as mentioned in the last item, may have greater prospects for success than otherwise suspected. Then regions organized functionally to problems central to the nation's concerns may be increasingly advisable. This broad, intractable effect may be the most important issue in the future of transportation planning.

This has been an introductory study. The complex undertakings represented by the regional agencies reviewed required further and closer examination to determine confidently their accomplishments, limitations, and prospects. Nevertheless, useful indications have emerged.

They suggest, among the possibilities for regional transportation planning in the United States, that state planning should be advanced toward the accomplishments that the states' ample breadth of powers makes possible. It is the area where the deficit of good analytical tools and strategic procedure is most evident and the one that would profit the most quickly from expertise of this sort. It is clear that the Federal Government should provide guidance for interstate collaboration, but except in special cases this apparently does not imply multi-state agencies that would add another level to the hierarchy.

Metropolitan transportation planning appears to be in limbo. It needs to be retooled. But we must await evidence from such creative undertakings as the Boston Restudy to be sure of appropriate directions. Meanwhile, methodological studies on the matter are worthy of attention. Care must be taken with the natural tendency for metropolitan planning techniques to be exported to the regional planning agencies, so that recipients are aware of previously discovered limitations on these techniques. Whether the current concerns will produce metropolitan regions that are larger than the present ones and of a scale appropriate to regionalization at the multi-state level remains to be seen. Investigations of the usefulness of such larger metropolitan regions would repay the effort because of the aforementioned pressures in this direction. In view of the coherence of the regions, and the size of the investment at stake, metropolitan planning clearly must be continued.

Corridor planning is clearly confined in applicability to the two largest ones. Any further "corridors" would be planned by means basically different from the Northeast Corridor, and appear to have very doubtful prospects of success. But the Northeast Corridor—or the sections of it above and below New York, if one prefers—is as viable a planning region as can be established on a multistate level. Its important contributions to choice of technology may well constitute an important contribution to the field, and enhance the feasibility of various kinds of regional transportation planning in the future.

The experiment of economic development regions is not yet complete. There have been important evolutionary changes in their approaches that require fuller evaluation and the generating of further evidence before they can be properly qualified as transportation planning regions. The fact that they are organized to meet the highest priority problems of policy at this scale recommends the use of resources to give them the best possible opportunities for success. These remarks apply, however, only to the most viable of them. There seems little hope for a number of additional ones to attain a good level of effectiveness.

The approach of this paper has been confining as a means of generating concepts for future regional transportation planning. If, instead of reviewing existing efforts, we had taken a course such as the assembly of specific transport markets over geographical space, by mode and activity system, different conclusions might have emerged. Conceivably, a territorial problem might have appeared that would have been so compelling as to recommend a new kind of agency that would break through the the obstacles we have cited.

We find little basis here, however, for encouraging the creation of much more widespread regionalization for transportation planning, such as an exhaustive regionalization of the United States. If real warrant exists, it has not been discovered here.

Notes

1. Secretary John Volpe's "Statement before the Senate Commerce Committee Regarding S. 2425," on April 15, 1970 is a well argued position of this type with reference to the proposed multi-state regions.

2. The basic codification of this approach appeared in Robert B. Mitchell and Chester Rapkin, URBAN TRAFFIC: A FUNCTION OF LAND USE, Columbia University Press, New York, 1956.

3. The first generation of them are reviewed in Richard M. Zettel and Richard R. Carll, SUMMARY REVIEW OF MAJOR METROPOLITAN AREA TRANSPORTATION STUDIES IN THE UNITED STATES, Institute of Transportation and Traffic Engineering, University of California, Berkeley, 1962.

4. Some of the most articulate critics have been David E. Boyce, et al., David Seidman, and Aaron Fleisher. See the bibliography.

5. A number of suggestions have been made about the forms of such extended metropolitan regions. See, for example, John Friedmann and John Miller, Constandinos Doxiadis, and Richard L. Meier in the bibliography.

6. David E. Boyce, et al., METROPOLITAN PLAN MAKING, p. 111. See bibliography.

7. John Friedmann and John Miller, "The Urban Field," JOURNAL OF THE AMERICAN INSTITUTE OF PLANNERS, November 1965.

8. Among his 55 to 60 Daily Urban Systems, approximately 25 are multi-state areas. Constandinos Doxiadis, in NATIONAL TRANSPORTATION ACT, HEARINGS BEFORE THE COMMITTEE ON COMMERCE, UNITED STATES SENATE . . . ON S. 2425, 1970.

9. Richard L. Meier, MEGALOPOLIS FORMATION IN THE MIDWEST, Regional Development Studies V, School of Natural Resources, University of Michigan, Ann Arbor, 1965.

10. This issue is discussed in more detail by Aaron Fleisher in "Influence of Technology on Urban Forms," in Lloyd Rodwin (ed.), THE FUTURE METROPOLIS, J. Braziller, New York, 1961.

11. Melvin Levin, "The Big Regions," JOURNAL OF THE AMERICAN INSTITUTE OF PLANNERS, Vol. 34, No. 2, March 1968, p. 68.

12. The only exception to this appears to be the case of New York City. Information on this matter was reviewed by Karl Robard, thesis draft, MIT, 1970. His review included: City of Philadelphia, GROUND TRANSPORTATION TO PHILADELPHIA INTERNATIONAL AIRPORT—NOW TO 1992, 1968; Port of N.Y. Authority, DOMESTIC INFLIGHT SURVEY, 1967-1968; 1969; Office of High Speed Ground Transportation, DOT, WASHINGTON-BALTIMORE AIRPORT ACCESS SURVEY, GRP, 1968; McLeod, A COMPREHENSIVE SURVEY OF PASSENGERS FLYING FROM TORONTO INTERNATIONAL AIRPORT, MAY-JUNE 1968, Institute for Aerospace Studies, University of Toronto, Tech. Note 141, 1969; Landrum and Brown (consultants), LOS ANGELES INTERNATIONAL AIRPORT ACCESS SURVEY, Cincinnati, March 1968; Port of N.Y. Authority, NEW YORK'S DOMESTIC AIR PASSENGER MARKET, 1965.

13. The problem receives comprehensive and case-descriptive attention in Kenneth R. Geiser, Jr., URBAN TRANSPORTATION DECISION MAKING: POLITICAL PROCESSES OF URBAN FREEWAY CONTROVERSIES, The Urban Systems Laboratory of MIT, Cambridge, 1970. New efforts to solve the

problem have been attempted by the Bureau of Public Roads in the form of Joint Development Programs in cooperation with other federal agencies. Among the most important research projects taking place at the present time is the Highways and Community Values Project at the Urban Systems Laboratory of MIT under the direction of Professor Marvin Manheim.

14. See the AMERICAN INSTITUTE OF PLANNERS' NEWSLETTER, Vol. 5, No. 11, November 1970.

15. A recent well reasoned position on the appointment of a strong state secretary of transportation was developed by the Governor's Task Force on Transportation (Massachusetts), headed by Alan A. Altshuler. See REPORT TO GOVERNOR SARGENT, Part II, The Task Force, Boston, June 1970.

16. Public Works Committee, U.S. Senate, SENATE SUBCOMMITTEE HEARINGS OF THE PUBLIC WORKS COMMITTEE ON ECONOMIC DEVELOPMENT REGIONS, U.S. Government Printing Office, Washington, D.C., 1967, p. 101.

17. David E. Boyce, et al., METROPOLITAN PLAN MAKING, op. cit.

18. National Capital Transportation Agency, RECOMMENDATIONS FOR TRANSPORTATION IN THE NATIONAL CAPITAL REGION, November 1962.

19. Penn-Jersey Transportation Study, PROSPECTUS SUPPLEMENT, The Study, Philadelphia, 1960.

20. Tri-State Transportation Commission, REGIONAL DEVELOPMENT GUIDE, The Commission, New York, October 1968.

21. An excellent case study of this experience appears in David E. Boyce, et al., METROPOLITAN PLAN MAKING, Study Summary VII, pp. 406-426.

22. Marvin L. Manheim, et al., SEARCH AND CHOICE IN TRANSPORT SYSTEMS PLANNING: SUMMARY REPORT, MIT School of Engineering, Cambridge, June 1968, pp. 65-158.

23. U.S. Department of Transportation, NATIONAL TRANSPORTATION MANUAL, Manual A, General Instructions, Government Printing Office, Washington, D.C., July 1970. There are more manuals detailing the general instructions in the first: B. Highway Functional Classification and Needs Study, C. Urban Public Transit, and D. Airports and Other Terminals.

24. Appalachian Regional Commission, ANNUAL REPORT 1968, U.S. Government Printing Office, Washington, D.C., 1969, p. 2.

25. Committee on Public Works, House of Representatives, ECONOMIC DEVELOPMENT ACTS, U.S. Government Printing Office, Washington, D.C., 1967, p. 21.

26. Appalachian Regional Commission, STATE AND REGIONAL DEVELOPMENT PLANS IN APPALACHIA, U.S. Government Printing Office, Washington, D.C., 1968, p. 49.

27. Ibid., passim.

28. Much of this literature is usefully synopsized in New England Economic

Research Foundation for the U.S. Department of Commerce, REVIEW OF REGIONAL ECONOMIC RESEARCH AND PLANNING ON NEW ENGLAND, U.S. Government Printing Office, Washington, D.C. (no date—1968?).

29. Ibid., p. i.

30. New England Regional Commission, REGIONAL TRANSPORTATION NEEDS, prepared by the Systems Analysis and Research Corporation, The Commission, Boston, 1968.

31. Real Estate Research Corporation, THE DEVELOPMENT AND ECOLOGY OF SMALL-URBAN NEW ENGLAND, The New England Regional Commission, Boston, August 1970.

Bibliography

The Metropolitan Agencies

Boyce, D.E., N.O. Day, and Chris McDonald, METROPOLITAN PLAN MAKING: AN ANALYSIS OF EXPERIENCE WITH THE PREPARATION AND EVALUATION OF ALTERNATIVE LAND USE AND TRANSPORTATION PLANS, Regional Science Research Institute, Philadelphia, 1970.

Creighton, R.L., "Have We Learned Anything From Transportation Studies?" PLANNING 1963, American Society of Planning Officials, Chicago, 1963, pp. 181-185.

DeLeuw, Cather and Associates, Report to National Capital Transportation Agency on RAIL RAPID TRANSIT ON THE ALEXANDRIA-SPRINGFIELD ROUTE, March 1963.

National Capital Transportation Agency, Appendix to the 1962 Report, ORGANIZATION AND FINANCE, Vol. 6, Washington, November 2, 1962.

————, RAIL RAPID TRANSIT FOR THE NATION'S CAPITAL, Washington, January 1965.

————, RECOMMENDATIONS FOR TRANSPORTATION IN THE CAPITAL REGION, FINANCE AND ORGANIZATION, Washington, No. 1, 1962.

————, THE REGIONAL DEVELOPMENT GUIDE, 1966-2000, Washington, June 1966.

Penn-Jersey Transportation Study, PENN-JERSEY AREA SYSTEMS by Britton Harris, P-J Papers, No. 14 (February 8, 1962); REPORT ON THE ACTIVITIES ALLOCATION MODEL by David R. Seidman, P-J Papers No. 22 (November 1964).

————, REPORT ON STUDY PROCEDURES, DATA COLLECTION PHASE, P-J Reports, No. 1, Philadelphia, March 1961.

————, P-J Reports, VOLUME 1, THE STATE OF THE REGION, April 1964; VOLUME 2, 1975 PROJECTIONS, September 1964; VOLUME 3, 1975 TRANSPORTATION PLANS, May 1965.

Rodwin, Lloyd, "New Towns, Urban Strategies and Transportation," WORKSHOP ON TRANSPORTATION FOR NEW TOWNS AND COMMUNITIES, Institute of Public Administration, New York, 1969.

Seidman, D.R., THE CONSTRUCTION OF AN URBAN GROWTH MODEL, DVPRC Report No. 1, Delaware Valley Regional Planning Commission, Philadelphia, 1969.

Tri-State Transportation Commission, ANNUAL REPORT, 1969, New York, August 1969.

————, ANNUAL REPORT, 1970, New York, September 1970.

————, DESIGNS FOR GROWTH, A REPORT ON THE TRI-STATE TRANSPORTATION COMMITTEE 1961-1966, New York, May 1967.

341

Tri-State Transportation Commission, MEASURE OF A REGION, New York, May 1967.

———, REGIONAL DEVELOPMENT ALTERNATIVES, New York, March 1967.

———, REGIONAL DEVELOPMENT GUIDE, GOALS AND PLAN FOR THE TRI-STATE REGION, New York, October 1968.

———, REGIONAL FORECAST, 1985: THE FUTURE SIZE AND NEEDS OF THE TRI-STATE REGION, New York, December 1967.

———, TRI-STATE TRANSPORTATION 1985: AN INTERIM PLAN, New York, May 1966.

———, Mass Transportation Demonstration Grant Projects—Final Reports: PARK'N RIDE RAIL SERVICE, May 1967; COORDINATED BUS RAIL SERVICE, June 1965; STATION FARE COLLECTION, June 1965; SUBURBAN SERVICE ADJUSTMENT, New York City, November 1967.

U.S. Statutes at Large, 86th Congress Bill No. 86-669, 1960; 89th Congress Bills Nos. 89-774, 89-173, 1965-66. Bills giving origins and powers of NCTA, WMATC, WMATA.

Watt, P.C., and S.O. Carroll, "The Tri-State Regional Planning Program," PLANNING 1970, American Society of Planning Officials, Chicago, 1970, pp. 193-198.

Zettel, R.M., and R.R. Carll, SUMMARY REVIEW OF MAJOR METROPOLITAN AREA TRANSPORTATION STUDIES IN THE UNITED STATES, University of California at Berkeley, 1962.

Corridor Transportation Planning

Barton-Aschman Associates, Inc., GUIDELINES FOR NEW SYSTEMS OF URBAN TRANSPORTATION, VOLUME 1: URBAN NEEDS AND POTENTIALS, prepared for the United States Department of Housing and Urban Development, May 1969.

———, JOINT PROJECT CONCEPT, INTEGRATED TRANSPORTATION CORRIDORS, prepared for the United States Department of Housing and Urban Development, Chicago, January 1968.

Bruck, H.W., S.H. Putnam, and W.A. Steger, "Evaluation of Alternative Transportation Proposals: The Northeast Corridor," JOURNAL OF THE AMERICAN INSTITUTE OF PLANNERS, Vol. 33, No. 6, November 1966, pp. 322-333.

Manheim, M.L., and E.R. Ruiter, SEARCH AND CHOICE IN TRANSPORTATION SYSTEMS PLANNING, Summary Report, M.I.T., Department of Civil Engineering, June 1968.

M.I.T., THE GLIDEWAY SYSTEM, Interdepartmental Student Project in Systems Engineering, 1965.

————, HIGH SPEED GROUND TRANSPORT, Survey of Technology, Part 1, June 1965.

Meier, R.L., MEGALOPOLIS FORMATION IN THE MIDWEST, Regional Development Studies, 5, School of Natural Resources, University of Michigan, December 1965.

Peat, Marwick, Livingston and Company, NORTHEAST CORRIDOR TRANSPORTATION: PROBLEMS AND PROSPECTS, Northeast Corridor Transportation Project Report No. 210, Department of Transportation.

————, STATUS OF THE TRANSPORTATION SYSTEM AND PLANS IMPROVING INTERCITY TRANSPORTATION IN THE NORTHEAST CORRIDOR, Northeast Corridor Transportation Project Report No. 211, Office of High Speed Ground Transport, U.S. Department of Transportation, December 1969.

Putnam, S.T., E.H. Greenman, S.T. Libson, D.L. Marshall, S. Rapport, and W. Steger, CONSAD Research Corporation IMPACT STUDIES, Northeast Corridor Transportation Project Report No. 218, Volume 4, Part A, Office of High Speed Ground Transport, U.S. Department of Transportation.

Rothenburg, M.J., NORTHEAST CORRIDOR TRANSPORTATION FACTS AND STATISTICS, Northeast Corridor Transportation Project Report No. 212, Office of High Speed Ground Transport, U.S. Department of Transportation.

Ruiter, E.R., "Prototype Analysis," SEARCH AND CHOICE IN TRANSPORTATION SYSTEMS PLANNING, Volume 2, M.I.T., Department of Civil Engineering, Cambridge, June 1969.

U.S. Department of Transportation, Office of High Speed Ground Transport, NORTHEAST CORRIDOR TRANSPORTATION PROJECT REPORT, SUMMARY REPORT, Washington, April 1970.

————, Office of the Secretary, CORRIDOR TASK FORCE REPORT FOR THE OFFICE OF THE ASSISTANT SECRETARY FOR POLICY DEVELOPMENT, Washington, June 12, 1968.

State Transportation Planning

California. Business and Transportation Agency, CALIFORNIA STATE HIGHWAY SYSTEM-FINANCING, Sacramento, January 1970.

————, Department of Public Works, THE CALIFORNIA FREEWAY AND EXPRESSWAY SYSTEM, 1968 PROGRESS AND PROBLEMS REPORT, Sacramento, March 1969.

————, Division of Highways, PRELIMINARY DRAFT OF THE ANNUAL HIGHWAY PLANNING REPORT, Sacramento, August 1970.

Governor's Task Force on Transportation, REPORT, Sacramento, November 1968.

Connecticut. Connecticut Interregional Planning Program, CONNECTICUT: CHOICES FOR ACTION, Chapter 1, "Transportation," Chapter 2, "Highlights," and Chapter 3, "Goals and Objectives," 1967.

State Highway Department, PLANNING FOR THE FUTURE: CONNECTICUT'S MAJOR CORRIDOR NEEDS, PRESENT TO YEAR 2000, Hartford, September 1968.

Massachusetts. Governor's Task Force on Transportation, REPORT TO GOVERNOR SARGENT ON IMMEDIATE ACTION OPPORTUNITIES, Boston, January 1970, PART II, Boston, June 1970.

New Jersey. State Department of Transportation, A STATEMENT ON TRANSPORTATION, Trenton, January 1970.

U.S. Department of Transportation, NATIONAL TRANSPORTATION PLANNING MANUAL; A. GENERAL INSTRUCTIONS, U.S. Government Printing Office, Washington, D.C., July 1970.

Wisconsin. State Highway Commission of Wisconsin, HIGHWAYS NO. 11: THE PLAN, Wisconsin Development Series, Madison, 1968.

Wyoming. State Highway Department, STATEWIDE HIGHWAY TRANSPORTATION PLANNING PROCESS, ANNUAL REPORT 1969, Cheyenne, January 29, 1970.

Economic Development Regions

Ford, T.R., (ed.), THE SOUTHERN APPALACHIAN REGION: A SURVEY, University of Kentucky Press, Lexington, 1962.

Fromm, Gary (ed.), TRANSPORT INVESTMENT AND ECONOMIC DEVELOPMENT, Brookings Institution, Washington, 1965.

Ganz, Alexander, NEW ENGLAND URBAN DEVELOPMENT, New England Regional Commission, New England Research Foundation, Boston, 1969.

Haefele, Edwin T. "Transport Planning and National Goals," in Edwin T. Haefele (ed.) TRANSPORT AND NATIONAL GOALS, Brookings Institution, Washington, 1969.

Harwitz, Mitchell, and A.P. Hurter, TRANSPORTATION AND THE ECONOMY OF THE APPALACHIAN REGION, Transportation Center of Northwestern University, Transportation Center Report No. 66, Evanston, Illinois, 1964.

Levin, M.R., "The Big Regions," JOURNAL OF THE AMERICAN INSTITUTE OF PLANNERS, Vol. 34, No. 2, March 1968.

New England Governor's Committee on Public Transportation, PUBLIC TRANSPORTATION FOR NEW ENGLAND, reports submitted to the New England Governor's Conference 1955-57, Boston, November 1957.

New England Regional Commission, ANNUAL REPORT 1967, Washington, 1967.

_____, ANNUAL REPORT 1968, Washington, 1968.

————, REGIONAL TRANSPORTATION NEEDS, prepared by the Systems Analysis and Research Corporation, November 1968.

————, STATEMENT AND SCHEDULE OF WORK, Part II, Section F, "The East-West Highway Study," Boston, 1970.

Pegrum, D.F., TRANSPORTATION ECONOMICS AND PUBLIC POLICY, Richard D. Irwin, Inc., Homewood, Ill., 1963.

U.S. Appalachian Regional Commission, ANNUAL REPORT 1968.

————, ANNUAL REPORT, 1969.

————, STATE AND REGIONAL DEVELOPMENT PLANS IN APPA-LACHIA, U.S. Government Printing Office, Washington, D.C., 1968.

U.S. Congress, ECONOMIC DEVELOPMENT PROGRAMS UNDER JURIS-DICTION OF THE COMMITTEE ON PUBLIC WORKS, U.S. House of Representatives, U.S. Government Printing Office, Washington, D.C., June 1970.

U.S. Department of Commerce, Economic Development Administration, AN-NUAL REPORT, 1967, Washington, 1967.

————, REVIEW OF REGIONAL ECONOMIC RESEARCH AND PLANNING ON NEW ENGLAND, prepared by the New England Economic Research Foundation, U.S. Government Printing Office, Washington, D.C., 1967.

————, Office of Regional Economic Development, NEW ENGLAND DEVEL-OPMENT BIBLIOGRAPHY, prepared by the Area Development Center of Boston University, U.S. Government Printing Office, Washington, D.C., 1966.

U.S. House of Representatives, ECONOMIC DEVELOPMENT PROGRAMS, U.S. Government Printing Office, Washington, D.C., June 1970.

U.S. President's Appalachian Regional Commission, APPALACHIA, A REPORT, 1964, U.S. Government Printing Office, Washington, D.C., 1964.

U.S. Senate, Committee on Public Works, ECONOMIC DEVELOPMENT ACTS, U.S. Government Printing Office, Washington, D.C., October 1967.

————, HEARINGS OF SPECIAL SUBCOMMITTEE ON ECONOMIC DEVELOPMENT, January 24, 25, 26, 31; February 1, 2, 3; September 25, 26, 27, 1967 and January 19, 21, 1968.

————, REGIONAL ECONOMIC DEVELOPMENT LEGISLATION, July 3, 1969.

————, REVISING AND EXTENDING THE APPALACHIAN REGIONAL DEVELOPMENT ACT, April 6, 1967.

————, SUMMARY OF LEGISLATIVE ACTIVITIES AND ACCOMPLISH-MENTS, December 31, 1966.

Wilson, George (ed.), THE IMPACT OF HIGHWAY INVESTMENT ON DEVEL-OPMENT, Brookings Institution, Washington, 1967.

The Focal Regions—Ports

Association of American Railroads, ECONOMIC AND TRANSPORTATION PROSPECTS, January 1946.

Corps of Engineers, U.S. Army, THE PORT OF NEW YORK, N.Y. and N.J., U.S. Government Printing Office, Washington, D.C., 1966.

_____, PORTS ON LAKE MICHIGAN, U.S. Government Printing Office, Washington, D.C., 1962.

Fogel, Robert, RAILROADS AND AMERICAN ECONOMIC GROWTH: ESSAYS IN ECONOMETRIC HISTORY, Johns Hopkins Press, Baltimore, 1964.

Hedden, Walter, MISSION: PORT DEVELOPMENT . . . WITH CASE STUDIES, American Association of Port Authorities, Washington, 1967.

Metcalfe, James, THE PRINCIPLES OF OCEAN TRANSPORTATION, Simmons-Boardman Publishing Co., New York, 1959.

National Academy of Sciences–National Research Council, INLAND AND MARITIME TRANSPORTATION OF UNITIZED CARGO, Washington, 1963.

O'Loughlin, Carleen, THE ECONOMICS OF SEA TRANSPORT, Pergamon Press, Inc., New York, 1967.

Robard, Karl, "Airport Development and Environmental Quality," Dissertation draft, M.I.T., unpublished.

U.S. Department of Commerce, Maritime Administration, UNITED STATES SEAPORTS: ATLANTIC COAST, U.S. Government Printing Office, Washington, D.C., 1963.

The Focal Regions–Airports

Civil Aeronautics Board, "New England Regional Airport Investigation," Docket 13494, et al., June 5, 1964.

The Port of New York Authority, AIRPORT REQUIREMENTS AND SITES TO SERVE THE NEW JERSEY-NEW YORK METROPOLITAN REGION, New York, December 1966.

_____, A REPORT ON AIRPORT REQUIREMENTS AND SITES IN THE METROPOLITAN NEW JERSEY-NEW YORK REGION, New York, May 1961.

The Thompson and Lichtner Co., Inc., SUMMARY REPORT: A MASTER PLAN FOR REGIONAL AIRPORTS TO SERVE SCHEDULED AIR TRANSPORTATION NEEDS OF NEW ENGLAND, prepared for the New England Council, Boston, June 1961.

Tri-State Transportation Committee, GENERAL AVIATION AIRPORTS FOR THE FUTURE, New York, March 1965.

8

The Future and Its Implications for Regional Transportation Planning

John R. Meyer,
*National Bureau of Economic
Research and Yale University*

Introduction and Statement of Methods

The design of a proper framework for transport planning has never been well understood. Among the many difficulties are specifying the objectives, reconciling different objectives where they conflict, determining the relationship between different policy instruments and their consequences, and, perhaps most basically of all, understanding the simple functional relationships between transport and economic development. The difficulties of these chores has always been heightened by the fact that transport tends to be one of the most interdependent or interactive of man's systems: modifications in one part of a transport network can have many unexpected or unforeseen ramifications elsewhere in the network and can condition economic development in many diffuse ways that are difficult to forecast.

A further complication is simply that transport technologies have hardly been static, so that any specification of the underlying behavioral relationships could quickly become dated. Indeed, transport technologies have been among the most rapidly changing in our society. The airplane and the internal combustion engine in the automobile, bus, and truck are perhaps the most dramatic representations of these changes, but they hardly exhaust the list: the pipeline, the giant bulk-cargo ship, long-distance high-voltage power transmission grids, containerized freight, and the diesel engine are less dramatic but also highly important technological developments in transportation. Perhaps the best single indication of the extent and scope of this technological change is that the average rate of productivity increase per unit of labor in transport has been estimated to be about 6 percent per year in the twentieth century, while the overall average for the economy has been placed at approximately 3 percent per year.[1]

A striking aspect of transportation that heightens the appeal of a planned or controlled approach to its development is that transport is an activity with many obvious externalities, both negative and positive. It is clear, for example, that transport developments bestow upon adjacent property either heightened values due to increased accessibility, or reduced values due to noise, smog, or other blights.

347

It is, then, within this framework of interdependencies, technological change, conflicting objectives, and externalities that an appeal for a "regional" approach to transportation planning must be fitted. Interdependencies suggest a regional or geographic framework of sufficient scope to embody the major interactions of importance for a particular planning objective. Rapid technological change suggests that what would be appropriate at one time as a proper functional area for planning may not be appropriate at another. Multiplicity or conflict of objectives would suggest that a region that is appropriate for one planning purpose may not be appropriate for another. Externalities would suggest that the region be sufficiently extensive to incorporate all the major external ramifications that can emanate from any transport modification or development under consideration.

The particular emphasis of this paper will be upon technological or other expected changes that can have implications for regional transportation planning. In particular, this paper will discuss the implications of future developments—ranging from transportation technology to population distribution to changes in industrial location—that may have implications for the efficacy of regional transportation planning.

In short, this paper is concerned with what one might describe as the "trends in transportation." Obviously, this is a very broad topic. To do it less than superficially requires a systematic analysis of all those forces that might be expected to condition the demands for various modes of transportation over the next few years. Obviously, this is no small task and one which to be done at all properly requires some sort of analytic framework.

An Analytic Framework for Forecasting Transport Demands

Certain techniques are conventionally used in estimating future transportation demands. These are summarized in rough schematic form in Figure 8-1. In essence, this is a flow chart of a conventional demand forecasting model for transportation services.

The demand for transportation usually arises because of technological relationships or needs involved in the production, distribution, and consumption of other goods and services. This principle applies almost without exception to freight transportation; it applies with only minor exceptions to passenger transportation. The obvious first step, therefore, as shown on the left hand margin of Figure 8-1, when estimating future requirements for various kinds of transportation services is to estimate what people would produce, distribute, and consume and where they will do so.

In order to do this, some systematic analysis is needed of the present and potential economic base of the area or economy under inspection. The emphasis of these "base analyses" may vary, needless to say, depending on whether one is

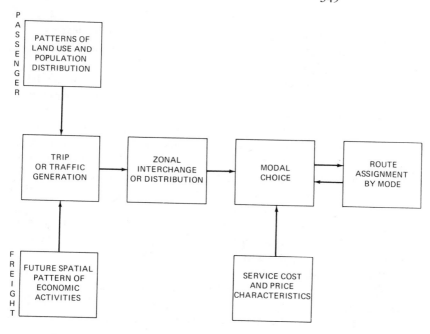

Figure 8-1. Demand forecasting model

primarily interested in projecting passenger or freight activity—though it should be recognized that the spatial location of passenger and freight traffic sources will be subject to certain common influences. In passenger studies, the emphasis is usually on the spatial distribution of population and so-called patterns of land use. For freight, the requisite economic "base survey" would normally include an appraisal of natural resources, population, labor force characteristics, and existing industrial opportunities.

The second major step in most demand forecasting exercises is to convert estimates of the future location of population and industry into physical estimates of the transportation requirements generated and terminated at different points in the geographic space under analysis. The conventional nomenclature for this exercise, as noted in Figure 8-1, is "trip generation"; in this, the emphasis is strictly on the estimated travel requirements to serve specific points in the system. For example, when forecasting freight, this means estimating how many tons of freight must be transported into a plant in order to manufacture certain commodities, and how much transport away is required to remove final goods or commodities from production sites to markets. In the case of passenger trip generation, the conventional unit of analysis will be the household and the forecasting exercise will seek to estimate how many trips the members of the household will make to school, work, places of recreation, for shopping, and so forth. In essence, the trip generation exercise provides a picture of the origins and destinations of different trip and travel demands but not of the flows or interchanges between different points within the system.

For estimating these flows or interchanges, several procedures are available. They can range all the way from very formal mathematical programming techniques to rather simple extrapolations of present flows or travel patterns. Whatever the method, the usual practice is to begin any attempt at estimating zonal interchanges by mapping the actual flows over the existing transport network, as based on the existing patterns of origins and destinations. Unfortunately, we have notoriously little data on either the patterns of origins and destinations or on these flow patterns for the U.S. economy—except for urban travel in a few selected cities for a few selected years.

The next conventional step in forecasting future transport demands is that of specifying modal choices. This requires an intensive investigation of the basic economic service characteristics of the different available systems or modes. Modal choice therefore, introduces major considerations on the supply side of the transport market, that is on the assessment of the capacity, cost, and performance of the existing or proposed transport systems. For forecasting, therefore, major technological improvements in different forms of transportation must be analyzed for their impact upon estimates of future transport requirements.

The final box in Figure 8-1, "route assignment," in essence describes a more precise form of zonal interchange in which zonal interchanges are given specific modal characteristics. The important aspect of route assignment from the standpoint of forecasting—as denoted by arrows going in both directions between route assignment and modal choice in Figure 8-1—is the fact that route assignment *does* interact with modal choice. As flows in a transportation network change, the cost and performance characteristics of the network also change. For example, as flows increase on a freight network, unit cost and service times usually are modified. Depending upon the mode and the overall volumes involved, an increase in flow may be associated with an increase or decrease in unit cost and an improvement or deterioration of service times. The point, simply, is that these effects of improvement or deterioration must be reflected back upon the modal choice and demand estimates.

Indeed, interactions and interdependencies permeate the whole framework. As noted before, improvement in transportation and other technologies can be expected to alter locational choices. These in turn can alter the basic economics of different transport systems and therefore modal choices and investor decisions to supply different kinds of transportation services. Indeed, the same can be said of any change, technological or other, that modifies the relative service cost, and price characteristics of different modes or routings. Any move toward either substantially more or less regulation of transport, for example, would almost certainly have such an impact. In fact, even a substantial reorganization of transport planning procedures, along regional rather than national lines or vice versa, might have such an impact. Accordingly, a fairly accurate demand forecast requires some specification of assumptions about technological change, regulatory procedures, the planning framework, and so forth. To some extent, then, the objective of this paper—to outline the implications of the future for regional transportation planning—poses an almost impossible task, since one might logically as well ask what are the implications of regional transportation planning for the future of transportation in general. Clearly, the hope is that future technological or regulatory changes are reasonably independent of whatever choices might be made about regional transportation planning practices; nevertheless, it should be recognized that an interdependency or specification problem exists in this matter.

Similarly, a considerable improvement in the quality of any transport demand forecast might be expected if one could reassess land use or economic base studies in the light of results obtained from performing the subsequent transport demand analyses. Unfortunately, we know very little about how to model these feedbacks or interdependencies.[2] Nevertheless, they can obviously be important and seriously condition the quality of any demand forecast one obtains.

In short, it is very difficult and hazardous to predict future patterns in transportation demands since there are so many dimensions and complexities to be comprehended. Any forecast is a guess at best and must be evaluated in that light. The analytic framework outlined in this section, hopefully, organizes these guesses somewhat more systematically than usual.

The Basic Economic, Social, and Demographic Trends Influencing Transport Demand

Population Trends

One obvious place to start when forecasting almost any economic or social phenomena is with the question of aggregate population growth, but it should be immediately recognized that demographic forecasts for the United States have long been a rather hazardous undertaking. The United States Bureau of the Census, in fact, provides different forecasts of future population growth based upon different assumptions about future birth rates. For the year 2,000, the lowest of these would place the United States population at about 260 million while the highest would be at 310 million.

The current vogue in aggregate demographic forecasts for the United States is a belief that the net reproductive rate will decline. By way of calibration, a net reproductive rate of 2.1 children per female eventually would stabilize the population. At the present time (1972) the United States figure is only very slightly above this level, so that the lower (260 million) Census forecast is perhaps the "best bet."

The economic implications of a stable population, or even of a tendency toward a stable population, derive mainly from what this would mean for the distribution of the population between different age groups. Above all, such a trend would greatly decrease the number of people in the younger age brackets, somewhat increase in relative terms those in the older age brackets, and very drastically, particularly at first, increase the relative number of people in the working ages, that is between approximately eighteen and 65 years of age. Some relevant comparisons of the age distribution effects of different population growth rates are shown in Figure 8-2. Just exactly what this change might imply for the growth and composition of transportation demand is a bit difficult to specify. There is some evidence, though, that a high rate of economic growth associated with a high birth rate tends to favor growth in freight transportation demands while a high rate of economic growth not strongly associated with a high birth rate has not been so favorable for the growth of freight transportation. Specifically, freight transport grew more rapidly than GNP in the late 1920s, declined more rapidly than GNP in the depression of the 1930s, expanded more rapidly than GNP during the post-war baby boom of 1945 to 1955, and declined quite markedly in relative terms as the economy expanded in

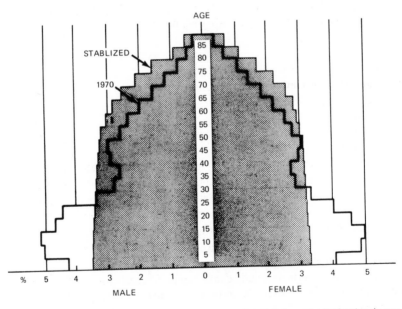

In a stablized population with low death rates, equal numbers of births and deaths, and no immigration, the number of 50-year-olds would be nearly as large as the number of 5-year-olds.

Figure 8-2. Age distribution (percent of total population)

the 1960s while the birth rate declined. To some extent these observations depend upon what one wishes to use as a measure of transportation output, but in general these conclusions seem sustained by available statistics, some of the more relevant of which are summarized in Tables 8-1 and 8-2.

The implications of a lower rate of population growth and therefore of a somewhat older population for passenger demands are not quite so obvious. However, it seems highly likely that such a shift should increase the relative demand for passenger transportation, everything else equal, because young adults, the retired, and childless families seem to travel relatively more than families with children. In particular, one might expect it to have very favorable

Table 8-1

Growth of Freight Transport Compared to Growth of GNP: 1889 to 1946

Year	Index of Freight Transport (1939=100)	GNP (Constant 1929 Dollars)
1889	16.5	27.3
1920	96	73.3
1921	72	71.6
1922	81	75.8
1923	96	85.8
1924	91	88.4
1925	97	90.5
1926	104	96.4
1927	102	97.3
1928	103	98.5
1929	108	104.4
1930	95	95.1
1931	79	89.5
1932	62	76.4
1933	68	74.2
1934	74	80.8
1935	77	91.4
1936	92	100.9
1937	101	109.1
1938	87	103.2
1939	100	111.0
1940	114	121.0
1946	176	166.8

Source: *Historical Statistics of the United States Colonial Times to 1957*, Bureau of Census Index of Transportation Output: Freight p. 427, GNP in Constant 1929 Prices, p. 139.

Table 8-2
Various Indices of the Growth of Intercity Freight

Year	GNP in $ Billions (Constant 1958 Dollars)	Tons of Intercity Freight Per $1000. of GNP (Constant Dollars)	Ton-Miles of Intercity Freight Per $1.00 of GNP (Constant Dollars)	Average Length of Haul Per Ton (Miles)	GNP in $Billions (Current Dollars)	Dollars of Intercity Freight Revenue Per $100 of GNP (Current Dollars)	Average Revenue Per Ton-Mile of all Intercity Freight (Cents)
1939	209.4	8.763	3.174	362.2	90.5		
1940	227.2	9.098	3.276	360.1	99.7		
1941	263.7	9.276	3.412	367.9	124.5		
1942	297.8	8.287	3.281	395.9	157.9		
1943	337.1	7.398	3.157	426.7	191.6		
1944	361.3	7.116	3.109	436.9	210.1	4.917	0.920
1945	355.2	7.179	3.072	427.9	211.9	4.835	0.939
1946	312.6	8.199	3.272	399.1	208.5	4.946	1.008
1947	309.9	9.571	3.638	380.1	231.3	5.717	1.173
1948	323.7	9.419	3.559	377.9	257.6	5.940	1.328
1949	324.1	8.463	3.168	374.3	256.5	5.879	1.469
1950	355.3	8.914	3.317	372.2	284.8	6.372	1.540
1951	383.4	8.954	3.388	378.4	328.4	6.126	1.549
1952	395.1	8.469	3.215	379.6	345.5	6.196	1.685
1953	412.8	8.525	3.234	379.4	364.6	6.386	1.744
1954	407.0	8.140	3.111	382.1	364.8	6.043	1.741
1955	438.0	8.292	3.264	393.6	398.0	5.936	1.652
1956	446.1	8.727	3.382	387.5	419.2	6.195	1.721

1957	452.5	8.480	3.283	387.2	441.1	6.108	1.814
1958	447.3	7.903	3.057	386.9	447.3	5.806	1.899
1959	475.9	7.739	3.005	388.3	483.7	5.654	1.912
1960	487.7	7.677	2.974	387.4	503.7	5.473	1.901
1961	497.2	7.548	2.892	383.2	520.1	5.390	1.949
1962	529.8	7.388	2.827	382.6	560.3	5.308	1.986
1963	551.0	7.416	2.863	386.1	590.5	5.245	1.963
1964	581.1	7.445	2.860	384.2	632.4	5.189	1.974
1965	617.8	7.271	2.837	390.1	684.9	5.245	2.050
1966	557.1	7.198	2.832	393.4	747.6	5.150	2.069
1967	673.1	7.069	2.773	392.2	789.7	4.922	2.083
1968	706.7		2.739		860.6		

Source: Unpublished Ph.D. dissertation of Alexander L. Morton, Harvard University.

ramifications for longer distance intercity or international travel. Of course, in the longer run, a stable population should inhibit the overall growth rate in passenger travel demands.

Perhaps more importantly, a shift in the basic demographic distribution of the United States population by age groups might influence the regional or geographic distribution of population. To a very considerable extent, the geographic distribution of population has almost as many or more implications for the total demand for transportation as the scale or the extent of population growth. Important changes have been and are taking place, of course, in the distribution of the United States population. The historic drift from east to west continues. It has, though, been greatly supplemented and complicated by migrations from the South to the North and West by American Negroes and from the Northeast to the South and West by whites. Indeed, it is one of the more striking aspects of recent migration movements that southern rural blacks tended to move to northern cities to a much greater extent than southern rural whites, who have more often simply moved from a southern rural to a southern urban location. Basically, though, these movements away from the rural south, and to a lesser extent the continuous move toward the West, involve a movement from rural and small town environments to big cities. Metropolitan area dwellers represented about 70 percent of the United States population in 1970; the best guess is that they will be about 85 percent of the total by the year 2000.

Somewhat paradoxically, though, at the same time that this general shift from rural and small towns to larger cities is occurring, the very central parts of most of our cities are becoming less populated. It is the suburbs of our cities that have been growing rapidly. Central cities have not increased their percentage of the total United States population in recent years, even though they have grown geographically due to annexations. Contrarily, suburbs now account (depending upon definition) for roughly one-third to one-half of the United States population today contrasted with under one-quarter as recently as 1950.

One of the many unanswered aspects of any pronounced shifts in the demographic distribution of the population into different age groups is whether it will have an important impact on this distribution between suburban and central city locations. Superficially, it could be argued that with a decline in aggregate population growth there will be fewer children and fewer families with children as a relative proportion of the total population; in turn, this might reduce the attractiveness of suburban locations. At any rate, it has been historically true that childless couples, whether young or old, have tended more toward apartment house or multiple family dwelling units and that these units have customarily been more available in central portions of cities. However, in the last decade there has been a strong trend toward construction of multiple family units, particularly garden apartments, in suburban areas so that the clear-cut distinction between suburban single-family dwelling units and central-city apartment dwellings is not quite so clear as it once was. Of course, it must also be recognized that rising incomes have customarily been associated with choice of more suburban residential locations, and there is no reason to expect a marked reduction in income growth.

Technological Trends

Locational patterns are undergoing change because of fundamental technological as well as economic or demographic changes. These technological changes have modified the profit or utility maximizing calculations of the important decision units in our society, households and business firms. It can hardly be overstressed that these locational changes have not been determined exclusively by technological developments in transportation. Changes in manufacturing and other production technologies, in the composition of economic activity that have occurred with growth and development, and in patterns of consumer taste have been at least as important as transportation in creating these locational shifts.

At the earliest stage of United States development, as in most economies, agriculture and raw material exploitation was emphasized. Essentially, each region of the nation participated in the national expansion on the basis of its comparative advantage in raw material and agriculture resources. From a locational standpoint, the outstanding feature of agricultural and raw materials extraction is that these activities need a physical location near required land and resources. Basically, the development of such activities, particularly agriculture, implies a dispersal of population over the land surface of the economy undergoing development.

Furthermore, early manufacturing development in the United States prompted some additional dispersal. The primitive character or nonexistence of technologies for transmitting power in the nineteenth century, and the consequent need to almost totally rely on waterfalls for early manufacturing power, meant that manufacturers had to be located nearby—virtually upon—the falls or rapids of rivers. The pattern is particularly evident in New England but is also observable in most other parts of the country, even including the Far West. The relatively early development of heavy industries with a strong raw material orientation, such as steel, also tended to develop urban nodes that were largely dictated by transportation considerations in relation to sources of basic raw material inputs. In the jargon of location theory these were resource- or process-oriented rather than market-oriented industries. In short, site locations for early manufacturing activities in the United States were, like those for agriculture and mining, not particularly dictated by the location of markets or any great need to be near existing urban settlements. They tended rather to be located near whatever raw materials, power sources, or agricultural land was required.

A very fundamental change occurred in development patterns with profound implications for transport choices near or just before the beginning of this century. Our economic development shifted toward lighter industries and service activities. For both light industries and services the locational advantage tends to be near major markets and sources of labor. And, as illustrated by the projections shown in Table 8-3, there is every reason to expect these sectors to continue to grow.

The newer and lighter industries developing at or around the turn of the century also found it advantageous to avail themselves of the externalities of urban locations, that is of so-called urban agglomeration economies. These were particularly important as they affect the recruitment and the development of a flexible or adaptable work force. Considerable economies of scale were also present in the development of certain types of urban public services; these ultimately could or would reflect themselves in lower cost at an urban location. This is not to argue that such economies of scale could not or have not been exhausted in very large urban agglomerations. The point is, rather, that given the status of urban development at the beginning of this century, reasonably high qualities of urban facilities were more inexpensively developed in or around our largest and medium sized cities than by starting *de novo* with new cities or by expanding sharply on the limited basis of small towns. These developments meant that the larger commercial, transportation, and manufacturing nodes that had developed earlier, that is during the nineteenth century for the most part, tended to become growth points as the twentieth century began.

These trends were heightened by an exodus from the countryside induced by relatively rapid rates of productivity improvement in agriculture, transportation, and heavy manufacturing. The relative importance of these basic activities not only declined within our economy, but the manpower requirement per unit of

Table 8-3
U.S. Gross Product Originating by Major Industrial Sectors, Actual 1960 and Projections for 1975 (Millions of 1964 Constant $)

	1960	1975	% Change
Agriculture	22,027.7	26,750.8	21.44
Mining	10,722.7	17,036.8	58.88
Construction	27,866.6	47,034.3	68.78
Manufacturing	143,572.7	284,493.4	98.15
Transportation, Communications, and Public Utilities	46,969.9	101,425.3	115.9
Trade	94,679.8	158,705.4	67.62
Finance, Insurance, etc.	64,196.8	123,382.7	92.19
Other Services	59,732.5	108,981.7	82.45
Government	59,693.2	97,299.9	62.99
All Industries	529,461.9	965,110.3	82.28

Source: National Planning Association.

output also tended to decline relatively more rapidly than for service or most light manufacturing industries.

Regionalization and Import Substitution

Another important locational trend also began somewhere near the turn of the century. This is a so-called "decentralization of industry" alluded to in several empirical studies.[3] This phrase describes a spreading of industries more evenly over the country. Activities once heavily concentrated in a particular region were attracted to or appeared in new areas.

To a considerable extent, decentralization of industry represents a type of import substitution that occurs on a regional or local basis in almost any economy as the size of local markets grow (in terms of both population and purchasing power). For example, as population has drifted toward the western and southwestern portions of the United States, the metropolitan centers of these regions have increasingly found themselves capable of supporting an even wider range of efficient manufacturing industries and services at the local level. That is, these newer growing regions have become more self-sufficient industrially.

Decentralization is also partly explained by causes tending to make industries more mobile, more footloose: these are attributable among other things to changes in production technology, to shifts in demand, and to the greater availability of technical talents and civilized amenities at more and more locations throughout the country. Coupled with the fact that labor costs have historically been somewhat lower in the South (and perhaps other localities with labor "surpluses" being released from agriculture), many industries, particularly the "footloose" and labor intensive, have migrated south in search of lower production costs, better climates, etc.

Population and industrial growth in the West and Southwest also relate to another important aspect of recent locational patterns. Specifically, resource-oriented development of new commercial centers or cities has never been totally arrested in our economy. While of far more relative importance during the nineteenth century than thus far in the twentieth, the development of new resources and products, particularly petroleum, woodpulp, and paper, has kept in motion certain basic population dispersal tendencies in our economy; it also has helped create new transportation and commercial nodes of considerable importance. These, in turn, create a new base for development of market-oriented local industries via the classic import-substitution mechanism.

Urban Location Patterns

Another major trend in American locational patterns refers to population and workplace distributions within our major urban areas. At base, these changes are attributable to advances in transportation, communications, bookkeeping, manufacturing, and retailing technologies which have tended to make different parcels of land within our urban areas increasingly homogeneous for most productive functions. The same is often increasingly true of residential locations as well.

The relevant point for present purposes is that these changes have tended to make location at points of very high density within central cities relatively less attractive than location at peripheral urban sites of medium to low density. A more uniform distribution of activities over the urban surface is the result. This has been achieved *both* by reducing concentration of existing points of maximum activity density (e.g., so-called central business districts) and increasing densities of less central sites within our urban areas. Thus, if we were to plot density of residences, workplaces, or of most other activities along the vertical axis of a two dimension diagram, and distances from the central business district along the horizontal and to the right, we would increasingly find that the functional relationship between these two variables is becoming less steeply inclined, dropping on the left and rising on the right.

Another interesting technological change with some implications for location, but almost certainly of a second order compared to those already discussed, concerns communications and jet air travel. Specifically, it is increasingly simple to centralize control of managerial or other functions at one point in space. One major impact of this development has been to make district offices less useful relative to regional offices and regional offices less important in relation to national offices than was previously the case. Thus, office and managerial functions have tended toward some centralization at the same time that manufacturing activities have become more regionally dispersed. In large measure, it is probably this pehnomenon that explains the widely observed and commented upon boom in office construction in a few of our large cities, particularly New York, Los Angeles, and Chicago.

Summary

On balance, the net effect of these different locational forces operating in the context of a modern economy or technology is not too difficult to discern. To begin, they suggest the development of a society that is increasingly urban. On the other hand, the maximum point densities of population or workplaces within these urban areas is declining or, at most, remaining stable; in other words, the activity and population densities of our urban areas are becoming increasingly uniform. This combination implies the emergence of a few very large multi-city conurbations containing a very substantial proportion of the nation's population.

It is difficult to assert with any confidence exactly where and what geographical extent these various conurbations might have. Obviously, though, one will be the so-called megalopolis of the Northeast. Another is clearly emerging at the opposite corner of the country, that is along the coast line in Southern California. Another will be or is located somewhere in or around Chicago with its associated industrial heartland. Still others are emerging along the Gulf coast and on a lesser scale in Florida and the Puget Sound region.

Wherever they might be located, the basic point is that we see two fundamental trends at work. One, so to speak, is pushing population toward our larger urban agglomerations and the other is pushing downward on the maximum point densities of population and workplaces within these agglomerations. It should be underscored that these trends are the product of many technological and economic changes at work in our society. Changes in transportation technology, which are so often singled out as the prime cause of location changes in many popular discussions, are influential but are not the only operative forces. Basic trends in the mix of industrial and economic activities and changes in productive technologies employed in producing goods and services are also most important.

Transport Demand Forecasts

Trip Generation: Freight

A most important set of implications for the generation of freight traffic derives from changes expected in the industrial mix of the economy. Some relevant figures on past growth and projected future rates of development by industrial sector are shown in Table 8-4. Industrial sectors that have been expanding rapidly and are expected to continue to expand at a high rate in the near future are services, finance, public utilities, communications, and manufacturing. By contrast, mining, agriculture, forestry, and fisheries will grow more slowly, even declining absolutely by such measures as employment.

The striking thing about these figures from the standpoint of transportation is that two sectors that traditionally have been important consumers of freight services—mining and agriculture—are very emphatically among the slowest growing sectors. However, they will still grow, if not in employment at least in output. Accordingly, their needs for freight transportation will also grow but almost certainly at a slower rate than the general economy. On the more optimistic side, manufacturing, another sector which generally has fairly substantial freight transportation needs, may accelerate its rate of growth in the next decade. Nevertheless, the general picture is one in which the amount of freight tonnage originating in our economy will probably not grow at as rapid rate as the economy as a whole. This will be especially true if demographic effects behave as postulated previously.

Technological changes should also reinforce these tendencies. To begin, a

Table 8-4

Changes in U.S. Industry Employment: 1947-62 and 1962-75

One-Digit Sectors	1947-62		1962-75	
	Change %	Rank[a]	Change %	Rank[a]
Government	72.3	1	52.0	1
Services	67.3	2	44.7	3
Finance, Insurance & Real Estate	59.5	3	50.7	2
Construction	31.6	4	43.4	4
Trade	21.0	5	27.0	5
Manufacturing	6.1	6	17.2	6
Transportation, Comm. and Pub. Utilities	−8.8	7	1.2	7
Mining	−31.2	8	−12.5	8
Agriculture, Forestry and Fisheries	−37.3	9	−27.5	9

[a]Employment rate change is ranked from the highest to the lowest.

Source: "State Employment by Industry: A Revised Series, 1947-62," National Planning Association, REPS Report No. 64-IV.

trend may exist toward what has been called "miniaturization" in manufacturing which could sharply reduce the physical transport requirements per dollar or unit of manufacturing output. The exact definition or empirical extent of miniaturization is difficult to determine. It seemingly relates, though, to the commonly observed phenomenon that lighter metals and smaller pieces of machinery are increasingly supplanting heavier and bulkier predecessors. It perhaps also connotes certain substitutions within the manufacturing sector of one kind of good for another, e.g., substitution of airplanes for passenger railroads, of microcircuits for transistors and transistors for vacuum tubes, etc. It also suggests some shift in the general composition of manufacturing with activities such as electronics and electrical machinery, products with relatively high value per pound, becoming increasingly important as other products such as food and beverages, with relatively low value per pound, becoming relatively less important. It perhaps also connotes simple quality upgrading as incomes per capita rise. In general, the best available evidence generally suggests that physical freight requirements do not expand proportionally with manufacturing output. Specifically, the physical freight requirements per unit of manufacturing output seem to increase by about 0.95 of a percent for every 1.0 percent expansion of manufacturing output. The evidence, though, is very aggregate and approximate.

A technologically induced decline in transport may also occur because of expected changes in electrical energy production. In particular, coal should become less important in relative terms as a source of fuel; by contrast, nuclear energy will expand rapidly. It should be noted, though, that while coal's relative share of the energy market may decline, coal consumption should not decline in absolute terms. Also, natural gas and oil, fuels which require considerable transportation, should hold their share of the market and continue to grow quite sharply in absolute terms. In large part, though, these fuels will move in tankers or pipelines, particularly natural gas. On balance, therefore, only modest growth in demand for carriage of coal seems likely, but there is strong probability of a considerable increase in demand for bulk movement of oil and gas by pipeline, barge, or tanker.

As an additional consideration, a nationwide energy grid increasingly seems feasible and, indeed, is actually emerging. This, coupled with more efficient long distance transmission of electrical energy, implies more location of electrical energy production closer to the sources of thermal energy, whether coal or natural gas. Naturally, this would reinforce any tendency toward reduced movement of coal tonnage for energy production and could even reduce pipeline requirements in the long run.

The basic pattern is clear: freight transportation is not by the usual standards a "growth sector" in the economy. It is, of course, always possible that certain technological or other changes may reverse this pattern. However, there is no particular reason for expecting such a reversal. Accordingly, in planning for future transportation one can fairly safely expect that freight transportation will be a relatively less important concern for the United States economy.

Passenger Trip Originations

A more positive picture emerges when one looks at passenger trip originations. Overall, people spend more money on passenger travel as their incomes increase, preferring more and better transport. International air travel and tourist travel in general seem to be major beneficiaries. Business travel has tended to follow the business cycle but with a strong upward trend, though improved communications eventually might slow this trend. To date, however, both communications and air travel have been improving and growing rapidly, almost seeming to complement one another rather than being competitive. Private planes may actually be the major threat facing commercial air travel. On balance, the high recent growth levels in air travel, roughly between 8 and 15 percent per year, seem quite sustainable for the near future—though in years of business recession the rates can decline precipitously. The only discernible damper on passenger travel growth in the long run, and then in the *very* long run, would be any tendency toward population stabilization. Indeed, in the short run a declining rate of population growth should stimulate passenger trip originations for reasons already explained.

Trends relating to passenger travel in urban areas are not quite so obvious.

The best guess would be that the total demands for trips in urban areas should continue to increase, at least slowly. In particular, as incomes increase, one would expect that more trips would be made for social and recreational purposes and for shopping and personal business.

As an offset, some decline could occur in work trips. The great unknown is whether the recent flirtation with 4-day and 3-day work weeks will spread and, if it does, what the reaction will be in terms of work force participation. For example, how many workers, if any, will simply shift to two 3-day jobs per week if a 3-day work week becomes increasingly prevalent? Or will a 3-day work week entice more housewives to enter the labor force?

Whatever happens, the number of worktrips *per job*, and probably per member of the work force, should not increase in the near future. Thus, if there is any change it will be towards some decline in the number of worktrips per week per participant in the labor force. Whether this will translate into a decline in the total number of worktrips per capita per work week is not so clear. In fact, it is reasonably clear that if the aggregate demographic trends outlined earlier prove to be true, then the number of worktrips per capita would probably increase, mainly because of a shift toward age brackets in which labor force participation is relatively high. On the other hand, the same demographic factors should tend to offset or reduce the number of urban trips made in the second large category of daily "commuter trips," those for attendance at school.

The net effect of all these forces on the pattern of urban trips is very difficult to discern. The best guess would be some "flattening" in the diurnal cycle for urban trips coupled with an increase in total trips. In particular, the peaks attributable to work and school trips should probably decline in relative importance (e.g., as a percentage of total trips during the 24-hour day) and off-peak trips, particularly during the work day (that is between 9 a.m. and 4:30 p.m.) should increase. Needless to say if this prediction proves true, that is if a flattening of the diurnal trip cycle occurs, it would mean that the problem of meeting the demands for urban trips would be somewhat attenuated since the major difficulty has, and continues to be, that of supplying sufficient facilities to meet the peak period demands.

Interzonal Interchange: Freight

The pattern of interzonal interchanges within any economy will be influenced in the first instance by the distribution of economic activities and people within the economy. In this connection the striking thing is the tendency toward regionalization of industry and the closely related phenomena of growing urbanization. Regionalization, as noted, seems largely a form of import substitution, made possible by regional market growth. Urbanization represents a general form of population concentration that facilitates local market growth. To put the matter in quantitative terms, the ratio of so-called "export products" to total output is normally smaller in large cities than in small. To take matters to an extreme, a market-oriented large-scale farming enterprise will have 80 percent or more of its total production in export activities; by contrast, a large city will have approximately 20 to 30 percent or so of its total economic activity in so-called export production.

Urbanization can also simplify the process of secondary distribution. As more and more people live within cities, intercity freight mileage needed to move products from urban centers to small town and farm locations will decline. Indeed, a significant negative statistical relationship usually is found between measures of urbanization and total demand for intercity rail and water ton miles on a per capita basis.

The basic point seems irrefutable. Urbanization in general, and continued growth of local or regional production, both tend to reduce the total number of miles that freight must be transported in order to meet consumer requirements.

The pattern of interzonal interchange within an economy is also influenced by technological changes over time. In particular, any innovations in transportation technologies that tend to affect the relative cost of short as against long haul freight influence these interchanges. For example, if short haul transportation becomes relatively cheaper as compared to long haul transportation, one would expect to witness more regionalization of industry. A relative reduction in long haul transport cost would, of course, work in the opposite direction.

There has been a good deal of speculation about the relative trends in long and short haul transportation costs.[4] The development of the internal combustion engine and highway transport certainly reduced short haul transport costs and tariffs more than long haul. The increasing availability of private and contract carriage added an important impetus to shipper realization on this development. On the other hand, improvements in pipeline and water transport have tended to lower long-haul bulk transport costs relatively more than short haul.

As one looks to the future conflicting trends are discernible in these cost relationships. There is every reason to expect, for example, that truck transport will continue to experience reasonably steady improvement in productivity through better vehicles and highways. In particular, improved urban highways will probably work to reduce short haul costs relatively more than long haul since, by almost any measure, an urban expressway effectuates sharper improvements in performance relative to its predecessors than most intercity expressways. In addition, urban or suburban metropolitan highways may be expected to take a larger share of total highway expenditures, at least in the near future.

A major offset, however, could be the continued development of containerization. Containerization, in essence, makes it possible to specialize each transportation technology more intensively in those particular areas where it has the greatest advantage. Containers make the long haul or line haul economies of water and rail transport become more readily accessible and therefore work to reduce long haul costs relative to short haul. Needless to say, continued development of pipeline and water transport would tend to work in the same direction.

It is difficult to guess how these different forces will net out. Probably the best guess would be that they will largely offset one another. In short, probably no major change will occur in trip distances due to changes in the relative costs of short and long haul transportation. Looking back at Table 8-2, stability in length of haul has, in fact, been characteristic recently. There may be some slight tendency for long haul costs to drift downward more than short haul. But this judgment reflects not only guesses about the relative strengths of the different technological forces at work, but also a suspicion that the regulatory structure is such that there is more room for or likelihood of downward revision of long haul than short haul tariffs.

The various forces altering the demand for freight transportation can be summarized under two major headings: shifts in industrial or output composition and structural changes (ranging from decentralization of industry to use of more efficient transport modes). The aggregate effects attributable to these two influences can, in fact, be analyzed by comparative input output techniques, something which has been done for the United States post-war experience by Alex Morton in an unpublished Harvard Ph.D. thesis. Some of the more striking of his results are reproduced in Table 8-5. An estimate of the losses of freight traffic due to shifts in industrial composition can be calculated as the difference between growth in the transport needs of an industry and that which would have occurred if the industry had grown as rapidly as gross domestic output, structure held constant. In Table 8-5 this is shown in the first and fourth columns respectively, and described as the "loss due to changing composition of final demands." The second major component of change, "loss due to structural change," can be represented as loss in transport due to changes observed in input-output coefficients over the time periods in question, final demands held constant. Results shown in Table 8-5 pertain only to the 20 industries with the largest total transportation requirements, but in sample analyses conducted of other industries Morton obtained more or less the same results.

There are several striking aspects of Morton's findings. First it would appear that the decline in transportation requirements attributable to shifts in industrial composition and to structural change are roughly equivalent for the post-war period. Second, structural change as a cause of a decline in transportation requirements was quite pervasive; the negative entries in the structural change column are few.

Finally, the changes in transportation needs due to changing industrial composition more or less conform to expectations. Resource industries known to have been expanding, such as petroleum refining and utilities, have contributed importantly to the expansion of total transport demands. And, of course, the largest single industry contribution to the decline in total transportation demands shows up within the transportation and warehousing industry itself, where the cumulative improvements in transport efficiency or effectiveness as shown by structural changes reduce the industry's own demands for its own services.

Interzonal Interchange: Passengers

While there are many reasons for expecting the length of interzonal interchanges of freight to shorten over the next few years, opposite trends seem at work in both intercity and urban passenger transportation. For example, as incomes increase, there is every reason to expect increasingly longer vacation trips. This tendency will be further strengthened by the greater availability of high speed transport, whether on the surface or by SST or lower cost subsonic jets. Of course, longer vacation periods should also accentuate this trend.

Longer urban trips may also be expected. This has certainly been the trend of the recent past. For example, average time required for worktrips in American cities has seemingly remained constant even as the length of the worktrip has increased. That is, urban commuters have tended to consume improvements in urban transportation systems more by lengthening worktrips than by shortening the time required for these trips. This, of course, is not unrelated to the increasing popularity of lower density residential suburbs. One small offset to this trend may be found in industry itself moving more and more to suburban locations. To the extent this happens, workers may be able to have their "cake and eat it too," that is, they may be able to not only live in low density residential suburbs but also may be able to reduce the distance between their homes and their workplaces. On balance, though, the probability is for somewhat longer worktrips. Furthermore, concentration of retail units into larger supermarket and shopping centers, combined with lower density residential living, may create somewhat longer trips for shopping and other non-worktrip purposes as well.

Modal Choice

In general, one must assume that modal choice for freight will be based upon economic rationality. That is, shippers will select that particular mode or combination of modes that will minimize their total cost. Cost, moreover, must be construed broadly so as to include all or at least most of the relevant expense of distributing goods within the system; in particular, one mode may have higher directly assignable costs for performing a transport service but savings in handling, packaging, inventory and other distribution outlays may more than

Table 8-5
Freight Loss Due to Changing Composition of Final Demand and Structural Change Among the Twenty Industries with the Largest Total Transportation Requirements

Industry	1947-1958			1958-1963		
	Loss Due To Changing Composition of Final Demands	Loss Due To Structural Change	Total Loss	Loss Due To Changing Composition of Final Demands	Loss Due To Structural Change	Total Loss
	(Millions of 1958 Dollars)			(Millions of Current Dollars)		
Transportation & Warehousing	3492	-115	3377	1681	-282	1399
New Construction	-764a	634	-130	285	421	706
Food and Kindred Products	620	151	771	811	403	1214
Wholesale & Retail Trade	280	1055	1335	7	71	78
Motor Vehicles & Equipment	174	-11	163	-361	166	-195
Real Estate & Rental	-135	682	547	-2	175	173
Petroleum Refining	-246	121	-125	135	92	227
Medical, Educ. Services & Charities	-89	289	200	-87	106	19
Electric, Gas, Water & Sanitary	-212	127	-85	-37	-1	-38
Apparel	76	173	249	49	125	174
Finance & Insurance	-15	39	24	-22	143	121
Hotels, Lodging & Pers. Services	46	4	50	10	38	48
Drugs, Cleaning & Toilet Prepn's	-95	133	38	-28	31	3
Aircraft and Parts	-210	61	-149	8	14	22
Radio, TV, & Communictn Eqpmt.	-86	58	-28	-152	110	-42

Maintenance & Repair Constructn.	-11	82	71	35	-40	-5
Other Transportation Eqpmt.	102	-12	90	-6	21	15
Agricultural Products[b]	48	146	194	42	17	59
Business Services	20	25	45	-67	13	-54
Household Furniture	25	53	78	14	18	32
Total	3020	3695	6715	2315	1641	3956

Source: Alexander Morton, Unpublished Ph.D. thesis, Harvard University.

[a]Minus sign indicates a gain.

[b]Exclusive of livestock.

compensate. The essence of the so-called revolution in physical distribution practices now underway is closer calculation of the trade-offs between different kinds of distribution practices; that is, lowest cost total solutions to distribution problems are increasingly sought and discovered.

Rather similar comments apply to the choice of passenger modes. Any good analysis must recognize that time savings and comfort play a role in passenger choices as well as cost in the simple or direct sense. In this connection, one would hope that we have almost heard the last of such remarks as "one lane of capacity relegated to rail transport can carry 40 times many people as the same amount of land devoted to highway passenger transport and that, therefore, it is obvious that the efficient solution to passenger transportation problems is to use rail." Such gross oversimplification simply will not do for forecasting passenger demands in the modern world.

Actually, there are no major reasons for expecting pronounced shifts in modal choice characteristics in the near future. But there is every reason to expect that some slow but steady trends of the recent past will continue to be manifested. In large measure (particularly for freight transport), these modal choices simply reflect what is best (lowest cost or highest utility) for individual shippers or travellers making the selection.

As already noted, for example, pipeline transportation is likely to continue its growth in relative and absolute terms. Only unexpectedly quick development of the electric auto could possibly reverse this trend by sharply reducing the total market for petroleum products. This seems highly unlikely; most of the available evidence suggest that it will be cheaper to cure the pollution characteristics of the internal combustion engine or to develop alternative thermal engines (steam, Wankel, turbine, etc.) that use petroleum fuels but may pollute less.

Some shift may also be discernible toward pipelines, induced, say, by technological improvements that make it increasingly possible to move bulk commodities in pipes. In short, the last may not yet have been heard of coal and other mineral slurry pipelines. Much depends upon the kind of competitive responses that the railroads, barges, and other traditional bulk commodity carriers make to any new pipeline proposals of this type and exactly where new commercial mineral resources are discovered and developed. Development at more remote sites tends to bestow some advantage on slurry pipelines as compared with rail or truck.

One would expect, too, that containerization and related piggybacking concepts will induce some substitution of rail for longer truck hauls. If and when the railroads fully organize themselves to provide a high performance service in longer haul piggybacking, the impact might be dramatic. As piggybacking becomes more freely available to all modes of truck transport—private, contract, and common carrier—any such development could accelerate.

Certain other improvements in railroad marketing and operational procedures may also facilitate a shift from truck to rail for longer hauls. In particular, so-called liner services, volume discounts, and rent-a-train concepts may facilitate such a development. Any pronounced deregulation of rail rate-making practices, as proposed in recent legislation advanced by the Nixon administration or in the 1962 Message on Transportation by President Kennedy, would also facilitate such changes. Basically, all these shifts have in common a tendency to relate rail rates more closely to rail costs and therefore facilitate rail ability to compete with trucks for longer distance shipments.

Some dramatic alteration in modal choices for freight transportation might occur in the upper spectrum of higher valued commodities now moving by truck. Here, the potential truck competitor would be air cargo. Thus far, of course, most air cargoes represent development of new traffic rather than a diversion of traffic from older modes. However, the application of the jet engine, with its low maintenance and operating costs, to very large cargo planes in the form of the C5A and Boeing 747, may create a new stage in air cargo development in which air freight becomes quite competitive with some surface transport. Taken together with any tendency toward increased used of rail piggybacking, long-haul truck transport could face, as a consequence, some substantial competitive challenges in the next ten or fifteen years.

The impact of cheaper and more widely available air cargo may be even more important in international markets. Among other possibilities air cargo could open up more opportunities for tropical and subtropical countries to supply fruit and other produce, particularly during off-season, to cities in temperate climates. In particular, one might speculate that with lower cost air cargo Central and South America, part of Africa, and Asia might become major sources of produce for major cities in Europe and North America, as well as for major cities in their own continents now served from these sources. Similarly, the whole industry of livestock growing and fattening might be considerably altered by the availability of low cost air transport. In general, many examples of similar possibilities might be cited. In essence, low cost air cargo opens up a whole set of new possibilities for international or regional specialization and interchange of goods not now commonly traded.

Continuation of recent modal choice patterns seems even more likely for passenger than freight transport. The airlines are now the major mode of public intercity transport and there is every reason to expect that they will consolidate and extend that position in the near future. Indeed, intercity air transport will increasingly compete with the automobile for tourist and vacation travel.

Development of somewhat higher speed ground transport *may* increase the share of total intercity public travel by rail or other conventional ground transport modes in certain local areas. There seems, though, little reason to expect that this will be a major development. The considerable speed advantage of air travel, now and for the foreseeable future, would seem to give it a very substantial advantage for almost all trips of 200 miles or more in length. To put the matter in perspective, large expenditures to develop high speed ground transport are difficult to justify when a technology rendering 500 to 600 mile an hour performance is available off the shelf at relatively moderate cost. This view seems further accentuated when one considers that most of the plans for high speed ground transport aim at achieving speeds of only 300 or 400 miles an hour at maximum.

This is not to say, however, that high speed ground transport operating at 100 or 150 miles per hour or so might not be a potential competitor for trips between 75 and 200 miles in length, especially where fairly large volumes are now moving by public modes. To some considerable extent, the future of rail and other high-speed ground transport will depend on the availability of government subsidies for either technological development or operating costs. For example, if enough public money is put into Amtrak, the steady attrition or erosion of available intercity rail passenger services may be substantially arrested. Without a considerable infusion of funds, however, it seems highly unlikely that intercity rail passenger travel will survive much beyond 1980, except in a few very dense corridors and for some rail commutation in and around major cities.

Meanwhile, the automobile should remain a most effective competitor for intercity trips of 50 to 100 miles or even longer, particularly when and if family or other small groups are involved. The automobile's advantage in shorter trips derives from low costs per available seat mile and almost infinite schedule flexibility and ubiquity. In general, it is very difficult to imagine that the automobile's present share of intercity passenger travel, approximately 90 percent of the total, will decline markedly in the next decade.

Shifts in intercity total shares, if any, are far more likely to occur within the 10 percent of the total market that is in the public sector. In particular, for the reasons already suggested, one can expect that air travel probably will absorb an increasing share of this public intercity air travel.

Actually, air travel may, at the margin, even erode some automobile intercity passenger travel. In particular, certain technological changes in the offing may substantially increase the effectiveness of air travel for shorter trips. In particular, there are some very good reasons for believing that so-called short takeoff (STOL) or vertical takeoff (VTOL) aircraft may become increasingly economic to operate. The natural niche for STOL or VTOL aircraft would seem to be roughly that now filled by the rapidly emerging so-called third level air carriers, or it could provide so-called air taxi services. In essence, both third level carriers and the air taxis serve more or less the same market, trips of rougly 50 to 150 miles supplementing or connecting with longer distance air line services between cities.

The unknown is whether these air taxi and third level air carriers may take up new activities in addition to their present supplementary role in conjunction with major inter-city airlines. Specifically, can we expect these carriers to meet demands now met by buses or autos? There are some reasons for believing that this might occur. Of course, the initial expectation would be that these services would not totally displace existing bus services. Furthermore, one might expect new air services to emerge first wherever water, urban congestion, or other barriers impede the flow of existing land transport.

Automobile transportation is not quite as dominant for urban as for intercity trips but it still accounts for a substantial majority of all urban trips made: approximately 60 to 70 percent of work trips and an even higher percentage of non-work trips. The automobile should acquire an even more dominant role in urban areas if work places and residential densities continue to decline as they have in the recent past.

Public transportation in cities is at its greatest advantage in serving dense residential areas and very highly concentrated workplaces. Planned improvements in public transit, moreover, will probably not change this in any major way so that modal choices in urban areas should remain more or less as they are. The availability of more government subsidy for public transportation may more or less offset the trend toward more use of automobiles attributable to continued decentralization and rising incomes. In sum, there may be some slow but steady increase in auto use for urban trips, but perhaps at a slightly slower pace than in the recent past, due to increased subsidization and government emphasis on public transportation.

Summary

Obviously, all this discussion does not result in any definitive quantitative description of future transportation trends and requirements. Indeed, for reasons outlined, this would be a very difficult and perhaps even impossible task. At best, given the number of technological and other uncertainties involved, one can only guess.

Still, on balance, railroads might expect a stagnation or very slow growth in demand for many of their basic raw material and agricultural commodity shipments. The railroads' best hopes of growth should occur through expansion of piggybacking and containerization to improve their competitive position in the longer distance hauling of manufactured products. Trucks, by contrast, may experience some relative reduction in longer hauls but should benefit, and quite substantially, from the increased regionalization of industry and urbanization— developments which reduce length of haul requirements.

One can also speculate that the use of the passenger automobile may not only continue to grow but at the same time become more functionally specialized. For example, the auto may lose some of its present role in vacation and other longer haul intercity trips. As vacation trips lengthen in response to longer vacation periods and higher incomes, a combination of air and car probably will be increasingly used for pleasure touring and related trips. On the other hand, the automobile, perhaps with some specialization in its design to meet pollution and similar problems, should continue to be quite competitive in urban areas for shopping, recreational, personal business, and even commuter trips.

Finally, airplanes should continue to grow in popularity and scale, both as carriers of passenger and freight. The "airline revolution" in transportation has probably just begun. The main problems are those of financing growth and properly adjusting the roles of private and common carriage. Proper development and efficient utilization of the public investments in airports and airways is also a most pressing problem.

The picture, therefore, for most modes is rather mixed. Only urban public transit and intercity rail passenger travel seem to have a thoroughly limited future. Even these modes, however, could have selected areas of expansion and increased popularity. Contrarily, the only problems one can foresee for the airlines is how to cope with the difficulties, particularly financial, of rapid growth. Pipeline transportation seems to be in a similarly favorable position but with fewer financial problems. For trucks, railroads, and barges much will depend on how well they adapt to changing circumstances. The successful management will be that which anticipates new technologies and locational patterns and plans carefully for the transitions that they imply.

Implications for Regional Transport Planning

Future developments in transport, as just outlined, are rather different or contradictory in their planning implications for different types of transport or travel requirements.

For example, to the extent that there really is a trend toward regionalization of industry via import substitution, one could argue that a regional basis for transportation planning becomes increasingly feasible. In particular, a regional approach might become even more sensible in planning freight transport for manufactured goods. Perhaps, too, the same kind of regional grouping might make sense for urban and short haul passenger travel. This is far from obvious, however, for the relevant regions for planning purposes of short haul passenger, urban passenger, and light freight transport may well be very different. For example, the commuter shed might define a relevant region for urban passenger transportation, while the regional conurbation or megalopolis was the relevant region for short haul passenger transport planning. But the regional conurbation or megalopolis might also be a good approximation of the relevant planning region for most freight as well.

However, even this two tier planning concept, say of a regional conurbation with sub-divisions of specific commuter watersheds, might not be entirely satisfactory for all aspects of transport planning, even for urban, short-haul passenger, and light freight. For example, the "ecological reach" of regional and urban transportation systems may greatly exceed the limits of the regional conurbation itself. Probably this is best illustrated by electricity and gas utility generation and their interaction with transportation requirements, as in the case of long distance transmission from a hydro-electric or thermal plant reducing transport requirements for fuel and simultaneously ameliorating local urban air pollution. At the same time, however, long distance transmission may have an adverse environmental effect in terms of reducing the attractiveness of the countryside, transmission towers not usually being regarded as esthetic or attractive. Similarly, if the distant source is a thermal plant, one might expect it to generate heat or air pollution that could be considered unattractive at the distant location. Or, if hydro-electric power is used, this might encounter conservationist or sportsmen objections because of what a dam can do to wild life, fish reproduction cycles, and so forth. In short, the trade-offs involved could have an areal reach well beyond any conventional definition of a regional urban conurbation or megalopolis.

More generally, it is not at all clear that a regional approach would be particularly sensible, let alone increasingly desirable, for many transportation activities. Specifically, a regional approach might create as many problems as it would solve if applied to fuel or energy traffic, long distance intercity passenger travel and light manufactured goods moving by air cargo or containers. Indeed, for most of these a move toward more international planning in lieu of national planning may be the preferred development. Moreover, the regional approach seems to be particularly inapplicable in growth sectors increasingly sensitive to externalities, e.g., fuel or energy traffic.

Container and air cargo traffic do point, though, toward an increasingly important special problem, which might be particularly appropriate for regional planning, namely that of developing terminal facilities for intermodal interchanges. For example, development of large regional airports which serve international and air cargo requirements in environmentally and otherwise suitable locations might be well conceived as a regional problem, and one for which the regional conurbation or megalopolis might be *approximately* the right planning unit. An additional argument for a regional approach to planning terminals is that a need usually exists to coordinate at the regional level the feeder or distribution networks needed for proper development of traffic going to and from such terminals.

In short, it is difficult to generalize about the proper level of planning for different transport modes and functions. For some modes and functions more international rather than national planning is needed; and for others more regional rather than state or local planning is needed; and for still others more regional rather than national planning may make sense. Moreover, the growth of environmental concerns is likely to heighten the demand for more local participation in certain decision processes even if technological or efficiency arguments suggest a shift toward higher level planning; perhaps this is best illustrated by the problems of choosing sites for major international airports.

Efficiency considerations may also conflict at different planning levels, particularly for multi-purpose facilities. For example, high performance urban highways might be differently designed and located to serve commuters than for intercity through traffic; or a major airport might be located differently if its primary function is to serve people in the immediately adjacent urban vicinity rather than as a port-of-entry or transfer point for originating and terminating international flights serving a much broader constituency.

Almost all transport facilities serve many purposes and the proper level of planning for some purposes may be quite different than for others. This suggests, in turn, that the planning process be devised so as to insure consultation or involvement of the many very different constituencies that are likely to be affected. To illustrate, planning an international airport probably requires consultations at the international level, some at the level of the regional conurbation or megalopolis, and probably some at a very local or grass roots level, (e.g., the neighborhood in the vicinity where a new airport might be placed). Similarly, the planning of highways within a state has long been recognized as involving compromises between the objective of serving local traffic, that is to say within the state, and serving longer distance or thru traffic; the traditional way of accommodating these diverse constituencies within the United States has been through extensive consultation between the Federal Bureau of Public Roads and State Highway Departments plus a considerable involvement in what has come to be called "congressional log-rolling." While effective, it is hardly very scientific.

As an alternative, transport planning might start by identifying its relevant constituency. To a first approximation, the possible constituencies might be identified in (roughly) rising order of scale or of geographic coverage as: (1) the neighborhood; (2) the city (or the commuter watershed); (3) the urban conurbation or megalopolis; (4) the ecological or environmental region; (5) the nation; (6) the international community.

It could be expected that different transport facilities would involve these different constituencies to a greater or lesser degree. Thus, as noted, planning of a new international airport would probably involve virtually all of them. Planning the resurfacing or improved curbing of local streets, by contrast, might usefully involve only the first group or possibly the second as well. Development of a new wilderness road into, say, a national park or wildlife preserve, might be primarily of interest to the fourth and fifth constituencies, that is the ecological community and the nation. The development of a high performance highway facility within a city might or might not involve all constituencies up through the fourth and fifth, depending upon environmental characteristics and the extent to which the highway is to serve through rather than purely local urban traffic. Planning to cope with problems of, say, oil pollution in sea water surely should involve the two largest constituencies, national and international, but also might involve some environmental constituencies as well.

It should be stressed that these illustrative examples of possibly relevant constituencies are not meant to be exhaustive. Indeed, the constituency idea need not be restricted to those defined by geography. The relevant constituencies deserving some sort of consultation in the planning process could as well be defined on functional or other lines. Indeed, to some considerable extent the environmental or ecological constituency is as much a functional as a geographic definition. Other constituencies that might be quite relevant in certain kinds of transport planning problems could be sportsmen or recreational groups, minority groups (which may or may not be consistent with a simple neighborhood definition), groups with particular interest in preserving historical sights, and so forth and so on.

In essence, what makes the transport planning function so difficult is that so many externalities tend to be involved. This, in turn, means that there are many different groups that legitimately (or sometimes illegitimately but nevertheless vocally) claim that they need to be consulted about transport developments before they occur. The essential problem in transport planning, then, is to identify these relevant interests or constituencies and devise means to represent their views *without unduly restricting or immobilizing the entire planning and development process.* The essential challenge for transportation planning in the next few years will be the development of planning devices at different levels of government to serve different modes and functions in such a way that these are properly articulated, coordinated, and cognitive of the many diverse interests involved. Political acumen, if not science, of the highest order may well be required.

Notes

1. Kendrick, John W., assisted by Maude R. Pech, PRODUCTIVITY TRENDS IN THE UNITED STATES, National Bureau of Economic Research, 1961.

2. Meyer, John, D. Kresge, M. Straszheim, P. Roberts, TECHNIQUES OF TRANSPORT PLANNING, Vols. 1 and 2, Brookings Institution, 1970.

3. H. Perloff, et al., RESOURCES AND ECONOMIC GROWTH, Johns Hopkins Press for Resources for the Future, 1960.

4. B. Chinitz, FREIGHT AND THE METROPOLIS, Harvard University Press for the Regional Plan Association, Cambridge, Massachusetts, 1960.

Political and Administrative Realities of Regional Transportation Planning

Norman Wengert,
Colorado State University

Decisions with respect to whether there will be regional transportation planning; what its characteristics will be; what regional boundaries will be drawn; how such regional planning will be accomplished; what its objectives and methods will be—all these decisions, and many others are, by definition, public sector or governmental decisions. Hence the various outcomes can only be understood in the context of an understanding of the political decision-making process. Thus, although this volume is concerned with regional transportation, it is desirable to examine the political and administrative realities affecting regional planning as a special case of the forces and factors that influence and shape public sector decisions in general.

The approach taken is analytical and interpretive, seeking to apply general concepts and theories about the political process to the more specific subject of regional transportation planning. Much of this essay is deductive; some of it is normative; very little is empirical. Except in a special sense explained below, no regional political science has developed comparable to regional economics or regional sociology. No theories of regional politics nor analytical schemes for ordering regional political data have been formulated.[1] In short, the literature on the political or administrative aspects of regionalism in general, or of regional planning in particular, is meager.[2]

To be sure, political scientists have always dealt with geographic or spatial units. Towns, cities, districts, counties, and states are types of political regions, and such political units, singly and in combination, have been traditional subjects for political studies. Since World War II, a number of political scientists has researched metropolitan problems. The results of these studies are of importance to regional analysis in general and to understanding the politics of regional transportation planning in particular, although they have not dealt directly with problems of decision-making in a regional context as part of a national system.[3] One must conclude, therefore, that a theoretical or conceptual basis for a regional political science has not yet been formulated (save perhaps with respect to certain types of area studies in international relations).

Regional political phenomena (including those directly relevant to transportation planning) must be considered as analogues of other political phenomena. This paper, therefore, applies general theories and concepts of the political process to the specific subject of regional transportation planning.

The literature of public administration (as distinct from political science) also lacks in-depth treatments of regional problems.[4] Little theoretical analysis has been conducted, and issues of regional organization, regional coordination, regional policy development, regional planning, or decision-making have not been explored to any great extent. The 1935 report of the National Resources Planning Board, *Regional Factors in National Planning*,[5] remains one of the classic explorations of these questions. The monographic literature consists largely of case studies and descriptions of administrative practice, including studies of river basins and regional economic development programs.[6] The "doctrinal" literature on such subjects as decentralization, delegation, field-headquarters relationships, etc., may often be useful in making judgments concerning questions of regional planning and administration. Similarly, administrative practice and experience with respect to regional planning and organization of federal and state programs also provides useful information. But empirical data is lacking and levels of analysis and generalization with respect to governmental practice and experience leave much to be desired. Much of the writing is descriptive, promotional, or simply hortatory, seeking to explain or justify policies and approaches of particular agencies, departments, or bureaus.

Propositions and Premises

Proposals for integrated approaches to transportation planning and management assume that transportation is a single commodity, a single service, or a single system, and hence can be analyzed on a unified basis. The question whether this is a necessary and proper assumption must be dealt with explicitly. While ultimately everything may relate to everything else, the simple assertion, or the attachment of definitions and labels does not really settle the question of system boundaries. The assumptions underlying functional analysis, therefore, are crucial to whether (or to what extent) regional transportation planning makes sense.

One can argue that a metropolitan region may benefit from unified transportation planning as it relates to intra-regional movement of goods and people, without proving the case for extending regional planning to air, truck, rail, bus, and private car transportation moving into the region from outside. That inter-regional transportation may affect the region needs little proof, but whether it should be dealt with by regional planning and new government structures requires proof.

The transportation situation is now characterized by highly pluralistic planning, involving decisions by many individual firms, and by a variety of federal, state, and local public agencies. The role of consumer and other pressure groups in dealing with the private firms and with the government agencies is important, as are the interests of investors, financial agents, and labor unions.

Partly because it tends to be typical of American society and of American government, and partly because of the pluralistic, uncoordinated structure of transportation, a dominant characteristic of governmental relationships to transportation is the tendency to respond positively to every demand without worrying about total costs or total benefits (consequences) or considering alternatives. The "squeaking wheel gets the grease." But coordination, to be meaningful, requires choices; whether on a local, a regional, or a national basis. It must deny the "something for everyone" approach of the present system.

Undoubtedly in every nation, but certainly in a nation as large as the United States, governmental (and much private) activity takes place in spatial units of less than national scope. Much action occurs at a point in space and has its initial impact at that point. The idea that a regional approach (i.e., combining counties or states) to a wide range of political problems might be conducive to their solution has in recent years gained popularity for several reasons:

- ° Numerous regional studies conducted by the government, such as those dealing with water development spearheaded by the Water Resources Council[7] under the Water Resources Planning Act of 1965[8] have interested politicians, bureaucrats, and planning professionals, and the general public in regional problem solving.
- ° Regional development planning has been given considerable stimulation through a series of recent Congressional enactments such as the Appalachian Regional Development Act[9] and Title V of the Public Works and Economic Development Act (which created other regional development commissions).[10]
- ° Considerable attention has also been focused on urban-metropolitan problems defined in regional terms, e.g., much of the discussion of urban-metropolitan transportation problems has been in a regional frame of reference.[11]

It is, therefore, not surprising to encounter suggestions that all transportation might better be dealt with through a network of regional transportation planning agencies. The question that needs evaluation is, of course, whether such organizational changes would result in fundamental improvement.

The Transportation Crisis

If an opinion survey were conducted on the question, it would very likely indicate that large segments of the public believe that the nation is confronted with transportation problems of crisis proportions requiring drastic government action at many levels. In the view of many, the national transportation crisis would probably consist of a number of subproblems summarized in the following bald statements:

1. Highway transportation in urban-metropolitan centers is highly congested, the congestion is increasing, and the major cause of this problem is the private automobile. Congestion of air traffic is a serious problem associated with large urban-metropolitan communities.
2. Private automobiles in urban-metropolitan centers are a major cause of air pollution.
3. The poor, particularly in urban-metropolitan centers, suffer inequalities in access to transportation that contribute to their unsatisfactory living situations, increasing difficulties in access to jobs, markets, other service facilities, and to recreation.
4. Public transportation services in metropolitan areas are substandard, including railroad passenger service for both commuting and intercity travel.
5. The financial status of public transportation systems, particularly those involved in passenger transportation, is precarious.
6. There is no effective integration or coordination of modes of transportation, the dominant organizing concept of the transportation sector being that the several modes compete with each other. Government intervention, though extensive, has not dealt successfully with problems of integration and coordination, despite substantial subsidies granted to many modes of transportation.
7. It is probably also quite widely held that present government policies and programs are inadequate, and may often contribute to intensification of transportation problems rather than to their alleviation. It was politically feasible to create the U.S. Department of Transportation in part because views of this kind were widespread. And the current interest in a variety of regional transportation approaches reflects a similar belief that present approaches are not working.

Other items might be added to this list, depending to a large extent on the point of view and values of the person stating the definition.

Problem Solving

It is a commonplace that the American political system is oriented to pragmatic problem solving, rather than being ideologically motivated. Among the consequences of this orientation is the fact that he who defines the problems, sets the agenda for social action and plays an inordinately important role in formulating solutions. A further implication of this situation may well be that, like beauty, problems are initially only in the eyes of the beholders. Another consequence of this emphasis on problem solving may be insufficient attention to the capacity and ability of government; all problems are believed solvable. On the one hand, this contributes to the optimism often associated with the American character. But on the other hand, when results are not up to expectations it ultimately stimulates a hypercritical negativism that can create public pessimism, frustration, disillusion, and the destruction of confidence in governmental processes and institutions (alienation).

To illustrate: Most anyone can prepare long lists of what is wrong with the national transportation system, but such lists depend in part on the measures one applies. In terms of such measures as ease of movement or the possibility of securing food and manufactured goods from almost anywhere in the world, or the freedom possessed by most individuals (because of the automobile) to come and go when and where they choose, perhaps one might conclude that the American system performs better than that of any other nation. A glass of milk may be half empty or half full depending on one's psychological outlook! No transportation system (any more than any machine) can be frictionless (i.e., problem-free). A reasonable test balances inputs against outputs as related to or qualified by basic concepts of equity and fair distribution of costs and benefits. Gross figures are not enough; distributional data must be examined to determine *who* benefits and *who* is burdened.

And how should transportation planning deal with the private auto? Is it a transportation problem, or by designating it a problem, do we obscure more fundamental and more real problems of which the auto is but the symptom, e.g., inadequate land-use and housing patterns, absence of effective planning with respect to labor markets, industrial location, and job security?

There are many signs that national values may be changing, although one must cautiously recognize that signs may be misread. Hardly a day passes when someone does not assert that we must change our priorities to include protecting the environment and improving the quality of life. Sometimes explicit, and always implicit, in such statements is a criticism of a presumed past emphasis on economic development, and on the application of economic efficiency measures (GNP) for determining the state of well-being of the nation.[12]

An illustration: The State of Colorado created an Environmental Commission that in its first annual report outlined sixteen recommendations for legislative action, including one for the creation of a state transportation department.

The Commission, being critical of the lack of action with respect to mass transit in the state, castigated the continuing preponderance of private automobiles and consequent air pollution. Thus the Commission said:

A disproportionate share of the state's resources go for highway construction simply because there is little alternative for transportation to the automobile. The expenditure of funds and resources almost exclusively for highways perpetuates the heavy dependence on the automobile . . . The decision-making process ultimately becomes self-defeating: lack of alternate modes of transportation leads to the need for more automobiles and more highways, and thus for more highway construction and widening and the dedication of more highway-user monies to highway construction, at the expense of other modes of transportation.[13]

As a step toward breaking the vicious circle, the Transportation Department was to have authority to integrate operation of air, highway, bus, rail and various forms of mass transit.

A Review of Regional Planning Trends

As a technical term with a particular meaning, "regionalism" is relatively new in the vocabulary of the social sciences.[14] Lewis Mumford once told a group of graduate students (of which this author was a member) how he came back from Europe in the early 1920s excited about the concept of "regionalism" as he had encountered it in France. But when he visited the New York Public Library to see what was available on the subject, he discovered that "regionalism" and "regions" were not then catalog categories!

An interest in regionalism developed at the University of North Carolina in the 1920s, and several articles with "regional" in their titles appeared in the *American Political Science Review* at about that time.[15] But major stimulus to regional thought undoubtedly resulted from New Deal interest, first, as represented by the TVA Act (May 1933), and then from the work on the subject undertaken by the National Resources Planning Board. The initial emphasis on *river basin regions* was reinforced by the Flood Control Act of 1936,[16] just as the concern for small watershed regions, important to its program from its earliest days, was evidenced in the Soil Conservation Service.

Although there were some strong advocates for expanding regional approaches (most federal agencies were, of course, administered on some kind of a regional basis, e.g., the Federal Reserve Banks), a general policy of regionalization of federal functions, including effective decentralization, was not adopted. Instead regionalism came more and more to be associated only with river basin development and the management of water. World War II postponed further implementation of any regional concepts, although it did encourage more rapid development of some public hydro-electric power projects. Once the war was over, a number of important persons sought to restore and even strengthen the idea of regional development. But, in fact, the emphasis continued to be on the river basin as the unit for development.

Perhaps the strength and persistence of the watershed or river basin as an effective unit for planning is attributable to the fact that almost from the founding of our government, it has been Constitutionally and politically possible for the National Government to make funds available for water development and to handle the resulting programs directly. Public works expenditures have always appealed to the Congress, since they provide tangible evidence of what a representative or senator is doing for his home constituency. And once the Supreme Court accepted the definition of a navigable stream (and hence one subject to federal jurisdiction) as one capable of floating a log, the Constitutional basis for river development expenditures (even without the *carte blanche* ultimately provided by the "spending power") served as an increasingly viable basis for federal construction programs. First navigation, then flood control, then irrigation, then power were included in the scope of federal interests. And as these interests broadened, the technology of water management also broadened with the result that, in hydrological terms, the watershed logically became an even more appropriate focus of attention. Even though the congruence of watersheds with social and economic problems was often not clear, the availability of federal funds for watershed development tended to force regional planning into the watershed mold, and made possible the evolution of watershed planning institutions. It has thus been politically desirable from the point of view of federal agencies and politicians to equate regional planning with river basin planning. A high point in this effort was the 1950 Report of the President's Water Policy Commission.[17] Regional water development continued to have support in some sectors, as indicated by the 1965 enactment of the Water Resources Planning Act,[18] which authorized a variety of regional planning efforts. But following the enactment of this statute, water development has seemed to decline in importance, probably for reasons which include the fact that most of the nation's water resources have been substantially developed.

Even where water problems continued to be pressing, they were defined in new terms, such as pollution control, and recreation. In the last few years, a hostility to "development" also began to be voiced, with environmental preservation being considered more important. Partly in response to these new policy interests, approaches to water planning have begun to change, with emphasis on issues other than efficiency in national economic development. The Water Resources Council, for example, took the lead in seeking to reformulate evaluation criteria to include environmental preservation, income distribution, and regional development as objectives of water development.[19]

But while these changes were occurring with respect to water planning, a completely independent thrust, involving fundamentally different concepts of regionalism, was being formulated in connection with the recognition that in urban-metropolitan regions were to be found some of the nation's most pressing and difficult problems. This approach stressed the "nodal" region and concentrated on a broad spectrum of interrelated problems in the metro area. It was problem-oriented and not primarily developmental. As coordinated and intergovernmental approaches to problems of the metropolis were emphasized, the sources of federal interest and funding shifted from water development agencies to new agencies with new programs, different statutory authority, and different constituency support. For a variety of reasons, these new programs tended to be carried out with and through existing governmental units: cities, counties, special districts, and states. The water development programs of the Corps of Engineers and of the Bureau of Reclamation were essentially direct action federal programs, with varying degrees of deference to local governments and local interests (often deliberately stimulated to provide legitimization for the federal activity), but the newer urban-metro oriented programs were carried out by existing governments and reflected their perspectives and interests.

Focus on Intergovernmental Relations

That the relationships were not always smooth is indicated by the substantial post-war interest in "intergovernmental relations," and in the still vehement debates about whether federal agencies should deal directly with local governments or only through state agencies, and about citizen participation in program formulation. A variety of patterns have, in fact, been followed with the position that the federal government should deal with the states tending to be more favorably regarded (i.e., receiving more political support). The power struggles between existing local governments (The Establishment) and newly stimulated community organizations in connection with the so-called "Poverty Program" shed light on the general questions of urban-metropolitan regional organization,[20] and an examination of certain aspects of these controversies follows in a subsequent section of this paper.

Of even more long-run significance to regional planning have been several other developments of recent years that have strengthened the role of both local and state governments vis-à-vis federally funded programs, emphasizing regional approaches—regional in this context meaning planning on a basis that transcends the boundaries of any single local governmental jurisdiction—and stressing the importance of coordination in both planning and action. Thus, the nodal metropolitan region has become a focus for many federal, state and local programs.

A significant thrust for dealing with problems on an area basis came from the Advisory Commission on Intergovernmental Relations, which in a series of careful studies over the past decade called attention to the need for better coordination and planning at the metro level. The Commission's studies have dealt with functional problems, such as sewage and water supply,[21] and also with organizational arrangements that it felt would contribute to more effective regional planning and decisions in metropolitan areas. In the area of organization, for example, the Commission reviewed the utility of Councils of Governments and encouraged their formation as coordinating mechanisms.[22]

At the same time, reflecting a variety of values and pressures, other federal programs began to emphasize the need for intergovernmental action at the metropolitan level. It is not appropriate here to review the wide range of federal programs that provide grants, loans, and technical assistance to local governments, but it is significant to note the growing insistence on regional or interjurisdictional collaboration as prerequisites to federal assistance.

In one of its studies, the Advisory Commission on Intergovernmental Relations stressed that fragmentation and proliferation of special service districts posed an acute challenge to planning in metropolitan districts. The Commission pointed out that the Standard Metropolitan Statistical Areas (SMSA) each averaged almost 100 local government units, which overlap, intermingle, intersect, and generally form a very confusing picture.

As the problems of government in metropolitan regions became more apparent after World War II, the first reforms were in the direction of the so-called "Toronto Plan," in which a new unit of government was proposed for the metropolitan area. But the incentives for consolidations of this sort have been few, and initial enthusiasm for this approach has waned. A degree of cooperation has been achieved through so-called "COG" organizations—Councils of Governments—but their performance remains to be appraised. It is clear, in any case, that their success in integrating planning and action on a metro basis will to a large extent reflect federal pressures. More recently, state governments have begun enacting statutes and creating agencies to facilitate integrated regional planning transcending local jurisdictional boundaries.

A landmark in this effort to insist on regional coordination and collaboration was the Federal Intergovernmental Cooperation Act of 1968,[23] the legislative history of which remains to be written. This Act is designed to, among other things, ". . . establish coordinated intergovernmental policy and administration of development assistance programs." Title IV sets out a national policy of considering local, regional, and state interests in administering federal aid programs for local development. At the time the Bureau of the Budget listed some fifty programs dealing with such subjects as open space development, airports, water supply and distribution, sewage facilities and waste treatment, highway and other transportation (including mass transport) grants, water development, and land conservation and planning—that were to be coordinated.

Circular A-95[24] of the Office of Management and Budget in implementing this Act, emphasized the need for sound, orderly development of urban and rural areas of the nation, and directed that "to the maximum extent possible, consistent with national objectives, all federal aid for development purposes shall be consistent with and further the objectives of state, regional, and local planning." Although the tone is one of deference to state and local interests, in fact the Circular went on to spell out the terms and conditions under which federal aid would be made available.

First, a *Project Notification and Review System* was to be established to facilitate coordination of state, regional, and local planning and development. Second, a system of *Intra-State, Multijurisdictional Planning and Development Regions* was to be provided to coordinate action on both an area and a functional basis. Finally, a system for *Grant-in-Aid Information* for any state desiring it was to be devised, with a designated single state agency to serve as the reception point for such information. This latter provision resulted in a system of clearinghouses through which applications for federal aid must pass. Through them concerned units of government, other than those directly applying for aid secure information, confer, comment, and identify conflicts. And within a particular state, machinery was indicated that would permit the development of regional plans and programs effectively transcending local jurisdictional boundaries.

The Colorado Experience

How this system was implemented is suggested by the Colorado experience. In August 1969 the governor designated the Office of State Planning as the responsible state agency. This office then established a network of regional metropolitan planning and development clearinghouses for the entire state. Eight regions were initially proposed, consolidating the fifteen that had existed prior to this reorganization. The boundaries for the eight proposed regions were the result of careful review and analysis by the Office of State Planning, and reflected the application of specific planning and development criteria. Space does not permit a discussion of these criteria, nor of the procedure followed. But one subsequent step deserves mention.

The Office of State Planning recognized that public support for the regions was essential—particularly support by the local government officials and other local influentials who would be affected by this pattern of regionalization and who would have to work within the regional framework. For this reason, the Office of State Planning undertook a widespread program to discuss its proposed regions with the people who were to be affected, with the purpose not only of passing on information to them, but of getting reactions, so that factors that may have been overlooked might be considered and errors in regional definition corrected. With no field staff of its own, the State Planning Office turned to the Colorado State University Extension Service to take responsibility for discussing the regionalization proposal in the counties and communities. Many meetings were held for discussion and exchange of views. These meetings permitted various groups to review the appropriateness of the proposed boundaries and to explain how they might affect their interests.

The direct results of this process—an increase in the number of planning regions from eight to twelve—were announced in the fall of 1970. It is too early to determine what the long-run effects will be, but several agencies have announced that they will conform their planning activities to the regional structure thus developed, and there is reason to expect that uniform regionalization of Colorado may ultimately result, contributing to the coordination of planning and action envisaged by the Intergovernmental Cooperation Act and

OMB Circular A-95. (Since the initial determination of twelve planning regions, unhappiness with their boundaries has been mounting and it is likely that changes may be made and perhaps additional regions designated.)

The point to emphasize in the context of this paper is that the impact of urban-metropolitan problems, and the apparent need for planning and co-ordinated action on an areal basis encompassing many traditional local juris-dictions, have led to a regional approach that gives promise of significant long-run benefits. It is important to note, moreover, that the resulting state regions are significantly different from the river basin regions of the Water Resources Planning Act and from the regions proposed to deal with regional transportation planning.

If one might hazard an opinion, it seems more likely that the regionalization under the Intergovernmental Cooperation Act and OMB Circular A-95 will come nearer to dealing effectively with pressing transportation problems than the proposed large transportation regions.

Regions, Politics, and Political Decisions

Decisions defining regions, decisions creating regional agencies, decisions assign-ing functions on a regional basis, decisions concerning programs and agency organization on a regional basis, decisions setting standards and spelling out procedures for regional action—these, and many other decisions concerning regions, are at some point political. They are outputs of a political process.

The stuff of politics is power—who governs and how, the reciprocal relationships of authority and obligation between the governors and the governed as well as between different sets of governors and among the governed themselves. The product of political interaction is more than a series of particular policies like foreign aid or civil rights [or regional planning] ; it is a way of life.[25]

Somewhat irreverently, Harold Lasswell many years ago defined politics as "who get what, when, how."[26] To his list should be added "where," to stress the importance of the geographical allocation of benefits and costs, which is a major dimension of political decisions with respect to regions and regionaliza-tion.

For some twenty-five years, political scientists have concentrated on the study of the process, on the interactions involved in "getting," and on the "what," the "when," the "how" but only to a slight degree on the "where," and quite generally neglecting the "who" and the normative and equitable issues implicit in any distribution of government advantages and disadvantages. Reflecting the logical-positivist mood of the post World War II era with its strong distinction between facts and values, decision-making research concentrated on process and avoided value questions. Goals and objectives, program content and program consequences provided a backdrop for process studies but little more. More recently, however, an awareness has been developing that while the processes by which decisions are made and the forces and factors affecting decisions are important, the content and consequences of decisions also require attention. In short, there is a renewed concern for the "public interest." In this new view, it is not enough simply to be concerned with "the authoritative allocation of values"—and with how the system achieves this allocation, but attention is also being directed to value consequences and alternatives and the equity, efficiency, and effectiveness of allocation decisions.

Politics is decision-making in the public sector. The term applies to the total process by which public-governmental decisions are made—decisions with respect to government goals, as well as structure, with respect to administration and with respect to policy, with respect to program content and program execution. Many factors and forces, concepts and ideas, values and beliefs, myths and symbols, institutions and customs may interact to influence the character and direction of public-governmental decisions. But all of these influences, whatever they may be, are perceived and understood by people. Hence of critical importance are the roles, perceptions, and personalities of the decision-makers, and of the publics comprising their constituencies. The substantive issues themselves (problems), the manner in which they are defined, the structure, mechanisms, techniques, procedures, and practices of government, as well as the many participants in the process and their goals and aspirations—all may affect the outcome, all may be significant elements in political decision-making.

Proposals to establish regions for whatever purpose, like proposals for organization or reorganization generally, involve a variety of strategic and technical considerations with a wide range of possible political inputs. The advantages anticipated by those supporting such proposals, as well as costs and benefits to those affected, must be considered. And a part of the decision, where the political content is high and awareness acute, may involve interrelationships between the Executive Branch and Congress, and between existing federal agencies and proposed regional organizations. And, of course, the relationships to state and local governments are not neutral. Traditions and what might be called a kind of "institutional culture" are involved. Linkages among agencies, and between the bureaucracy and the Congress may be important. In short, the rhetoric of efficiency, of better program administration, of improved coordination, cannot be permitted to cloud the fact that regionalization decisions are politically determined and may vitally affect the allocation of power and influence; they may decide who gets what, when, where, and how.

Yet, not all political decisions have identical impact; not all involve the same intensity of issues; not all involve significant alterations in the distribution of advantages and disadvantages.

The following classification of public sector decisions is a heuristic device that may help to identify decisions that might profitably be considered for political analysis.

○ There are in our complex society, first, what may be classed as *automatic (or autonomous) decisions*. These are decisions where the facts seem clear or undisputed, the precedents well-established, the consequences generally accepted, and hence choices are virtually non-existent. The absence of alternatives may simply reflect previous decisions, institutionalized behavior, or ignorance of the consequences. But in any case, decisions of this type involve few choices, arouse no hostility or opposition, and hence are not involved in the political process. Because of the ever present span of attention limitations, there is a constant psychological pressure to move decisions into this category.

○ A second type, which may be designated *pseudo-automatic decisions*, are those in which the decisionmaker *assumes* that the facts are clear and that no choices are involved, but for a variety of reasons (perhaps because neither information, nor techniques, nor institutions for challenging such decision exist) society tends to accept these decisions until some crisis arises causing a reexamination of decision premises. Common instances of such decisions are those made by scientists presuming their data to be more reliable and conclusive than they in fact are or those in which the decision-makers ascribe their own values to society at large and are thus unaware of the need for choice.

○ A third category of *decisions* are those where *conditions of uncertainty* prevail, and the decisionmakers recognize the need for choosing, for exercising judgment without knowing for certain what the consequences are going to be, or how the chosen action in fact relates to individual, group, or societal interests.

○ A fourth category, difficult to distinguish from the third, involves decisions under conditions of *uncertainty*, but where the *decision-maker knows what he wants* and rationalizes his goals as being in the "public interest," *public* as well as *interest* often being undefined. Decisions in this category often involve self-seeking and personal gains and advantage, extracting group or individual benefits from the system.

As a matter of societal goals, there is a strong thrust to move decisions into the first category by increasing rationality and thus certainty. At the same time, the decisional universe grows, reflecting more reliable problem diagnosis, as well as increasing complexities of life, changing value systems, and new priorities. Thus while the number of autonomous decisions may increase, the ratio of autonomous to other categories may not change—or may even decrease. In this connection it is noteworthy that we know too little about man's propensity for non-rational behavior.

This classification of decisions is in contrast to a more frequently encountered approach which characterizes decision processes rather than decisions. Thus Paul Diesing speaks of "Technical Rationality," "Economic Rationality," "Social Rationality," "Legal Rationality," and "Political Rationality."[27] This seems to be too static an approach, establishing rigid walls among the several types of rationality. The typology we have suggested, even though only heuristic, recognizes social strivings to move decisions to the autonomous category through research and other means for increasing knowledge.

The Public Interest

In recent years it has been fashionable among many social scientists to reject the concept of "the public interest," the premise being that in political decisions everyone seeks his own advantage, manipulating the system so that he will get the most out of it. That decisionmakers can only act on the basis of their own perceptions of what is good and bad, needs no proof. But that no one has the capacity to consider the interests of society, that it is impossible to assess advantages and disadvantages or costs and benefits is quite a different matter. The ethical issues aside, one can recognize institutional and cultural constraints, ideals, and commitments—all may contribute to a system that can strive to seek the "public interest" and in some cases realize it.

At the same time, it is not possible to assert with respect to public sector decisions, as does economic theory with respect to market decisions, that the result of *all* seeking their *own advantage* will automatically result in achieving the public good. The important distinction in the public sector is that we are dealing with the application of power and influence, rather than with the calculation of interests guided by profit and loss accounting. He who has power and believes in the rightness of his cause (to paraphrase the late Justice Oliver Wendell Holmes), or perhaps simply he who has power, will use it to his advantage, particularly in a situation in which public interest values do not serve as effective constraints.

Perhaps those who reject the concept of the public interest as a viable principle confuse its measurement with its reality. Perhaps they do not recognize that personal perceptions need not be limited only to personal interests or that individual values may be broadened by ideals, by education, by analysis and study, and may include an interest in the community, the organization, the party, etc.

Thus to take account of the non-rational way in which political decision-making processes operate, with all these limitations, frictions and imperfections, is not to deny that the ultimate goal is the search for the public interest. Clearly, the processes involve compromise, negotiation, bargaining, conflict, and struggle. But while asserting that the search for the public interest is the end of politics (in many situations an item of faith, and one that is often sorely tried), it is this very search that requires critical analysis, clarification, and definition so that more reasonable and perhaps more rational decisions may be made with respect to the distribution of advantages and disadvantages, and allocation of costs and benefits, so that judgments may be made with respect to what are sound and desirable policies and programs. It is perhaps significant that new concepts of "the public interest" are being written into law and established by judicial decision with respect to emerging environmental values.

Pragmatic Definitions

It may well be that at some future time in a "Brave New World" mankind and governments will know enough to make social value choices entirely by nonpolitical means. (One of the important attempts at defining "the public interest" involves the search for "social indicators," the literature on which is growing apace.) But, borrowing Madison's figure of speech, till angels govern men, the political process as here described and as we know it in the United States will continue to be the way in which public-governmental decisions can best be made. This is not a matter of blind adherence to the *status quo*, nor simply a question of tolerating corruption and irrationality or of living with second-best choices, but rather accepting a process that takes into account the diversities of democratic life, and that is sufficiently flexible to permit examination and reexamination of values, goals, methods, and techniques. The political process, thus conceived, is necessary for refining and clarifying objectives for permitting countervailing forces to organize and to operate (however ineffectively) and for ultimately arriving at working definitions of public goals and objectives, i.e., the public interest.

In this view, politics is a process in which trades and negotiations must take place; individual, group, and community interests are weighed against each other; costs and benefits are assessed; and finally choices are made. Like the economic market place, the political market place is also concerned with allocation, not of resources directly, but of power, authority, and influence over the decisions of government that will disadvantage some and advantage others. In this political market, competition is imperfect because of inadequate knowledge, power inequities, and other impediments, frictions, and distortions. And like the economic market process, so too the political process often appears confused, illogical, and inequitable, rather than neat, logical, reasonable, and systematic. And certainly the political process also suffers from man's inability to foresee the future, to consider all relevant consequences, to account for all effects.

In the face of these frictions and deficiencies, the openness of the process is important. Equally important is a recognition of the rules of the game for the system can only work if *due process* is accepted as an overriding value.

This pluralistic view of politics and the political processes leads to several derivative propositions, stated here in summary fashion:

First, the points of decision in the system are many and shifting, scattered through the government structure at all levels, and through society itself, for political activity is not restricted to the formal government, but at some time may involve private sector actors mobilized for particular program and policy matters.

Second, groups are dominant participants in the process, providing support and legitimation.[28]

Third, struggle, competition, bargaining, tradeoffs, negotiation and alignment and realignment of factors and forces are characteristic of the on-going process of government, reflecting the complexity of individual and group goals, and uncertainties as to how these may best be achieved.

Fourth, decisions occur and can only be understood in the social context or setting from which they have emerged. Simply, the political system must be analyzed as a system, with planning representing the effort to apply reason and rationality so that better, wiser decisions may result.

In summary, then, while the political process is primarily concerned with "getting" (to use Lasswell's word), it is only a partial view to overlook the ability of man to analyze and judge consequences and to deal with society's interests about who should share in the benefits of public programs and who should share their burdens. The effects of socialization, the constraints of institutions, and the influence of the "rules of the game" (*due process of law*)—all may be important.

As the interest in process, narrowly defined, is broadening, so a renewed interest is developing in questions of "what is government for," and in the competence and capacity of government. It has been too easy to say "if you want something, organize a pressure group to attain it," or if there is a problem, "pass a law directing government to solve it," just as in the context of our affluent society it has been too easy to say "if you want to pay for it, you can have it."

Long before Lord Acton said that "power corrupts, and absolute power corrupts absolutely," political philosophers had dealt with the moral and ethical goals of society and how they might be attained. But the wave of logical positivist thought that dominated political science after World War II resulted in a rejection of the normative content of political decisions and avoided distributive issues of equity and justice. While one may concede that it was urgently necessary to raise questions about the viability of such concepts as "the public interest," "rationality," and "objectivity" in the formulation and administration of public programs, one must also recognize that discrediting normative political science left nothing in its place. It has clearly been useful to examine the structure of power and influence, to analyze the techniques and uses of political power, and to take account of the variables subsumed under the rubric of "political behavior." Perhaps, as Dr. Samuel Eldersveld has written, we are now in the "post-behavioral" period in which we must begin to develop better techniques for program and policy analysis and viable criteria for judging effectiveness and consequences. This means a revived interest in program goals, distributive goals, distributive effects, and due process.

One of the consequences of putting normative issues aside is that fundamental values are often assumed as given or as already determined, and attention is then directed to questions of efficient goal achievement, to operational problems of relationships, and to the interactions among established organizations and institutions. Those in the bureaucracy have been particularly prone to operate in this fashion, rationalization becoming a substitute for rationality.

The sophistication of aggregative economic analysis, for example, reinforced the avoidance of distributive and equitable questions. For the bureaucrat, assumptions of this nature may be particularly comfortable, if not necessary, for they permit him to do "his job" without worrying too much about ethical questions of who benefits and who pays—just so long as the ratio of total or averaged costs to benefits is at least unity. Perhaps recent concern for environmental consequences has again begun to bring these value issues to the fore—although I am not sure that we know how to handle them any better than forty years ago when the Great Depression presented policy makers with similar kinds of value choices.

Perhaps one way of confronting these problems is to focus on the *agenda of politics* as distinct from the processes of politics. Both are important; both can benefit from much more knowledge than is now available to us. But decisions in both areas (agenda decisions and process decisions) must be made. We cannot wait until we know all things. So perhaps being sophisticated about the process can alert us (society) to the dangers of simply responding to the loudest clamor, or of reacting on the basis of myths and shibboleths, slogans and catch phrases. And in this view of the political process, one can begin to ask meaningful questions concerning regionalization of government functions and activities.

Governmental Goal Setting

Setting of public goals to be implemented by governmental means (i.e., by encouragement, by prohibitions, by sanctions, by subsidies, etc.) is an important function of the political process. The factors and forces relevant to an analysis of substantive goals and the processes by which they are determined include: the state of technology and information; the organizational structure, what it is and what it is not, what it can do and what it cannot do; the interests involved in the formulation and implementation of particular goals; social values, popular perceptions and expectations; the capacity of government; and the institutional forces affecting social values.

None of these factors is static. They interact on each other and respond to changing times and circumstances. Most goals, moreover, are ultimate from some points of view, relative or instrumental from others. And goals, whether accepted or rejected, are not necessarily wise, rational, good or correct.

Transportation, for example, is a means to other ends: production, sales, freedom of movement, freedom to live virtually anywhere, etc. For this reason, transportation can be regarded as a service function and government intervention justified as seeking to improve service, i.e., to better realize public interests in the movement of goods and people. If present patterns of transportation create problems, these can be minimized either by dealing with transportation as such, allowing the service concept to continue to dominate, or by dealing with the activities that transportation is seeking to serve. For example, a traditional solution to highway congestion has been to build more highways (i.e., provide more service), but decentralization of economic activity, as Lewis Mumford long ago argued, may also solve the congestion problem. Congestion at airports can be solved by providing more airports or by rationing access.

Another illustration: urban living congestion and other undesirable housing conditions can be dealt with by attempting to improve the transportation network, or it can be dealt with by controlling land use development. Air pollution resulting from automobiles can be reduced by limiting automobile use in smog-prone areas, encouraging or requiring the use of mass transit, or by installing pollution control devices on automobiles, or by shifting settlement patterns.

The volume of freight, as well as the means by which it is moved, can be controlled in a variety of ways. The exigencies of World War II, for example, indicated that the consumer can do without many products, and thus it is possible to influence transportation patterns by dealing with the need for the things a transport system moves. It can be argued, in fact, that planning for transportation cannot be carried out effectively without also giving attention to the things and people transported, and to the purposes for which they are transported.

It certainly is clear that planning is impossible without first stating the goals that the plans seek to achieve. Even if the stress is simply on problem solving (which may avoid more difficult goal formulation) choices must nevertheless be made among alternative means of solving the problems, including among the alternatives the possibility of eliminating the causes of the problems. If, for example, there is a problem of shipping oranges from California to Chicago, one possible solution is not to ship them. One of the aspects of the so-called "affluent society" is the tremendous range of substitutability of products, and consequently the wide range of choices open to solve many problems. Humans need vitamin C, they probably do not need oranges! Such decisions with respect to goals as well as with respect to the means for achieving them are political decisions, almost inevitably involving conflict over both ends and means. And those involved in the struggle to resolve the conflict will constantly need to analyze, persuade, build alliances and alignments, so that action may be taken and programs legitimated. Legitimation, in our system, depends on communication, on socialization, on institutions that make possible support and acceptance of proposed courses of action, resting on values in which tolerance and confidence in the equity of the system are widely shared.

The Politics of Area and Space

Boundary decisions are concerned with space and hence are an important component of regional analysis. Thus, many discussions of regional planning begin by examining or defining the basis for the region to be planned. Typically, the factors to be considered in drawing regional boundaries are identified, and from these regional limits tend to emerge. But such analytical regions usually rest on the stated or unstated premises of the analyst, with little systematic recognition being given to the perceptions, attitudes, and expectations of residents. Save perhaps in the delineation of "cultural regions," behavioral influences are also not given much attention. But such deficiencies are not the necessary result of regional analysis. In many cases, indeed, to achieve viable, effective regional planning, such influences may be of critical importance. It is important to recognize, therefore, that determining boundaries involves choices and hence is not a neutral decision, any more than administrative organization or reorganization decisions are neutral.[29] Regionalization, just like departmentalization, is to the advantage of some individuals, groups, interests, and programs, and to the disadvantage of others. The issues are not simply matters of efficiency or effectiveness, but include fundamental determinations with respect to costs and benefits and how these are to be allocated. For this reason, the justification and equity of particular allocative decisions require careful analysis. And those engaged in such analysis must assess not only aggregate costs and benefits, but also the distribution of costs and benefits among specifically identified individuals and groups, among the various geographic areas of the nation, and in relation to program goals and objectives.

A few illustrations, chosen more-or-less at random, suggest the kinds of factors that historically would seem to have been important. At the international level, many wars have dealt at least in part with questions of where boundaries between two nations should be set, and the motivational content of such decisions, if one can believe nationalistic historians, has been of considerable importance. The use of force to settle disputes over feudal relationships to which boundary questions (i.e., legal relationships to land) were sometimes critical was not unusual in Medieval times. Many modern wars have been concerned with boundary changes although dynastic control, or religion, or trade and economic advantage have also been important. Yet in many cases, whatever the dominant *casus belli*, the resolution of particular conflicts often resulted in boundary changes. Thus, questions of where and how to draw national borders was an important element of the peace settlement. The constraints of physical geography, as well as strategic considerations, frequently led to the use of rivers as boundaries.

Most boundary changes resulting from war have been rationalized in terms of economic and prestige aggrandizement of the victor and retribution to the vanquished. "Eye for an eye and tooth for a tooth" has remained an important value in international law.

It would be interesting to study the processes by which particular boundaries were determined and to lay bare the factors and forces that influenced choices, distinguishing among real and purported reasons, between fact and rhetoric. Among questions to which answers might be sought are: Why was the new boundary located where it was? Who stood to gain? Who to lose? What was the nature of gains and losses? What kinds of analyses went into the decisions? What were the rationalizations? What were the bargaining components? Did bargaining occur, or was the settlement "imposed" as a result of "unconditional surrender," or because of political commitments to victorious constituents? What factors were considered by the victors? How adequately were consequences considered? What kind of consequences? How did the peacemakers perceive the boundary decisions? (To anticipate, similar questions are relevant at the intranational level, where boundary problems also may be crucial.)

But many boundary decisions in the international world have been made without war or even the threat of force. A classic example, perhaps, was the decree of Pope Alexander VI in 1493 (confirmed in 1494 by the Treaty of Tordesillas between Spain and Portugal), dividing the New World between Spain and Portugal. Among the consequences of this decision is the fact that Brazilians speak Portuguese rather than Spanish. Not much less in arrogant, yet also accepted, were the grants that determined the boundaries of the original thirteen English colonies in North America.

The treaty settlement of 1783 established the initial boundaries of the United States, and over the next 75 years to the sizeable area thus marked out was added new territory by purchase, annexation, and conquest. The story of "Manifest Destiny" is, of course, familiar. Not so familiar are the negotiations and bargains that were involved in setting the boundaries of the added areas and later of the 50 states into which the total was ultimately divided. Within the states the lesser boundaries of counties, townships, and urban incorporated places similarly often involved complex decisions based on political negotiations, bargains, and judgments. While in part these decisions involved conscious deliberative processes, they also reflected the traditions, expectations, and institutions of the times in which the decisions were made. For example, the boundaries of urban places reflect to a considerable extent fundamental concepts of the law of municipal corporations with its strong emphasis (in the United States) on self-determination, even as counties are often regarded as "little states" rather than convenient divisions of the states.

The literature of regionalism (regional planning and regional science) is replete with discussions of what are "proper" regions and how one should go about drawing regional boundaries. But little of this discussion deals with political realities. The National Resources Planning Board in 1935 concluded that there were no general criteria for regional administrative boundaries, and that generalized regions could probably not be determined. In many respects, we have advanced little in dealing with the issues of regional boundaries identified in that early report.

TVA was the first major experiment in regional river basin development in the United States. Although its *major* functions were navigation, flood control, and hydro-power generation, the TVA Act included language granting general planning power and extending its planning authority beyond the watershed of the Tennessee River to the contiguous area. And TVA was a symbol of American regional planning for many years. But in general, the watershed lines were most easy to defend, especially against bureaucratic attack. Except in two cases (first, electric power distribution, where pragmatic opportunities served to delimit the service area, and, second, certain fertilizer activities, where a tenable interpretation of the statute was that responsibilities were not regional but national in scope), TVA adhered strictly to the watershed—to the point of giving free seedling trees for reforestation for only that part of a farm that actually drained into the Tennessee River!

At the Federal level generally, partly due to the work of the NRPB and partly as a consequence of the Flood Control Act of 1936, regional planning was often regarded as equivalent to watershed or river basin planning. Undoubtedly this reflected the pragmatic reality that this was one area of planning which 1) was not labelled radical, 2) had much traditional political support, and 3) reflected the fact that everyone lived in a watershed. Yet many interested in regional planning have challenged the watershed as the "proper" approach.

As already pointed out in the last several decades, new emphasis has been given to metropolitan regions as more useful and more effective areal units for planning. On the pragmatic side, while everyone lives in a watershed, more people live in metropolitan areas, and it is people, not acres that count. Moreover, many of the largest metropolitan areas are located in areas where "the watershed" is not an important factor. In the tidewater area from Boston to Washington, in the Great Lakes cities, and probably in many other metropolitan centers on the coasts, the "river basin" is not a realistic concept, and the role of the "river" as an important influence is not recognized or perceived. In these centers, most water and watershed related decisions are in fact "invisible," being left to engineers and other technicians.

Analytical and Decisional Regions

It may be useful to distinguish several kinds of regions in order to provide a basis for some generalizations about those of similar type.

First, *analytical regions* are those identified and described by the analyst, people living or working in the region not being particularly aware of its regionality until it is pointed out to them. Two subcategories of analytical regions may be identified: those determined by social or natural data, an illustration of the former being an ethnic or cultural region, and an illustration of the latter being a soil region or a river basin; and those evolving from human behavior without particular thought to areal factors, a metropolitan region being in this category (although a metro region might also be identified by data analysis).[a]

Second, *decisional regions* are regions determined by deliberate, considered governmental or private action. A sales or service district would be an illustration of a decisional region in the private sector; a state or a county would illustrate public sector decisions with respect to regional boundaries, as would a Federal Reserve District or a Soil Conservation District.[b] The point to emphasize is that "regionality" flows from a constituent act and is comparable to the kind of act involved in creating a corporation, although a corporation need not have spatial or areal specifity. Municipal corporations tend to be spatially oriented, although some states grant them limited functional extraterritoriality.

In economic and sociologic analysis, regional boundaries are often established more-or-less clearly from data generated by more-or-less independent actions of individuals. A trade area, for example, has definite and statistically determinable boundaries that emerge from the facts of trading behavior. The statistics simply mirror behavior.

Similarly, cotton politics, corn politics, wheat politics, etc., provide a basis for studying certain limits of political activity on a regional basis. The pre-World War II isolationism of the Midwest appears to have been a regional political phenomenon. The labor politics of the industrial northeast and the irrigation politics of the semi-arid west, to mention a few examples, exhibit similar political "regionality." V.O. Key could write impressively on *Southern Politics*[30] believing (and proving) that this region provided a logical and proper basis for generalization about its politics. In fields like history, art, and literature, the identification of "regionality" is primarily a conclusion of the observer who sees uniformities which may not be quantifiable but are nevertheless real.

But many regions exist simply because of political-governmental decisions. If a region is defined as a unit of space delimited by one or many homogeneous factors, then, the political unit—the nation, state, county, city, township, district—is a decisional region. Similarly, by definition, the geographically defined unit for governmental administration may be considered a region and analyzed as such. In time, such "arbitrary" regions affect social and economic behavior and activity.

[a]Human behavior may be affected by social or by natural (environmental) phenomena.

[b]Initially, Soil Conservation Districts were to have followed watershed boundaries, but this was often not acceptable to local decisionmakers, so many districts have been drawn on township and county lines.

Purposes Underlying Regionalization

A listing of some of the purposes which lie behind regionalization suggest the complexity involved in defining regions, whether analytically or decisionally, and it begins to indicate why agreement on regional boundaries is difficult.

To begin with, of course, regionalization in the United States reflects the tremendous area of the country, the diversity of its physical geography, and historic contrasts in culture and in social, economic, and political conditions. It also reflects span of attention limitations. Thus administrative convenience as well as effectiveness of public and private activities require regionalization. But, of course, the need for dealing with parts of the country does not automatically provide a basis for defining those parts.

Closely related to the size of the country is the nature and characteristics of problems to be dealt with, since many problems confronting government can better be identified and dealt with on a less-than-national basis. In part this may simply reflect the desire for visibility and attention, but in part it reflects the fact that, like pain, social problems are often local and can best be identified and dealt with on a less-than-national basis (analytical regions).

Undoubtedly coordination has often been a purpose behind a regional emphasis. Two different approaches often are involved: the one focusing on more effective integration within the regional system; the other focusing on the linkages to other systems.

Finally, regionalization, like all organizational decisions, is often concerned with arranging and controlling power and influence. How an area is structured may determine who dominates the decision-making situation. A common illustration of this is the decennial struggles associated with legislative reapportionment and the drawing of legislative district boundaries.

Like decisions with respect to the organization of government departments and agencies, so geographic, spatial, or regional decisions may serve as substitutes for more difficult policy and program decisions. Regionalization, like reorganization, is no panacea. And whether altering organization structure through regionalization will contribute to the solution of defined problems, or bring about more efficient or effective government requires analysis and proof. Too often changes in organization are not accompanied by changes in authority to act. The same weakness has often been present in actual or proposed regionalization. It is a truism that planning should not be separated from action; and yet it is not unusual to create complex planning machinery without facing up to the problem of authority. This has been the situation with respect to much of the planning effort of the Water Resources Council and its related regional organizations; it is likely to be the situation with respect to the proposed regional planning program for transportation.

Boundaries and Data

Unit boundaries are important to political analysis, since most governmental activity takes place within rigidly defined spatial units. The boundaries of the administrative and political units of government provide an integrating force that solidifies the basis for analyzing regional aspects of activity within and among the units. It should be noted, too, that political boundaries and the activities within them may act as strongly linked features that in fact determine a multi-factor region, influencing its development, and structuring many other activities within its boundaries.

In some respects, this may make political regional analysis easier than other types. Vance has stated, for example, that:

In political science the problem of relating wholes is clarified by the fact that political entities have legal boundaries. In much of our social science analysis we deal with natural areas whose boundaries must be determined by research into the characteristics and functions of the regions under consideration. Given this advantage, history and political science have been able to specialize in the analysis of international and interregional relations in terms of formal structure and formal functions . . . [31]

In this light a substantial amount of political research is regional, *ab initio*.

Vance also points to an important consequence of the decisions with respect to political boundaries (regions):

Regions are delineated in terms of statistical indices of important cultural, economic, or social conditions. Since these figures are gathered on the basis of administrative areas, such as enumeration districts, urban census tracts, minor civil divisions, and counties, the process is one of building up small political units into homogeneous subregions.[32]

Vance might have with equal validity included states in his list of administrative statistical areas, for a substantial amount of important data is available only on a state basis, and thus states become significant analytical units. With respect to water law, for instance, building up of "water law regions" (i.e., homogeneous combinations of sub-units) can only be done by combining states with similar legal concepts.

Political and administrative units are in many respects comparable to farm units, firms, or other social units. Although arbitrarily delimited in the first instance, each develops its own integrity and becomes a distinct entity over time. Natural, physical and environmental factors are the molds that shape the blocks from which the units are built, while the mind of man, analyzing and synthesizing, makes of these basic forms a region. Of politically determined regions the late John Gaus said:

... the often derided political jurisdiction is as much a region as one determined by climate. Once a political boundary is drawn, human interests—political ambitions, areas of common services, and tax rates—adhere to it. It becomes as 'natural' a fact as a rainfall line. . .[33]

He was alluding to the fact that some of the literature on regionalism had criticized political and administrative boundaries on the grounds that they were impractical, unrealistic, and inconsistent with analytically determined regions. Since political and administrative boundaries are the result of more-or-less deliberate decision (rather than the result of converging natural, social and economic forces as reflected in data), the question of the logic and propriety of particular political boundaries is more readily criticized, if not altered. But many political boundaries when drawn had sound reasons behind them.

The county boundaries of Tennessee, for example, were drawn so that every resident would be no more than one day's journey from the seat of government. These boundaries persist even though the automobile made them obsolete. The drawing of county boundaries often occurred before areas were populated, but nevertheless determined social and economic relationships from then on, and in many cases, these relationships would have been upset by boundary changes.

Boundaries are important determinants of the structure of government, and also of the relationships of residents to governmental processes, most obviously in setting up geographical districts for representation. Under recent judicial doctrine ("one man, one vote") the boundaries of representative districts have been redrawn by the courts or as a result of court decisions, but basic jurisdictional units have not been changed, i.e., county, township, city, and school and special district boundaries have as yet not been altered by court action.

Finally, for many activities, the important point is that *some* boundaries be drawn, and only secondarily where they will be drawn. Yet once drawn, vested interests develop in their stability. This is true not only with political boundaries, but with respect to any activity to which boundaries are significant. Two salesmen selling the same product want to know the limits of their respective territories. A regional analyst must know what spatial data to include, and once the boundaries for statistical collection are set, only a major upheaval will warrant changes. Although for some purposes fluid boundaries might seem preferable in order to take dynamic patterns and change into account, analysis and appraisal require stability of boundaries.

Other Regional Determinants

With few exceptions, practical approaches to regional definition, as well as most of the literature on the subject, have sought to find objective factors to delimit appropriate regional boundaries. These regional determinants might be a single factor, or a set of inter-related factors, or, if the approach is considered to be "comprehensive," then an attempt is made to deal with many factors. Among those considered relevant have been physical environment and economic activity (e.g., the Cotton South, the corn belt, the soft coal areas, etc.). Sometimes a set of problems, such as poverty or flooding, have been utilized to delimit program regions (e.g., Appalachia, the Great Lakes Cut-over Area). In many cases, however, familiarity, convenience, political advantage, and personal perceptions seem to be of major importance.

There are many different kinds of regions, even though it is often implied that there are distinctive regional phenomena which automatically delimit regions for planning. Perhaps for this reason most of the literature fails to deal explicitly with the question of alternative approaches to regional delimitation, and with alternative consequences.

Proposals to regionalize government activities may serve many different agendas and, where possible, these should be identified. Central to an understanding of most proposals for regional organization are the basic assumptions made by proponents concerning the importance of particular area or space arrangements to program goal accomplishment. Often inability to solve problems at the center leads to the hope of success by focusing on a smaller area, assuming that the policy problems are more manageable on this smaller scale. And as a result, arguments over organizational structure may mask basic disagreements over program objectives.

As discussed elsewhere in this paper, proposals to regionalize federal functions rarely include structural changes with sufficient delegations of authority, thus manifesting an incomplete understanding of the governmental system, of institutional behavior, and of the tactical and strategic uses of organizational arrangements as instruments of politics, position, and power. Since regional commissions, committees, or agencies generally lack machinery for authoritative policy decisions equivalent to those of an elected representative legislature, the issue of how policy direction will be received, and what the relationship of the new agencies will be to the President, the Congress, and their state and local equivalents is usually ignored. Thus, such proposals fail to come to grips with the delicate and necessary relationship between the bureaucracy and the legislature, seeming to assume that planning and administrative coordination will eliminate problems that have their roots in the need for policy decisions.

Federal programs and organizational decisions usually have overt and covert multiple objectives. Disagreements about priorities and about the shares of the available budget are a major source of conflict. The ideal of a neat, logical frictionless organizational allocation of responsibility is a myth.

Organizational arrangements are not neutral. We do not organize in a vacuum. Organization is one way of expressing national commitment, influencing program direction, and ordering priorities. Organizational arrangements tend to give some interests, some perspectives, more effective access to those with decision-making authority, whether they be in the Congress or in the executive branch.

Assignment of administrative jurisdiction can be a key factor in determining program direction and ultimate success or failure. Each agency has its own culture and internal set of loyalties and values which are likely to guide its actions and influence its policies.[34]

Support for a regional approach to certain kinds of transportation problems has emerged logically from data presented in many studies of problems in many communities describing them in regional terms (i.e., transcending established political boundaries), and it is therefore not unexpected that solutions should be developed in such terms. The study data usually contain a special bias, which is not to say that it is incorrect, but simply to suggest that more attention should be devoted to possible alternatives (e.g., deliberate policies of population dispersal). In addition to biases implicit in the manner in which and the purposes for which data and information are gathered, decision-makers (influentials) express judgments and beliefs that regional approaches will result in more effective solutions to transportation problems, often before studies are completed. Hence, it is necessary to consider motivations that may underlie support for a regional approach to transportation problems if such pressures are to be understood.

First, as already indicated, there are those who believe for whatever reasons that a regional approach will result in a solution to what is regarded as a bad situation. But motivations for particular forms of political action may include an interest in benefits to oneself, one's friends and associates, one's supporters and constituents, and somewhat less specifically for the allocation of costs and burdens to others than those now bearing them. In political decisions, the allocation of secondary benefits are often of greater significance than the allocation of primary benefits—although not sufficient research into the relationship of secondary benefits to political action has been undertaken. In economic terms, political decision-makers (elected officials and bureaucrats) are often interested in such questions as who gets government contracts, where contract activity is to be undertaken, payrolls involved, individuals and firms who will benefit, effect on land values, etc. Decision-makers are also concerned with the effect that particular decisions may have on their power and influence. And since most governmental decisions have a spatial dimension, they seek locational orientations that will most enhance their own power and influence. This can obviously mean an emphasis on the district or state, but it can also mean (in the case of a Congressman or Senator) the enhancement of power and influence in the Congress or with the bureaucracy or with particular interest groups.

An important psychological motivation can be the indirect affect on one's constituency. A "do nothing" Congressman may court defeat as much as a "do nothing" Congress. Our system puts a premium on *action*, on doing something whether right or wrong, seeking simply to avoid obvious and apparent negative effects. Not only the pyramid builders wanted to construct monuments; many an American political decision-maker seeks psychic rewards in the action programs he initiates or supports without being constrained by more subtle negative consequences and relationships. Then, finally, there is always the constituency demand/response relationship, whether of the elected representatives, or of the many constituency oriented agencies and offices in the government structure. "What's good for General Motors is good for the nation" reflects a psychological set of many beside the president of that corporation. Despite progress in recent decades in program analysis, a concern for doing what constituency groups *consider* to be in their interest (even when it may not in fact be, viz., the revival of tariff proposals) remains a dominant force in American political decision-making.

It is in the context of these comments on motivation that a critical analysis of proposals for regionalization of transportation planning needs to be considered. One needs to ask *why* regionalization is proposed and supported; by whom; what expected benefits are considered to be; etc.

Regionalization may, for instance, merely be a symbol obscuring a struggle for power and influence. Proponents of a particular plan may be seeking to enhance their status among constituents or to gain new supporters. Those seeking or already dependent on federal benefits may use regionalization as a device for manipulating decisions in order to maximize control and thus benefits.

At the administrative level an analytical approach to the delineation of regions requires attention to human (social psychological and political) motivational factors as these influence decision. Human behavior, human aspiration, values, choices, and preferences must be taken into account. The extent to which behavioral information may be important is suggested by the following comments on the interpretative role that decision-makers play with respect to certain kinds of data:

1. *Physical data.* Most approaches to regional planning include some recognition of the physical situation as perceived by particular planners, and ultimately by political decisionmakers. Thus, if a city council, or a county governing board is not truly concerned about the need for and utility of an effective mass transit system, or if a city council has a weak perception of the pollution of the stream into which it discharges its sewage, then it makes little difference how the planner may perceive such physical data relevant to these situations, except that such limitations in perceptions may involve him in public controversy and establish for him an agenda for public education.

2. *Socio-economic data.* Much planning rests on socio-economic data but data rarely speak for themselves, and political responses to such data will obviously be affected by the personality, understanding, and perceptions

of those who have to act on such data. And the process of collection involves selection, choices, and often reflects biases of the compiler.

3. Similarly, the perceptions of decisionmakers with respect to *goals, problems,* and *opportunities* are important influences in decisional processes. The Chamber of Commerce Secretary or the Railroad General Counsel will bring to public decisional roles the views and values that he has built over his life span, even as the planners or the nationalist has "built-in" biases and preferences.

In each of the above instances, the term "perceptions" is used. Political analysis requires attention to what may shape perceptions of decision-makers in confronting areal decisions (regional boundaries). Such analysis also may produce the kind of information and research that would contribute to a better understanding of political factors involved in boundary decisions.

Of basic importance (but difficult to handle in any specific decisional situation) is the socialization of the specific decision-makers. "Socialization" research has forced the social scientist in the direction of individual case studies and tended to make unmanageable the demands for unique personal data, raising questions of whether the investment of time in such investigations is warranted. To study the socialization of a president or governor may be manageable, but to prove the socialization of hundreds, even thousands, of local decision-makers in an open, democratic decisional system may seem an insurmountable and unrewarding task. Perhaps one can discover uniformities and patterns of behavior that permit generalization on the basis of key sociometric indicators.[35] Even then, to complicate the situation, one needs also to deal with responses to particular environmental stimuli. Clearly, these are areas of investigation with respect to which we now know very little. In any case, most of what we know may only be useful for interpreting past decisions (history) and not for predicting future behavior.

More manageable, perhaps, is the kind of information one can secure through survey research and similar data gathering techniques that permit description of the values, preferences, attitudes, motives, motivations, rationalizations, beliefs, etc., of the public, various groups, and particular types of decisionmakers. These can often be correlated with sociometric data so that, although causal links are not established, reliable judgments and probability predictions may be possible.

But survey research has definite limitations. It is often not possible to separate out rationalizations for self-seeking behavior from firmly held conclusions with respect to social goals; opportunism and expediency may not be distinguishable from conscious bargaining strategies seeking conflict resolution and synthesis of goals at higher levels. Time perspectives of those interviewed may be very short run, for discounting the future seems to be a characteristic of most decision-makers, as well as of the general public. Thus, when dealing with public policies (e.g., with respect to natural resources and the environment, or with respect to long-term capital investment) in which time is an important dimension, how decision-makers perceive time may be a critical variable.

There is no evidence to suggest that behavioral influences affecting regional boundary decisions are substantially different from those affecting political decisions generally. The point simply is that boundary decisions, too, need to be analyzed in behavioral terms, if they are to be fully understood and if some of the pitfalls of a false rationalism are to be avoided. Try as we will, we cannot escape the fact that boundary decisions are made by humans, subject to all of the influences to which humans are subject.

That boundaries may determine the agenda for social action is suggested by discussions of urban problems in terms of core city-suburban relationships which probably reflect an over-emphasis on jurisdictional boundaries. One may wonder what might happen to some of the more simplistic analyses if present jurisdictional boundaries were assumed away and data were organized in terms of other categories perhaps reflecting such factors as age of the several parts of the metro area, economic status of the several parts, dwelling types, employment and communication patterns, service levels and needs, etc. But of course the jurisdictional boundaries do exist, and much social and economic data for both the private and public sector is organized in terms of these boundaries—often in such a way that "unscrambling" is difficult, expensive, or impossible. Clearly, he who controls the structuring of data also may often control the design of programs in response to such data. Consider another example: what would be the political, economic, and social effects of including Chicago in Wisconsin? How differently data aggregates would appear; how differently problems would be defined; how differently the resulting agendas for social action and the patterns of political behavior!

The impact of boundaries on data analysis was cogently made by Professor Charles L. Levin in a report prepared for the Institute for Water Resources (U.S. Army Corps of Engineers).[36]

> . . . the distribution of effects by region clearly would depend upon the way in which we defined regions. . . . Let us assume that one of the objectives of Appalachian development policy is to cause an increase in the ratio of per capita income in Appalachia to per capita income in the United States. [To achieve this] . . . all we need do is to redefine Appalachia, say, as an area about 100 miles wide stretching from Philadelphia to St. Louis, and we will find that our desired ratio has increased substantially under a policy that would have no cost whatsoever.[c]

Although not often made explicit in discussions of cost-benefit analysis, it seems reasonable to assume that certain individuals and groups may be better able to bear costs, just as certain individuals, and groups have a higher claim to the distribution of certain benefits. Similarly, some geographic areas may

---

[c]That is, the result flows simply from the way in which the region is defined.

logically be given primary consideration in the distribution of certain benefits, while other areas may be better able to bear certain additional costs. "Ability to pay" is more than simply an income tax principle! It can be a viable standard for allocative decisions, if fundamental equity is to be achieved. It can be a crucial element in determining policies and program emphasis as among regions.

Regions and People: Participation and Representation[37]

This section of the paper deals with several important concepts and symbols of American democratic government as these are related to regionalization of government programs. Attention is directed, *first*, to the subject of *citizen participation*, particularly in planning, which has become an important issue in recent years. As mentioned earlier, one justification for regionalizing government programs has been not only that they may be more effective, but that they will be more closely related to the values of the citizens they serve.

Attention is directed, *second*, to the more traditional issue of how regions and regional agencies relate to concepts of *representative government* and to *systems of representation* as these have been established at federal, state, and local levels.

Both topics are discussed from a point of view that challenges currently popular views. In the first case, the rhetoric and the operational practicality of participatory democracy as conducted by administrative agencies is examined. In the second case, the question is posed as to whether the problems to which regionalization and regional planning are directed are administrative problems to be dealt with by means of administrative manipulation of spatial organization, or whether they are, in a much more fundamental sense, governmental, requiring a clearly identified structure for political decision-making, which in a nation of 200 million people necessitates the use of formal systems of formal representation and the creation of politically responsive governmental units.

The phrase "maximum feasible participation" was inserted in the Economic Opportunity Act of 1964[38] without much attention to its political or administrative implications, according to the account of Daniel Patrick Moynihan who was personally involved in developing the Johnson "War on Poverty."[39] But whatever its origin, the phrase soon became a rallying cry, first in connection with welfare and programs affecting the poor, and then with respect to many other public programs and activities.

It is paradoxical that at the time when population numbers and density in the United States are reaching new highs, theories of public involvement are being promoted without regard to their practicality or to more traditional concepts of representation and majority rule. The motivations for this new emphasis on citizen involvement are complex. However unrealistic and unworkable the concept may be, it is clear that for many, increasing citizen participation reflects a recommitment to what are perceived as democratic ideals, particularly because many believe that the views and interests of some segments of society (particularly racial minorities) have till now been neglected. For some, participation is a therapeutic technique to decrease alienation, and its espousal may reflect guilt over past elitism. For others, quite obviously, citizen involvement was a response to the politics of violence and confrontation. For still others it probably means simply "getting on the bandwagon." And for some, it is clear, citizen involvement is a means for getting "power for the people"—a euphemism for attacking "the establishment." Who *the people* are, and how they will use the power, is usually not articulated, and one must at times be concerned that the symbols of democracy are being used for other than democratic purposes, the real goal being simply to alter the power structure.

Some segments of the federal bureaucracy are among those seeking to ride the "bandwagon," as measured by their lack of serious attention to the implications of participation for policy, for politics, or for administration, and the lack of concern for developing participatory arrangements meeting criteria of due process and equal protection. As one observer has noted, public agencies ". . . are being shaken by the call for participation." And he points out that ". . . efficiency and participation do not necessarily converge."[40] Neither equity nor justice follow automatically from increased participation. Nor does participation assure wiser decisions. Somehow questions of community welfare and of the common good must be dealt with explicitly, and the basic questions about the capacity of government and the effectiveness of its programs need careful examination.

Small group concepts applied to problems of a nation of 200 million people appear to be rhetorical substitutes for a careful consideration of the issues involved in the calculus of consent. To use involvement for purposes of social therapy and to talk about "rights" to participate pose far-reaching questions of what government is for and what constraints may limit effective government. The statement in a recent issue of the *American Behavioral Scientist* is axiomatic:[41]

In all societies, and under all forms of government, the few govern the many. . . . Because the symbols and concepts of American politics are drawn from democratic political thought, we seldom confront the elemental fact that a few citizens are always called upon to govern the remainder. . . . It is somehow undemocratic to think of elites and masses and to differentiate between them. . . . [Yet] elite-mass interaction is the very heart of the governing process.

Herbert Kaufman has suggested that the pendulum is simply swinging away from the dominant values of the preceding period to a new trend seeking greater "representativeness" in the administrative process.[42] Other values, dominant in other times (according to Kaufman), have included attempts to secure "neutral competence," and attempts to secure better "executive leadership." To him, current emphases are analogues to the situation in the Jacksonian era when the struggle for greater representativeness was also a major thrust. The Jacksonians, however, were able to implement their beliefs (especially through the election of even the least important public officials), but there is serious doubt that present goals of those urging participation can be realized in a nation of 200 million with about 10 million public employees. The result of the effort will, therefore, simply be to shift power relationships. In any case, very little attention has been directed to designing viable procedures and methods for participation consistent with other widely held values and beliefs.

A university professor recently asserted: "The right of people to participate in decisions which affect their lives is a central value of democracy." High sounding, but impossible to implement. Good rhetoric, but impossible to achieve. "No taxation without representation" was a polemic slogan of the American Revolution; but at least it could be made operational.

An assistant secretary of a federal department, discussing weather modification asserted: "A basic moral question then concerns the rights of an individual not to have man-made precipitation fall on his property without his having a role in the decision." The U.S. Constitution says simply that property shall not be taken for public purposes without just compensation—a principle that can be and is readily implemented.

It is a strange paradox that the receipt of public benefits is believed to carry with it the right to exercise public power, while shouldering public costs by paying large amounts of taxes apparently does not. Such euphemisms as "decentralization," "grass-roots administration," and "power to the people," serve to justify the former with little effort to consider the equally valid interests of the latter. Due process and equal protection of the laws would seem to require a concern for both.

Most public agencies have over the years developed a variety of relationships with particular "publics," with clients and clientele groups, and with other levels of government. Until recently, bureaucracies tended to describe such relationships as involving "the people." But as demands for new patterns of participation have developed, bureaucracies have been re-examining the adequacy of their relational patterns. Traditional "hearings" required by many laws have been recognized as inadequate. At the same time, most bureaucracies, except perhaps those involved in the community action and related poverty programs, have been puzzled about how to achieve fuller public participation.

In terms of equity, a necessary step would seem to be to identify specifically those individuals and groups who may benefit from particular programs, as well as those who will pay the costs or be burdened by them, and involve these groups at some stages of planning. At the same time, the fact that there is and always will be a silent majority cannot be overlooked by a responsible government. It is clearly no longer enough simply to identify aggregate costs and benefits. Those who will be helped and those who must make sacrifices (including payment of heavier taxes) need to be identified,[4,3] whether or not they are active or articulate. And since both costs and benefits are in many cases distributed geographically, this kind of analysis can be particularly important to regional planning.

Many agencies are experimenting with a variety of approaches to increasing public participation. One such experiment that deserves special mention because of its regional focus was that sponsored by the Corps of Engineers in formulating its plan for development of the Susquehanna River Basin.

Seeking to learn the preferences of residents, the Corps employed the University of Michigan to undertake sample studies in five counties. Standardized techniques for identifying the so-called "influentials" were used, but instead of simply surveying them for their views, the research team sought to increase informational inputs for sounder judgments, holding a series of workshops and public forums over a period of months.

Unquestionably, this approach has many advantages over the formal hearing. It was novel, in that the Corps presented to the region three alternative development possibilities, rather than a single well-crystallized plan. But the approach used hardly meets the test for increasing participation of *the public*. Even the most careful selection of "influentials" has built-in "establishment" biases and fails to take into account the possible need to encourage new leadership and new activist groups. Identification of "influentials" is essentially static, failing to deal with the issue as to who *ought* to be involved in planning decisions. A not unimportant question is what individuals and groups are likely to be affected. These are researchable questions.

It is not adequate, as in the Susquehanna, to assume that those most concerned with development decisions are those who happen to live in the watershed. To illustrate: water supply from the Susquehanna is of major importance to the more than one million people living in Baltimore; the recreation potential of the basin is probably of most importance to urbanites in New York, Philadelphia, Pittsburgh, Washington, and Baltimore; and clearly the entire nation has a stake in the economic development of the basin.[4,4]

Planning—whether local, regional, or national—must seek to consider the views and interests of *all* the people affected by plans and proposals. A two-way flow of communication must be an essential part of sound planning. But identifying those affected by plans and programs requires careful research and analysis, since only a few of those affected will voluntarily speak out. Clearly where one happens to reside, or how loudly one may shout, are not the sole criteria for identifying those whom government programs may affect. Even the techniques for identifying and recording citizen views are not simple. Neither the traditional stilted hearings, nor town meeting discussions are sufficient. And for different reasons, survey research cannot be adequate.

The challenge remains *the search for the public interest*, to the definition of which the attitudes and expectations of articulate citizens are important but not sufficient. And a variety of techniques and procedures may be required in this search for the public interest, including: (1) careful research and analysis, (2) opinion surveys of a broad range of affected and concerned publics, (3) simulation of social decision-making, (4) organization and encouragement of groups not presently expressing their views, (5) advocacy planning and use of "ombudsmen," (6) adversary proceedings, (7) hearings. Probably other techniques could be listed. But even after all such techniques have been utilized to the fullest, the administrator and planner cannot avoid the responsibility for judgments and recommendations, weighing citizen views, technical and expert opinions, and research findings in the context of time perspectives (since plans often will affect generations yet unborn).

So-called plebiscitary democracy may provide an important input for planning and decision processes, but it is a mistake to regard such participation as the total process. Citizen participation does not avoid the need for leadership—it may only produce different leaders. Nor does it change the motivational patterns of the leaders. The slogan "power to the people" has often been simply a cloak for authoritarian dictatorship (viz., Nazi Germany, Communist Russia, Castro Cuba).

Decision-making is ultimately a political responsibility, and administrative processes like planning must be assessed in terms of their contributions to supporting *all the values of our system.* Responsiveness to citizen demands is but one of these values. Due process, equal protection of the laws, equity, justice, and the preservation of the kind of pluralism and diversity that is a necessary concomitant of an open society are other crucial values.

Regional administration and planning can encourage a more effective recognition of local interests and views and may result in articulating regional interests more clearly. But linkages to other regions cannot be ignored in planning or in action. A region is not an independent nation. Advantages of regionalization must be weighed in the context of the total national interest. The fundamental test, perhaps, is how specific regional proposals contribute to making the total governing process more effective.

Regions and Representation

A necessary characteristic of a viable government is ability to act to accomplish public purposes properly and legitimately determined. A test for any organization proposal is the extent to which it increases government's ability to act effectively. In the case of regionalization of transportation, the question is ultimately whether government will be more effective, whether transportation will, as a result, better meet specifically identified needs of specifically identified people in specific parts of the nation.

The many units of government in the American federal system receive their authority either from constitutions (in the case of the national government and the fifty states) or from statutes generally based on constitutional provisions, as in the case of lesser units such as counties, townships, special districts, and municipal corporations.

In a distinctly different category are the departments and agencies of government, whether established by constitutions or general statutes. The primary differences between a unit of government and a department or agency of government are three: territory; independent financial authority; and a popularly elected, independent governing body, whether designated a board, a commission, a council, or a legislature. It is the method of selection, the relationship to constituents, and the extent of autonomy, and not the title that is important and that distinguishes the unit of government from the administrative agency. Fixed territorial jurisdiction, not subject to easy alteration and often determined by constituent processes, also distinguishes the unit of government from administrative departments, agencies, or bureaus. And it is with respect to units of government that Supreme Court doctrines of "one man, one vote" become significant. In other words, *representation is crucial to a unit of government; it has not been so construed with respect to administrative agencies.*

No regional organization to date can be considered a unit of government. A fundamental question with respect to any attempts to "regionalize" governmental functions is therefore whether, to be effective, a "region" ought to be constituted as a unit of government, or whether it is enough to be created for administrative convenience and effectiveness. The issues are fundamentally ones of relationship to constituents and of authority to act. Autonomy and financial independence are measures of authority, and independent governing authority demands consideration of popular control and representation.

Although an independent agency, the Tennessee Valley Authority is still a long way from being a unit of government. It does have some financial independence, but it does not have autonomy, and its governing board has no popular constituency, being appointed rather than selected by the people of the valley. TVA is, of course, popular with the people of the valley, but this is not the proper test. The status of the Port of New York Authority is similar to that of TVA. It does have financial independence, but its governing board is not an elected body. A few compact agencies also seem to approach the status of units of government, but most will not meet the tests outlined above. Similarly, federal regional commissions and committees do not qualify as units of government, but are simply administrative agencies. Their budgets are subject to Congressional or State legislative approval; their governing bodies are appointive; and attempts at involving citizens in their activities fall far short of formal representation. In all these cases, formal requirements of "one man, one vote" are irrelevant.

In some respects, certain regional administrative bodies are really reversions to pre-1789 patterns of confederation, for votes have been given to states (or governments) rather than to people. (The Councils of Governments are of this type.) In some cases, the obvious concession to "states' rights" has been modified by giving federal executive representatives one vote, the right to share the chairmanship of the body, and sometimes a veto. This, of course, involves the assumption that federal interests are equal only to those of a single state, that area is more important than people, even when most funding comes from national sources. But there is no basis in reason or experience to expect regional agencies set up on this basis to be any more effective in serving the public interest than was the Continental Congress.

In fact, after 1789 we have not been innovative in developing arrangements for making multi-jurisdictional decisions in the context of the national system. The "Pork Barrel" approach, based on tradeoffs among sections, states, or lesser areas is dominant. Undoubtedly, it is this expectation that has contributed to some of the political support for the idea of regional agency approaches to transportation. For example, by extending the principles of "Senatorial Courtesy" to regional agency decision, Senators of particular regions may hope to control the expenditure of substantial amounts of money with minimal interference from outside the region and equally minimal accountability to the people within the region.

Lack of attention to regional problems on the part of Congress has certainly been the experience of TVA. But a similar lack of interest (which may simply reflect a span of attention problem) is to be found at the executive level. Over the years, the TVA Board has been reluctant to "bother" the President. At the same time, it has resisted inclusion of TVA in any executive department or agency for fear of losing independence and identity.

Many problems (including transportation) may be regional in character and scope and may be amenable to regional solutions, but simply creating regional administrative agencies or commissions does not guarantee that they will be dealt with more effectively. One might even harbor the concern that creation of regional transportation agencies will result in less effective or less responsible action with respect to regional problems.

One might wish for regional governments with clear governing authority and responsibility to the people through elected representatives. But moves in this direction seem unlikely.

The Constraints of the Federal System

As indicated elsewhere in this paper, the states and their subunits may be regarded as political regions. The dispersal of authority and responsibility to approximately 80,000 units of government in the United States has created a fractured plural system that severely constrains national, state, regional, or local planning.

The design and administration of government programs at all levels has been and continues to be significantly affected by these values of the American federal system. The processes of politics and the patterns of decision with respect to both what government does and how it does it mirror the constraints of that system. Unquestionably, too, the evolution and structure of the federal system has had a considerable impact on the growth and development of government planning, shaping both the focus and the methods of planning and the organizations and processes for planning.

The boundaries of the original thirteen states were drawn in response to the desires and needs of the granting monarchs with no attention to resources or growth potential. But even if fuller information had been available in the 1600s, the technological and social changes in the interim would have negated decisions made at that time. The boundaries of the remaining 37 states were set on the basis of considerations equally irrelevant to today's needs. Rivers as boundaries seemed sound when bridge building was still a primitive art, but the logic of 100 years ago may be nonsense today, yet boundaries then established persist. Survey townships—those rectangular boxes—seemed neat and sensible, when it was quite generally assumed that "Manifest Destiny" means population scattered in patterns of more or less uniform density across the face of the continent, and when a primary public goal was privatizing the Public Domain.

The rectangular survey with its sections and townships based on latitude and longitude certainly provided a land record system unequaled anywhere in the world. And in the horse and buggy era, the survey townships served as a framework for local government and school administration that worked reasonably well. But for most purposes today, township government (particularly in the Midwest) prevents achieving social goals and meeting public needs.

Someone has suggested that an East and a West Dakota would have been wiser than a North and a South Dakota, if natural homogeneity had been used as a criterion. But, of course, the movement of population, the construction of railroads, the need to maintain contact with Eastern points and many other economic, social, and political forces contributed to a dominantly East-West structure of commerce and communication.

The states and the institutional structure that has developed around them are the result of many complex forces, some of which are no longer operative, but the residual effects of which are still recognizable.

Most observers agree that the Federal system established by the Constitutional Convention was truly the work of creative statesmen, providing a governmental structure which has stood the tests of time. But two views about the nature of that system are prevalent. The one view, less popular today than 50 years ago, regards the system as nearly perfect, and attributes a kind of prescience to the Founding Fathers. In this vein, for example, Dean Roscoe Pound wrote that no nation of continental expanse could be governed democratically except by means of a federal system like the American. And others who held this view were prone to suggest that problems of democracy in most corners of the world might be solved by following the American Federal model.

The other view with respect to the decisions of 1787 is that, rather than being an ideal conception of how to govern a large country, they were the best that could be obtained at the time. The politics of choice (the bargaining, the negotiations) was only too evident when the new Constitution almost failed of adoption in several states.

In this view, the *Federalist Papers*, while still recognized as great political writing, are, like the Constitution itself, regarded as pragmatic responses to a tough political situation. They are rationalizations of a proposed structure that first and foremost was to deal with immediately pressing problems as perceived by the proponents of the new constitution. For example, almost every one of the powers granted to the National Government in Article One, Section Eight—still the chief source of federal power—was a response to the exigencies of the times. The Founding Fathers, like most of their heirs today were pragmatic realists. Much of the "theory" that has been read into the Federalist Papers and into the Constitution itself is largely an *ex post facto* rationalization of decisions made to solve particular problems of the 1780s.

One need but to refer to one of the so-called "Great Compromises"—that involving equal representation of the States in the Senate and representation on the basis of population in the House—to illustrate how a pragmatic response of 1787 has, in popular folklore, been raised to the level of a grand theory of government. Equal representation of the States in the Senate was no grand principle; it stemmed simply from the fears (widely held at the time) that the large states would dominate the small ones. We do not know whether they might have done so if the system had been different. But the pragmatic bargains relating to representation in the National Congress within only a few years became a principle of government extended in most state constitutions to the formation of counties giving representation to area rather than people. Only recent Supreme Court decisions have begun to free us from the consequences of this misreading of history and of democratic principles.

Another constraint of the federal system on new regional approaches in responding to present day problems is the necessary reliance of the national government upon the "spending power" as the basis for many of the newer governmental programs. Most constitutional lawyers agree that there are few if any limitations on the spending power. As a result, the grant-in-aid has become the major technique for federal intervention into a wide range of problems. But grant-in-aid programs themselves reflect the constraints of the federal system, as suggested by the various grant formulas, all of which contain components that recognize the existence of the states as political entities and in varying degrees distort the relationship of federal funding to the problems to be solved. This is the price we pay for maintaining a federal system with political institutions organized on a state basis. A related consequence is that states may establish

organizational arrangements for spending grant monies that they might otherwise not have established, and such arrangements persist long after the problems
have changed because the federal funds continue to be available. In a superficial
way, the persistence of an agricultural experiment station and an agricultural
extension service in Rhode Island illustrates the point.

The federal system also has numerous political consequences, one being the
extent to which the federal system (and its modified counterpart in state-
county-city relationships) obscures the relationships between public costs and
public benefits. Many federal programs have as a primary purpose a redistribution of income, but the federal system permits program decisions without a
deliberate and forthright confrontation of who benefits and who pays. Politics is
undoubtedly concerned with "who gets what, when, how and where," but the
issues of politics, the struggles, the conflicts, the bargains and negotiations rarely
overtly deal with the issues of "getting." Even less frequently emphasized are
adverse effects of public programs (the costs and who bears them). Except for
the Federal income tax, with its philosophy of "ability to pay," few federal
programs deal explicitly with problems of income redistribution. Cost-benefit
studies within the bureaucracy identify some of the factors involved in program
proposals, and discussions of fiscal policies touch on aspects of this important
policy area, but we do not have an articulated policy or set of policies that state
what the objectives of income redistributions should be. Nor have goals been
formulated that identify this as an important subject for public policy decision-
making, even though direct subsidy, as well as indirect benefits, are a major
aspect of many federal programs, including those in transportation. The federal
system contributes substantially to this obscurantism.

A special area of federal influence on governmental institutions and decisions
can be observed in the area of regionalism and regional analysis. There is little
doubt but that the constant promotion by the federal government of a regional
approach to a host of problems, particularly in the resources field, reflects both
substantive logic and political interests.

As suggested earlier, a basic problem involved in regional analysis is that of
determining regional boundaries, and in terms of establishing organizations for
regional transportation planning, we must ask whether a regional approach is
"logical," and identify the purposes it may serve—including possible political
benefits. This question should not be confused with the question of whether
special programs and organizations for dealing with them are needed, or with the
less frequently stated question of who will benefit from a regional approach.

It is difficult, for example, to relate the transportation regions proposed in S.
2425 with the concept of the nodal urban-metro region where many of our
transportation problems are most acute. The ten largest Standard Metropolitan
Statistical Areas, accounting for well over 50 million people, are only vaguely
related to the proposed regions. And if consideration is given to the several
different transportation modes—private cars, mass local transit, intercity buses

and trucks, rail, barge, and air—it is not at all clear how regional action will resolve the problems involved. Regional analysis is necessary, but this is quite different from regional decision-making.

Regions and the Coordination of Government Programs[4][5]

Among the premises for a regional approach to governmental problems have been, on the one hand, the position that public programs are not and cannot be effectively administered from the center in Washington and, on the other hand, the belief that more effective planning and coordination can and will take place "at the grass roots," where problems are real, and where the people affected can interact with government personnel. This was a major argument of David Lilienthal in explaining and justifying the so-called "TVA approach." It is a recurring theme today in connection with many public programs, particularly those dealing with or affecting the environment.

These premises are also implicit in proposals for a regional approach to transportation planning. It is assumed that with less geographic area to be concerned about, with more concrete and perhaps simpler problems, with fewer people, and with closer proximity to them, planning and coordination will be more effective, and action will be more responsive to their needs and desires.

As already suggested, the belief is widespread that federal programs in general, and transportation programs in particular, are neither well planned nor well coordinated. Much of the planning and coordination that has been occurring, even with a nominally unified Department of Transportation, is *pro forma* and superficial. Although programs relating to the several different modes of transportation have obvious interrelationships, the agencies within the Department of Transportation planning and administering separate programs do not (and perhaps cannot) work together on eliminating conflicting statutory goals and objectives, or in exploring innovations that might make it possible for several subsystems of transportation to collaborate more effectively. As is so often the case, the pluralism in our society is mirrored in the activities of government agencies dealing with the range of transportation programs from highways, to airports, to railroads, to safety, and so on.

General social planning in the United States has never had the kind of political support that would have encouraged the identification and then the resolution of policy and goal conflicts. In fact, the tremendous increase of narrowly focused, problem-oriented government programs over the past forty years has intensified the need for coordination to the point where one might almost despair of effective improvement at either policy-making or administrative levels. In this connection, it is worth emphasizing that the expectation that organizational and administrative techniques can achieve more effective coordination may rest on a misdiagnosis. Perhaps more powerful tools are needed! The fundamental problem may be political and may reflect the inability or unwillingness of the system to make hard choices. Something for everyone is an appealing though costly formula. At the same time, administrative arrangements (improvements?) *may* contribute to more effective coordinative efforts.

Two relatively recent administrative changes affecting transportation give some promise of encouraging improved coordination in this field. The first of these, the creation of the Department of Transportation, will take years to have any considerable effect, if the experience of other "conglomerate departments" is any guide, and the second is the strengthening of state regional planning best typified by the Intergovernmental Cooperation Act of 1968[46] with the supporting Office of Management and Budget Circular A-95 (July 24, 1969), as amended. And undoubtedly the probable enactment of one or another of the planning and land use control acts now pending in Congress (July 1972) will provide further impetus to State planning, with possible consequences for transportation.

Coordination and Choice

In considering regional coordination and the effectiveness of coordination devices, the point to stress is that coordination is not simply a matter of administrative arrangements and processes. The word "coordination" is used so freely by drafters of statutes and by organizational specialists that it is easy to fall into the error of assuming that if only people can be brought together, coordination will automatically result. There are, in fact, numerous impediments to coordination, as the following paragraphs suggest. While in one sense everything is ultimately related to everything else in a continuous web of action and interaction, as a practical matter administrators can only deal with the limited range of factors they assume to be interrelated and perceive to be important. Their judgments usually reflect a narrow span of attention and are characterized by lack of information and by lack of data on causes and effects and on reactions and consequences.

Despite several decades of social psychological research in decision-making, there is still a strong tendency, particularly in the federal bureaucracy, to conceive of the process of deciding as rational and comprehensive, involving a progression of logical steps: (1) recognition and diagnosis of the problem, (2) determination of *all* possible alternatives, (3) careful accumulation and investigation of *all* the facts relating to each alternative, (4) weighing of the consequences expected from each alternative course of action, and (5) selection of the best possible solution.[47]

Similar premises undergird much discussion of coordination, it being assumed that agreement will follow from exchange of ideas and full exposure of all the facts.

That such rational-comprehensive premises are unrealistic has been well stated by Anthony Downs, who points out the limited amount of time for decision-making, the limited amount of information, the limited span of attention of most decision-makers, and their involvement in more activities than they can consider carefully at any one time, the difficulties of organizing and retrieving relevant information, the costs of securing relevant new information, and the difficulties of dealing with the uncertainties of the future.[48]

Most frequently, perhaps, coordination efforts run aground on the shoals of differing goals, differing program premises, conflicting values, and differing perceptions of the problems to be dealt with. It is at this point where better information is not enough, and where political choices would seem to be most appropriate. It is one thing to know that the construction of an expressway through a city is likely to have some effect on the economy, the sociology, the politics of the city; it is quite another matter, of tremendously greater difficulty, to identify the specific consequence of such construction and to act with such knowledge in mind. Even more difficult is reaching agreement on whether the consequences, chosen from a range of possibilities, are desirable or undesirable.

One of the most frequently ignored aspects of coordination is *time.* Coordination of activities in contemplation of future needs, problems, and developments is particularly difficult because the character of that future is so uncertain (i.e., involves so many assumptions); and so many independent, unanticipated variables will undoubtedly shape that future. Agency orientations and perceptions of administrators may vary widely. A source of conflict involving the time dimension may be differing operating mandates of agencies and their responsibilities for immediate impacts and achievements as compared to longer-range considerations.

Coordination at early program formulation stages is often recommended by administrative analysis since program content is then still fluid and less structured. But most agencies are reluctant to involve others (agencies or the public) at such early stages because the needs and opportunities for coordination are not clear, and it is just at this stage that fear over the possible loss of program control is very real. Important at this stage, too, is the lack of information on the specifics of what other agencies might contribute to program results. Hence little staff time is devoted to early stage coordination. Later coordination, among programs well set in the authority framework of particular agencies, is much more difficult.

Difficulties of the kind suggested are often compounded by the lack of both organizational arrangements and procedures for program coordination—even such as would simply involve a systematic exchange of information. But the point to stress is that *motivation for coordination is weak* because programs that to an outside observer seem to be interrelated in their impact may actually be seeking different—even conflicting—goals probably have substantially different statutory authorizations and appropriation structures and are probably supported by different clientele and interest group configurations.

It is against the background of these comments that the conclusion is again worth re-emphasizing: *organization and reorganization, including decisions with respect to regions, are not neutral.* They affect the relationships of influence and power within the system; they alter the allocation of costs and benefits; and they run risks of a wide range of unanticipated consequences, especially with respect to agency and program integrity.

Coordination as an objective of administration may be considered to have two primary purposes: first, to improve programs and program administration by providing better information, avoiding duplication, and improving the action base; and second, to minimize or eliminate conflict—conflict among objectives, among approaches, and among individuals. But this aspect of interagency relationships is reluctantly recognized partly because the bureaucratic system is not anxious to admit conflicts (and has not learned the constructive use of conflict), and partly because in many situations not too much can be done about conflicts, since these often have their roots in agency policies and positions not amenable to ordinary coordinative processes, because decisions and choices are required. Arrangements and mechanisms for making such decisions and choices often do not exist. And the need is easily dismissed, for if the problems are not solvable, why bother to discuss them! The nature of some of these interagency and intergovernmental conflict situations and the implicit difficulties in dealing with them through normal administrative devices and procedures in the *absence of authoritative decisional power*, are suggested by the following descriptive list of factors that may be involved:

1. *Ideology, Goals, and Values.* Undoubtedly, each participant in the power struggle may be contending for his particular views of society. They may be pro- or anti-governmental in orientation; and they may have a wide range of value content. American politics is not strongly ideological in its orientation, but some participants in the political struggle are motivated by essentially ideological concerns and seek value-based goals.

2. *Allocation of Costs and Benefits.* More often than not, the struggle for power involves a struggle over who will control the allocation of costs and the distribution of benefits (economic and non-economic) flowing from government programs. In this connection, control of access to points of decision in the legislative and administrative branches is of crucial importance, and the relation of benefits to re-election hopes of legislators is obviously important.

3. *Bureaucratic Self-Preservation.* Power struggles to increase or preserve bureaucratic advantages (agency size, budgets, importance of programs, and so on) are not unusual.

4. *Technological Biases.* These may involve beliefs that certain specialists are better able to solve a particular range of problems.

5. *Leadership and Personality Factors.* Although difficult to describe, it is

clear that the personalities of particular political and bureaucratic leaders may be important factors in particular power struggles. The Soil Conservation/Agricultural Extension controversy of twenty-five years ago would have been unthinkable without a Hugh Hammond Bennett at the head of SCS. TVA would not have become a reality without the persistence of Senator George W. Norris, and its direction would have been much different had Arthur Morgan, rather than David Lilienthal and Harcourt Morgan, won the 1936-1939 power struggle.

Coordination may be helped or hindered by the authority, responsibility, and jurisdiction of the agencies and agents involved in particular situations. Put negatively, many problems of coordination simply reflect the fragmented character of authority, responsibility, and jurisdiction of those involved, and the absence of any clear-cut identification of how such differences may be remedied or how authoritative decisions may be reached.

In the American system, two factors contribute to this situation. One is the pragmatic and piecemeal way in which government programs tend to develop. The result of this is that authorizing statutes do not often deal with program and policy relationships, only occasionally declaring that coordination shall take place or providing primitive coordinating mechanisms without changing the allocation of responsibility and authority for decisional choices. Machinery alone cannot achieve coordination where goals and values conflict, and where authority to make decisions has not been granted. The other factor, discussed in a separate section of this paper, involves the constraints arising from the federal system with its approximately 80,000 units of government.

Experience, as well as research, supports two conclusions with respect to both interagency and interlevel conflicts. First, arguments as to what level of government should act (the classic "states' rights" issues of the federal system) often reflect differences between overt and covert objectives and interests; and second, conflicts among agencies with similar program responsibilities (e.g., welfare or education) at any level are less frequent than among agencies with different programs and between the administrative, executive, and legislative branches.

Coordination at the center (i.e., in Washington) may be reasonably successful, particularly in the large agency or department where mechanisms for coordination have been developed and occasions for hard decisional choices have been provided (e.g., the budget process). But even at this level, many of the same kind of factors that make interagency field coordination difficult may also be at work. Creation of the Department of Transportation (like earlier action with respect to Defense; Health, Education, and Welfare; and Housing and Urban Development) offers promise of more coordinated transportation policies. But clearly time and effective leadership are needed before the fruits of this reorganization may begin to be realized. To expect "frictionless" operation is, in any case, unreal.

In some situations, coordination in the field may be more effective. A field perspective may be more highly sensitive to concrete reality than the point of view at the center. At the point where programs take effect, specialists can more readily comprehend how their several interests may be related. They may perceive adverse consequences of going separate ways and may recognize the logic of supportive effort by others whose program authority and responsibility may complement their own.

The opportunities for coordination at the "grass roots" may benefit from policies of decentralization that stress delegation to the field as an antidote for remote control and inflexible decisions based on abstractions. This problem was recognized 135 years ago by de Tocqueville: "However enlightened and however skillful a central power may be, it cannot of itself embrace all the details of the existence of a great nation."[49] Similar views were associated with the "Jacksonian revolution," which stressed the devolution of power and authority (not simply administration) to the lowest levels of government. In the field of management, Mary Parker Follett emphasized advantages that may flow from attention to concrete realities (made possible by delegation) as contrasted with action based on abstract general principles. Unquestionably, one of the difficulties with federal programs is that as formulated and administered in Washington they are often so highly generalized that they do not meet the specific needs of any particular area. Substantial pressures make Federal programs nationally uniform, rationalized on the specious basis that uniformity results in equality of treatment. In fact, the failure to develop varied policies and programs adjusted to differing local needs may reflect bureaucratic timidity more than anything else.

But field coordination may also suffer from limitations that are operative in Washington. Program rigidities, embedded in statutes or administrative rules, administrative timidity, clientele pressures—all may work to restrict the scope of field coordination, particularly when no mechanism for authoritative decisions has been developed. The various committees and commissions dealing with regional water resources program coordination have impressive records of frustration and ineffectiveness.

The regional agency idea, as reflected in TVA and developed by David E. Lilienthal and Gordon Clapp, placed great emphasis upon the role of the regional agency in developing resources of the region on a coordinated basis. But, however impressive, it must be admitted that TVA results have been considerably more modest than doctrine would suggest.[50] For one thing, the TVA statute was just not broad enough to permit it to assume leadership among federal resource development agencies operating in the valley. Where TVA could not persuade federal agencies to share or coordinate responsibilities, it tended to be ignored. Today the TVA program emphasizes public power. While TVA is still interested in the watersheds making up the region and in the regional economy, it is not in a position to do much about such broader concerns, nor even to exercise much leadership with respect to them. An impressive exception is its development of the "Land Between the Lakes" recreation area. That TVA was regarded as a threat to regular federal resource agencies is apparent in the record of their opposition to proposals to expand this device. It is evident that the ideal of using regional agencies modeled on TVA as a means for more effective coordination of federal programs is dead.

To summarize, then, desires for logical neatness press in the direction of complete coordination and full program integration and stress comprehensiveness. But limitations of intellect, of time, of institution, the divergence of values, and the politics of program decision, conspire to make plural programs and heterogeneous agencies avoid the problems of coordination as well as the limitations on coordination.

This gloomy picture with respect to coordination is not meant to minimize the need for as much coordination as possible. Nor is it meant to discredit attempts to secure better and more effective coordination. Its purpose has been, rather, to present realistically the very substantial problems involved in coordination and to suggest a basis for even greater effort in this direction by identifying the complexities to be encountered in effective regional planning and indicating the need for decisions on more than simply organizational structure.

The fundamental challenge in seeking better coordination is to deal effectively with conflicting goals and purposes, resolving them if possible, but choosing from among them when necessary. In this connection, it must be accepted that a plurality of values and goals is endemic to our society. And choices from among them are not easy, especially since techniques for choosing are often too primitive or non-existent. It must also be recognized that many forces support a pluralistic system in which integrative decisions are avoided, even at the expense of program conflicts, inconsistencies and inefficiencies (and this may not be all bad!).

A common example of tolerance for inconsistencies is evident in conflicts between local and national interests. Most resource decisions, most economic development decisions (despite sophisticated economic analysis) are determined on a local basis. Consider, for example, the way in which the Rivers and Harbors bill is put together.

In many cases, secondary benefits flowing from federal expenditures are of greater political significance than primary benefits, for it is the secondary benefits that most directly affect local interests. In addition, program and project justifications usually stress benefits while deliberately ignoring costs and who bears them. It is an acceptable tactic to tout benefits and seek to disperse the costs so that those on whom they may fall will be unaware of the impact (compare the historic strategy of those supporting higher tariffs).

Our system just has not provided for making decisions based on a large national interest when this is alleged to be contrary to strong local interests. Nor is the premise generally accepted that local interests should at times be

426

subordinate to national interests. As the only elected national spokesman, the President finds resolution of conflicts between local and national interests difficult, expensive, time-consuming, and often impossible. The assumption is widely held that the sum of local advantages is the measure of the national interest. But this is clearly not the case. Coordination is more often by addition than by integration; pluralism rather than tightly reasoned neatness remains a dominant feature of most government programs.

To repeat, true coordination, whether on a regional or on a national basis, requires choice. And choice processes are political processes. To operate effectively, they must be structured to permit bargaining and tradeoffs in the process of resolving conflicts. Thus, a fundamental question with respect to proposals for regionalizing transportation planning (and action) are whether they, in fact, will make possible more effective political decisions.

Notes

1. For one attempt to develop a theoretical approach to spatial problems, see Arthur Maass (ed.), AREA AND POWER, The Free Press, Glencoe, Illinois, 1959. Another significant collection of essays is Merrill Jensen (ed.), REGION-ALISM IN AMERICA, University of Wisconsin Press, Madison, 1951, which while emphasizing historical aspects of regionalism, also presents its philosophical dimensions.

2. A landmark study of the subject is Advisory Commission on Intergovernmental Relations, MULTISTATE REGIONALISM, April 1972, A-39. U.S. Government Printing Office, Washington, D.C. (sn 5204-0041). Hereafter cited as "ACIR-1972."

3. Chapter I of ACIR-1972 presents an up-to-date review of "The Concept and Growth of Multistate Regionalism," citing some of the relevant historical literature on the subject. The view presented is somewhat more optimistic with respect to the conceptual basis for regionalism, although the report does not deal explicitly with regionalism as a political theory.

4. Two early works on the subject are James Fesler's AREA AND ADMINISTRATION, University of Alabama Press, 1949, and Schuyler Wallace's FEDERAL DEPARTMENTALIZATION, Columbia University Press, 1941.

5. National Resources Committee, REGIONAL FACTORS IN NATIONAL PLANNING AND DEVELOPMENT, U.S. Government Printing Office, Washington, D.C., 1935.

6. Norman Wengert, VALLEY OF TOMORROW: THE TVA AND AGRICULTURE, University of Tennessee, 1952. See also Charles McKinley, UNCLE SAM IN THE PACIFIC NORTHWEST, University of California Press, 1952; and Henry C. Hart, THE DARK MISSOURI, The University of Wisconsin Press, 1957. These and other studies that might be listed are illustrative of descriptions of particular regional programs.

7. The approach of the Water Resources Council is indicated in many of its publications; see especially, HANDBOOK FOR COORDINATION OF PLANNING STUDIES AND REPORTS, 1969.

8. P.L. 89-80. This Act authorized the establishment of River Basin Commissions and provided generally for the coordination of water resources planning, stressing the watershed approach.

9. P.L. 89-4. See ACIR-1972 for a review of experience under this Act.

10. 42 USC 3121.

11. The regional emphasis is evident, for example, in a number of the studies of the Advisory Commission on Intergovernmental Relations, e.g., URBAN AND RURAL AMERICA: POLICIES FOR FUTURE GROWTH, U.S. Government Printing Office, 1968. See also Lyle C. Fitch, URBAN TRANSPORTATION AND PUBLIC POLICY, Chandler Publishing Company, 1964; J.R. Meyer, et al., THE URBAN TRANSPORTATION PROBLEM, Harvard University Press, 1966; Wilfred Owen, THE METROPOLITAN TRANSPORTATION PROBLEM, The Brookings Institution, 1966; California Division of Highways, LOS ANGELES REGIONAL TRANSPORTATION STUDY, 1963; J.D. Carroll, Jr., CHICAGO AREA TRANSPORTATION STUDY, 1959; Penn Jersey Transportation Study, THE STATE OF THE REGION, 1964.

12. This view is explicit in D.H. Meadows, D.L. Meadows, J. Randers, and W.W. Behrens, THE LIMITS TO GROWTH, Universe Books, New York, 1972; and in P.W. Berkley and D.W. Seckler, ECONOMIC GROWTH AND ENVIRONMENTAL DECAY, Harcourt, Brace, Javanovich, Inc., New York, 1972.

13. From a summary in the Rocky Mountain Center on Environment, OPEN SPACE REPORT, Vol. 6, No., 9, December 1970, p. 1.

14. For a recent history of Regionalism in America see, Jensen (ed.) op. cit., and also ACIR-1972, Ch. I.

15. In 1926, Charles A. Beard wrote "Some Aspects of Regional Planning" in the AMERICAN POLITICAL SCIENCE REVIEW, Vol. 20, p. 273ff. The same year S.M. Harriss wrote "Some Regional Problems and Methods of their Study," also in AMERICAN POLITICAL SCIENCE REVIEW, Vol. 20, p. 156. A search of the CUMULATIVE INDEX, 1906-1963, indicates only three other articles with the word "region" or "regionalism" in the title, except as related to international relations studies. In addition, several articles dealt with TVA, planning development, and other key words of some relevance to regional investigations.

16. 49 Stat. at L. 1570.

17. REPORT OF THE PRESIDENT'S WATER RESOURCES POLICY COMMISSION, U.S. Government Printing Office, 1950 (three volumes).

18. P.L. 89-80.

19. FEDERAL REGISTER, Tuesday, December 21, 1971 (Vol. 36, No. 245) Part II: "Water Resources Council, Proposed Principles and Standards for Planning Water and Related Land Resources," states that the overall purpose of water and land resource planning is to reflect society's preferences for enhance-

ment of (A) national economic development, (B) environmental quality, and (C) regional development (at p. 24145).

20. The so-called "War on Poverty" was authorized by the Economic Opportunity Act of 1964, P.L. 83-253. For a discussion of how this Act was formulated (from the point of view of one of the participants) see Daniel Patrick Moynihan, MAXIMUM FEASIBLE MISUNDERSTANDING, The Free Press, Glencoe, Illinois, 1970. Also see Advisory Commission on Intergovernmental Relations, INTERGOVERNMENTAL RELATIONS IN THE POVERTY PROGRAM, U.S. Government Printing Office, Washington, D.C., 1966.

21. Many reports of the Advisory Commission on Intergovernmental Relations have a significant relationship to metropolitan regionalism. One of these reports (ACIR-1972) has already been cited several times. Of additional note (suggesting the breadth of the Commission's approach) are: INTERGOVERN-MENTAL RESPONSIBILITIES FOR MASS TRANSPORTATION FACILITIES AND SERVICES IN METROPOLITAN AREAS, 1961; ALTERNATIVE AP-PROACHES TO GOVERNMENTAL REORGANIZATION IN METROPOLI-TAN AREAS, 1962; INTERGOVERNMENTAL RESPONSIBILITIES FOR WATER SUPPLY AND SEWAGE DISPOSAL IN METROPOLITAN AREAS, 1962; PERFORMANCE OF URBAN FUNCTIONS: LOCAL AND AREA-WIDE, 1963; THE PROBLEM OF SPECIAL DISTRICTS IN AMERICAN GOVERN-MENT, 1964; METROPOLITAN SOCIAL AND ECONOMIC DISPARITIES: IMPLICATIONS FOR INTERGOVERNMENTAL RELATIONS IN CENTRAL CITIES AND SUBURBS, 1965; METROPOLITAN AMERICAN: CHALLENGE TO FEDERALISM, 1966; A HANDBOOK FOR INTERLOCAL AGREEMENTS AND CONTRACTS, 1967.

22. Advisory Commission on Intergovernmental Relations, METROPOLI-TAN COUNCILS OF GOVERNMENTS, 1966.

23. P.L. 90-577.

24. Originally released July 24, 1969, by what was then "The Bureau of the Budget." The Circular has been revised in detail but not in substance.

25. Quoted from Robert K. Carr, et al., ESSENTIALS OF AMERICAN DEMOCRACY, Holt, Rinehart, and Winston, New York, 1961, p. 1. See also Norman Wengert, "The Politics of River Basin Development," LAW AND CONTEMPORARY PROBLEMS, Spring 1957, Duke University School of Law; and ibid., NATURAL RESOURCES AND THE POLITICAL STRUGGLE, Doubleday, 1955.

26. Harold D. Lasswell, POLITICS: WHO GETS WHAT, WHEN, AND HOW? McGraw-Hill Book Company, 1936.

27. Paul Diesing, REASON IN SOCIETY, University of Illinois Press, Urbana, 1962.

28. Group theories of politics tend to overlook the large "silent majority." Some of these theories seek to solve this problem by speaking of "potential groups," but even in an open society this is only partly satisfactory. For a cogent

critique of group theories, see Mancur Olson, Jr., THE LOGIC OF COL-LECTIVE ACTION, Harvard University Press, Cambridge, Mass., 1965.

29. A realistic analysis of Federal organization and reorganization may be found in Harold Seidman, POLITICS, POSITION, AND POWER: THE DYNAMICS OF FEDERAL ORGANIZATION, Oxford University Press, New York, 1970.

30. V.O. Key, Jr., with Alexander Heard, SOUTHERN POLITICS, Alfred Knopf, New York, 1949.

31. Rupert B. Vance, "The Regional Concept as a Tool for Social Research," in Merrill Jensen (ed.), REGIONALISM IN AMERICA, University of Wisconsin Press, 1951, p. 122.

32. Ibid., p. 129.

33. John M. Gaus, "Introduction to Part IV," in Jensen, op. cit., p. 314.

34. Seidman, op. cit., p. 14.

35. For a careful review of socialization research, see John A. Clausen, "Recent Developments in Socialization Theory and Research," THE ANNALS OF THE AMERICAN ACADEMY OF POLITICAL AND SOCIAL SCIENCE, Vol. 377, May 1968, p. 139 ff.

36. DEVELOPMENT BENEFITS OF WATER RESOURCE INVESTMENTS, A report submitted to the U.S. Army Engineer Institute for Water Resources by Washington University, St. Louis, Missouri, edited by Charles L. Leven of the Institute for Urban and Regional Studies, November 1969, p. 8.

37. This section of the paper is based in part on Norman Wengert, "Public Participation in Water Planning: A Critique of Theory, Doctrine, and Practice," WATER RESOURCES BULLETIN (Journal of the American Water Resources Association), Vol. 7, No. 1, February 1961, p. 26 ff; and on Norman Wengert, "Where do we go with Public Participation in the Planning Process?" in PROCEEDINGS, American Water Resources Association, 1961, National Symposium on Social and Economic Aspects of Water Resources Development Proceedings Series No. 9.

38. P.L. 88-253.

39. Daniel P. Moynihan, MAXIMUM FEASIBLE MISUNDERSTANDING, The Free Press, New York, 1969.

40. S.M. Miller and Martin Rein, "Participation, Poverty, and Administration," PUBLIC ADMINISTRATION REVIEW, Vol. 29, No. 1, 1969, p. 15.

41. AMERICAN BEHAVIORAL SCIENTIST, Vol. 13, No. 2, November-December 1969; entire issue devoted to "Elite-Mass Behavior and Interaction"; quotation is from "Editors' Note," p. 167.

42. Herbert Kaufman, "Administrative Decentralization and Political Power," PUBLIC ADMINISTRATION REVIEW, Vol. 29, No. 1, 1969, p. 3-14.

43. Robert Dorfman in Hearings before the Subcommittee on Economy in Government of the Joint Economic Committee, 91st Congress, 1st Session, May 12 and 14, 1969.

44. Revised from the author's article in WATER RESOURCES BULLETIN, op. cit., pp. 30-31.

45. This discussion on coordination is in part based on a paper presented in March 1965 at a Conference-Seminar at Indiana University on the topic "Political Dynamics of Environmental Change." The paper was entitled "Reflections on Perennial Problems of Federal Coordination." It has been reprinted in Leslie L. Roos, Jr. (ed.), THE POLITICS OF ECOSUICIDE, Holt, Rinehart and Winston, Inc., New York, 1971, pp. 116-130.

46. P.L. 90-577.

47. From Felix A. Nigro, MODERN PUBLIC ADMINISTRATION, 2nd ed., Harper and Row, Publishers, New York, 1970, p. 172.

48. Paraphrased from Anthony Downs, INSIDE BUREAUCRACY, Little, Brown, Boston, 1967, p. 75.

49. As quoted in David Lilienthal, TVA, DEMOCRACY ON THE MARCH, Harper, 1944, p. 149.

50. See John R. Moor (ed.), THE ECONOMIC IMPACT OF TVA, University of Tennessee Press, 1967, especially Chapter 4 by Norman Wengert, "The Politics of Water Resource Development as Exemplified by TVA."

Index

Accountability, political, 5, 167
Acton, Lord, cited, 394
Adams, R. B., cited, 104, 106
Administration and administrative forms,
    1–2, 6, 11–12, 15, 106, 161, 168,
    306–309, 314, 379–380, 390, 402, 409,
    413, 421–422; railroad, 41–43, 320
Adversary proceedings, 15, 413
Advertising, kinds of, 31
Advisory Commission on Intergovernmental
    Relations, 307, 386–387
Advocacy planning, 15
"Affluent society," 396
Africa, 371
Age groups and distribution, 352, 356
Agencies: central, 29, 334, 414; federal, 313;
    local, 329; metropolitan, 1, 306–307,
    314; multistate, 333–335; national, 293;
    public, 380; short-term, 335; state, 1, 8,
    12, 225, 307–314, 326, 335
Agricultural Extension Service, 418, 423
Agriculture, 153, 211, 247–248, 274,
    361–362; areas of, 106, 116, 128, 179;
    chemicals used in, 221, 223; products of,
    182, 219, 235, 238, 373; resources in,
    357; shippers and shipping in, 182, 233
Agriculture, Department of, 238, 240
Aid: to farmers, 62; federal, 15–16, 202,
    209, 230, 253, 261, 388; financial,
    195–199, 206, 208, 213–214, 231, 250,
    254, 271–272; matching, 251; public,
    204, 229. *See also* Grants
Air: cargo, 254, 325, 371, 374; congestion,
    57; costs, 61; travel, 37, 54–55, 64, 96,
    123, 131, 180, 201, 254, 371–372
Air cushion vehicles, 321
Aircrafts and carriers, 4, 92, 96, 134, 180,
    199, 258, 276
Airline industry, 44–46, 51, 64, 155, 178,
    236, 242, 254–255, 371, 374
Airmail, contracts for, 231, 253–254; sub-
    sidies for, 273
Airports, 66–69, 178, 181, 183, 229, 250,
    256, 258, 269, 292; adequacy of, 326;
    civil, 271; construction of, 216, 266,
    275–277, 304; international, 375–376;
    large, 230; local, 254; location sites for,
    157, 261, 322; management of, 303;
    regional, 330
Airways, 229, 309, 332–333
Akron, Ohio, 130
Alabama, 302
Alaska, 179, 220–223
Albany-Schenectady-Troy area, 130
Allegheny Mountains, 230
Allentown-Bethlehem-Easton area, 130
Allocation: of benefits, 14; geographical,
    389; of investments, 12, 328; of man-
    power, 292; of resources, 6, 22–24, 30,
    34, 168, 222, 229; traffic, 10

Alonso, William, cited, 5–6, 17–18, 177–193
American Behavioral Scientist, 410
American Political Science Review, 384
Ames, Iowa, 116
Amsterdam, New York, 331
Amtrak Rail System, 158, 168, 372
Analytical regions, 399–402, 406, 421
Anti-trust laws and policies, 9, 30, 65, 190,
    245, 270
Appalachia, area of, 12, 17, 143, 154,
    181–182, 186, 201, 204, 209, 214, 216,
    220–223, 268, 272, 295–296, 304, 312,
    328–329, 335, 404
Appalachian Regional Commission, 161,
    214–216, 295, 302, 312–313, 328, 334
Appalachian Regional Development Act, 295
    295, 381, 408
Appalachian Studies, Office of, 330
Appalachian Throughway, 330
Area Redevelopment Administration,
    212–213
Arizona, 154, 217, 300
Arkansas, 217
Arkansas-Verdigris Navigation System, 182,
    191
Asia, 371
Asheville, North Carolina, 181
Atlanta, Georgia, 4, 96, 126, 130, 133–134,
    143, 255, 260
Atlantic Ocean, 300; seacoast of, 143, 186,
    204, 230, 261, 273
Authority and authoritarianism, 15, 22, 35,
    141–142, 154, 156, 164, 209, 250, 292,
    314–315, 389, 413, 423–424
Automobile: 97, 106, 110, 372–373; pri-
    vate, 380, 382–383; revolution in use of,
    95, 133–134, 211, 223, 248, 252, 261,
    266, 347, 373, 403
Autonomy, measures of, 99, 164, 205, 209,
    216, 414
Australia, central, 179

Balanced growth and coordination, 1, 183,
    330
Baltimore, 126–128, 130, 220, 330, 412;
    Port of, 205–206
Baltimore and Ohio Railroad, 204–208, 220
Bankruptcy, effects of, 246, 259, 268, 274
Bargaining, components of, 398, 417, 426
Barges and bargeline firms, 58, 250, 256–257,
    275–277, 363, 370, 374, 419; operating
    costs of, 37–40, 264
Behavioral influences, 13, 397, 408
Benefits and costs analysis, 7, 15, 18, 66,
    200, 202, 208–213, 222, 225, 255–256,
    264, 266–267, 271, 275, 389
Bennett, Hugh Hammond, cited, 423
Berry, Brian J. L., cited, 98, 102, 116–118,
    122–128, 135, 144, 147, 153, 217
Bicycle revolution, hypothetical, 93–94

431

Selected Rand Books

Bagdikian, Ben. THE INFORMATION MACHINES: THEIR IMPACT ON MEN AND THE MEDIA. New York: Harper and Row, 1971.

Bretz, Rudy. A TAXONOMY OF COMMUNICATION MEDIA. Englewood Cliffs, N.J.: Educational Technology Publications, 1971.

Dalkey, Norman C. (ed.) STUDIES IN THE QUALITY OF LIFE: DELPHI AND DECISION-MAKING. Lexington, Mass.: D.C. Heath and Company, 1972.

Downs, Anthony. INSIDE BUREAUCRACY. Boston, Mass.: Little, Brown and Company, 1967.

Fisher, Gene H. COST CONSIDERATIONS IN SYSTEMS ANALYSIS. New York: American Elsevier Publishing Company, 1971.

Judd, William R. (ed.) STATE OF STRESS IN THE EARTH'S CRUST. New York: American Elsevier Publishing Co., Inc., 1964.

McKean, Roland N. EFFICIENCY IN GOVERNMENT THROUGH SYSTEMS ANALYSIS: WITH EMPHASIS ON WATER RESOURCE DEVELOPMENT. New York: John Wiley & Sons, Inc., 1958.

Meyer, John R., Martin Wohl, and John F. Kain. THE URBAN TRANSPORTATION PROBLEM. Cambridge, Mass.: Harvard University Press, 1965.

Novick, David (ed.) PROGRAM BUDGETING: PROGRAM ANALYSIS AND THE FEDERAL BUDGET. Cambridge, Mass.: Harvard University Press, 1965.

Pascal, Anthony H. (ed.) RACIAL DISCRIMINATION IN ECONOMIC LIFE. Lexington, Mass.: D.C. Heath and Company, 1972.

Pascal, Anthony H. (ed.) THINKING ABOUT CITIES: NEW PERSPECTIVES ON URBAN PROBLEMS. Belmont, Calif.: Dickenson Publishing Company, 1970.

Quade, Edward S., and Wayne I. Boucher. SYSTEMS ANALYSIS AND POLICY PLANNING: APPLICATIONS IN DEFENSE. New York: American Elsevier Publishing Company, 1968.

The Rand Corporation. A MILLION RANDOM DIGITS WITH 100,000 NORMAL DEVIATES. Glencoe, Illinois: The Free Press, 1955.

Williams, John D. THE COMPLEAT STRATEGYST: BEING A PRIMER ON THE THEORY OF GAMES OF STRATEGY. New York: McGraw-Hill Book Company, Inc., 1954.